CLIMATE-CHANGE POLICY

Climate-change Policy

Edited by
Dieter Helm

OXFORD
UNIVERSITY PRESS

OXFORD
UNIVERSITY PRESS

Great Clarendon Street, Oxford OX2 6DP

Oxford University Press is a department of the University of Oxford.
It furthers the University's objective of excellence in research, scholarship,
and education by publishing worldwide in

Oxford New York

Auckland Cape Town Dar es Salaam Hong Kong Karachi
Kuala Lumpur Madrid Melbourne Mexico City Nairobi
New Delhi Shanghai Taipei Toronto

With offices in

Argentina Austria Brazil Chile Czech Republic France Greece
Guatemala Hungary Italy Japan Poland Portugal Singapore
South Korea Switzerland Thailand Turkey Ukraine Vietnam

Oxford is a registered trade mark of Oxford University Press
in the UK and in certain other countries

Published in the United States
by Oxford University Press Inc., New York

© Oxford Review of Economic Policy and Oxford University Press, 2005

British Library Cataloguing in Publication Data

Data available

Library of Congress Cataloging in Publication Data

Data available

Typeset by the author
Printed in Great Britain
on acid-free paper by
Biddles Ltd, King's Lynn, Norfolk

ISBN 0–19–928145–9   978–0–19–928145–9
ISBN 0–19–928146–7 (Pbk.)   978–0–19–928146–6

1 3 5 7 9 10 8 6 4 2

Contents

Contributors

Scott Barrett
Scott Barrett is Professor and Director of International Policy at the School of Advanced International Studies, Johns Hopkins University, in Washington, DC. His research focuses on the ability of the international political and legal system to address transnational and global issues, particularly in the environmental and public health areas. He also advises a number of organizations on these topics. In addition to climate change, he has recently been writing on such topics as high seas overfishing and disease eradication. He received his Ph.D. in economics from the London School of Economics.

Christoph Böhringer
Christoph Böhringer is head of the research department 'Environmental and Resource Economics, Environmental Management' at the Centre for European Research (ZEW), Mannheim. He studied Economic Engineering at the University of Karlsruhe and received his Ph.D. in economics from the University of Stuttgart in 1995. Between 1995 and 1998 he supervised the research group 'Energy Economics' at IER (Institute of Energy Economics), University of Stuttgart. In 2002, he received his habilitation and *venia legendi* in economics from the University of Regensburg. Since 2004, he has been professor at the University of Heidelberg. His research focuses on the quantitative impact analysis of environmental, energy, and trade policies. He has published widely in international journals on these topics.

Michael Finus
Michael Finus is assistant professor in economics in the Institute of Economic Theory at the University of Hagen. His academic interests include games theory, coalition theory, and environmental economics.

Dieter Helm
Dieter Helm is currently a fellow in economics at New College, Oxford. His career to date has spanned academia, public policy, and business. His interests include utilities, infrastructure, regulation and the envi-

ronment, and he concentrates on the energy, water, and transport sectors in Britain and Europe. He holds a number of other advisory board appointments, including the Prime Minister's Council for Science and Technology, the Defra Economic Academic Panel (Chair); the DTI Sustainable Energy Panel Advisory Board; and the Ministerial Task Force on Sustainable Development.

Cameron Hepburn

Cameron Hepburn is a junior research fellow in economics at St Hugh's College, Oxford. His research interests include environmental economics, behavioural economics, discounting and intergenerational equity, time-consistency of environmental policy, and international trade and the environment.

Chris Hope

Chris Hope is director of the management studies tripos at the Judge Institute of Management at the University of Cambridge. He has been involved in the Integrated Assessment Modelling of climate change since 1990 through the development and use of his PAGE model. He is a lead author and review editor for the Third Assessment Report of the IPCC and is on the editorial board of *Integrated Assessment, Transport Policy*, and *Energy & Environment*.

Alan Ingham

Alan Ingham is senior research fellow in the economics division of Southampton University and is a member of the Tyndall Centre for Climate Change, which is the national UK centre for trans-disciplinary research on climate change. His work there is on the effect of learning and precaution on adaptive investments related to climate change. Other recent work relates to the effect of climate change and water extraction for wetlands in Central Asia.

Nick Johnstone

Nick Johnstone (Ph.D., Cambridge) is a policy analyst in the National Policies Division of the OECD Environment Directorate. He has led a number of large multi-country empirical studies in the area of environmental economics, in both OECD and non-OECD countries. His research has focused on the economics of environmental policy instrument choice. His current research interests include analysis of the links between environmental policy and industrial organization, market failures in secondary material markets, and the economic analysis of the use of environmental policy mixes. He has contributed chapters and is the principal author of a number of books with leading academic publishers (Routledge, Blackwell, Edward Elgar), and has published in leading journals in the field (*Land Economics, Environmental and Resource Economics, Energy Economics, Ecological Economics, Natural Resources Journal, Transport Policy*).

David King

Professor Sir David King ScD, FRS, FRSC, FinstP was appointed as the Government's Chief Scientific Adviser and Head of the Office of Science and Technology in October 2000. Born in South Africa in 1939, he spent his early career at the University of Witwatersrand, Imperial College, and the University of East Anglia, before becoming the Brunner Professor of Physical Chemistry at the University of Liverpool in 1974. In 1988, he was appointed 1920 Professor of Physical Chemistry at the University of Cambridge and subsequently became Master of Downing College (1995–2000), and Head of the University Chemistry Department (1993–2000). He retains his position at Cambridge as 1920 Professor of Chemistry, where he is still active in research.

Richard Mash

Richard Mash is a fellow and tutor in economics at New College, Oxford. His research is primarily concerned with monetary policy but he has a particular interest in time-inconsistency issues in policy towards climate change.

Robert Mendelsohn

Robert Mendelsohn is a resource economist who specializes in valuing the environment. He has taught at the Universities of Washington and Michigan, and for the last 20 years at Yale University, where he is now the Edwin Weyerhaeuser Davis Professor in the School of Forestry and Environmental Studies. Over the last 12 years, he has concentrated on measuring the impacts from climate change. He has also worked on valuing recreation, non-timber forest products, and hazardous waste sites. Together with Drs Nordhaus and Shaw, he invented the Ricardian technique, a cross-sectional analysis that reveals the climate sensitivity of agriculture. With other academic colleagues he has worked on combining an ecological model of forests with a dynamic economic model of the economy to predict a path of timber effects from climate change; using cross-sectional information from households and firms to measure the impacts of climate change on energy; studying the effect of climate change on the United States economy; and calculating climate response functions.

Ian W. H. Parry

Ian Parry is a senior fellow at Resources for the Future. He received a Ph.D. in economics from the University of Chicago in 1993 and an MA in economics from Warwick University in 1987. Parry specializes in environmental, transportation, energy, and tax policies. His recent work has analysed gasoline taxes, fuel economy standards, transit subsidies, alcohol taxes, policies to reduce traffic congestion and accidents, environmental tax shifts, the role of technology policy in environmental protection, the incidence of pollution control policies, and the costs of the tax system.

David Pearce

David Pearce is Emeritus Professor of Environmental Economics at University College London. He is the author or editor of more than 50 books, mainly in the fields of environmental economics and cost–benefit analysis, and more than 350 papers in refereed journals. In 2005 he will be given a lifetime achievment award by the European Association of Environmental and Resource Economists.

Jos Sijm

Jos Sijm holds a Ph.D. in development economics from the Tinbergen Institute (Erasmus University Rotterdam, 1997). He conducted research in several African countries on food security and agricultural policy issues. Since 1999, he has been employed as a scientific researcher at the department Policy Studies of the Energy Research Centre of the Netherlands (ECN). He has been actively involved in a variety of research projects, either as a project leader or economic expert, dealing with energy and climate policy issues, such as the burden sharing of future mitigation commitments, the performance of the Kyoto Protocol, the implementation of the Kyoto mechanisms, and the EU Emissions Trading Scheme (EU ETS).

Steven Sorrell

Steve Sorrell is a research fellow in the Environment and Energy Group at SPRU (Science and Technology Policy Research), University of Sussex. He joined SPRU in 1990, following an earlier career in electronic engineering, and now conducts research on energy, climate, and environmental policy, with particular emphasis on energy modelling, environmental economics, and the implementation of industrial pollution control. He has acted as consultant to the UK Department of the

Environment on the use of tradable permits for controlling sulphur emissions, and to the Department of Trade and Industry on industrial combined heat and power. He has also acted as a consultant to the European Commission, industry, and NGOs, and his recent publications include *The Economics of Energy Efficiency: Barriers to Cost Effective Investment* (Edward Elgar, September 2004).

Tom Tietenberg

Tom Tietenberg is professor of economics at Colby College, Maine. He is the author or editor of 11 books (including *Environmental and Natural Resource Economics*, one of the best-selling textbooks in the field, and *Emissions Trading*, one of the most widely cited books in the tradable permits literature) as well as over a hundred articles and essays on environmental and natural resource economics. Elected President of the Association of Environmental and Natural Resource Economists in 1987–8, he has consulted on environmental policy with the World Bank, the InterAmerican Development Bank, the Agency for International Development, and the US Environmental Protection Agency, as well as several state and foreign governments. He was the principal investigator for the United Nations' study to facilitate the implementation of Article 17 of the Kyoto Protocol, the article that uses emissions trading to control climate change.

Richard S. J. Tol

Richard Tol is the Michael Otto Professor of Sustainability and Global Change at the Centre for Marine and Climate Research, Hamburg University; a Principal Researcher at the Institute for Environmental Studies, Vrije Universiteit, Amsterdam; and an Adjunct Professor at the Center for Integrated Study of the Human Dimensions of Global Change, Carnegie Mellon University, Pittsburgh. He has 71 publications in learned journals and many other ones. An economist and statistician, his work focuses on climate change, particularly detection and attribution, impact and adaptation, integrated assessment modelling, and decision and policy analysis. He is an editor of *Energy Economics* and *Environmental and Resource Economics*. He has played an active role in international bodies such as the Stanford Energy Modeling Forum, the Intergovernmental Panel on Climate Change, and the European Forum on Integrated Environmental Assessment.

Alistair Ulph

Professor Alistair Ulph is Vice-President of the University of Manchester and Dean of the Faculty of Humanities. He has written extensively in the field of environmental and resource economics, most recently in the areas of trade and environment, and acted as consultant and adviser to a number of government bodies and private companies. He was elected President of the European Association of Environmental and Resource Economists for 2000 and 2001.

Preface

DIETER HELM

This volume has its origins in an earlier issue of the *Oxford Review of Economic Policy*, published in autumn 2003. Those earlier contributions have been revised, and brought together with new chapters which flesh out the main themes — the science of climate change, the social cost of carbon, the choice of policy instruments, and the appropriate institutions. The result is an integrated set of analyses, which bring out the richness of the contribution that economic analysis can bring to what is perhaps the most challenging problem of our times.

In editing this volume, I am extremely grateful to Alison Gomm, who has brought her calm and professional skills to bear on the complex task of coordinating so many contributors and copy editing. I am also grateful to Cate Dominian for her support.

Introduction

DIETER HELM*

The importance of climate change is now widely accepted. From being a research topic, it has moved to the political stage, and while most politicians have yet to see it as a 'greater threat than weapons of mass destruction', the main political parties of almost all developed countries have accepted that emissions of greenhouse gases will have to be curbed to avoid serious climate change.

What is less widely accepted is what needs to be done. Policies remain largely *ad hoc*, focusing on energy efficiency, renewables, and, in some countries, nuclear power and clean coal. To support these, a host of measures has been introduced, ranging from carbon and energy taxes, emissions trading schemes, and subsidies, to obligations to purchase selected technologies, tax concessions, and R&D expenditure. These policies are intended to achieve aspirations, targets, and, for those countries that have signed up to the Protocol, the Kyoto caps. The relationship between the measures and the objectives is, at best, poorly defined, and many of the aspirations and targets not very credible. In the case of Kyoto, only one or two countries in Europe are on track, and there are no serious penalties for those who fail.

In the wider scientific context, the gulf between the scale of the problem and current objectives and measures is enormous. Scientists suggest that, with emissions now at around 370 parts per million (ppm) of carbon dioxide (CO_2), relative to around 250 ppm before the Industrial Revolution, the aim should be to stabilize at around 550 ppm rather than permit a business-as-usual scenario of around 750 ppm during the course of this century. David King, in chapter 2, sets out the rationale for this view.

* New College, Oxford.

This science-driven target is open to challenge, but at present there is, in any event, little evidence that it will be achieved. The USA, China, and India currently contribute, respectively, around 25, 19, and 8 per cent of the world's CO_2 emissions, and none is committed to a cap on its emissions. Over the course of the century, the world population is likely to rise from the current 6 billion to 9 billion, or perhaps more. Most of these extra 3 billion people will be in the developing world, with perhaps as many as 1 billion each in China and India. China's GDP has been growing at around 9 per cent per annum for over a decade, and much of its growth has been based on coal, steel, and other energy-intensive industries. Soon, China will exceed the USA in its share of world CO_2 emissions.

In tackling this enormous gulf between objectives and policy, there have been intense debates between scientists and economists, with little meeting of minds. To economists, the 550 ppm target has little justification without supporting evidence on costs and benefits. The economy substitutes man-made for environmental capital—that is, what economic development and the industrial and post-industrial transformations have been about. The optimal quantity of pollution is typically not zero, and how much pollution is 'optimal' depends upon a careful evaluation of the nature of the problem, the risks and uncertainty, and the valuation consumers place on both the climate and on the things that they consume which damage the climate. Scientists are interested in the physical consequences—how emissions and climate interact. Economists are interested in the value of the consequences.

With a problem of such a scale, neither scientists nor economists can have much confidence in their standard tools. Modelling the climate *as a whole*, including not just the atmosphere, but also the oceans and their currents, and the impact of land masses, is a task which requires global climate models. Estimating economic valuations of uncertain costs and benefits in a global context, where information and understanding by consumers is often (very) poor, stretches existing techniques. Devising policies to address these problems at the global level, with technical change at the heart of the problem, is analytically and empirically very demanding.

Nevertheless, despite these difficulties, the starting point is not one of pure ignorance. In science, understanding of the recent ice ages and the relationship with changes in atmospheric concentrations of greenhouse gases has advanced significantly, with new evidence from ice cores. This has built upon the theoretical foundations of the relationship between greenhouse gases and climate developed in the late nineteenth and early twentieth centuries.[1] Though the science is continually advancing, the Intergovernmental Panel on Climate Change (IPCC) report, *The Scientific Basis* (IPCC, 2001), provides a summary of what is the consensus view. The differences that remain between scientists have noticeably shifted from disputes about whether climate change is taking place to a narrower focus on the extent to which human causes are responsible, and the roles of specific greenhouse gases, carbon sinks, and other components of the process of climate change.

In economics, valuation techniques have also advanced, as there has been a steady increase in the number of studies and supporting data. Governments now widely recognize, at least in principle, the need to support targets and policies with cost–benefit analysis (CBA), even if this is sometimes more an effort in *ex post* justification than an *ex ante* search for the 'correct' target. An example is the paper by Clarkson and Deyes (2002), which identified a social cost of carbon of around £70 per tonne, consistent with the government's Kyoto target. As David Pearce (chapter 5) demonstrates, more robust estimates point to a much lower valuation, and this result is borne out by other studies. Robert Mendelsohn (chapter 6) and Richard Tol (chapter 7) provide further support for such lower estimates.

The Pearce result for the social cost of carbon is in stark contrast to the sorts of targets suggested by scientists, reinforced by the Royal Commission on Environmental Pollution (RCEP, 2000). There have been various attempts to explain this gap. The first takes the CBA estimate at face value and claims that the revealed willingness-to-pay reflects underlying consumer preferences. Put simply, people value the polluting activities (the use of fossil fuels, such as in cars, air travel, coal- and gas-fired electricity generation, and chemicals) more than the damage caused by them. Thus, the 'gap' is not so much an indication that scientists are wrong, as a reflection of the costs and benefits of the consequences.

A second view is that the CBA studies reflect the ignorance of the general public about the way climate and ecosystems work. Experts understand these relationships, rather as doctors understand how the human body works. CBA studies, on this view, mistake the nature of the choice people actually make. For public-policy issues, such as climate change, people exercise their choice through voting, enabling politicians to select targets and policies on the basis of the best information and advice available. The choices that result are what people would have made—and be willing to pay for—had they had the necessary scientific and economic training and the information available to them.

---

[1] See Weart (2003) for the history of climate-change science.

Although the amount of information will inevitably 'frame' the result of CBA studies, there is an inherent difficulty with this second line of argument. The gap can only be closed if people (as consumers and voters) are willing to accept the consequences. Recent examples of policies which have run ahead of voter's willingness-to-pay include the imposition of VAT on domestic fuels and the fuel price escalator. To the extent that this second view is correct in explaining the gap, the policy implication is a public education policy to improve general understanding of climate change and its consequences.

The third view is that the gap arises because of a mismatch between the nature of the climate-change problem and the marginal nature of economic analysis. To many scientists, climate change is anything but marginal; it is macro and global in its effects. By contrast, CBA technologies are designed to address marginal changes in a partial equilibrium context. This distinction has been further sharpened by recent research into the possibility of rapid climate change.

Each of these three views adds something to the debate between scientific and economic outlooks. Actual preferences matter, since it is relatively ill-informed people, living today, who will have to change their behaviour. Information and greater understanding will probably alter attitudes and choices, and inevitably experts have a role in advising governments and educating people as to the consequences of global warming. And CBA is a very limited — but useful — technique, especially in this particular context.

Together, the three views illustrate a central characteristic of climate change — that it is a multi-disciplinary problem, and it requires multi-disciplinary approaches. The science is essential to any economic policy response, and the economics provides the way forward in identifying least-cost (and therefore politically acceptable) solutions. But although this may seem obvious, it is an exception rather than the rule to see it reflected in practice. There are few, if any, genuinely multi-disciplinary examples. Even the IPCC process has the science conducted largely as a separate exercise to the economics. This separation of research effort reflects the structure of universities and, indeed, the structure of academic disciplines, and feeds right through to the lack of promotion, career prospects, and supporting academic journals for multi-disciplinary studies. In the chapters below, it is reflected in the absence of costs and benefits in the scientists' analyses, and the absence of much science in the economists' contributions. This is not a criticism of any of them individually, but rather an illustration of the gap between the analytical approaches, which mirrors the gap between the policy recommendations which emerge.

But whatever the gap, and however weak the emphasis on multi-disciplinary analysis has been, the two sides do have to be brought together — neither science nor economics can make much progress without the other. Two examples of the ways in which this can be advanced are in the treatment of the risks and uncertainties which are reflected in the science and economics; and in trying to build models which combine both.

Let us start with risk and uncertainty. Although our knowledge is limited, it is not zero. Probabilities can be attached to potential outcomes, and estimates can be made of costs and benefits. As time goes on, we will learn more, and uncertainty may (although not necessarily) reduce. Some have argued that the fact of uncertainty and the possibility of learning mean that there is a benefit to delaying action. We should 'wait and see' or perhaps 'learn then act'. This may have merit, but also has a cost. While we wait, concentrations of greenhouse gas rise faster than they would if we had acted sooner. The costs of dealing with higher concentrations may be greater.

But we also need to bear in mind that they might not — it may be cheaper to deal with an admittedly greater concentration later, as new technologies are developed. And the interventions may be better targeted as our scientific and economic knowledge increases. Alan Ingham and Alistair Ulph make this point in chapter 3, and they show that even when irreversibility and catastrophe are introduced, the intuitive response of greater immediate action is not obvious. The precautionary approach may be ambiguous: precaution is as much about how to head off possible adverse consequences as about incurring costs which may turn out to be excessive.

Even for catastrophe — a high-impact, low-probability event — the implications of uncertainty are complex. In a rational analysis, the value to be attached to a catastrophe (the negative utility) is the result of multiplying two numbers: the probability of the event and the damages that result. The former is small, the latter large. It has to be weighted against other factors in the calculation, such as the discount rate. For example, the catastrophe might be several centuries away, by which time all sorts of technical progress may have taken place. By then, for example, carbon sequestration might be a very easy option. On the other hand, if sudden climate change were to be imminent, the case for rapid action would not be outweighed by the discount rate.

These considerations of uncertainty provide considerable insights into research priorities. They tell scientists what it is that policy-makers need to know more about. Timing is of the essence; it may be at least as important as the scale of the consequences. Whether the Arctic will be free of ice within the next 70 years, whether the Antarctic ice sheets will break off, and what would be the consequent expected rise in sea level this century—these are all questions that bear directly on how much immediate action should be taken.

Research agendas are, therefore, much better defined by considering the questions thrown up by a multi-disciplinary approach. But a further step in integration of different disciplines has been through the creation of 'integrated assessment models' (IAMs). These are described in chapter 4 by Chris Hope, and they come in a host of different sizes and shapes. At one level, IAMs are little more than the integration of a simple damage function into an economic model to assess costs and benefits, and the consequences of different policy responses. At another level, more complex models integrate the dynamics of climate models (global circulation models), and the feedbacks between ecosystems over time. Policies themselves have feedbacks, and there can be an integration of these into the models. Debates abound on the relative merits of simple and complex models, and probably both have their places. What IAMs add is the ability to change parameters and test out policies, to try to quantify what happens if, for example, the discount rate changes. They provide tools to investigate flexibility and to allow more precise questions to be asked about specific interventions.

Analyses of the social costs of carbon, of the nature and implications of uncertainty, and IAMs, all help to inform the policy question of what should be done. For many reasons, it is unlikely, however, that the essentially political process of setting objectives and targets will be much more than a crude one. Recognizing this political reality, perhaps economists' largest contribution to date comes once the objectives and targets have been set. Much research has concentrated on the question of delivering least-cost means of achieving the goals of policy—the optimal policy instruments.

The conventional economic literature focuses on the choice between carbon taxes and tradable permits. The former sets the price of carbon, letting the quantity adjust. Permits start the other way around and, since the targets are set in quantities, it is an obvious—and largely erroneous—conclusion to draw that, therefore, permits are preferable. A flexible carbon tax can be adjusted to achieve a given quantity, just as a permit system can be adjusted to deliver a desired price. The choice between the two instruments depends in theory on the shape of the marginal damage- and marginal abatement-cost functions, and on the uncertainty associated with these functions. Climate change, in the absence of sudden deteriorations, tends to have steeper, shorter-run marginal cost functions than marginal damage functions, and, hence, in theory carbon taxes are to be preferred to permits. In practice, however, the politics, and the relation to international agreements, plays a significant and ultimately determinant role.

In the debate between taxes and permits, the detailed design of policy matters considerably, as the chapters by Ian Parry (10), Tom Tietenberg (8), and Nick Johnstone (11) illustrate. In particular, a key theme is whether permits are grandfathered. Grandfathering limits the scope to adjust other, typically labour, taxes, since the initial income effect is zero. It also has important consequences for competition, since permits have strategic value to incumbents. For both reasons – the lack of an initial income effect, and the entry-deterrent potential – incumbents tend to favour permits, and, indeed, this has been reflected in industry lobbying.

The European Union Emissions Trading Scheme (EU ETS) is perhaps the most ambitious attempt yet to design an economic instrument to address climate change. But, as Steven Sorrell and Jos Sijm set out in chapter 9, it is being introduced into a context which is already crowded with other overlapping policy instruments. It is the interactions with these other policies which is important in considering what its impacts will be, rather than simply treating it as a textbook trading model.

The EU ETS has other complications, too. The scheme has reserved permits for entrants who may or may not appear. It is for an initial period (2005–8) and will then be revised from 2008 to 2012 on a basis and permit allocation yet to be agreed. And, perhaps most significantly, it will accommodate purchases of carbon reduction from outside the Kyoto European countries through the Clean Development Mechanism and Joint Implementation. Given that the European countries are mostly not on target to meet their Kyoto 2012 targets, and given that the price of permits is likely to be very high were those off target determined to achieve them through the EU ETS, the obvious political solution is to buy in carbon reductions from outside, and thereby keep the permit price within 'politically acceptable' boundaries. Thus, by adjusting quantity, an implicit 'target price range' might be achieved – and hence what is deemed a permit scheme may, in fact, turn out to be more like a carbon tax. With Russia now ratifying Kyoto, surpluses can be purchased from Russia and Joint Implementation schemes developed with Russia, thereby allowing EU countries to meet the Kyoto target, keep the permit price low, and (ironically) provide Russia with funds to finance its developing oil and gas (carbon) industries.

The Kyoto Protocol does not in itself do much to address global warming. Its overall target is weak, and very different from the 550 ppm target recommended by scientists. With Russia on board, it has legal force, but the absence of China, India, and the USA from binding targets weakens its effect further. Not surprisingly, there has been an intense debate in the economic literature on the pros and cons of Kyoto. Christoph Böhringer and Michael Finus, in chapter 12, put the case for the defence. They see it as a flexible, broad-based, international mechanism — a first step towards a future, more effective, climate policy. In effect, Kyoto is learning by doing, even if what is agreed initially is minimal. Such arguments have not, however, found much favour outside the EU, for a variety of geopolitical and economic reasons. Europe has largely been through the industrialization process, and the relationship between economic growth and energy and carbon intensity has been weakened. Large-scale energy-intensive industries have been slowly closed down and have declined as a proportion of GDP. The coal industries of Britain, France, and even Germany have been substantially pruned back. Thus, for the EU, the costs of reducing emissions are lower and, in any event, economic growth itself is widely expected to be lower for the Kyoto period up to 2012 in Europe, compared with the USA, China, and India.

By contrast, developing countries, such as China and India, with rapid population growth, have been growing apace — roughly 9 per cent per annum for a decade for China. China and India have many of the energy-intensive industries which once dominated European economies, and both are reliant on coal as a major energy input. Absolute caps on carbon emissions (such as Kyoto limits in Europe) are very difficult to envisage practically without a more significant effect on growth *in their economies*, and politically probably impossible.

Between the EU on one side, and China, India, and developing countries on the other, lies the USA. With its current higher growth rate than Europe, energy dependency on oil imports, and very large reserves of cheap coal, it has so far rejected absolute caps, too. Its main emphasis has been on supply-side technology policy, notably clean coal, sequestration and hydrogen. For Kyoto to provide the flexible starting point, as Böhringer and Finus claim it does, rather than a blind alley, a way of bridging the gap between these three blocks of players needs to be found.

In contrast to Böhringer and Finus, Scott Barrett, in chapter 13, argues that Kyoto is, in any event, conceptually flawed, and that these flaws can be identified by considering the characteristics of international agreements generally. Barrett advocates a multi-track agreement, with a series of mutually reinforcing protocols — what he calls 'Kyoto plus', rather than 'Kyoto only'. This is more than a minor modification of approach. Barrett argues that Kyoto is flawed in trying to do too much too soon, which will not be delivered. However, his is a more fundamental critique about the ways of building up agreements gradually and internationally in a context that is fraught with the conventional problems of cooperative agreements such as free-riding, cheating, monitoring, and enforcement, in the absence of international property rights and credibility. And, in addition to this general critique about the way to construct international agreements, Barrett also challenges the incentive structure in Kyoto and, in particular, its short-term time horizon and the related lack of incentives for R&D and technology.

The question of credibility is not just about policy design: it is about institutional design, too. Carbon taxes, tradable permits, and international treaties on climate change affect behaviour only to the extent that economic players believe them. In many cases, there is a classic time-inconsistency problem: tell people *ex ante* that policy will be set to achieve a target, but then *ex post* renege on the target. The carbon tax example illustrates this, discussed in chapter 14 by Dieter Helm, Cameron Hepburn, and Richard Mash. Suppose a government announces that it will set a carbon tax at whatever level necessary to meet an emissions target. If producers and consumers believe the government, they will invest in non-carbon technologies accordingly. But now suppose that the carbon tax will be politically painful: voters may react negatively. Because the government has the political incentive to cheat, producers and consumers do not believe it. Hence, they do not invest in non-carbon technologies. Helm *et al.* propose a possible solution to this problem—by delegating the policy instrument to an independent agency. This is analogous to the delegation of interest-rate setting to independent central banks, with inflation targets.

Institutional design matters not only for credibility reasons—whether at the national or international levels—but also because climate-change policy tends to operate in the context of other market failures, and therefore other instruments, too. In the energy sector, as I discuss in chapter 15, there are also concerns about security of supply, competitive prices, and fuel poverty. Multiple market failures give rise to multiple objectives and multiple instruments. Where these are each addressed separately by different institutions, inefficient resource allocations typically result from the interplay of competition between institutions, lobbying and overlapping policy instruments. Internalizing these multiple objectives and instruments within a single agency helps to reduce these costs.

The chapters in this volume bring together the science, the cost–benefit analysis, the role of uncertainty, and the choice of policy instruments with the design of international agreements such as Kyoto and associated institutions. Together, they reveal how much is already known about how to address the problem of climate change, and the depth of our ignorance. Enough is already known to mandate early action, but there is enough uncertainty about the optimal policies to give a strong preference towards general, broad-based policies, putting a price on carbon (directly through taxes or indirectly through permits), rather than detailed and often *ad hoc* policy interventions. In intervening now, the 'learn-then-act' strategy is not thereby rendered irrelevant. We need both to act now in a flexible fashion, *and* learn to modify the levels and forms of intervention. In both cases, the crude tools of science and economics will need to be refashioned, and the approach will necessarily need to be multi-disciplinary.

Climate-change Policy: A Survey

DIETER HELM*

1. Introduction

Climate change presents a challenge to policy-makers of an altogether different kind to the day-to-day business of intervention in the economy to correct market failures. It is characterized by major and multi-dimensional uncertainties (in the science, the economics, and the politics), it is an externality created by almost all production and consumption, and it requires international cooperation on an unprecedented scale. Arguably, there is no other economic problem on this scale—save perhaps the related one of population growth. Furthermore, while economic analysis focuses on changes at the margin, many argue that the consequences of climate change may be anything but marginal. Climate change is likely to have a massive impact on biodiversity, it may alter oceanic currents, and it may displace whole populations and significantly reduce the economic prospects of our grandchildren.

Unsurprisingly then, the usual economists' toolbox looks puny against the scale of this challenge, and will require very considerable review and development. There will be no easy read across from existing economic theory and empirical evidence to policy. Just as the experience of the unemployment of the 1930s required a reinvention of much of macroeconomics, climate change will need new thinking, too. Environmental economics is in its infancy.

For many environmentalists, the conclusion that follows is that conventional economics has little to add; that the problem is largely a scientific, and a moral one. Scientists should, on this view, determine the 'correct' level of emissions, and then this level should be imposed

* New College, Oxford.

I would like to thank Christopher Allsopp and David Pearce for helpful comments. Any errors remain mine.

through direct intervention. Where doubts may arise as to the wisdom of such an approach, moral philosophy, not economics, provides the necessary intellectual input: we have a duty to ensure that future generations are treated at least as well as our own on grounds of intergenerational equity. We should not discriminate between individuals according to the time period in which they happen to live. And, in recognizing uncertainty, we should be guided by the precautionary principle. Thus, it is argued, sustainable development—leaving future generations at least as well off as the present—mandates, first, the achievement of a stable level of greenhouse-gas emissions, and then a reduction.

This is the sort of reasoning that lay behind the Framework Convention on Climate Change in 1992, which set in motion a process which produced the Kyoto Protocol in 1997. Targets were fixed and allocated for the period 2008–12, as a first stage in what was envisaged to be a permanent process of negotiations, agreements, and enforcement (Grubb, 2003). An element of flexibility was built into the targets, to be further extended in subsequent negotiations.[1] Unsurprisingly, perhaps, there has been a strong and divergent reaction by politicians and economists. While some scientists thought the reductions agreed at Kyoto were too timid, the USA opted out (despite being a principal architect of the Kyoto Protocol), and a number of economists questioned the wisdom of having targets at all, and, if there were targets, at the level agreed. They also pointed to the exclusion of the developing countries.

Climate change is, thus, not only a problem on a wholly new scale, but one which must—of necessity—be an interdisciplinary one. Without the science, there can be no serious understanding of what the problem is; without the politics, there can be no strategy for reaching a global consensus to reduce emissions and, hence, defining international property rights; and without the economics, scarce resources are likely to be wasted on badly designed policy instruments. New science, advances in the understanding of international agreements and institutions, and new economic techniques are all required.

Though there are natural fluctuations in CO_2 levels and temperatures, the main cause of the rise in CO_2 emissions is economic activity and, in particular, the transformation of economies in the twentieth century. Since 1900, the global population has more than tripled and the consumption of energy (largely fossil fuels) has increased more than ten

[1] There are three flexibility mechanisms in the Kyoto Protocol—joint implementation, the Clean Development Mechanism, and a facility for emissions trading. The Kyoto targets are for greenhouse gases and not just CO_2. However, for simplicity, throughout the article we concentrate on CO_2.

fold.[2] Climate change has been caused by the way resources have been consumed, and climate-change policy necessitates a substantial change in the allocation of resources. Furthermore, while scientists may suggest the appropriate level of emissions to stabilize the climate, they have little to say about the optimal resource-allocation path to achieve such targets, given that it is impossible to move to a substantially non-carbon economy quickly.

This chapter focuses on the three core components of climate-change policy: the targets, the instruments, and the institutional structures. Respectively, the questions are: what is the optimal path for reducing CO_2 emissions? which policy instruments, or combination of instruments — taxes, permits, and command-and-control — are likely to be most efficient within the political constraints? and how might institutional arrangements and structures be designed to facilitate international agreements and credible global climate-change policies?

2. How Much Should We Reduce CO_2 Emissions?

In designing policy targets, there are two separate but related questions which arise: what is the optimal amount of CO_2 in the atmosphere? and how fast should we move from the current level to the optimal? They are separate in that it makes sense to identify what the ideal level would be, but related, since the optimal level is path-dependant.

Let us start with the optimal level, which is where most scientific discussion begins. A reasonable amount is known about long-term trends in CO_2 levels. We know that the pre-industrial levels were of the order of 270–80 parts per million by volume (ppmv), and that the number has substantially increased since the industrial revolution, and particularly in the twentieth century, and is now around 370 ppmv. On current emissions trends, this could exceed 500 ppmv in the current century and even, eventually, 750 ppmv (see IPCC, 2001a). We also know that over longer periods the levels have fluctuated. An obvious starting point might be to regard the pre-industrial level as 'normal' and to take this as 'optimal'. Indeed, some environmentalists make the further connection that we should therefore adopt production and consumption patterns consistent with such a pre-industrial society.[3] But such an approach is not politically or economically plausible, and an alternative is to take current emissions levels as the base line, and to

---

[2] See Cohen (1995). McNeill (2000) provides an accessible summary of aggregate data on the main environmental trends in the twentieth century.

[3] This preference for a pre-industrial society is often linked to a wider claim about the virtues of an Arcadian life style.

attempt in the first instance to hold that line. This is the Kyoto approach. Subsequent steps might involve reductions in emissions, and a number of suggestions have been made, notably the RCEP (2000) proposals — carried over into the 2003 Energy White Paper (DTI, 2003a) — that UK emissions should not exceed levels consistent with a concentration of 550 ppmv, which would entail a 60 per cent reduction in emissions by 2050.

These numbers are subject to uncertainty. The precise levels over the last few thousand years are estimates from ice cores and other sources. Atmospheric CO_2 is a stock with inflows and outflows. The increase in emissions arises from diverse and often diffuse sources, and trends in emissions are particularly uncertain because they depend upon future policies, technologies, and population trends. These have to be included within climate models, where the simultaneous dependencies and feedbacks are crucial. Radical discontinuities are, by their nature, harder to model: a suspension of the gulf stream, changes in storm and cloud patterns, and the impact of deforestation and melting of the polar caps are examples which some scientists think are plausible within the century time frame (see IPCC, 2001a, pp. 15–16, 570–6).

These uncertainties are about the numbers and trends. But there is the additional step from the numbers about CO_2 concentrations to climate, on the causal relationships inducing climate change and its effects. Higher levels of CO_2 do not translate in a simple way into higher global temperatures. For this, a model of the climate and the causal mechanisms is needed. Some commentators — and several lobby groups — have focused on the problems with the science of climate-change models and suggested that even the direction of the relationship between CO_2 and temperature is questionable. This extreme position has gradually given way, as the climate-change models have developed, to a recognition that the uncertainties now lie with the scale, not the direction of change. But the range of temperature changes predicted remains wide and subject to substantial revisions, and some sceptics suggest we should focus on research to reduce the uncertainty of the science first, before changing policies.

Economists naturally focus on uncertainty in policy design, and there has been a tendency to see economic arguments as challenging the scientific approach. There are two reasons for this: the first, to do with the scientific uncertainties; and the second to do with the introduction of costs and benefits. On the former, it is important to recognize that the uncertainty in economic models of climate change is probably at least as great as that of the science (De Canio, 2003). The economic uncertainties are enormous: attempts to create general equilibrium models which can simulate the effects of a change in climate on the world economy —

termed integrated assessment models (IAMs) — tend to involve heroic assumptions. Over a longer run, such models need to simulate the path of technology and of demand, and to include the feedbacks from policies, including taxes on carbon, depletion of resources, and population trends.

To some, such attempts are too demanding to yield meaningful results, and clothe an inherently unpredictable path in a cloak of scientific and technical sophistication. General equilibrium models addressing more immediate and smaller-scale changes, such as tax changes, have had limited success. Politicians and the wider public, having little understanding of the technicalities of such models, may place too much faith in their predictions.[4] While this danger is widely manifest, the problem with this response is that it leaves policy design to the whims of political selection, and it provides no guidance as to the optimal level of emissions and emissions control. A central insight which environmental economics brings is that the optimal level of pollution is not normally zero: it is where the marginal costs of abatement equal the marginal costs of the pollution. Given that the marginal costs of abatement are unlikely to be negligible — and, indeed, may be very large — and that the marginal costs of pollution are not infinite, it follows that the optimal level of CO_2 in the atmosphere is unlikely to be the pre-industrial 270 ppmv. It may be 500 ppmv or more or less. Thus, although the IAMs may be imperfect, they provide a starting point for trying to estimate the optimal point — if only to see the simultaneous consequences of a series of assumptions. They provide valuable inputs into the policy process, but should not be decisive.

Economic analyses also demonstrate that such calculations vary greatly between countries and regions. Some countries are likely to be net gainers from climate change as agricultural productivity increases (through increases in warmth and the benefits to plants of CO_2 itself), as heating requirements fall, and because the offsetting costs of emissions are relatively smaller in economies which are more industrialized. Others may be worse off, and some much worse off.

The idea that CO_2 emissions have costs and benefits naturally leads to the idea that CO_2 is a commodity, which can be valued and traded like any other. This means that it has a price, which is the outcome of its supply and demand, and is amenable to application of the traditional economics tools of valuation. The price is a *social* one, in that it needs to incorporate the social dimensions — the externalities and distributional effects across the current populations and over generations.

---

[4] See, on the institutional incentives and structures, Wildavsky (1979).

There have been a number of attempts in the literature to arrive at the social cost of carbon. David Pearce (chapter 5 in this volume) summarizes the evidence and suggests that the value lies within the range of £4 per tonne of carbon (tC) to £27 tC. The importance of this calculation is illustrated through his critique of the approach by Clarkson and Deyes (2002), who estimate £70 tC, an estimate which the Department for Environment, Food and Rural Affairs subsequently used (Defra, 2002a). His analysis provides not only a critique of the government number — suggesting that it should be much lower — but also an insight into the core issues raised by the cost–benefit exercise. The main issues are: the use of discount rates and the way in which future generations' interests are taken into account; equity weighting and the interests of developing countries; catastrophe and the possibility of non-marginal changes; innovation and technical progress; and assumptions about continuing economic growth.

It is important to recognize that these are all issues amenable to analysis and modelling, and not merely criticisms. There is, for example, a voluminous literature on the use of discount rates, and the social cost of carbon can be modelled against different assumptions. The climate-change debate has focused on the issue of whether to discount the future at all and, within discounting, on whether to use discount rates that decline over time.

On equity weighting, the consequences are highly significant to the valuation exercise. This conveys an important policy lesson: the extent to which carbon emissions are reduced is to a significant degree a question of the global redistribution of resources to poorer countries. Whether this is best achieved by developed countries reducing CO_2 emissions or by direct wealth transfers is far from clear. The catastrophe problem is less amenable to modelling precisely because it is non-marginal. However, there are many examples of small-probability, large-cost events that confront policy-makers, such as a nuclear accident, a collision with an asteroid, or a virulent virus. The 'catastrophe' in the climate-change case is not likely to be the end of all human life: it is more likely to be a sharp reduction in welfare over a short time frame. How much resource should be devoted to such low-probability, high-cost events is controversial, but it is not infinite. Faced, for example, with new evidence of a rapid slow-down of the gulf stream, it is unlikely that a zero-emissions policy would be adopted and successfully implemented immediately (see Ingham and Ulph, chapter 3 in this volume).

The treatment of innovation and the assumptions about economic growth are linked: economic growth over the long run has conventionally been linked to technical progress, and the pushing out of the production frontier. Innovation in the context of the social cost of carbon is particularly important, because the 'solution' to climate change is likely to lie in large part with supply-side substitution to non-carbon energy technologies (assuming that demand for energy continues to grow).[5] The costs of reducing emissions over time are, therefore, greatly affected by the technology assumptions, and the policy implication is that efforts should focus on inducing more rapid technical progress.[6]

These issues can all be incorporated and organized within IAMs. Different assumptions will produce different estimates of the social costs of carbon. There remain substantive objections in principle to the whole exercise. These focus mainly on the nature of the information used — whether based on willingness to pay or willingness to accept.[7] Cost–benefit analysis is a technique which attempts to elicit the preferences of current individuals. The choices they make depend upon the information available to them and the way it is presented (the framing effect). Some environmentalists argue that climate change is a problem which is both so complex and large-scale, and so serious in its consequences, that we cannot rely on the choices people make now. Preferences should either be reflected through the delegation of the political process — electing people to choose on our behalf — or directly by 'experts'. Choice, on this view, should be restricted to those with superior information. There are many problems which are addressed in these ways — notably military and medical ones — but in the case of climate change, since the economic effects of policies to mitigate global warming are likely to be large, electorates will need to be persuaded to absorb the costs, and a useful starting point remains the information about their preferences from cost–benefit analysis studies. If results turn out to be very sensitive to the framing effect, then this conveys useful information, too.[8]

These considerations affect the choice of the number and the reliance placed upon it. But whatever the number chosen, there is an important

---

[5] Technology is also important on the demand side, enabling more efficient energy utilization.

[6] An example of the impact of assumptions about technical progress is seen in the MARKAL model which informed the 2003 Energy White Paper (DTI, 2003a). On MARKAL, see DTI (2003b) and Helm (2004, ch. 22).

[7] Willingness to pay and willingness to accept differ in part because willingness to accept assumes an ascription of property rights. There may, however, also be important framing effects issues.

[8] The literature on the application of cost–benefit analysis techniques to environmental problems is voluminous. See Bateman and Willis (1999) for a summary.

consequence of having a single number – and that is *consistency*. If the same number is applied across the range of policies – as it should be, since the social cost of a tonne of carbon is roughly the same wherever it is emitted – then the outcome should ensure that the substitution effects are efficient. The corollary of this point is that since existing policies implicitly assume a social cost of carbon, and since these assumptions vary enormously, current policies are likely to be very wasteful. We return to this point in section 5 below, in critiquing current policy.

A second policy implication is that the number is likely to vary over time. The marginal cost of emitting a tonne of carbon, given the current concentrations, is likely to be different (less) than if the pollution takes place in the future when concentrations have gone up. The social cost will rise through time (Mendelsohn, chapter 6 in this volume). Any carbon policy – whether permits, taxes, or command-and-control – should therefore be designed so that it can be ratcheted up through time, a point which turns out to have considerable implications for policy credibility and institutional structures.

A third policy implication of having a number is that this lends itself to economic instruments – arguably it is the optimal carbon tax. Or, put the other way around, an economic instrument requires a number – either a price or a quantity (which implies a price). If the social cost is, say, £4 tC (as per the lower bound of Pearce, chapter 5), then a price of carbon of that level would internalize the externality. If, however, Clarkson and Deyes (2002) are right, then a carbon tax of over £70 tC is indicated – or other forms of intervention which have equivalent effect. The effects would be very different, especially in the short run.

3. What Sort of Policy Instruments Should We Have?

A social cost of carbon may lend itself to a carbon tax, but it does not necessarily require one. The social cost can be integrated by a planner into command-and-control policies. These can take the form of designating technologies, or the less informationally demanding form of fixing the total quantity of emissions. The former is very informationally demanding; the latter assumes that the path to the optimal quantity is known, i.e. that the policy-maker knows the quantity of emissions which would come about as a result of the decisions of firms and individuals confronted with the price. If the quantity is translated into property rights, then a price of permits will emerge, though this will not necessarily be equivalent to the social cost of carbon.[9]

Almost all existing climate-change policies have command-and-control elements, involving choices of technologies and quantities, which is somewhat counter-intuitive in the context of the weight of the economic literature, which favours market-based instruments.[10] The fact that this is true in a wide variety of economies suggests that there is likely to be some rational (political) explanation. To see what this comprises, we need first to reiterate the standard case for economic instruments and then consider the particular features of the carbon case.

The starting point is to recognize uncertainty (in certainty, the planner can choose the optimal outcome, since all the demand and supply functions are known). Above, we noted a series of sources of uncertainty: about the optimum level of CO_2 in the atmosphere, about the transitionary path to reduce emissions, and about the costs and benefits of climate change. We noted, too, that the social cost of carbon was sensitive to the discount rate, equity weightings, innovation, and the economic growth path. The errors in climate models were compounded by the errors in economic models.

Faced with so much uncertainty, the planner's problems are immense. The market will have problems, too, but the great merit of the price mechanism in such circumstances is that it economizes on information, and it reveals information. It economizes since it decentralizes decision making to each firm and household, and each only needs to know the price, not everyone else's production and utility functions as does the planner. It reveals information, in that the policy-maker can see what happens when the price of carbon is imposed, so that the optimum can be better determined, and the instrument can be adjusted accordingly. The planner, by contrast, will observe queue shortages or surpluses. It is likely that there is learning-by-doing.

Economic instruments decentralize decisions about carbon abatement, with several important consequences. The market dictates which supply- and demand-side responses are cheapest, and which forms of pollution are marginal. It is neutral between adaptation and abatement. If the policy is credible (see below), then it encourages responses through time, benefiting non-carbon R&D. It is likely that, in the short run, adjustments will be on the demand side (since capital is fixed), but over time the supply side will respond as the capital stock is replaced.

[9] The difference between the carbon tax and the permits prices depends on the income effect.

[10] The forms of environmental regulation are discussed in Helm (1998), Heyes (1998), and Pearce (1998b). They are collected together in Helm (2000); see also HM Treasury (2002).

A credible economic instrument signals both. And, as noted above, if the marginal cost of carbon is expected to rise over time, then a low tax now can mitigate the costs in the short run when capital is fixed, while signalling a higher rate in the future.

In the literature, the choice of economic instrument is classically presented as one between adjusting prices or quantities for a particular commodity.[11] The policy-maker can fix the price and allow the quantity to adjust, or vice versa. Under uncertainty, the choice is an empirical one, dependent upon the expected shapes of the marginal damage function relative to the marginal costs of abatement, and the degree of relative uncertainty between marginal costs and marginal damages. If the damage function is expected to be steep (for example, the effects of a small dose of mercury in a water course can wipe out aquatic life), then a quantity restriction is preferable. If—as with climate change—the damage function is expected to be fairly flat (a small increase in CO_2 now arguably makes little difference to global temperatures), and if the costs of further abatement are, in the short run at least, very high at the margin, then a price mechanism is to be preferred.[12]

Ian Parry (chapter 10) provides an analysis of the carbon taxes versus permits debate, emphasizing the importance of the income effect. The revenues raised from carbon taxes can reduce distortions elsewhere— what has become widely known in the literature as the *double-dividend* effect—notably labour-market distortions resulting from income taxes. This holds for tradable permits, too, but crucially only if they are auctioned. In practice, it is highly unlikely that they will be, except at the margin.

It is, therefore, somewhat surprising that, despite these reservations, permit schemes have dominated climate-change policy developments. There are two reasons, both with important political elements. The first is that international agreements tend to be set in quantities rather than prices. The second is that carbon taxes are explicit and involve substantial income effects, which are disguised in the grandfathering of permits schemes. That a carbon tax might overcome these obstacles, and that it might, as noted above, also be more efficient, does not necessarily mean that it will be adopted. It needs to overcome the political and institutional obstacles, too.

The international dimension of the climate-change problem lends itself to quantity solutions for good economic reasons. The essential problem is that of an oligopoly, with poorly defined property rights.

[11] The classic articles are Weitzman (1974) and Roberts and Spence (1976).

[12] These assumptions may change over time: in the future the costs of non-carbon technologies may fall, while, as noted above, the marginal cost of carbon may rise.

The objective is to reduce output of CO_2. Countries, however, have different initial endowments, different capital structures, and face different marginal cost and benefit functions. Everyone (or almost everyone) has an incentive to cheat—to get others to reduce emissions while maintaining their own levels. The solution mimics an oligopolistic collusion or cartel: there must be accurate monitoring of emissions, cheating must be detectable, and punishment must be enforceable. In such circumstances, political negotiations will inevitably start with measurable quantities and look for a direct linkage between the overall objective (which is a quantity reduction) and the policy instrument. Using prices rather than quantities adds a further element for cheating, especially if there is a lack of credibility in the *ex-post* adjustments in taxes to meet the target (see below).

In an international agreement,[13] elements of equity as well as political power come into play. The burden of emissions reductions needs to be shared. From the economic theory perspective, the cheapest solution is independent of who has the initial rights. Trade will ensure that the marginal costs are minimized. But from a political perspective, the initial rights are crucial—politics is conducted as much in terms of the income effect as the substitution effect. Each country considers how much it will gain or lose by cooperation and, indeed, Russia's recent ratification of the Kyoto Protocol has been explicitly tied to the pay-offs. Climate-change agreements are, ultimately, the assignment of property rights—the starting point of emissions-trading schemes.

With the focus on the different costs and benefits between countries, the problems of enforcement, and equity considerations, it is not difficult to see why Kyoto has been so hard to negotiate. Following the Framework Convention in 1992, the developing countries effectively opted out of the first phase of Kyoto for 2008–12, as eventually did the USA. China's programme of economic expansion, largely based upon coal-fired electricity generation, left it outside, too,[14] while Russian involvement has had to be negotiated on the basis of the 'hot air' credits for the rapid falls in emissions associated with the collapse of the communist system at the end of the 1980s. Interestingly, those countries most in favour of Kyoto are either those with few immediate costs, or those with arguably a greater equity weighting on the welfare of developing countries.

The income effect explains why large corporations have typically favoured permits over carbon taxes. There are two factors at play here.

[13] Barrett (2003*a*) provides a comprehensive analysis of environmental agreements, protocols, and treaties. See also Barrett's chapter 13 in this volume.

[14] On China's energy programme, see IEA/OECD (2000) and Kroeze *et al.* (2004).

First, a carbon tax reduces profits by increasing costs, unless demand is inelastic. Thus, while electricity generators and oil companies may be able to pass through the tax, companies facing international competition—predominantly large energy-users in chemicals and manufacturing—may not be able to do so. Where this competition comes from developing countries outside the Kyoto framework, the effect may be considerable. There are companies where the share of energy in total costs is large, and where there is little prospect of non-carbon fuel sources replacing their fossil-fuel sources in the short to medium term. Permits, by contrast, are grandfathered, reducing the initial impact of the policy and perhaps even providing a windfall in the event of plant closure for other reasons.[15]

Grandfathered rights have the further benefit to incumbents of being particularly powerful barriers to entry, benefiting in this case the electricity generation and oil companies, where entry comes significantly from within the Kyoto boundaries. Permits raise entrants' costs, a well-known entry-deterring strategy in oligopoly theory.

For these reasons, emissions-trading schemes have had a good press, encouraged by intense lobbying. The UK experimented with its own scheme, providing a subsidy to large users to take additional reductions in emissions beyond those in the command-and-control plant-level emissions controls provided through the integrated pollution-control system. It excluded electricity generators and renewables, to avoid damage to the coal industry and to protect the high cost of renewables, and had very limited effect.

A better-designed system is the European one (see CEC, 2003a). This is more comprehensive in two senses: it includes the electricity sector, and it includes all the EU members. As such, it has a number of the desirable general features discussed by Tom Tietenberg (chapter 8). It will, however, still face the core challenges of such schemes. Rights have to be allocated, trades have to be regulated, revisions will be needed, and adjustments to take account of other policies incorporated in the scheme's design. The adjustment problem will be especially difficult in the UK, from the existing partial scheme to the comprehensive one, since the primary impact in the UK will be on coal power stations, which are likely to be crucial in maintaining security of supply in the second half of the first decade of the twenty-first century.[16]

In practice, though a permits scheme will play a central role in climate-change policy within the EU, and more generally in respect of

---

[15] This has been the experience of the UK Emissions Trading Scheme — see section 5 below.

[16] See Helm (2004, chs 16 and 23) and also DTI (2003c).

the future development of the Kyoto framework, it will be hedged around with other policy instruments. Steven Sorrell and Jos Sijm, in chapter 9, consider how these plural instruments will mesh together. The starting point is to recognize that the policy process does not typically conform to the economist's rational framework, where objectives and instruments are consistently matched. On the contrary, policy is almost always a piecemeal process—problems arise, and when politically acute, beget 'solutions'.

Thus, in the UK, there is an Energy Saving Trust (EST) with associated energy-efficiency policies; there is a Carbon Trust to spend monies on low-carbon technologies; there is a Renewables Obligation to support, predominately, wind power. In addition, there has been *both* a UK Emission Trading Scheme (ETS) *and* an energy tax, the Climate Change Levy. As noted above, the inconsistency of policy—and its inefficiency—can be seen by comparing the very different implied social costs of the policy measures against each other, and against the estimates for the level of the social cost of carbon. (We return to the point in section 5.)

A further characteristic of policy is that reform does not tend to happen wholesale. It is unlikely that at the international level Kyoto will be completely abandoned; and it is improbable that energy efficiency and renewables policies will be abandoned in favour of the European Emissions Trading Directive as the *sole* instrument of policy. Politics creates interests which support each policy; in economic terms, policies have rents. As a result, in the policy process, reform tends to be incremental.

These considerations have important consequences for policy analysis. Some inconsistencies are more inefficient than others and these costs can be estimated and ranked, so that priority can be given to the most significant distortions. Some policy rents are so large that they create insurmountable obstacles to change. And some overlap may be desirable, once the multiple market failures are identified. For example, there is considerable evidence of 'barriers' to take up for energy-efficiency measures, ranging from the landlord–tenant incentive problem, to capital market failures, and lack of information (see, for a summary, EST, 2001*a*). But, in such circumstances, the correct approach is to deal with each of the main market failures, and then tackle the carbon problem through the main policy instrument. It suits the vested interests to confuse climate change with other market failures, but they are analytically distinct and should be addressed separately.

4. What is the Appropriate Institutional Structure?

So far, we have argued that, although a permits scheme may be economically inferior to a carbon tax, its political advantages are considerable, including the fact that it is in sympathy with quantity-based international agreements. Signatories to agreements such as Kyoto could achieve their allocation in a number of ways, but there are considerable practical difficulties with all of them. Using any instruments requires that governments have credibility, both to firms and individuals within the country, and internationally to other parties to such agreements. International agreements typically lack the facilities to enforce quotas, and given that the free-rider problem is pervasive, some other mechanism will be required to induce confidence among the other parties.

Though not sufficient, it is necessary that the parties have confidence that instruments will be set and adjusted to meet the nationally allocated targets.[17] Dieter Helm, Cameron Hepburn, and Richard Mash (chapter 14) provide one such mechanism. They consider the credibility problem in terms of multiple objectives and time inconsistency and, with the analogy of monetary policy in mind, suggest that some form of delegation to an agency may be required credibly to commit to carbon targets. Such an agency might be given a single target for carbon emissions (as, in monetary policy, central banks are given inflation targets), and the setting of the appropriate instrument, such as a carbon tax, might be delegated too (analogous to the interest rate in the monetary policy example). Transparency of reporting would aid credibility further.

Such institutional reform would contribute to international credibility, too, and help to overcome the obstacles to a global climate-change agreement. But, as noted, it would not be sufficient: the process of negotiating the original 1997 Kyoto Protocol, and the subsequent attempts to gain ratification, have demonstrated how hard it is to achieve the necessary political buy-in. Many economists have suggested that the Kyoto Protocol is so flawed that it should be heavily circumscribed or abandoned in favour of other options. Among the critics, McKibbin and Wilcoxen (2002), Nordhaus and Boyer (2000), Victor (2001), and Barrett (2003a,b; and chapter 13 in this volume) have analysed the economic inefficiencies embedded within Kyoto and suggested alternative approaches.

---

[17] In the EU ETS these are set in National Allocations. See DTI (2003c) for details of the initial UK proposals.

The 'flaws' are not hard to identify. As noted above, in addition to the exclusion of the developing countries, notably China and India, the USA has decided not to ratify, and Russia has sought to maximize its economic leverage. Even after the post-1997 renegotiations, with the elements of flexibility (notably emissions trading, joint implementation, and the Clean Development Mechanism) further developed, it remains the case that the USA, as the source of around 25 per cent of global emissions, and China, which in 2003 alone plans to add around 50 GW of coal power stations to its electricity system (about the same as the total capacity on the British system), will continue outside Kyoto, while many of their industrial competitors, notably the EU, will be constrained by the targets. And even among those inside, it is unlikely that the net effect will be even stabilization at the 1990 levels. Add to the partial coverage, the absence of any serious enforcement mechanism for those countries that do sign up, and a notable absence of credible policy commitments to deliver the targets, and it is easy to see the critics' point of view.

But whereas the economic inefficiencies of Kyoto are easy to identify, the alternatives are not much more convincing. McKibbin and Wilcoxen (2002) advocate unilateral hybrid policies for emissions permits; Nordhaus and Boyer (2000) develop the idea of a harmonized carbon tax; Victor (2001) advocates emissions trading with a safety valve; and Barrett (2003*b*) advocates R&D and standards protocols with an adaptation fund. However, the problems that confront Kyoto are common to most, if not all, of the solutions on offer. Most countries are better off if others reduce emissions and they themselves do not, at least in the short run. For most governments, elections are a far more immediate concern. Time horizons are short—typically less than 5 years; voters are ill informed; and politicians have little incentive to impose on voters the costs—and hence reduced living standards—that climate-change policies might entail. Elections are conducted largely in terms of short-term economic growth, not long-term environmental concerns, and take little account of the interests of future generations. Politicians are also exposed to the power of corporate lobbying and, in the carbon field, there are obvious large-scale businesses with an interest in undermining and delaying the implementation of policies to reduce emissions. The economic case for doing less now (reflected in the low cost of carbon) fits neatly with the political interest in avoiding confronting the polluters—the voters—with the consequences of their behaviour. The economic approach effectively boils down to doing little now, waiting for the social cost of carbon to rise, and then assuming action will be taken. At 370 ppmv the costs are assumed low, but perhaps not at 500 ppmv. But at 500 ppmv, the political incentives will be largely the same, and hence there can be no easy assumption that the necessary actions will then be taken.

Christoph Böhringer and Michael Finus (in chapter 12) provide a defence of the Kyoto agreement as a pragmatic move in the right direction. They point to what has been achieved, and consider Kyoto to be a first step towards a more comprehensive agreement: it allows iterative adjustments towards an evolving goal. In a sense, this is not entirely distinct from Victor's argument. While Victor emphasizes the gains in monitoring emissions, he does indicate that the Clean Development Mechanism can be built upon the framework already in place. What both have in common is a recognition that building up international agreements is a gradual process, which requires investment in credibility. The Framework Convention on Climate Change in 1992 was ambitious in attempting to set the course for dealing with climate change. What the Kyoto process has revealed is that trying to be too ambitious too early has left the main players—the USA, China, and Russia—on the sidelines. Bringing them back into the process requires either a watering down of the overall target, or large-scale pay-offs and concessions. Watering down means that the emissions will continue to grow at a faster rate for a longer period; concessions will either have the same effect or mean that some countries will have to bear more of the costs.

It is, however, not unreasonable for a political process to start off with the status quo. In political terms, given the long-run aim of stabilizing atmospheric concentrations, the Framework Convention started with trying to limit emissions at the 1990 level. It then moved on, at Kyoto, to try to negotiate reductions among developed countries to offset rises in developing countries for the period 2008–12, with the intention of thereafter making significant reductions. Gaining political consensus and going through the ratification process would be necessary steps (see Grubb, 2003).

In economic theory, solutions to free-riding problems typically involve compensation. The problem with climate change is that it is all about shuffling around the losses in economic output and growth. Without some element of international altruism, and with the major emitting countries better off if they do not curb their emissions, there is little chance of much progress. Indeed, it might be argued that it is surprising that Kyoto has come as far as it has, and that should sufficient countries ratify it so that it comes into effect, it provides perhaps the only credible means of exerting moral pressure on the USA. And if the USA were to participate, it is perhaps the only country powerful enough to exert pressure on China.

If the free-rider problem is overcome, then the next step is to enhance the credibility of Kyoto. In addition to the role that emissions trading might play, there is also the question of its institutional structure. This might fall within the ambit of existing international institutions such as the World Trade Organization or even the United Nations, or new environmental international bodies may be needed. The arguments for delegation of carbon objectives to avoid conflicting objectives and to overcome the time-inconsistency problem discussed above apply not just to the national level but internationally, too. An international carbon-trading regime will need institutional support to establish, monitor, arbitrate, and revise carbon property rights.[18]

5. Policy Implications

We have established that the optimal level of carbon emissions is uncertain, and depends upon the costs and benefits of emissions reductions. The social cost of carbon is disputed, too. We have established that consistency is likely to improve economic efficiency, and that, although carbon taxes are economically superior to emissions permits, there are good political reasons why permits are likely to dominate. International agreements are plagued with problems, notably free riding, credibility, and enforcement, and are likely to take much longer to bring into effect than the architects of the 1992 Framework Convention imagined. In the light of these conclusions, what should policy-makers do now?

The obvious starting point is to consider whether existing policies are well designed, and whether the current emissions reductions could be achieved at lower costs — or whether, for the current expenditure of resources, the level of emissions reductions could be higher.

In most European countries, mixtures of policy initiatives have been introduced. These comprise energy taxes, emissions trading, support for renewables and energy efficiency, low-carbon technology support, international environmental aid, and numerous command-and-control rules. These policies have typically been developed in an *ad hoc* fashion, have been subject to vigorous lobbying by vested interests, and have been supported by overlapping and multiple agencies of government and voluntary bodies.

In the UK, by way of example, domestic targets have been set for CO_2 reduction (20 per cent by 2010; 60 per cent by 2050), independent of the

---

[18] The EU ETS is one example of the kind of super-national structure required, based upon a legally enforceable directive.

Kyoto targets for greenhouse gases. None of these has been subjected to serious cost–benefit analysis, and the overlaps have not been explicitly considered. In terms of policies, there is an energy tax (called the Climate Change Levy, CCL) which excludes coal; negotiated agreements with large industrial customers to reduce the effect of the CCL by up to 80 per cent; a renewables obligation on energy suppliers to take 10 per cent of their electricity from renewable sources, subject to a buy-out price; several schemes to support energy-efficiency measures; and there has been a UK ETS which subsidizes large industrial companies to adopt more stringent pollution limits (thereby reversing the polluter-pays principle) and which excludes electricity generators (and hence coal). Responsible departments, agencies, and other public bodies include: the DTI, Defra, and the Treasury (responsible, respectively, for energy policy, energy efficiency, and fiscal mechanisms); the EST (which promotes energy efficiency and administers the various energy saving schemes) and the Carbon Trust (which spends monies from the CCL on non-carbon technologies); the Environment Agency (responsible for pollution control and licensing); and Ofgem (responsible for regulating the energy industries).

The gap between economically efficient and existing policies is undoubtedly very large within the UK and in Europe. Existing carbon reductions could be achieved at (probably) significantly lower cost. The gap between the various implied costs in the different schemes and their variance, compared with the social cost of carbon from recent studies, is very large.

For some economists, the conclusion that follows is that little should be done now – that there is time to figure out appropriate policies.[19] The failures of Kyoto should not, therefore, be an immediate concern and a number of existing policies should probably be abandoned, or at best not expanded. If, and when, the social cost of carbon rises over time, then – and only then – should substantive action be taken.

For scientists, environmentalists, and even some politicians, this conclusion is anathema. Some argue that the damage now and in the future is much larger than IAMs have assumed – notably in terms of loss of biodiversity and the possibility of catastrophe. Intangible non-market values should also be included. Others challenge cost–benefit analysis directly: the framing effect is argued to be very large, other moral values beyond utility need to be taken into account, and the preferences of future generations may be very different from current ones.

[19] The main studies referred to in section 4 (Victor, 2001; McKibbin and Wilcoxen, 2002; Nordhaus and Boyer, 2002) all stress that there is time to develop new policy regimes – while the marginal cost of carbon is low.

There are two ways to approach a resolution of the sharp divergence in the climate-change debate. The first is to engage directly with the IAM approach and address the criticisms, while also taking a precautionary approach. Recognizing that the economic toolbox to tackle global warming is very crude, recognizing that a lot is left out (including, notably, adaptation) and revising the estimates of variables already included, provides the basis for an interdisciplinary approach. The second is to reject economic approaches and, instead, to focus on the political process to deliver non-economic objectives and to use policies on the basis of 'the more the merrier'. This chapter has argued that the former is the better way forward.

Part One: Principles

2

Science Informing Policy on Climate Change

DAVID KING*

Temperatures are rising. Last year we experienced the warmest recorded day ever in the UK; over the past hundred years, average global temperatures have risen by 0.6°C, and the ten warmest years on record have occurred since 1990. In summer 2003, an unprecedented heatwave swept across Europe causing up to 30,000 deaths and 13.5 billion euros worth of damage (UNEP/DEWA~Europe, 2004) and was more than 2 degrees hotter than the previous record.

The consensus among climatologists is that we are now experiencing the first effects of global warming, and that more extreme events could well be on their way. I believe that global warming is the most serious threat facing our world today. In this chapter, I discuss the evidence for this bold statement, and describe the current attempts by the UK government to try to combat this menace both as an individual nation and as part of a concerted international effort.

How do we know that we are now experiencing the effects of global warming, rather than a natural blip in the climate cycle? After all, Europe experienced a 'mini ice age' lasting from the thirteenth to the nineteenth century; could this latest trend simply be part of a natural 'mini warm age'? The evidence strongly suggests otherwise. There has been a widespread retreat of mountain glaciers in non-polar regions, many dating back 12,000 years, during the twentieth century; this ice evidence for global warming over the past century corroborates global measurements of temperature. An icon in the climate-change debate is the so-called 'hockey stick', a graph showing the average annual temperature in the northern hemisphere over the last 1,000 years. Shown in Figure 1, it is based on direct measurements since 1860 and

---

* Professor Sir David King is the UK government's Chief Scientific Adviser and Head of the Office of Science and Technology.

Figure 1
Variations of the Earth's Surface Temperature: Years 1000 to 2000

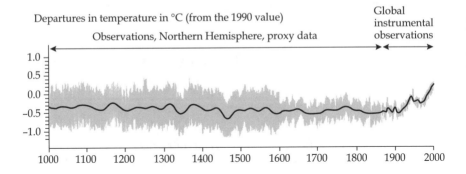

Departures in temperature in °C (from the 1990 value)

Observations, Northern Hemisphere, proxy data

Global instrumental observations

Source: Intergovernmental Panel on Climate Change.

proxy measurements, for example from tree rings, corals, and ice cores for the earlier period. The line shows the 50-year-averaged temperatures. (Mistakes in the original paper concerning the nature of the data included have recently been corrected (Mann *et al.*, 2004) but have no effect on the temperature trend shown.) All of this evidence demonstrates that we are facing a trend that is unheralded since the beginnings of our civilization 12,000 years ago. It seems that we have never had it so hot.

What is the origin of this warming? There is abundant evidence that we have brought it on ourselves. We have long known that atmospheric gases can affect the global climate. In the nineteenth century the French mathematician Fourier realized that the atmosphere naturally acts as a partial blanket for thermal radiation leaving the surface of the earth, keeping global temperatures about 21°C higher than they would be otherwise. Later a British scientist, Tyndall, demonstrated that the gases responsible for this were so-called 'greenhouse' gases, including water vapour, methane, nitrogen oxides, sulphur oxides, and, perhaps most importantly, carbon dioxide (CO_2). Critically, he demonstrated that the major constituents of atmosphere, nitrogen and oxygen, do not absorb the radiated energy and are not contributing to the greenhouse effect.

Figure 2
Carbon-dioxide Levels over the Last 60,0000 Years

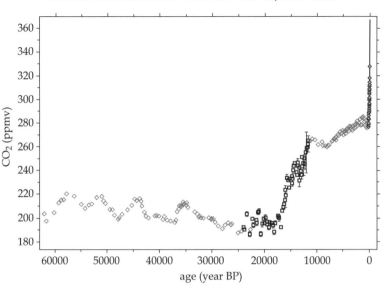

Source: University of Berne and National Oceanic and Atmospheric Administration.

Although CO_2 is not the most efficient of the greenhouse gases, its levels in the atmosphere have been rising very substantially in recent years thanks to human use of carbon, stored as fossil fuels ,as an energy source. The evidence for this comes from two sources. Ice cores, taken from the Antarctic and Greenland ice sheets contain a well-preserved record of the atmospheric composition dating back up to 740,000 years. Oxygen isotope measurements from these cores also provide a proxy for global temperatures. And since 1958, accurate direct data have been obtained at the Mauna Loa Observatory in Hawaii, chosen because of its distance from large human populations.

The data for the past 60,000 years are shown in Figure 2. Until around 1900, CO_2 levels lay in a perfectly natural range. According to the most recent ice-core data, CO_2 levels are always lower during the ice ages, and higher during the intervening warmer periods. Thus, between 60,000 and 18,000 years ago, which spans the last ice age, CO_2 levels were between 190 and 220 parts per million (ppm). From about 18,000 years ago, the levels rose to 265 ppm and from then onwards until 1900 lay in the normal warm period range of 260–280 ppm.

However, in the past 50 years the level has risen abruptly to around 379 ppm,[1] higher than at any point in at least the past 740,000 years. The

[1] http://www.cmdl.noaa.gov/

planetary atmosphere now contains a level of CO_2 that is a full 50 per cent higher than its pre-industrial levels, and it is still rising at an average of 1.84 ppm per year. Not surprisingly, therefore, much attention and work has been devoted to modelling the effect this will have on global climate.

The results are alarming. Even if CO_2 were stabilized at the present level, inertia in the climate system means that we would face at least a further 0.5°C rise in temperature over the next few decades. And if the levels continue to rise unchecked, current models indicate that, by 2100, temperatures will have risen by between 1.4 and 5.8°C (IPCC, 2001*d*).

One reason this range is so large is that the models have to incorporate complex climate feedbacks into their scenarios. For instance, rising CO_2 levels increase global temperatures, which also increase the rate of evaporation from the oceans, lakes, and rivers. This in turn raises atmospheric levels of water vapour—a potent greenhouse gas—in a positive feedback. The complication is how to incorporate cloud formation. Some types of clouds warm the planet, but others cause cooling by reflecting back solar energy into space. Satellite measurements support the notion that the average effect of cloud cover is a slight net cooling.

However, it is likely that these models predict a conservative outcome. Many of the non-linear complexities in the global climate system not included in the modelling to date would have a positive feedback on global temperatures. These include the potential loss of tropical forestation. There is evidence of a lowering of rainfall in regions of the Amazon which, extrapolated forward, may lead to significant losses, switching the forest regions from net CO_2 absorbers to emitters. Equally, warming the oceans may in turn lead to decomposition of deep-sea methane clathrates, resulting in an increase in atmospheric methane, another significant greenhouse gas. Increased melting of ice may change the salinity in the North Atlantic to limit substantially the circulation of the thermohaline current, the major heat conveyor which maintains high temperatures in Northern Europe. This would lead to an anomalous cooling in that region, while global temperatures continued to rise. Local weather patterns which are essential to local economies are also likely to be altered; an example is the Indian Monsoon. Finally, there is a growing interest among scientists in the possibility of attaining an average global temperature at which the irreversible melting of the Greenland ice sheet would be initiated. Loss of that land-based ice sheet alone would give rise to sea levels rising by about 6.5m (Gregory, 2004).

None the less, a small but vociferous group of global warming sceptics and lobbyists has been seizing on any legitimate mention of scientific uncertainties to lend fuel to their attempts to wreck the international scientific consensus. In my opinion, this is a particularly dangerous development. Although science has always progressed healthily by challenge, and this must be defended, the problem is that the voices of these sceptics are being very greatly amplified by particular economic/political interests, which have little to do with evidence-based scientific debate.

Interestingly, not all oil companies are giving support to the sceptic camp. Both John Browne, Chair and Chief Executive Officer of BP Amoco, and Lord Oxburgh, Chair of Shell, have made clear and uncompromising statements acknowledging and underlining the anthropogenic nature of global warming. Lord Oxburgh, for instance, said in a *Guardian* interview: 'No one can be comfortable at the prospect of continuing to pump out the amounts of carbon dioxide that we are at present. . . . You can't slip a piece of paper between David King and me on this position.' Each of these companies is involved in efforts to reposition themselves as 'energy' companies, with financial investments in renewable energy sources such as photovoltaics and hydrogen for transport.

For most climate scientists, the case for global warming has now been made. In an exhaustive and detailed review of the science in 2001, the UN Intergovernmental Panel on Climate Change (IPCC) concluded that 'there is new and stronger evidence that most of the warming over the last 50 years is attributable to human activities'. This represents the consensus of climate experts around the world.

Global warming is occurring on a scale unprecedented at least over the period of our civilization, dating back to the end of the last ice age; and it is largely caused by our determined exploration for, and burning of, carbon stored within the earth's crust as oil, coal, and gas over the past millions of years.

There are clear signs that our wanton exploitation of these resources is already having alarming environmental effects. Take the heatwave in Europe in 2003. On a random basis it is calculated that such a summer would occur once in about 800 years; climate change means that by the 2040s at least one year in two is likely to be warmer than 2003 (Stott *et al.*, 2004). The UK Meteorological Office's world-renowned Hadley Centre has shown that the human signal of climate change can be found on all continents. Extreme events are becoming more frequent. Glaciers are melting. Sea ice and snow cover are declining. Permafrost is melting and animals and plants are responding to an earlier spring.

In addition, melting glaciers and warming oceans have already caused sea level to rise by up to 20 cm during the last 100 years, and the rate will continue to increase. Even modest rises in sea level ensure that flooding from extreme storms reaches farther inland. UK insurers are already declaring new swaths of land to be unofficial flood plains, which could leave residents unable to receive cover for their properties. In 2002, I convened a team of national experts to investigate the specific threat of increased flooding and coastline vulnerabilities that we are likely to face from global warming. The panel concluded that, in the highest emission scenario, by 2080, flood levels that are now expected only once in 100 years could be recurring every 3 years (Office of Science and Technology, 2003).

By 2100, sea levels could have risen enough to pose a direct threat to 100m people around the world living in low-lying areas. In the longer term, even partial melting of the Greenland and West Antarctic ice sheets could cause further catastrophic rises. It has been predicted that, if temperatures across Antarctica continue to rise, the whole West Antarctic Ice Sheet could eventually collapse leading, to a rise in sea levels of 5–6 metres.

As if the risk of climate change were not enough, there are further dangers in relying so heavily on carbon-based fuels to run our industrial economies. Oil reserves are diminishing. According to Shell projections, oil supply will no longer meet demand in 25–30 years, and independent analysts predict that this could happen in just 15 years. What is more, oil is a relatively insecure resource, with much of the world's supplies coming from politically very unstable countries. I believe it is time for the world to kick its carbon habit.

All of these arguments point towards the same, unequivocal goal. The UK government believes that it is now urgently necessary to curtail greenhouse emissions. As a result the government announced in 2003 in the Energy White Paper (DTI, 2003a) a path towards reducing CO_2 emissions by 60 per cent of 1990 levels, by 2050. Let me explain why we chose this figure, and how we plan to achieve it.

CO_2 levels in the atmosphere are rising and will continue to rise, and other greenhouse gases, such as methane and nitrogen dioxide, are also at historic highs. The increased concentration of these gases is undoubtedly due to human activity—there is no other plausible explanation.

Whatever action is taken now, it is already too late to stop the initial manifestations of climate change. Inertia in our climate system means that the CO_2 we have released into the atmosphere will stay there for centuries, and we cannot escape the warming it will bring (Caldeira *et al.*, 2003). Our goal must be to reduce emissions urgently, to ensure that we do not make matters worse.

When setting a long-term target for reducing emissions, the first step is to attempt to stabilize greenhouse gases at some advanced level. Herein lies the first difficulty; there is as yet no international consensus as to how much atmospheric CO_2 we could reasonably adapt to, and what constitutes dangerous climate change.

The present atmospheric CO_2 concentration is 379 ppm, rising on average by 2 ppm per year with global emissions projected to rise more rapidly if no additional international restrictions are agreed. If we allow levels to rise to 550 ppm, about twice the pre-industrial concentration, models suggest that global temperatures will rise by between 2 and 5°C. At the higher end of this range, we would expect severe impacts from climate change, with a significant increase in extreme climate events, and most people adversely affected. The European Union has indicated that 550 ppm should guide global reduction efforts. The UK's Royal Commission on Environmental Pollution (RCEP, 2000) has also recommended the same limit for CO_2 levels. I should point out that this is not to imply that we are striving to achieve a level of 550 ppm. Rather we see this as an absolute upper limit, to be regarded as an initial rather than ultimate target.

For stabilization to occur, global emissions will have to equal natural uptake, and all countries will eventually need to take action to reduce their emissions to well below current levels. By ratifying the Kyoto Protocol, the UK had already committed to reducing emissions by 12.5 per cent below 1990 levels by the period 2008–12, and we had also set the national goal of a 20 per cent reduction in CO_2 emissions by 2010. Estimates suggest that if all industrialized nations make equal percentage emissions reductions (with developing countries later following suit), a figure of 60 per cent reduction by 2050 should lead to stabilization of CO_2 at 550 ppm some time in the next century. The 2003 Energy White Paper (DTI, 2003a) set the UK on the path towards this reduction. However, if the climate system turns out to be at the higher range of model sensitivities, still greater reductions will be needed to avoid the more severe impacts.

The UK government believes that action, far from being expensive, could be an excellent economic investment. An extensive review by the IPCC suggests that stabilizing atmospheric CO_2 at 550 ppm would lead to an average gross domestic product (GDP) loss for developed countries by 2050 of only around 1 per cent. This figure should be more than offset by the savings from reduced environmental damage. For example, if just one flood broke through the Thames Barrier today, the Environment Agency estimate the cost of the damage could be as much as £30 billion.

Environmental changes and severe weather events are already affecting the world insurance industry. Swiss Re, the world's second largest insurer, has estimated that the economic costs of global warming could double to $150 billion each year in the next 10 years, hitting insurers with $30–40 billion in claims.

It is a myth that reducing carbon emissions necessarily makes us poorer. Tackling climate change can create economic opportunities and higher living standards. Between 1990 and 2002, the United Kingdom's economy grew by 36 per cent, employment increased by 4.8 per cent, and our greenhouse-gas emissions fell by 15.3 per cent (Defra, 2002b) This example does not just apply to industrialized nations. During the same period, the Chinese economy grew by over 60 per cent, while its emissions intensity fell.

Although a 60 per cent reduction in CO_2 emissions may seem an ambitious target, we have already put in place measures that should help us achieve it. The first such measure is to reduce emissions by improving the efficiency of our industrial and domestic energy use: a win–win situation.

Sixty per cent of the energy in the UK grid is used for heating, lighting, and cooling buildings. However, with the standard set-up of widely separated power stations and long-distance cables, some 55 per cent of this is lost in transmission. It is ironic, indeed, that power stations have large cooler systems to enable them to lose heat to the environment, when the electricity they generate is later used to heat buildings. One way to improve this is for energy companies to provide combined heat and power, with more widely distributed power stations contributing the heat they generate directly for central heating and hot water. At present, only about 5 per cent of the energy supply on our grid provides this combination, but the UK government is using fiscal measures to encourage companies to increase this proportion. In Denmark, for instance, 50 per cent of electricity supply comes from combined heat and power (Szokolay, 2004).

The UK government is also introducing regulations for new buildings and refurbishments, to ensure that they exhibit the highest possible energy efficiency. The economic and social case for new housing is compelling, but it is also important that our approach is environmentally sustainable. In 2002 the government raised the minimum standard for the energy performance of new buildings by 25 per cent, and next year we will raise it by another 25 per cent. The challenge now is to work with the building industry to make sustainability an important factor in the design of all new housing.

The second strand in our strategy for reducing greenhouse emissions is to encourage the development of energy technologies that can replace fossil fuels. There are many possible ways to provide energy from low-emission or renewable sources, and I should emphasize that we should not attempt to second-guess which of these will finally win the race. Rather, the British government intends to set up the right economic framework and let the marketplace figure out the best technology or combination of technologies.

The UK's target is that, by 2010, 10 per cent of the country's electricity sales will come from renewable sources of power, such as biofuels, wind farms, tidal, and solar power. In 2002 the UK government introduced a Renewables Obligation, calling on all licensed electricity suppliers to provide a specific proportion of their electricity sales from renewable sources. Since many potential renewable resources are still at an early stage of development, we also recognize the importance of investing in research. The UK's research councils are establishing a new national energy research centre. Moreover, in its 2004 spending review, the government increased the annual science budget by 5.6 per cent, which, following the rise from £1.45 billion in 1997 to £2.4 billion in 2004, will see a further climb to £3.3 billion by 2007 in cash terms.

Meanwhile, the UK government's 10-year framework for science and innovation set the target of raising UK investment in R&D as a proportion of GDP from 1.9 per cent this year to 2.5 per cent by 2014 (HM Treasury, 2004). Government will fund part of this increase through its investment in the science base. But the private sector has an even bigger role to play. Our vision is to see industry's investment in research and development increasing from 1.24 per cent to 1.7 per cent of GDP over the same period.

One possible way to increase power output while reducing emissions would be to rely more heavily on nuclear power. Instead, however, we are currently in the process of decommissioning the country's nuclear power stations. By 2020 Sizewell B will be the only remaining nuclear power station on the national grid, and the nuclear contribution will have dropped from around 26 per cent to about 5 per cent—a reduction of some 20 per cent. Since nuclear energy generates no greenhouse emissions, the danger here is that, as a nation, we might only break even on carbon emissions, with increased efficiency and use of renewable technologies simply making up the nuclear gap.

As the 2003 Energy White Paper rightly stated, the UK government has not ruled out the possibility that at some point in the future new nuclear build might be necessary if we are to meet our carbon targets.

The problem of the nuclear waste legacy needs to be addressed, but modern power stations are designed to operate at much higher efficiencies than in the past; if the current fission power stations in the UK were replaced by, for example, a new fleet of Westinghouse AP1000, that would only add about 10 per cent to our current levels of nuclear waste over a period of 60 years.

Beyond that, the way forward could well be nuclear fusion, since this is a nuclear energy process that generates no radioactive waste and no carbon emissions. The UK has been a big part of the major European push towards promoting the development of electricity and hydrogen generation from nuclear fusion, particularly through the six-partner consortium to construct ITER (International Thermonuclear Experimental Reactor).

The third strand in our attempts to reduce emissions is to consider ways to capture CO_2 from the power station emissions and store it in some fixed form. One way to achieve this in the UK would be to make use of our depleted oil and gas fields in the North Sea. At present, the remaining stores of oil in these sites are forced to the surface using compressed air. If compressed CO_2 were used instead, the carbon removed as oil could be offset by CO_2 stored in its place.

Of the options for reducing emissions, capture and storage is the only one that would allow us to continue to burn fossil fuels far into the future. Since oil companies have the most to gain from this option, I believe they should be the ones to provide and fund the research. I also believe that CO_2 capture and storage should never become a fig leaf for avoiding the issue of how to replace a carbon-based economy. Sooner or later we will need to curb our dependence on fossil fuels.

Action on the part of the UK alone will not be enough; there is a clear need to secure action worldwide. Climate change is no respecter of national boundaries. We in the UK are showing leadership, and many other countries, including our European partners, are also in the vanguard. But we cannot solve this problem without the determined commitment of the international community.

The only international treaty currently on the table is the Kyoto Protocol, under the auspices of the United Nations Framework Convention on Climate Change (UN FCCC). The Protocol sets legal targets for all signatories to reduce emissions by around 5 per cent of 1990 levels in the period 2008–12. One criticism of the Protocol is that this reduction will not be enough to make a serious dent in greenhouse-gas levels. However, it is a valuable first step, providing a fiscally driven framework by which countries, individuals, the private sector, and multinationals can join forces to play their part in the international effort. Once emission trading is fully established, emission reductions can be ratcheted up to meet internationally agreed targets.

The Kyoto Protocol also makes provisions for carbon trading, whereby individual countries can exceed their own emissions quota by buying unused capacity from others. A particularly important form of this is the so-called 'clean development mechanism' (CDM), which is meant to come into effect in 2008. By this mechanism, a significant emitter country, such as the USA, could trade some of its emissions against providing carbon-free technology to developing countries.

Since developing countries contribute some 40 per cent to global greenhouse emissions, their role in tackling climate change has been contentious. Developed countries need to enable developing countries to leapfrog to cleaner technologies, and the CDM within the Kyoto Protocol is an excellent way to achieve that. It could make a significant difference to countries such as India and China, as anticipated in the 2008–12 phase of Kyoto. The UK government is in discussions with both countries and we feel most encouraged by their eagerness to address the problem of global warming. In particular, the Chinese government is demonstrating a considerable awareness of the dangers of environmental pollution, and has made significant strides in reducing its emissions intensity. Data published by the International Energy Agency show that, in China, the CO_2 emitted per dollar of GDP fell by some 47 per cent between 1990 and 1999, achieved by sustained improvement of energy efficiency and increased use of gas and hydropower.

In a very welcome move, Russia has now ratified the Protocol, which will swing into action from 16 February 2005. To date, the USA and Australia have not yet ratified. Both countries say that they remain faithful to the UN FCCC and Australia has said it will continue to work towards what would have been its Kyoto emissions targets.

The situation in America is very pressing. The United States is responsible for roughly 25 per cent of global greenhouse emissions, though it has only 4 per cent of the world's population. In January 2004 I published an article in *Science* (King, 2004) calling on the USA to play its leading part in the war on climate change. In a welcome response, Spencer Abraham, the former US Energy Secretary, published a piece recognizing the importance of global warming and its anthropogenic cause and spelling out the work by the USA on improving energy efficiency and developing technologies such as carbon sequestration (Abraham, 2004). He finished by saying 'The President remains committed to leading the way on climate change at home and throughout the world.'[2]

US emissions have risen significantly since 1990, so ratifying the Kyoto Protocol would appear to be an expensive step for them to take (although Spencer Abraham also acknowledges the potential economic damage to the USA from climate change). However, it is not enough for each country to act alone: global problems require global solutions.

At present, the Kyoto Protocol is the only game in town, and the UK is doing everything it can to support it, while recognizing the need to get all players on board. We would welcome discussions of alternative

[2] http://www.whitehouse.gov/news/releases/2001/06/climatechange.pdf

processes that might serve similar ends, but this must not be an excuse for delaying action. The Kyoto Protocol was 8 years in the making, and I believe that this is such an urgent issue that we do not have eight more years to spare developing a new system. Delaying action is not an option now that emissions trading is about to begin at the international level.

The UK government is, therefore, entering into discussions with the USA, Australia, India, and China about how to bring everybody fully back on to the international stage. In 2002 the UK set up the world's first economy-wide greenhouse-gas emissions-trading scheme. The rationale is to ensure that emission reductions take place wherever the cost of the reduction is lowest, thus lowering the overall cost of combating climate change. As a fiscal incentive, companies that meet their emissions targets, by buying excess capacity from others if necessary, receive an 80 per cent discount from the Climate Change Levy—a tax on the business use of energy. On 1 January 2005 a similar Europe-wide scheme will come into place, and the other Kyoto signatories will follow suit. With or without the participation of the USA this will be a very significant market, eventually worth trillions of dollars.

Ultimately, climate change will be everybody's problem. In January 2004, I made a comment that caught the headlines around the world. I said that, in my view, climate change is the most severe problem that we are facing today, more serious even than the most severe threat of terrorism. I firmly believe that this is true, and that all countries will eventually come to the conclusion that global emissions reductions are truly necessary. When that happens, countries such as the UK, which have already set their strategy in place, will have a distinct advantage over those that have not begun to set up emissions trading markets, or invested heavily enough in renewable technologies.

Meanwhile, Tony Blair has set climate change as one of two top priorities for the UK's G8 Presidency in 2005. He has also declared that his ambition is to build scientific and policy consensus among governments throughout the world, and to promote much more vigorous global action. The challenge is out there. All we have to do is meet it.[3]

---

[3] Recommended further reading includes Houghton (2004); Weart (2003); Victor (2004); and King (2002).

Uncertainty and Climate-change Policy

ALAN INGHAM AND ALISTAIR ULPH*

1. Introduction

One of the major issues in climate-change policy is the considerable uncertainty that surrounds many of the elements needed, in terms of the scientific understanding of the processes driving climate change, for example the risk of possible catastrophic effects of climate change, the impacts of any such changes on society and the economy, for example, the extent of adaptation that might take place, and the economic values to be attached to these impacts, for example the appropriate social discount rate or equity weights.

This raises the obvious first question of how such uncertainties should affect decisions about the current level of abatement of green-house-gas emissions and hence about the correct current value of the social cost of carbon (SCC). What would be the difference in policy if explicit account is taken of uncertainties, as opposed to ignoring such uncertainties? This question is addressed in section 2 of this chapter.

However, the issues surrounding uncertainty are considerably more complex than just comparing policy outcomes with uncertainty with policy outcomes when uncertainties are ignored. For some of these uncertainties will be resolved through the process of further research, for example as exemplified in the reports of the Intergovernmental Panel on Climate Change (IPCC). This process of learning raises a crucial timing question. On the one hand, it can be argued that society should delay taking action to reduce greenhouse-gas emissions, because if we subsequently learn that climate change is less serious than we had thought, we will have taken steps unnecessarily, while if we do

* Tyndall Centre for Climate Change Research and University of Southampton. This chapter is a revised version of a paper produced for a Defra international conference in London on the Social Cost of Carbon, July 2003. We are grateful to Michael Grubb and Dieter Helm for helpful comments on that earlier version, and to the Tyndall Centre for financial support.

learn that climate change is more serious than we now anticipate, we can always accelerate action then.

However, it is often argued that this 'learn-then-act' approach only makes sense if the accumulation of greenhouse-gas emissions is *reversible*, so that if we learn that climate change is serious we can 'undo' the effects of some of the emissions that were released while we were waiting to get this information. But the accumulation of greenhouse gases is often viewed as *irreversible*, so that by the time we learn that climate change is a serious issue, we may have built up such concentrations of greenhouse gases that we are faced with drastic consequences which cannot be readily undone.

The process of concentration of greenhouse gases in the atmosphere is not literally irreversible, but the usual models of climate change (e.g. underlying the DICE model) suggest that if emissions of carbon dioxide (CO_2) stopped, atmospheric concentrations would continue rising and only revert to current levels after 300 years, and to pre-industrial levels after 1,000 years. As Fisher (2002) points out, more recent analysis suggests that after rapid mixing of the atmosphere with the surface ocean, further removal of CO_2 from the atmosphere depends on the much slower mixing of surface ocean with deep ocean (Joos *et al.*, 1999). Schulz and Kasting (1997) calculate that CO_2 concentrations will be more than double their current level in a thousand years' time, and will still be higher than current levels for several thousand years. So, although there is a process of decay in CO_2 atmospheric concentrations, it is extremely slow.

This irreversibility in the climate process leads to calls for implementing a *precautionary approach* — that, far from delaying taking steps to reduce greenhouse-gas emissions while we wait for better information, we should take more steps now, to guard against getting bad news in the future and finding it is too late to do anything about it.

This statement of the precautionary principle makes it sound rather intuitively obvious, and the precautionary principle is often employed in debates on climate-change policy, particularly in support of calls for increased action by governments to reduce greenhouse-gas emissions. However, an important message of this chapter is that the intuitive argument is not necessarily correct. In section 3 we review the conceptual underpinnings of the precautionary approach and show that there are fundamental ambiguities in whether the precautionary principle implies that we should be accelerating action now to reduce emissions. There are some rather subtle technical reasons for this, which we try to explain in a straightforward way. A more readily appreciated argument is that, in policy terms, there are many quasi-irreversible stocks involved in climate change — stocks of greenhouse gases, stocks of capital which emit greenhouse gases, and stocks of capital which reduce emissions of greenhouse gases. How uncertainty and learning affects emissions will depend on how it affects all these stocks, and they have different effects on emissions.

Of course, the important question is how these ambiguities work out in empirical models of climate-change policy, and in section 4 we review the empirical work that is currently available and show that it does not support the precautionary principle, so that the prospect of getting better information in the future leads to a *reduction* in current abatement efforts. However, we draw on the conceptual review in section 3 to argue that the particular models used in the empirical work have perhaps understated what the impact should be.

Another argument often used in climate-change policy debates is the possibility that climate change may lead to catastrophic effects; for example, those caused by the melting of ice sheets. However, we show again that the simple intuition — that the risk of catastrophes should lead us to be more cautious about increasing greenhouse-gas emissions now — need not be correct. This depends crucially on what is meant by a catastrophe, and how the risk is modelled. Paradoxically, if one thinks that the concentration of greenhouse gases affects only the risk of a catastrophe, and that if a catastrophe occurs it results irreversibly in a radically lower level of welfare, which does not depend on the concentration of greenhouse gases (the kind of apocalyptic scenario sometimes associated with discussions of nuclear warfare), then this may lead to a reduction in abatement effort. We review the conceptual and empirical literature on this in section 5.

Throughout this chapter we draw upon standard economic tools of analysis of uncertainty (essentially cost–benefit calculations) in discussing climate change, and in section 6 we review a number of broader issues about whether this is an appropriate framework for thinking about climate change.

2. Uncertainty and the Social Cost of Carbon

In this section we assess the impact of uncertainty in the absence of learning, beginning with a brief sketch of the methodology involved, then illustrating the approach with a couple of studies, and finally addressing some methodological issues raised in the literature.

(a) *Approaches for Introducing Uncertainty*

Most models which have been used to compute optimal policies essentially use best-guesses or estimated values of uncertain parameters, and then compute policy as if these parameters were known with certainty. Such studies are referred to as 'certainty-equivalent' models. To recognize that there is significant uncertainty about these parameters, the obvious first step is then to conduct sensitivity analysis by varying one or more parameters from their best-guess or estimated values and then rerun the deterministic model to assess what effect this has. A more sophisticated form of sensitivity analysis is to assume that uncertainty about each parameter value can be captured by a probability distribution,[1] and then conduct sampling from these distributions. For any given set of parameter values from this sampling procedure one again uses the deterministic model to compute the optimal policy. This allows the analyst to build up a probability distribution of policy values, and one can then calculate the mean or median values of this distribution. The mean of the distribution of optimal policy values generated by this sensitivity analysis will usually be significantly different from the calculation of optimal policy derived from the certainty-equivalent model. This just reflects the fact the model is a non-linear function of parameters, so the expected value is not the same as using the expected value of parameter values.

While this is useful in building up a picture of how uncertainty affects things, it has to be emphasized that the calculation of optimal policy is still undertaken using a deterministic model, in which uncertainty is ignored. This form of analysis is what is referred to as 'learn-then-act' — the analyst calculates optimal policy and hence the SCC as if he or she has learned the true set of parameter values. To take account of uncertainty fully, one needs to model the situation where the decision-maker recognizes that the future flows of net benefits are uncertain, and maximize present value of expected utility of these future flows of net benefits. This corresponds to what is called 'act-then-learn', although for this stage in the chapter we assume that learning never takes place, so uncertainty is never resolved. (The next section of this chapter asks what happens when learning can take place.) The difference between 'act-then-learn' and 'learn-then-act' analysis is, first, that the decision-maker can choose only one set of actions now, not a different set of actions contingent on each set of parameter values. A second difference is that one can allow for attitudes to risk by the decision-maker. We now illustrate these different approaches by considering a couple of studies for estimates of the SCC.

---

[1] The distributions for different parameters are usually assumed to be independent of each other.

Table 1
Effects of Uncertainty on Social Cost of Carbon ($/tC)

Study	Year of SCC	Certainty equivalent	Learn-then-act Mean	Median	Std dev.	Act-then-learn
Schauer (1995)	n.a.	3.75	8.73	1.76	21.16	n.a.
Nordhaus and Popp (1997; full)	2000	n.a. ($3–4)	11.65	4.39	n.a.	n.a.
Nordhaus and Popp (1997; 5 SoW)	2000	n.a.	6.25	n.a.	n.a.	6.31

Note: SoW is states of the world.

(b) *Studies of Uncertainty and Social Cost of Carbon*

Schauer (1995) uses a climate model very similar to the well-known DICE model (Nordhaus 1993*a*, 1994*a*) to calculate the SCC as a function of eight parameters. To assess the uncertainty about these parameters he asked 16 experts for their estimates of the most likely value of these parameters, together with high and low estimates and assessments of the likelihood that actual values would lie above or below these upper and lower estimates. From this he constructed triangular distributions for each expert for each parameter, and these were then aggregated to form *Bayesian prior* distributions for each parameter.

Using the expected value of each of the uncertain parameters, Schauer used the resulting certainty-equivalent model to compute an SCC of $3.75/tC (see Table 1). He then conducted sensitivity analysis by assessing by how much the SCC would respond to a one standard deviation in each of the eight parameters, which showed that uncertainty about the social discount rate had the greatest effect on the SCC. By random sampling from the distributions of each of the parameters he built up a distribution of 10,000 values of the SCC, of which the mean value was $8.73/tC, the median $1.76/tC, the standard deviation $21.16/tC, and the range –$18 to $358. So the non-linearity of the model of the SCC causes the expected value of the SCC to be more than double the estimate derived from the certainty-equivalent model, and the degree of uncertainty about the SCC is substantial. Schauer compared this range of estimates for the SCC, derived from using uncertainty about the parameters of his model, to a direct assessment of uncertainty by asking the experts to provide their range of values for the SCC. This latter exercise produced a much higher mean value $112.5/tC, and a much higher standard deviation $49/tC. However, Schauer did not carry out any analysis maximizing expected utility.

Nordhaus and Popp (1997) use a version of the DICE model, called PRICE, designed to analyse decisions under uncertainty. They consider uncertainty about a number of parameter values in the DICE model: (i) cost of climate change; (ii) cost of mitigation; (iii) the link between CO_2 concentrations and climate; (iv) future population growth; (v) the growth of greenhouse-gas emissions per unit of output; (vi) the retention rate of CO_2; and (vii) the rate of productivity growth in the economy. Uncertainty about each of these parameters was derived from both surveys of the literature and surveys of expert opinion. They carried out Latin hypercube sampling from the distributions of parameters, and from 625 such samples calculated that the SCC, expressed as carbon tax that would be levied in 2000, would have a mean value of $11.65/tC, a median value of $4.39/tC, and 10th and 90th percentile values of $0.04/tC and $33.85/tC, respectively. Although they do not provide the SCC from the certainty-equivalent model, earlier work by Nordhaus (1994*b*) would suggest a figure in the range $3–4, so that the mean of the distribution of the SCC would be between three and four times the value calculated from the certainty-equivalent value. These results are broadly consistent with those of Schauer (1995) in terms of the shape of the distribution of the SCC, though the range of uncertainty is rather smaller.

It would not be tractable to use this kind of sampling approach to conduct expected utility analysis. To make analysis more tractable, the 625 estimates were grouped into five possible 'states of the world', ranked in terms of potential degree of damage. Using this much reduced analysis of uncertainty, the control rates for the year 2000 for these five states of the world under the learn-then-act approach would range from 3.9 to 45.8 per cent, with a mean of 10 per cent, and a carbon tax (SCC) from $1.21/tC to $44.26/tC, with a mean of $6.25/tC. Comparing this figure with the estimated mean value of the SCC of $11.65/tC shows the effect of substantially coarsening the treatment of uncertainty by aggregating the original 625 samples into just five states of the world.

Nordhaus and Popp then go on to conduct an 'act-then-learn' analysis, where policy-makers have to choose control rates or carbon taxes for 2000 to maximize expected utility, although for this analysis they assume that the true state of the world will eventually become known in 2045. They show that the control rate for 2000 will be 12 per cent (compared to a mean rate of 10 per cent from the learn-then-act approach) while the SCC in 2000 would be $6.34/tC, compared to a mean figure of $6.25/tC using learn-then-act. So using expected-utility maximization to deal with uncertainty can lead to slightly higher levels of controls, and hence SCC, than just taking expected value of the distribution of social costs that arises from the use of learn-then-act models. Part of this reflects risk aversion, and part the different timing of when information is learned, as we shall see in sections 3 and 4. In particular, in section 4, we consider a further experiment conducted by Nordhaus and Popp of changing the date at which uncertainty gets resolved.

Nordhaus and Popp also use their model to assess the value of getting better information, defined as the difference in present value expected welfare from having uncertainty resolved in 1995 compared to 2045. They calculate that the value of perfect information about all the seven parameters listed above is $86 billion, and that the benefit of resolving each individual source of uncertainty is in the order the variables are listed, with the first variable accounting for about half the benefits, the second variable half the remaining benefits, and so on.

These studies, therefore, suggest that allowing for uncertainty might raise the SCC by a factor of 2–3 compared to the values that emerge from certainty-equivalence models.

(c) *Methodological Issues about the Treatment of Uncertainty in Cost–Benefit Analysis*

Some concerns have been raised about the appropriateness of using expected-utility maximization, and hence conventional cost–benefit analysis, to deal with uncertainties about climate change. Tol (2003*a*) suggests that the standard approach of expected utility maximization adopted for modelling uncertainty and solving for an optimal policy is fundamentally flawed because of the possibility of infinite mean and variance for the value of discounted net marginal benefits. These infinities arise in his model basically because climate change can cause income in some regions in some time periods to fall to zero. This has three impacts on calculation of expected present value utility (see Yohe, 2003).[2]

(i)   The first arises from the social discount rate.[3] It is well known that the social discount rate for discounting future streams of income depends on the rate of economic growth. If environmental problems result in negative economic growth, then the social discount rate could be negative, and expected utility could become unbounded. This problem was also encountered by

[2] One reason why this can occur is that the random variable that underlies the process may be one with 'fat tails' so that there are relatively large probabilities of extreme values. An example of this, that is often used for counter examples, is that of the Cauchy distribution. In this section we shall discuss factors relevant to climate change that might cause these problems.

[3] The social discount rate at time t is defined by $\delta_t = \rho + \eta g(t)$, where ρ is the pure rate of time preference, η is the aversion to inequality, and $g(t)$ is the economic growth rate.

Schauer (1995) when random sampling for parameter values, including economic growth and the pure rate of time preference. He got round this problem by replacing random values by expected values to ensure the discount rate remained positive.

(ii) The choice of utility function can mean that the marginal utility of income becomes infinite as income tends to zero. Tol uses a logarithmic utility function, which has this property.

(iii) This second problem can be compounded by the use of equity weights, which take the form of global income divided by regional income, which obviously become infinite if income in a region falls to zero.

Tol suggests that infinite variance is more than just a theoretical possibility, and demonstrates that they arise in his Monte Carlo simulations, where one of the simulations has water supply for irrigation in central Europe, and hence income, going to zero. However, as Yohe (2003) notes, it can be argued that this problem arises because of a lack of economic instruments: a social planner would wish to use policies such as income transfers or technology transfers to avoid income falling to zero in some region, if the planner cares as much about low incomes as is implied by the objective function.

Azar and Lindgren (2003) support some of the criticisms that traditional cost–benefit analysis may be limited in its application to climate-change problems. Those related to the treatment of uncertainty are that most models fail to deal adequately with possible catastrophic effects of climate change, an issue we deal with in section 5, and that an approach which alternates between acting and learning may be more fruitful. Yohe (2003) also agrees that it is important to model learning, so that policy-makers would respond if they learned that income was falling rapidly in some regions, though of course this raises the question of whether, with irreversibilities, policy-makers would have time to act once they have learned. We turn to these issues of learning, irreversibilities, and precaution in the next two sections.

3. Uncertainty, Learning, Irreversibility, and Precaution

We now explore the implications of allowing for the fact that decision-makers know that, over time, they are likely to get new information which will help them to resolve some of the uncertainties about climate change. The standard intuition is that if one is making an irreversible decision under uncertainty, when there is the prospect of obtaining better information in the future, then this should reduce the extent to which one makes irreversible commitments in order better to exploit the information that will become available. In simple terms it pays to keep one's options open. This insight, which can also be viewed as a formal statement of the precautionary principle, was introduced into environmental economics in the seminal papers of Arrow and Fisher (1974), and Henry (1974*a,b*). The benefit derived from keeping options open so as to be able to adjust policies in the light of better information is referred to as 'option value' or 'quasi-option value', and is an additional source of benefit to be included in any cost–benefit calculation of the net benefits of different policy choices.

In relation to climate change, the precautionary principle would seem to imply the following. Suppose one has used standard cost–benefit analysis under uncertainty in which the social planner maximizes expected utility to calculate the optimal level of current abatement of greenhouse gases, as described in section 2. If there is the chance of getting better information, and the accumulation of greenhouse gases is irreversible, then the precautionary principle seems to suggest that the optimal level of abatement of greenhouse gases now should be increased; this is referred to as the 'irreversibility effect'. This decision would be reflected in the use of a higher value for the current SCC by adding to the previous calculation of the SCC a premium, which we shall refer to as a 'learning premium', which reflects the benefit of reducing the extent of irreversible accumulation of greenhouse gases so as to be better able to exploit new information when it becomes available.

Research in the last 30 years has shown that this simple intuition may be wrong, and the optimal current policy is more ambiguous. It may be the case that the prospect of obtaining better information in the future should lead to *lower* current abatement of greenhouse gases, and hence a *lower* value for the current SCC (the 'learning premium' might be negative). In this section we provide a relatively non-technical survey of the underlying conceptual developments, which both shows why the simple intuition behind the precautionary principle can fail and provides a basis for understanding the results of applying these concepts in models of climate change.

(a) *Fundamental Ambiguities in the Irreversibility Effect*

To illustrate why ambiguities might arise, we set out a simple model of climate change, similar to Ulph and Ulph (1997) and Gollier *et al.* (2000) in which there is a two-period model of a stock pollutant where damage costs (which occur at the end of period 2) are uncertain, but we expect to get better information between period 1 and period 2. The problem is thus:

$$\max_{e_1 \geq 0} u(e_1) + E_{\tilde{y}} \left\{ \max_{e_2 \geq 0} E_{\tilde{\theta}|\tilde{y}} [v(e_2 - \theta(\delta e_1 + e_2))] \right\} \qquad (1)$$

where e_i denotes emissions in period $i=1,2$, u and v are the net benefit functions or utility functions in periods 1 and 2 respectively, and θ is a parameter reflecting the damage that will be caused in the future by the future stock of greenhouse gases.[4] At the beginning of period 1, the value of θ is unknown, although we expect to get some new information, denoted by the random variable y, next period.

There are two key elements of this problem to note. First, the *irreversibility constraint* takes the form $e_2 \geq 0$ — there cannot be negative emissions in period 2; this is equivalent to saying that the stock of emissions at the end of period 2 cannot be less than δe_1, the stock of emissions inherited from period 1 allowing for a decay factor $\delta \leq 1$. The second key element is the *information structure*.[5] As noted, we start in period 1 with uncertainty about the extent of future damages from climate change, and our uncertainty is captured by an initial set of probabilities of different values of the parameter θ. We expect to learn some new information about how damaging climate change might turn out to be; this information is represented by the random variable y, since we cannot know now what science will tell us about the world, for if we did we would already have incorporated this information in our prior set of probabilities about how damaging climate change would be. Based on this new information we will be able to revise our probability distribution about how damaging climate change might be. We can classify different kinds of information structures in terms of how *informative* they will turn out to be, which means, loosely, how much we

[4] In this simple model damages from climate change arise only in the future. This is the natural focus for the the discussion of the precautionary principle. We could add damages in period 1 without any loss of generality.

[5] More technically, $\tilde{\theta}$ is the unknown damage-cost parameter, and let π be the initial (prior) set of probabilities the decision-maker has about possible values of $\tilde{\theta}$. Before the start of period 2 the decision-maker expects to get information, captured by the random variable $\tilde{y}$, which will allow the decision-maker to update the probabilities with which different values of θ might occur. For any particular piece of information we might receive, y, define π_y as the revised (posterior) distribution of $\tilde{\theta}$. Suppose there are two possible sets of information that might be received, captured by two different random variables $\tilde{y}, \tilde{y}'$. We say that $\tilde{y}$ is more informative (better information) than $\tilde{y}'$ if the set of revised posterior probability distributions conditioned on $\tilde{y}$ are more dispersed (roughly speaking closer to 0 or 1) than those conditioned on $\tilde{y}'$. The extreme comparison would be between *no information*, where, for any piece of information y', $\pi_y = \pi$ the decision-maker has the same probabilities after receiving the information as before, and *perfect information*, where for all values of y the posterior probabilities of different values of $\tilde{\theta}$, π_y, are either 0 or 1, so we know exactly what the true damage costs are.

can sharpen our estimates of climate-change damages based on the information. The information structure will be not very informative if our revised probabilities are rather similar to our initial probabilities. The information structure will be very informative if we can attach a very high probability to some narrow range of values for how damaging climate change will be. Note that in problem (1) we need to form two sets of expectations in period 2: we need first to consider what kinds of information we are likely to receive; and then, conditional on what information we learn, we need to assess what are the likely values of the damage-cost parameter.

Thus, problem (1) captures the two key features of our climate-change problem, albeit in a simple model: the fact that climate change is irreversible, and the fact that we are likely to get better information in the future.

We can now give a more precise statement of the precautionary principle. We want to know how the prospect of getting better information in the future affects our decisions on current emissions, given that current emissions are irreversible. Let $\hat{e}_1$ be the solution of problem (1) with one information structure, and $\hat{e}_1'$ be the solution of (1) with a less informative information structure. Then the precautionary principle or irreversibility effect would suggest that we should expect $\hat{e}_1 \leq \hat{e}_1'$, that is, the decision-maker reduces the extent of irreversible accumulation of emissions if there is the prospect of getting better information. Under what circumstances will the irreversibility effect or precautionary principle hold?

Suppose, first, that in problem (1) the objective function in period 2 does not depend on e_1, so that the objective functions of the two periods are *separable*, and e_1 affects the period 2 decision-making problem only through the irreversibility constraint. Freixas and Laffont (1984) showed that a sufficient[6] condition for the irreversibility effect to hold is that the utility function in period 2 should be quasi-concave. This is a relatively mild assumption and would be satisfied by most economic models. This was the set-up in which Arrow and Fisher (1974) and Henry (1974a,b) first derived the irreversibility effect.

However, it is the essence of climate change that future damage costs depend on cumulative emissions. With non-separable net benefit functions, it

---

[6] Freixas and Laffont actually claim their condition is necessary and sufficient for the irreversibility effect to hold, but their 'proof' of necessity is simply an example in which the objective function is not-quasi-concave and, indeed, the irreversibility effect does not hold. But Fisher *et al.* (2002) show it is possible to modify their example slightly so that the objective function is still not quasi-concave but the irreversibility effect does hold.

is more problematic whether the irreversibility effect holds. The seminal paper is Epstein (1980). Define:

$$V(e_1, \pi_y) = \max_{e_2 \geq 0} E_{\tilde{\theta}|y}[v(e_2 - \theta(\delta e_1 + e_2))] \tag{2}$$

as the maximum expected pay-off we can get in period 2, given emissions e_1 and particular piece of information y, where π_y is the probability distribution for different values of θ, revised in the light of the new information received. Problem (1) can then be written as:

$$\max_{e_1 \geq 0} u(e_1) + E_{\tilde{y}} V(e_1, \pi_{\tilde{y}}). \tag{3}$$

Epstein (1980) showed[7] that (i) if $V_{e_1}(e_1, \pi_y)$ is concave in π_y then $\hat{e}_1 \leq \hat{e}_1'$; and (ii) if $V_{e_1}(e_1, \pi_y)$ is convex in π_y then $\hat{e}_1 \geq \hat{e}_1'$. The problem is that these conditions have no very obvious economic intuition and so it is difficult to know when these sufficient conditions will be satisfied.

To make further progress it is useful to distinguish two different components of problem (1): the effects of better information and the effects of the irreversibility constraint. To study the effects of better information, suppose that in problems (1), (2), and (3) we can ignore the irreversibility constraint, so that if we learn that it is much more likely that damage costs from climate change are very high, it is possible immediately to reduce the stock of greenhouse gases. Then we are just isolating the effect of getting better information.

Gollier et al. (2000) used a particular class of utility functions, hyperbolic absolute risk aversion (HARA)[8] for period 2, which contain a parameter γ, which is a measure of relative risk aversion. They showed that $\hat{e}_1 \leq \hat{e}_1'$, if and only if $0 < \gamma < 1$, and that $\hat{e}_1 \geq \hat{e}_1'$ if $\gamma < 0$ or $\gamma > 1$, and that $\hat{e}_1 = \hat{e}_1'$ if $\gamma = 1$, i.e. $v(x) = \log(\eta + x)$. Thus, within this relatively restrictive class of utility functions, the effects of better information will lead to a reduction in period 1 emissions if and only if the decision-maker is risk averse, but not too risk averse.[9] Gollier et al.

---

[7] These results follow almost immediately by considering the first-order condition for problem (3) and the definition of a more informative information structure given in footnote 1.

[8] To be precise: $v(x) \equiv \dfrac{\gamma}{1-\gamma}(\eta + \dfrac{x}{\gamma})^{1-\gamma}.$

[9] With more general utility functions they show that if risks are 'small' in the sense that one can ignore higher moments than mean and variance, then $\hat{e}_1 \leq \hat{e}_1'$ if and only if the absolute coefficient of prudence $P(x) \equiv -v'''(x)/v''(x)$ is at least twice the coefficient of absolute risk aversion $A(x) \equiv -v''/v'(x)$. For HARA utility functions this is equivalent to the condition that the coefficient of relative risk aversion $R(x) \equiv xA(x) = \gamma$ lies strictly between 0 and 1.

note that econometric estimates of γ show that it lies between 0.1 and 100, and that values for γ which solve the equity premium puzzle would require γ around 30. So for plausible values of risk aversion, better information, without any irreversibility constraint, will lead to an *increase* in period 1 emissions. For later purposes, note that, with a logarithmic utility function, the prospect of better information has *no* effect on period 1 emissions.

Fisher *et al.* (2002) note that one limitation of the use of HARA utility functions is that they restrict the coefficient of relative risk aversion to equal the inverse of the elasticity of intertemporal substitution, so it is difficult to tell whether risk aversion or intertemporal substitution is driving results (Ha-Duong and Treich (2003) make the same point about modelling climate change, but not in the context of the irreversibility effect). Using a more general class of utility functions in which risk aversion and intertemporal substitution can be distinguished,[10] and working with one of the examples introduced by Epstein, they use numerical simulations to suggest that it is a low intertemporal elasticity of substitution rather than a high degree of risk aversion that is likely to cause the irreversibility effect not to hold.

Ulph and Ulph (1997) considered the extreme cases of no information and perfect information and used the following specification for period 2 net benefit function: $W(e_2) - \theta D(\delta e_1 + e_2)$ where W is the (gross) benefit from emissions in period 2 and D is the damage-cost function from the stock of emissions at the end of period 2. They showed that if we take the 'textbook' model of quadratic benefit and damage-cost functions (i.e. linear marginal benefit and damage-cost functions), then unambiguously $\hat{e}_1 \geq \hat{e}_1{}'$, i.e. without any irreversibility constraint, the prospect of better information would lead to higher emissions in period 1.

Readers wanting more intuition for this result can consult Figure 1 for the case where there are just two, equally likely, levels of damage costs, high and low. What we need to calculate is the expected marginal damage cost of a unit of emissions in period 1, given the optimal choice of policy in period 2. With no learning, the optimal choice of emissions in period 2 will be $\bar{e}_2$, and corresponding expected marginal damage cost is the distance OA. With perfect information, optimal policy in period 2 will be to choose emissions $e_2{}^l$ if it is learned that damage costs are low, and $e_2{}^h$ if it is learned that damage costs are high. So expected marginal damage costs are 0.5 (OB + OC). This will be less than OA if AB > AC, or equivalently, if $(e_2{}^l - \bar{e}_2) > (\bar{e}_2 - e_2{}^h)$, the amount by which emissions rise

---

[10] This class of utility functions does not satisfy von Neumann–Morgenstern axioms.

if we learn that damages are low, relative to no information, exceeds the amount by which emissions contract if we learn that damages are high. Simple geometry shows that this has to be the case.[11] Another rationale for the Ulph and Ulph result is that, as noted by Fisher *et al.* (2002), the quadratic gross benefit function and damage-cost function imply that relative risk aversion is infinite, so from Gollier *et al.* (2000) we would expect that $\hat{e}_1 \geq \hat{e}_1'$.

To summarize, the effect of better information, without any irreversibility constraint, may cause current emissions to be reduced or increased, and for the standard textbook model of linear marginal benefit and damage-cost functions, better information unambiguously causes current emissions to rise.

What happens if we now introduce the irreversibility constraint? As Ulph and Ulph (1997) and Gollier *et al.* (2000) note, the irreversibility constraint tends to reduce current emissions. The rationale is straightforward. If, in some states of the world, the irreversibility constraint bites, this must increase expected marginal damage costs of current emissions, so making it desirable to cut current emissions relative to the situation where no irreversibility constraint is imposed. This can be seen easily from Figure 1 where, if the irreversibility constraint $e_2 \geq 0$ is imposed, this will bite in the high damage-cost state, and marginal damage costs in that state will be OK, which is greater than marginal damage costs with no irreversibility constraint, OC.

Returning then to the full problem (1), where there is both better information and an irreversibility constraint, we have two effects which may go in different directions. If the prospect of getting better information would cause decision-makers to cut current emissions, then adding the irreversibility constraint just reinforces this. But if the prospect of getting better information leads decision-makers to increase current emissions without an irreversibility effect, then adding the irreversibility constraint gives an offsetting effect, and the overall effect is ambiguous. This is precisely what arises when we have the 'textbook' model of linear marginal benefits and damage costs, as noted by Ulph and Ulph (1997). Can this ambiguity be resolved? Intuitively this should depend on just how severely the irreversibility constraint bites. Ulph and Ulph (1997) showed that if the irreversibility constraint bites when there is no learning, then the irreversibility effect holds, $\hat{e}_1 \leq \hat{e}_1'$, so current emissions should be reduced when there is the prospect of getting better information. On the other hand, if the irreversibility

---

[11] By construction the distance JG equals GH. Construct equal triangles by drawing lines through J and H with slope $\bar{\theta}$ to meet W'. This shows that GF > EG.

Figure 1
Learning and Irreversibility

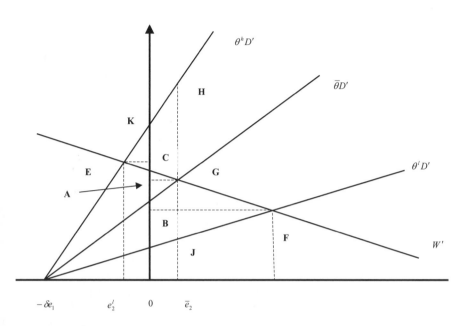

constraint bites for every possible value of θ, then current emissions are unaffected by the prospect of better information.

To summarize, even with the simplest specification of a climate-change problem, economic analysis does not provide general support for the precautionary principle that, faced with the prospect of obtaining better information, the correct response is to reduce current irreversible actions. It can be the case, for quite standard models, that the correct response to the anticipation of getting better information is to increase current emissions. What the correct response should be cannot be deduced just from general theoretical arguments, but is an empirical matter. However, if we want to ensure that the precautionary principle does apply, what this section suggests is that we either have to assume that agents are less risk averse than the data suggest they are, or we have to assume the irreversibility constraint is a serious issue, in the sense that we expect it to bite. Before turning to empirical models, we discuss a number of other factors that might affect whether or not the irreversibility effect holds.

(b) *Other Irreversibilities*

Suppose the precautionary principle holds for the 'environmental irreversibility', so that with the prospect of better information the decision-maker would want to reduce current build-up of irreversible emissions of greenhouse gases. In a sequence of papers, Kolstad (1993, 1996a,b) pointed out that, if the reduction of emissions of greenhouse gases involved investing in specific forms of abatement capital (e.g. investments in tidal energy, nuclear power plants, etc.), which could not be easily converted to other purposes if we subsequently learn that climate change is not as serious as expected, then the same precautionary principle suggests that, if we expect to get better information in the future, we should reduce our investment in such irreversible forms of capital. So, even if we accept the precautionary principle, we have two irreversibilities which go in opposite directions. Which one is stronger is an empirical issue, and Kolstad shows that the abatement capital irreversibility dominates the environmental irreversibility (we discuss this empirical modelling in more detail in section 4).

Pindyck (2000) reaches a similar conclusion using the real options framework. As in (1) there is a stock pollutant with a decay factor δ. The parameter θ, reflecting (unit) damage costs is subject to upward drift, and may also be uncertain. New information will arrive which will cause the evaluation of damages to change, though in this model uncertainty is never resolved. Society can decide to make a once-for-all, irreversible, investment, which will permanently reduce the future flow of emissions (in the simplest case he considers the investment will reduce emissions to zero). The question is when should society make this decision? Again there are two irreversibilities. The possibility of getting more information in the future provides the usual incentive to delay irreversibly sinking capital to reduce emissions, but this needs to be balanced against the benefit of early action to reduce the stock of pollution which decays slowly and imposes nearly irreversible costs on society. It turns out that there is a critical level of damage costs at which it will pay to make the investment. The presence of uncertainty about future damage costs raises this hurdle, i.e. the fact that we are uncertain about future damage costs, although we will learn more information in the future, causes society to delay its decision to invest, relative to a world where there is no uncertainty. In this sense, the capital abatement irreversibility dominates the environmental irreversibility. Pindyck shows that as δ increases, the pollution stock becomes less reversible, then the critical threshold at which society should sink abatement capital is reduced, again illustrating the tension between the two irreversibilities.

But, more generally, there is likely to be a wide range of irreversibilities in the climate-change problem. Ha-Duong *et al.* (1997), using a somewhat different approach, have considered the impact of significant inertia or costs of adjustment in the use of capital which generates greenhouse gases, and show that this will lead to increasing current abatement of greenhouse-gas emissions to avoid the future costs of rapidly increasing abatement if it is necessary to meet some critical target level of greenhouse-gas concentrations.

The general point then is that it will be the balance between the different sources of irreversibilities that will determine the extent to which current emissions of greenhouse gases with learning and irreversibilities should be higher or lower than the level which ignores learning and irreversibilities.

(c) *Catastrophic Effects*

Narain and Fisher (1998) argue that the above analysis of irreversibilities is limited because it ignores the possibility of catastrophic effects of climate change, and in particular the possibility that such risks depend on the stock of pollution, so that abating pollution reduces the risk of catastrophes — the risks are avoidable.[12] They argue that allowing for such effects would reduce the significance of the abatement capital irreversibility and increase the significance of the environmental irreversibility. Since the issue of catastrophic risks is an important one, we deal with this separately in section 5. We merely note here that, in general, allowing for catastrophic effects in general has ambiguous implications for the SCC.

(d) *Other Models of Learning*

In problem (1), as in much of the literature on irreversibility effects, the process of learning is purely exogenous — new information just arrives which allows decision-makers to adjust their probabilities. This is referred to as *passive learning*. Underlying this, of course, is the thought that such information is being gathered through some research process, and, indeed, the analysis of learning is used not just to assess how current emissions policies should be adjusted but to assess the *value* of better scientific information, and hence determine how much to invest in getting better information. However, the explicit modelling of the level of investment in research has not been carried out, as far as we are aware.

[12] They also argue that there are problems with the way that Kolstad captures the degree of irreversibility of abatement capital and pollution. Their treatment of this issue is not fully persuasive, so we do not pursue it.

A particular aspect of the way that research on climate change is conducted is through the observation of current climate events. This is known as *active learning*. Kelly and Kolstad (1999) and Karp and Zhang (2002) introduce such models. Since the results are derived mainly through numerical simulations of climate-change models, we discuss their results in section 4, but introducing active learning does not change the basic implications about the way the anticipation of getting better information affects current policy derived above.

(e) *Option Value in a Broader Context*

As noted in the introduction to this section, the seminal papers by Arrow and Fisher (1974) and Henry (1974*a,b*) introduced the concept of option value (or, as they called it, quasi-option value) to reflect the benefit of reducing or delaying making irreversible decisions if there is the prospect of obtaining better information in the future. The concept of option value has also been derived in the theory of finance and in the last 15 years extended to real investment decisions, reflected in the real options literature, and popularized by Dixit and Pindyck (1994). The option value in the real options approach again captures the benefit to delaying making an irreversible capital investment under uncertainty, in particular because of the benefit of being able to exploit better information. What is the link between these two concepts of option value?

Fisher (2000) addressed this issue by setting out a model of a once-for-all decision to develop or conserve an area of land, where development would irreversibly destroy any environmental benefits, although these benefits are currently uncertain, only becoming known next period. The model was based on Fisher and Hanemann (1986) and is similar to the original Arrow and Fisher and Henry models. Fisher derives the (quasi-) option value for this model, which he calls the Arrow–Fisher–Henry–Hanemann (AFHH) option value. He then sets out an example of a Dixit–Pindyck model of investment, where the future returns from the investment are currently unknown but will become known next period. He calculates the option value for this model using the Dixit–Pindyck analysis, and calls this the Dixit–Pindyck (DP) option value. He then claims that the two option values are equivalent.

It has been pointed out that this is not quite right (Mensink and Requate, 2003). Rather, the DP option value can be decomposed into two elements: the AFHH option value, which captures the benefit of better information, and a pure postponement benefit, which simply captures the fact that without any uncertainty and learning it may just be better to delay making an investment decision till later because the returns are higher.

(f) *Multiple Decision-makers*

Implicit in the modelling of irreversibility, learning, and the precautionary principle that we have outlined above, is the assumption that there is a single decision-maker. In the context of global warming this implies a single global social planner. That is also the context in which much of the analysis of the SCC takes place. Of course, in practice, the problem of climate change has to be tackled by persuading individual nation states to join some form of international environmental agreement (IEA), such as the Kyoto Protocol. This raises another important timing question: how does the prospect of getting better information affect the incentives for countries to join an IEA? Since this goes beyond the scope of this paper, we simply note that this question is only just beginning to be addressed (Ulph, 2004).

(g) *Summary*

The simple intuition, enshrined in the precautionary principle, is that, faced with a need to make an irreversible commitment where the (net) future benefits are uncertain, but there is a prospect of getting better information, society should reduce or delay its irreversible commitment so as to preserve its options to exploit that information. Applied to climate change this suggests that society should reduce the extent of current emissions of greenhouse gases, and this would be reflected by adding to the conventionally calculated SCC a (non-negative) learning premium. Early work in environmental economics supported this intuition. In this section we have reviewed developments in the literature over the last 30 years, and especially the last 10 years, which have shown that, for reasons that are relevant to climate change, economic analysis suggests that results are not quite as simple as this. Key factors determining whether or not the irreversibility effect holds (whether the learning premium should be positive or negative) are: (i) the nature of utility functions (risk aversion and intertemporal substitution); (ii) the extent to which the irreversibility environmental constraint bites; (iii) the extent of other irreversibilities in the stock of abatement capital and the stock of greenhouse-gas-generating capital relative to irreversibility in the stock of pollution; (iv) whether risks are avoidable and there are catastrophic effects. The general message is that one cannot simply deduce from economic theory that we should raise the SCC to take account of irreversibility, learning, and precaution: it may be optimal to reduce the SCC. This reinforces the view that to address this issue we need to turn to empirical modelling, and we do so in the next section. However our review of the theoretical literature will be important for understanding why the empirical models of climate change have so far not identified a significant positive learning premium.

4. Empirical Assessments of Irreversibility, Learning, and Precaution

In this section, we review the attempts that have been made to assess the implications of uncertainty, irreversibility, learning, and precaution in the context of empirical models of climate change. Obviously, such models are much richer than the simple theoretical models set out in the previous section, so while we suggest how some of the insights from those theoretical models might be used to explain the results obtained, this needs to be interpreted with considerable caution. For example, as we have seen, a lot of the theoretical literature works with two-period models, which are fine for illustrating conceptual possibilities, but results derived from such models may not carry over to multi-period situations. The results of these studies are summarized in Table 2.

We begin with studies by Manne and Richels and by Nordhaus. There were a number of early studies by Manne and Richels (1992) and Nordhaus (1994a), but we consider the more recent analyses they have done. Manne and Richels (1995) use their MERGE2 model to consider a simple model of uncertainty in which there are just two possible states of the world: a base case with low damages (doubling CO_2 concentrations leads to a temperature increase of 2.5°C, which would cost 2 per cent of GDP) and a high damage-cost scenario where a temperature increase of 1°C increase would cost 2 per cent of GDP, but a doubling of CO_2 concentration would cause a 5°C increase in temperature. There is a 95 per cent chance of the base-case scenario being true, a 5 per cent chance of the high-damage scenario being true. If there is no learning the decision-maker chooses a path of emissions to maximize present-value expected utility. Learning takes the form of being given perfect information at some date in the future. They compare the optimal policy when uncertainty is resolved in 2050 with resolution in 2020. The prospect of earlier resolution of uncertainty (i.e. getting better information) causes the optimal level of control (abatement) to *decrease*, from 9.6 to 5.7 per cent in 2000 and from 25.6 to 9.5 per cent in 2020. The reason for this result is that in the MERGE model the utility function is logarithmic, which as we have seen means that, in a simple two-period model, resolution of uncertainty by itself has no effect. Further, from the time paths of carbon emissions, it seems that the irreversibility constraint never bites, so that would not cause current abatement to rise. The decrease in abatement is due to the irreversibility effect associated with irreversible investment in capital to reduce emissions.

In section 2, we introduced the model Nordhaus and Popp (1997) used to assess the impact of uncertainty. In their model the decision-maker chose policies to maximize expected utility, taking account of uncertainty as expressed in five possible states of the world, but on the assumption that uncertainty will eventually get resolved in 2045. We now report the results of their experiment of considering what happens if uncertainty can be resolved at an earlier date, 2025. Optimal policies for the years 2000, 2010, and 2020 in terms of carbon tax and control rate for the two different dates of uncertainty resolution are shown in Table 2.

As can be seen, the effects of earlier resolution of uncertainty are negligible: control rate and carbon taxes fall, but very slightly. Like Manne and Richels, DICE uses a logarithmic utility function, and there is no evidence of irreversibility constraints biting. The DICE/PRICE models do not explicitly model irreversibility of abatement capital. These results are, thus, in line with what would be predicted from the theory. The corresponding effects on carbon taxes (SCC) are also small and negative. So learning in 2025 rather than 2045 causes the carbon tax in 2000 to fall from $6.34 to $6.31; in 2010 it falls from $8.81 to $8.78; and in 2020 it falls from $11.79 to $11.74.

Ulph and Ulph (1997) used an optimal control model of Maddison (1995), similar to the theoretical model set out in the previous section, but with a cubic damage-cost function, and introduced uncertainty about damage costs of global warming. There were three possible values: the middle value was set so that 2.5°C warming would cost 3.75 per cent of GDP (this was higher than in Maddison (1995) to ensure that the irreversibility constraint would bite in some cases); low damage costs were half this value; and high damage costs were either double or 12 times the middle value. Two sets of probabilities were used and two sets of discount rates, giving eight possible cases. There were four time periods, 1990–9, 2000–29, 2030–99, and 2100–∞, and either there was no resolution of uncertainty, or uncertainty was fully resolved after period 1. In four out of the eight cases, the irreversibility constraint did bite in the 'no learning' case (in period 3 in three cases and period 4 in one). From the simple theoretical model, it would be expected that this would cause the optimal abatement in the first period (1990–9) to be higher with 'learning' than with 'no learning'. The four cases where the irreversibility constraint bites with 'no learning' are shown in Table 2. In only one of these cases (case 2) was abatement in period 1 higher with learning than no learning (rising from 16.8 to 17.2 per cent). In the other

Table 2
Optimal Control Rates (%) and the Effects of Learning and Irreversibility

Name of study

Manne and Richels	Date of action	Learn in 2020	Learn in 2050
	2000	5.7	9.6
	2020	9.5	25.6
Nordhaus and Popp	Date of action	Learn in 2025	Learn in 2045
	2000	12.0	12.0
	2010	13.8	13.9
	2020	15.8	15.9
Ulph and Ulph		Learning	No learning
	Case 2	17.2	16.8
	Case 5	15.3	18.9
	Case 6	27.8	33.9
	Case 8	8.9	9.9
Kolstad	Date of action	Learning	No learning
	1995	5.0	7.25
Karp and Zhang	% Loss of GWP	Learning	No learning
	0.3	2.0	2.5
	1.33	8.0	9.8
	3.6	19.5	23.0
	Degree of uncertainty	Learning	No learning
	0.3	9.0	9.8
	0.6	8.0	9.8
	Variance of signal	Learning	No learning
	Low	8.0	9.8
	High	9.8	9.8

three cases where the irreversibility constraint bites (and all four cases where the irreversibility constraint did not bite with 'no learning') first-period abatement with learning was lower than with no learning. So even with relatively unrealistic assumptions designed to ensure that irreversibility constraints might bite, this was usually insufficient to cause abatement to rise with the prospect of getting better information.

Kolstad (1996b) uses an optimal control model very similar to the DICE model. There is uncertainty about damage costs which can be either low (in fact zero) or high, with prior probabilities 0.8 and 0.2 respectively. Learning is not perfect, but takes place over the first two periods (1995–2005, 2005–15). The rate of learning is controlled by a parameter λ, which varies between 0, 'no learning' and 1, 'perfect learning'. The degree of irreversibility of greenhouse gases is captured by the rate at which the stock of greenhouse gases decays (with non-negative emissions), set at 8.3 per cent per decade, and similarly the degree of irreversibility of abatement capital is captured by the rate at which the stock of abatement capital depreciates. What Kolstad shows is that if abatement capital is completely reversible, so there is only the environmental irreversibility, then the 1995 control rate for greenhouse gases is virtually invariant to the rate of learning, but if the stock of abatement capital is irreversible, then as learning increases from 0 to 1, the 1995 control rate declines from about 7.25 per cent to just under 5 per cent. So the abatement capital irreversibility effect is much stronger than the environmental irreversibility. The rationale for this would seem to be that, since this model is based on DICE, the use of the logarithmic utility function means that the pure learning effect is likely to be small, and if the environmental irreversibility constraint never bites, but the abatement capital constraint does, then one would expect the capital irreversibility effect to dominate.

The models surveyed so far have used models of passive learning, all except Kolstad taking the simple form of perfect information being provided at some specified date. Karp and Zhang (2002) consider a model of active learning, where the decision-maker can learn from previous observations of climate and damages about how damaging climate change is ultimately likely to be. However, observations of past climate change only provide imperfect information about true damages (there is a 'noisy signal'). They use a linear-quadratic model, calibrated to the same kind of data used by other modellers, but ignore irreversibility of the stock of emissions. Uncertainty is about damage costs, in particular about how much damage (per cent loss of gross world product (GWP)) would be caused by a doubling of pre-industrial stocks of atmospheric carbon. They use values of 3.6, 1.33, and 0.3 per cent as the decision-maker's initial best guess of true damage costs. Table 2 shows the optimal control rate in 1990–9 with and without learning, assuming the decision-maker's initial best guess of true damages is 0.3, 1.33, or 3.6 per cent of GWP. Again, initial abatement is always lower with learning than with no learning. They then show how the degree of uncertainty (variance) about the damage-cost parameter affects optimal current abatement, assuming the decision-maker starts with the assumption that damage costs are 1.33 per cent of GWP. As shown in Table 2, the degree of uncertainty about damage costs has no effect on the initial control level if there is no learning (9.8 per cent), but if learning is possible then the initial control will decline from 9.8 per cent to 8 per cent if the degree of uncertainty about damage costs (and hence potential scope to benefit from learning) is high, but from 9.8 per cent to only 9 per cent if the degree of uncertainty is more modest. Finally, Karp and Zhang analyse how an increase in the variance of the information (the signal becomes less informative) affects optimal current control. As shown in Table 2, the optimal current control with 'no learning' falls from 9.8 to 8 per cent, with a low variance of information—i.e. the signal is quite informative, but is almost unaffected by a high variance of information (very noisy signal, and hence little scope for learning). These results are again what we might expect from the theoretical literature, since with a quadratic model and no irreversibility constraint better information unambiguously reduced initial abatement.

Another interesting feature of the Karp and Zhang model is the speed of learning. To test this, they suppose that, initially, the decision-maker believes that damage costs are 1.33 per cent but the true value is actually 3.6 per cent. They calculate two benchmark paths of carbon stocks: (i) the path of carbon stocks if the decision-maker starts believing damage costs are 1.33 per cent but cannot learn; and (ii) the path of carbon stocks that the decision-maker would set if it were known for sure that damage costs were 3.6 per cent. They then compute the path of carbon stocks if the decision-maker starts with the belief that damage costs are 1.33 per cent but can learn. This path obviously starts out very close to path (i), but within five periods (each period is 10 years) it gets very close to path (ii).

Finally, Conrad (1997) implements a simple version of the Pindyck (2000) type of model discussed in the last section. He assumes that, in the absence of any action to deal with climate change, mean global temperature will evolve over time according to Brownian motion, and so will drift upwards with random shocks, with an expectation of an increase of mean global temperature of 2.5°C in 100 years. Damages are a convex function of mean global temperature, calibrated so that a 2.5°C increase in temperature causes a loss of 1.5 per cent of GDP. In Pindyck's model there is uncertainty abut both the evolution of climate change and about the damage costs. Conrad allows only for uncertainty about climate change, not about damage costs. Society has a number of policies ('bullets') it can introduce to reduce permanently either the level of upward drift, or the variance of climate change, or both, but it has to pay a large sunk cost for such a policy. He considers three 'basic bullets' of reducing mean upward drift of temperature by 25, 50, and 75 per cent at once-for-all sunk costs of $300 billion, $1,800 billion, and $6,000 billion, respectively, and asks what are critical values of temperature or damages at which such policies should be introduced, when is this likely to occur, and what is the option value of having such policies available? The earliest likely time for adopting such policies ranges between 35 and 112 years and option values lie between $600 billion and

$700 billion. However, he does not explore the issue of how variations in the rate at which learning might take place affect the critical thresholds for policy adoption.

To summarize, in this section we have reviewed a number of models which have attempted to explore the issue of how the prospect of getting better information in a world of uncertainty about climate change and irreversibilities might affect current policies to control greenhouse-gas emissions. Contrary to the simple intuition of the precautionary principle, with the exception of one scenario in Ulph and Ulph (1997), all these studies suggest that the prospect of getting better information (earlier resolution of uncertainty) should lead to a reduction in current abatement levels, although these effects are small. This suggests that the prospect of getting better information should cause either no change or a small reduction in the SCC, relative to calculations which ignore the issue of learning. However, the theoretical analysis of section 3 would suggest that these results are not very surprising given the choice of utility functions (either logarithmic or quadratic) and that the environmental irreversibility constraint does not seem to bite even in worst-state scenarios. Before being confident that one can rule out the possibility of a significant positive option value for climate change, it would be desirable to see some studies with different objective functions, and with parameter values where the environmental irreversibility constraint bites. So, as we noted earlier in section 3(a), what is needed for empirical models to confirm the precautionary principle would be the use of utility functions which imply more risk aversion than the simple logarithmic function widely used (but less than the empirical evidence suggests is warranted), and/or models of climate change which imply that the environmental irreversibility constraint is stronger than it appears to be.

5. The Impact of Catastrophic Effects

We now return to the issue of catastrophic events — events which have large impacts but may occur only with small probability, such as melting of West Antarctic Ice Sheet or the switching off of the Atlantic 'conveyor belt' — mentioned briefly in section 3(c). We begin by reviewing what economic analysis has to say about the introduction of catastrophic effects and then survey the few papers that have attempted to analyse such effects empirically, using models of climate change.

(a) *Theoretical Results on Catastrophic Effects*

How the risk of catastrophic events affects current policy towards a stock pollutant depends crucially on a number of features of how catastrophes are modelled: (i) what triggers catastrophic events; (ii) whether the risk of catastrophic events is avoidable; and (iii) what the impact of a catastrophe is, and in particular whether the costs of a catastrophe are reversible or irreversible – i.e. can the world eventually return to a scenario similar to what prevailed before the catastrophe occurred, albeit with a substantial transitory loss, or is it impossible to restore the kind of world that prevailed before the catastrophe, which is what seems to be envisaged in some of the discussion of the problem by environmentalists.

Cropper (1976) assumes that pollution stock accumulates in a stochastic fashion, but it is known for sure that once the stock level reaches a certain critical threshold, then a catastrophic event occurs, which causes a temporary, fixed, reduction in well-being. Below this critical level, the stock of pollution has no effect on well-being. However, the loss of well-being caused by the catastrophe is reversible, since the effect disappears once the stock falls back below the critical level. Cropper shows that compared to no catastrophe, policy requires a reduction in current emissions, to reduce the likelihood of triggering such losses.

Clarke and Reed (1994) consider a situation where, in the absence of catastrophe, well-being depends negatively on a stock of pollution. There is a probability (hazard) of a catastrophe occurring, and if it does occur well-being falls sharply to some base level, which does not depend on the stock of pollution, and well-being remains at this level for ever. In this sense, the catastrophe is *irreversible* in its effects. The probability (hazard rate) of a catastrophe occurring at any particular date is known, and may depend on the stock of pollution. They show that there are two effects at work. If a catastrophe occurs, the stock of pollution no longer affects welfare. This *reduces* expected marginal damage cost of current emissions. On the other hand an increase in emissions may increase the probability of a catastrophe occurring. This increases the expected marginal damage cost of current emissions. Thus, if the hazard rate is either independent of the stock of pollution, or varies very little with the stock of pollution, the first effect will dominate, and the optimal policy involves a *higher* level of emissions than if there was no risk of catastrophe. If the marginal effect of current emissions on the risk of a catastrophe is very high, so risks are easily avoidable, then the second effect dominates and optimal current policy should be to reduce emissions. In between, the effect is ambiguous.

Tsur and Zemel (1998) have the same structure of risks of catastrophes as in Clarke and Reed (1994). But they now allow for the effects of a catastrophe to be reversible, in the sense that a catastrophe just involves incurring a once-for-all penalty in terms of a loss of wealth. Moreover, if catastrophes are reversible they can also be recurrent. Tsur and Zemel (1998) show that reversible catastrophes, whether recurrent or not, always lead to a lower level of emissions than would be the case without catastrophes. This is perhaps not surprising since with reversible catastrophes one effectively gets rid of the first effect in the Clarke and Reed model. So, perhaps paradoxically, allowing for the more benign scenario in which it is possible to recover from a catastrophe makes it more likely that one wants to take more stringent action now to cut greenhouse-gas emissions.

Tsur and Zemel (1996) consider what happens when uncertainty is endogenous, in the sense that a catastrophe is triggered by a stock of pollution, but it is not known what that stock is. Of course, learning takes place, in the sense that if no catastrophe has occurred up to now, then the critical stock level must be at least as high as any past stock. A catastrophe has the same kind of reversible effect as in Tsur and Zemel (1998), i.e. society incurs a once-for-all penalty if a catastrophe occurs. Tsur and Zemel (1996) show that the optimal policy can be characterized in terms of an interval of steady-state stock levels. The upper end of this interval is the steady-state stock that would be set in the absence of catastrophes. If the initial stock of pollution is above this level, then society just aims for that steady-state and ignores catastrophes. The reason is simple — society knows that catastrophes cannot occur in the relevant range of stocks, so policy should ignore catastrophe. On the other hand, if the initial stock is below the lower end of the interval of steady-state stocks, society should move towards that lower end, but more cautiously than if there were no catastrophes. The interesting case is where the initial stock of pollution lies in the interior range of the steady-state stock levels. In this case, society should immediately freeze the stock of pollution. This calls for drastic action. The analogy might be that society has walked into a minefield, has not so far set off a mine, but should now stay where it is because the risk that the next step it takes will set off a mine is now very high.

In summary, this review of the impact of the risk of uncertainty on optimal pollution policy and hence on the SCC shows that, as with the analysis of irreversibility and learning in section 3, there are no unambiguous results. Depending on the features of catastrophes set out at the beginning of this section, compared to policy with no catastrophes the risk of catastrophe could call for weaker action now, no further action, somewhat tougher action, or drastic action to stop any further increase in the stock of pollution. However, the balance of results would suggest that the possibility of catastrophic effects should lead to a reduction in current emissions, possibly a very drastic reduction. Before reviewing what empirical models have to say, we deal with a further criticism of the use of expected utility to analyse optimal policy towards catastrophes.

(b) *Further Critique of Use of Expected Utility*

In section 2, we noted a number of criticisms about the use of the expected utility approach to assess climate change, and in this section we deal with another criticism concerned specifically with the treatment of small-probability high-impact events. The criticism is that, because expected utility is linear in probabilities, events with small probabilities become essentially negligible. The insensitivity to small risks axiom says that the modification of two alternative choices in states which occur only with small probability should not change the ranking of those choices. Chichilnisky (2000) argues that this is contrary to what is meant by catastrophic risks. These are seen as events which are large scale, possibly irreversible, to which social rankings should be sensitive. For example, the loss of all irrigation water and agricultural produce for the USA is calculated to lead to a loss of 2.5 per cent of GDP.

It is shown by Chichilnisky (2000) that if the axiom of insensitivity to low-probability events is replaced by one of being not insensitive to low-probability events, i.e. they can make a difference, and also not being insensitive to high-probability events, then expected utility is replaced by a criterion which is the sum of two components. The first is analogous to expected utility but does not apply to all states of the world. The second component is a function of utility in a particular state, e.g. the worst possible outcome. This second component accommodates the consequences for small probability events, but in a way which does not go to zero (or infinity) as the probability becomes very small. However, to the best of our knowledge this approach has yet to be implemented in empirical analyses of catastrophic risks.

(c) *Empirical Results on Catastrophic Effects*

The discussion in section 5(a) suggests that the way catastrophic events affect current policy and the SCC is ambiguous, although most studies would call for a reduction in current emissions of greenhouse gases, and, therefore, there is a need for empirical analysis. We report on two studies.

Gjerde *et al.* (1999) investigate an empirical model to consider the effect the possibility of a catastrophe has on optimal climate policy.

Table 3
Empirical Analysis of Catastrophic Effects
Gjerde *et al.* (1999)

Type of catastrophe	% Abatement 2020	% Abatement 2050	Risk of catastrophe by 2090 (%)
No catastrophe	24.0	50.0	12
Case A (unavoidable)	21.0	46.0	63
Case A (avoidable)	53.0	86.0	8
Case B	35.0	64.0	9

Climate change will cause damages, measured by a loss of 2 per cent of GDP for a temperature increase of 2.5° C above pre-industrial levels. In addition there is uncertainty about whether a single catastrophe will occur when a critical temperature level is reached. If the catastrophe occurs, there will be a loss of GDP for ever after. They consider four possible catastrophe scenarios. In scenario 1, there is no risk of catastrophe; in scenario 2 the catastrophe reduces GDP to 75 per cent of the level without the catastrophe, analogous to the effect of the Great Depression and equivalent to the curing costs model of Tsur and Zemel (1996); in scenario 3, the catastrophe reduces GDP to zero, analogous to the Clarke and Reed (1994) model; finally in scenario 4 the catastrophe reduces GDP to zero, but the hazard rate for this occurring is 1 per cent, independent of the level of greenhouse gases or temperature. The results are shown in Table 3.

Under all scenarios, emissions are significantly reduced from 'business as usual'. In catastrophe scenarios 2 and 3, where the risk is avoidable, emissions are reduced further than with no catastrophe. The risk of a catastrophe by 2090 is reduced from 12 per cent under scenario 1, to 8 and 9 per cent, respectively, for scenarios 2 and 3. With catastrophe scenario 4, where the risk is unavoidable, there are higher emissions than the no-catastrophe case. This reflects the theoretical result of Clarke and Reed that where future utility is unaffected by the stock of pollution and the risk cannot be affected by actions, it makes sense to bring forward welfare by increasing current consumption and pollution. Another way of interpreting this result is as a risk premium added to the rate of discount.

Mastrandrea and Schneider (2001) investigate whether the conclusion that only small changes in initial emissions, or a policy of waiting for uncertainty resolution, are justified when catastrophe is a possibility. They couple the DICE model to a simple climate–ocean model which generates one form of abrupt climate change through the multiple equilibria of ocean circulation, the thermohaline circulation (THC) effect in the North Atlantic. To capture the impact of the THC effect,

Table 4
Impact of THC on Social Cost of Carbon ($/tC) in 2005

Discount rate	No THC damages	THC damages 1% GWP	THC damages 5% GWP
4.0%	2.90	3.19	4.29
3.0%	5.43	5.99	8.17
1.5%	17.06	19.14	27.61
0.0%	101.01	118.06	210.20
Hyperbolic	67.39	78.54	137.80

they modify the shape of the damage function and make assumptions about the percentage loss of GDP that would be caused by the THC. Table 4 shows the effects on optimal carbon taxes (SCC) in 2005 of assuming different discount rates of different discount rates (0–4 per cent and hyperbolic discounting) and different assumptions about damages caused by THC: no damages (original DICE model), 1 per cent loss of GWP, and 5 per cent loss of GWP.

As this table shows, using relatively high discount rates (3 per cent or 4 per cent) the inclusion of THC does not have a marked effect on the SCC, if costs of THC collapse are either 1 per cent or 5 per cent of GWP. Mastrandrea and Scheider show that substantial effects from THC collapse (loss of GWP of 25 per cent) are required before there is a noticeable impact on optimal carbon taxes. The reason for this is the use of the high discount rates and the long lag in the working out of the THC collapse. Table 5 shows that the social cost of capital is very sensitive to different values for discounting, and while this is also true for the basic DICE model, the sensitivity to discount rate is somewhat greater in the THC-enhanced DICE model than in the model with no THC effect.

To summarize, the introduction of catastrophic effects into models of optimal climate policy can have ambiguous effects on the SCC, and these theoretical ambiguities are borne out in the empirical modelling of Gjerde *et al*. The work by Mastrandrea and Schneider suggests that incorporating some abrupt climate changes does cause the SCC to rise, although the effect of discounting is more important than how the damage effect is modelled.

Of course, the representation of catastrophes in both the theoretical and empirical literature surveyed above is extremely simple. Any serious analysis of the implications of potential catastrophic effects of climate change would need to be grounded in a much more detailed description of the scientific nature of the suggested catastrophes, including the timescales over which they might occur, and how they translate into economic damages. Our discussion here is intended to note that there may be some surprising implications of analysing catastrophes, the intuition for which is more readily understood using some simple models. Whether these implications would arise in a fully specified model of climate-change catastrophes is a matter for further research.

6. When Probabilities Are Not Known

To complete this analysis of how uncertainty, learning, and precaution might affect the SCC, we address very briefly another criticism that is sometimes made of the kind of models that we have employed so far: the assumption that it is possible to describe all conceivable events or states of the world that might be of interest in thinking about climate change, and to ascribe probabilities to such states of the world.

Kann and Weyant (2000) and van Asselt and Rotmans (1999) divide uncertainty into two separate types: parametric uncertainty, which is concerned with imperfect knowledge of the underlying processes, some of which may be resolved through learning, and stochastic uncertainty, due to the natural variability inherent in the process. Van Asselt and Rotmans give a full description of the different sources of uncertainty and variability that arise in integrated assessment models (IAMs). An important element of parametric uncertainty for the models and estimates that have been discussed is that of lack of knowledge of the probabilities and their underlying distribution. If this is the case, then expected utility cannot be calculated, even if it were an appropriate objective; nor can the alternative criteria, such as that discussed by Chichilnisky, or methods that replace uncertain variables by their expected values.

Kann and Weyant's main purpose is to compare models incorporating uncertainty analysis. Almost all of the approaches they consider have a requirement that probability is describable. They are concerned about the choice between models with learning and models without learning: between optimization models in which there is a 'learn now, then act' approach and policy evaluation models with an 'act now, then learn' approach. They point out that one of the main problems in incorporating uncertainty is the curse of dimensionality. For this reason, they advocate the use of sequential decision models, and show how other models can be seen as cases of this approach. This is very much consistent with the approach taken in sections 3 and 4 of this paper, where decision-makers start out with possibly very poor understanding of many aspects of climate change, captured by diffuse Bayesian prior distributions over parameters, but recognize that they are likely to get better information over time which will allow them to update their estimates. Sections 3 and 4 of this paper were concerned with the question of how such a sequential approach to decision-making would affect the choice of current policy.

Alternative approaches they discuss are *sensitivity analysis* and *scenario analysis*. Sensitivity analysis varies parameters and then records the resulting changes on output variables. Primarily, it is chosen as a way of determining which variables have greatest impact on the results of the model. It can then assess the impact of the sensitivity of the model results to those variables for which a probabilistic analysis is not possible. Kann and Weyant include discounting and underlying damage valuation within these. However, they regard this approach as having various shortcomings. Not all of the effects of uncertainty will be revealed if they occur for parameter values interior to the range chosen for the maximum effect of variability to be observed. Sensitivity analysis will not allow for modelling of stochastic variability, and assumes that the model structure is correct. Consequently, it cannot measure uncertainty arising from specification uncertainty. This is in line with our discussion in section 2.

The other main alternative to the use of probabilities that Kann and Weyant consider is that of scenario analysis. This consists of a combination of assumptions about different states of the world. It then compares the results of these. Scenarios can be generated either by judicious choice of parameter values, or by using a joint probability distribution on parameter values. Again in section 2 we showed how Nordhaus and Popp generated a number of scenarios from underlying probability distributions on parameters. However, scenarios need not be assigned probabilities, in which case it does not lead to a full analysis of uncertainty. There also needs to be a consensus about which scenarios should be chosen. So the discussion of how to do analysis under uncertainty by Kann and Weyant (2000) is consistent with the approach taken in this paper.

Van Asselt and Rotmans (1999) suggest that by using an approach of pluralistic uncertainty, some of the problems noted by Kann and Weyant can be resolved. Their main aim is to obtain results from IAMs that are robust. Van Asselt and Rotmans argue that, as most probabilistic analysis uses Bayesian analysis with a diffuse prior, to reflect lack of knowledge of underlying probability distribution, the output of these models suggest how probability distributions are transformed by the model, rather than what the output probability distributions actually are.

The pluralistic uncertainty approach that van Asselt and Rotmans advocate has several stages. The first is cultural theory, which develops a set of perspectives from which the model outcomes are to be assessed. The next stage is an analysis of controversy, which suggests areas of uncertainty that needs to be addressed by the uncertainty analysis. Together with a sensitivity analysis this gives the crucial uncertainties that form the model analysis. The outcomes of this give perspectives that are developed as questions posed to the model. The calibrated model is then used for model experiments as a way of building scenarios. These scenarios generate future paths for the variables in the model. These are evaluated as to whether they are significantly different from those derived from previous models. An attempt is then made to explain differences that arise. A set of possible future paths for the output variables of the model is then created. These are then used to develop a risk assessment, which gives insights independent of the preferences that decision-makers might have for the perspectives developed in the first stage. However, it is not clear just how flexible a tool this might be for reaching decisions in the kind of sequential process described by Kann and Weyant, where one wants quickly to assess the effects of making changes to underlying modelling assumptions.

7. Conclusions

In this chapter we have reviewed how uncertainty, irreversibility, and precaution might affect the calculation of optimal climate-change policy. On a number of key conceptual issues, such as the implications of the precautionary principle or irreversibility effect, and the implications of introducing catastrophic effects, we have shown that economic analysis yields ambiguous and sometimes counter-intuitive results. In particular, the introduction of uncertainty, irreversibility, and learning, or the introduction of catastrophic effects can lead policy-makers to increase current emissions. These effects are not mere theoretical curiosa – the empirical modelling of optimal climate policy confirms that policy may, indeed, require that the SCC be reduced when account is taken of factors such as irreversibility and learning or catastrophic effects. The benefit of reviewing the theory is to provide an explanation of why such results might occur. So, a first conclusion from this chapter is that results which standard intuition suggests might go in one direction may be more ambiguous.

A second broad conclusion from this chapter is that, based on the studies we have reviewed, estimates of optimal control rates for carbon emissions do not seem to be very sensitive to the introduction of factors such as irreversibility and learning or catastrophic effects, compared, say, to the well-known sensitivity of the SCC to assumptions about discounting.

However, there are two reasons why it may be dangerous to conclude that the control rate is inherently insensitive to the issues addressed in this chapter. The first is that, as our analysis of irreversibility and learning showed, the rather small empirical results found may be a direct consequence of the choice of modelling assumptions (e.g. logarithmic utility functions or quadratic functions) which predispose such effects to be small or go in one direction. More familiarity with the literature might, therefore, lead to alternative models which make results more significant. The second reason is the 'curse of dimensionality' problem. To make the analysis of optimal policy under uncertainty with irreversibility and learning tractable, analysts are forced to simplify drastically the representation of uncertainty: dealing with uncertainties about relatively few variables, or combining such uncertainties into a small number of scenarios or states of the world. This very coarse treatment of uncertainty may significantly underestimate effects. We are less optimistic that this problem can be tackled easily. Nevertheless, we hope that this review of the literature to date will help to guide directions for future research.

4

Integrated Assessment Models

CHRIS HOPE*

1. Introduction

Integrated assessment models (IAMs) of climate change are the formal, computerized, representations that have been created to understand and cope with this complex, global problem. 'The term Integrated Assessment (IA) . . . is a relatively recent creation, though much of the "discipline" is not new, dating back at least 25 years' (Kolstad, 1998, p. 268). What we would now call IAMs were used extensively to examine energy policy in the 1970s and the acid-rain issue in the 1980s. IAMs of climate change first emerged in the late 1970s, and have multiplied dramatically since the early 1990s under the twin stimuli of the Intergovernmental Panel on Climate Change (IPCC), which first reported in 1990, and the Framework Convention on Climate Change (FCCC) signed at Rio in 1992.

The IPCC and FCCC represented the first political recognition of the global scale of a problem which combines science and economics, and requires contributions from several disciplines if it is to be tamed. This chapter describes the main ways in which modellers have responded to this challenge, the capabilities of the models that have been produced, and gives an example of the social-cost results for several gases from one IAM. It concludes with some observations about the limitations of the models and the role of IAMs in the policy process.

2. The Definition of IAMs

Several attempts to define IAMs have been made. They are not totally in agreement, but do provide enough information to come up with a reasonable working definition.

* Judge Institute of Management, University of Cambridge.

(a) *Integrated Across Disciplines*

Weyant *et al.* (1996) have produced what is regarded as the most authoritative review to date for the IPCC. They say that IAMs 'all share the defining trait that they incorporate knowledge from more than one field of study' (p. 377). They also feel that 'integrated assessments can be integrated over different dimensions and to different degrees' (p. 375), and that different models 'vary greatly with regard to their scope' (p. 377).

For Kolstad (1998), 'an integrated assessment model is a model that includes both human activity and some key aspects of the physical relationships driving climate change' (p. 270). This is a more restrictive definition, which would exclude, for instance, a general circulation model (GCM) linked to an ecosystems model, or a model of an economy which can estimate the effect of a carbon tax. Edmonds (1998) feels it is too restrictive: 'It unnecessarily excludes models that are clearly interdisciplinary, and it is the interdisciplinary character of the research that defines IA, not the joining of social- and natural-science components' (p. 292).

(b) *Policy Orientation*

Other definitions emphasize the policy-oriented nature of the work. Schneider (1997*a*) points out that IAMs 'are purposefully constructed primarily to address real-world problems that lie across or at the intersection of many disciplines' (p. 230). He deduces from this a 'special obligation to make these tools as transparent as possible' (p. 230).

Weyant *et al.* (1996) agree that 'integrated assessment is distinguished from disciplinary research by its purpose, which is to inform policy and decision making rather than to advance knowledge for its intrinsic value' (p. 374). This prompts the question: how successful have IAMs of climate change been in this purpose? We return to this later in the chapter.

(c) *Integrating Climate Change with other Concerns*

Parson and Fisher-Vanden (1997) add a fairly obvious caution that 'IA modelling is not, and cannot be, all of assessment . . . IA models can contribute best to assessment when embedded in broader assessment processes that introduce more deliberation, criticism, diversity of views, and common sense' (p. 619). They also distinguish a different type of integration, which they call 'horizontal', 'between climate change and other issues, including both other atmospheric issues such as ozone depletion, acidification, or photochemical air pollution, and linked social issues such as health and development' (p. 594). They recognize that present attempts at this horizontal integration are 'preliminary' and 'moving some distance ahead of current structures of decision-making', but are clearly excited by the opportunity they present 'to sketch an integrated conception of sustainable development' (p. 594).

The most sensible course seems to be to accept the Weyant et al. (1996) definition of IAMs of climate change as models that incorporate knowledge from more than one field of study, with the purpose of informing climate-change policy.

3. Prominent IA Models

Table 1 (Table 10.1 in the original) shows the IAMs included in the review by Weyant et al. (1996). Although the versions of some of the models have changed in the meantime (for instance ICAM-2 has become ICAM-3, and PAGE has become PAGE2002), this list is still a fair representation of the range of models available.

The organizations developing IAMs are concentrated in two regions: the USA and Western Europe. Parson and Fisher-Vanden (1997) give a paragraph of description for most of these models; see Annex 1 for a condensed version of this. There are various ways to distinguish them.

(a) *Optimizing or Simulation*

Optimizing models endogenously compute the optimal level of control of greenhouse gases, within their restricted framework. Simulation models evaluate the effect on the economy and/or the environment of a particular policy to control climate change (Kolstad, 1998, p. 270).

It might seem from this description that optimizing models are superior—they can find the best policy rather than just explore the effects of a policy that is externally specified. In fact, optimizing models have to simplify drastically to be able to run: 'model size, detail and structure are limited by the numerical algorithms used to solve optimization problems' (Kolstad, 1998, p. 271).

For example, the original MERGE model was an influential optimizing model, but had no representation of impacts at all. It needed to be given a target for concentrations, and would then find the optimal way of meeting that target by emission cutbacks across regions and time (Manne and Richels, 1997).

Further examples from early versions of FUND are that additional malaria deaths were assumed to be linear in global mean temperature

Table 1
Models and Modelling Teams

Model	Modellers
AS/ExM (Adaptive Strategies/Exploratory Model)	R. Lempert, S. Popper (Rand); M. Schlesinger (U. of Illinois)
AIM (Asian-Pacific Integrated Model)	T. Morita, M.Kainuma (National Inst. for Environmental Studies, Japan); Y. Matsuoka (Kyoto U.)
CETA (Carbon Emissions Trajectory Assessment)	S. Peck (Electric Power Research Institute) T. Teisberg (Teisberg Assoc.)
Connecticut (also known as the Yohe model)	G. Yohe (Wesleyan University)
CRAPS (Climate Research And Policy Synthesis model)	J. Hammitt (Harvard U.); A. Jain, D. Wuebbles (U. of Illinois)
CSERGE (Centre for Social and Economic Research on the Global Environment)	D. Maddison (University College of London)
DICE (Dynamic Integrated Climate and Economy model)	W. Nordhaus (Yale U.)
FUND (The Climate Framework for Uncertainty, Negotiation, and Distribution)	R.S.J. Tol (Vrije Universiteit Amsterdam)
DIAM (Dynamics of Inertia and Adaptability Model)	M. Grubb (Royal Institute of International Affairs), M.H. Dong, T. Chapuis (Centre Internationale de recherche sur l'environnement et développement)
ICAM-2 (Integrated Climate Assessment Model)	H. Dowlatabadi, G. Morgan (Carnegie-Mellon U.)
IIASA (International Institute for Applied Systems Analysis)	L. Schrattenholzer, Arnulf Grubler (IIASA)
IMAGE 2.0 (Integrated Model to Assess the Greenhouse Effect)	J. Alcamo, M. Krol (Rijksinstitut voor Volksgezondheid Milieuhygiene, Netherlands)
MARIA (Multiregional Approach for Resource and Industry Allocation)	S. Mori (Sci. U. of Tokyo)
MERGE 2.0 (Model for Evaluating Regional and Global Effects of GHG Reductions Policies)	Alan Manne (Stanford U.), Robert Mendelsohn (Yale U.), R. Richels (Electric Power Research Institute)
MiniCAM (Mini Global Change Assessment Model)	J. Edmonds (Pacific Northwest Lab), R. Richels (Electric Power Research Institute), T. Wigley (University Consortium for Atmospheric Research (UCAR))
MIT (Massachusetts Institute of Technology)	H. Jacoby, R. Prinn, Z. Yang (Massachusetts Institute of Technology)
PAGE (Policy Analysis of the Greenhouse Effect)	C. Hope (Cambridge U.); J. Anderson, P. Wenman (Environmental Resources Management)
PEF (Policy Evaluation Framework)	J. Scheraga, S. Herrod (EPA); R. Stafford, N. Chan (Decision Focus Inc.)
ProCAM (Process Oriented Global Change Assessment Model)	J. Edmonds, H. Pitcher, N. Rosenberg (Pacific Northwest Lab); T. Wigley (UCAR)
RICE (Regional DICE)	W. Nordhaus (Yale U.); Z. Yang (MIT)
SLICE (Stochastic Learning Integrated Climate Economy Model)	C. Kolstad (U. of California, Santa Barbara)
TARGETS (Tool to Assess Regional and Global Environmental and Health Targets for Sustainability)	J. Rotmans, M.B.A. van Asselt, A. Beusen, M.G.J. den Elzen, M. Janssen, H.B.M. Hilderink, A.Y. Hoekstra, H.W. Koster, W.J.M. Martens, L.W. Niessen, B. Strengers, H.J.M. de Vries (Rijksinstitut voor Volksgezondheid en Milieuhygiene, Netherlands)

with no adaptation or delay, and that the economic costs of carbon abatement measures were assumed to be quadratic in the amount of abatement, and to decay exponentially over time as the economy grows accustomed to it (Tol, 1996, pp. 157, 161).

Most optimizing models do have some representation of impacts and focus on a cost–benefit paradigm of balancing the marginal costs of controlling emissions with the damages that result (Weyant *et al.*, 1996, p. 380). The simplifications they employ to be able to do this include a highly aggregated representation of damages (losses are a function of mean global temperature), limited spatial resolution (often the whole world is treated as a single region), and often no explicit treatment of uncertainty.

For instance, in DICE, the damage from climate change is described by a single quadratic function of global mean temperature, calibrated to 1.33 per cent of GDP at 3°C (Tol and Fankhauser, 1998). As Tol and Fankhauser comment, 'damage modules are often no more than ad hoc extrapolations around the 2xCO$_2$ benchmark' (p. 73).

(b) Deterministic or Stochastic

Uncertainty is a common problem for policy-making, particularly in the environmental area. But it is almost the main defining characteristic here. Parson and Fisher-Vanden (1997) state that 'uncertainty is central to climate change' (p. 609).

Two examples can illustrate this:

1. The second IPCC report was the first to go so far as to state that 'the balance of evidence suggests a discernible human influence on global climate' (IPCC, Working Group I (WGI), 1995, p. 4), and the third report strengthened this slightly to say that 'most of the observed warming over the last 50 years is likely to have been due to the increase in greenhouse gas concentrations' (IPCC, WGI, 2001a, p. 10). The caution in the use of language is obvious in both statements, and the third report formalized this by defining 'likely' as meaning a judgemental confidence estimate of 66–90 per cent chance (IPCC, WGI, 2001a, p. 2). In the modelling work, the equilibrium temperature response to a doubling of carbon-dioxide (CO$_2$) concentration 'is likely to be in the range of 1.5 to 4.5 degC' (IPCC, WGI, 2001a, p. 67) with significant voices arguing that the true value could still easily be higher or lower than the extremes of this range. When 16 leading climate scientists were put through a formal decision-analytic eliciting of their subjective probability estimates, most assigned a 10 per cent or so probability for large climatic sensitivities of more than 5°C (Schneider, 1997b, p. 47).

2. Plausible ranges of CO$_2$ emissions, in the absence of policies to cut them, span a range of 5–35 gigatons of carbon/year in 2100 (IPCC, WGIII, 2001c, p. 4). These are baseline scenarios, upon which any climate-change policies would be imposed.

It is clear that any climate-change models that do not incorporate uncertainty are missing a very large part of the issue. Weyant (1998) feels that 'these numbers [from IAMs] ought never to be used without some degree of sensitivity and uncertainty analysis' (p. 289). But there is a difference between a simple sensitivity analysis of an essentially deterministic model, and a model that incorporates uncertainty at its heart.

Table 2 (Table 10.4 in the original) shows the Weyant *et al.* (1996) division of models into simulation (which they call policy evaluation) or optimization, and deterministic or stochastic.

Table 2
Models by Type

Policy evaluation models
  Deterministic projection models
    AIM
    IIASA
    IMAGE 2.0
    MIT
    ProCAM
    TARGETS
  Stochastic projection models
    PAGE
    ICAM-2
    TARGETS

Policy-optimization models
  Cost–benefit and target-based models
    CETA
    Connecticut
    CERGE
    DICE
    FUND
    DIAM
    MARIA
    MERGE 2.0
    MiniCAM
    RICE
  Uncertainty-based models
    AS/ExM
    CETA
    CRAPS
    CSERGE
    DICE
    FUND
    ICAM-A
    MERGE 2.0
    PEF
    SLICE

(c) *Partial or Full*

Figure 1 shows a simple linear characterization of the climate change problem (Parson and Fisher-Vanden, 1997, p. 596). Weyant *et al.* (1996) state that 'models that attempt to represent the full range of issues raised by climate change are referred to as "full-scale" IAMs' (p. 377). So to qualify as a full-scale IAM, a model must address each of the boxes in the figure. Weyant *et al.* (1996) also specify a variety of other conditions, which properly come under the heading of complexity rather than scale (such as the inclusion of a range of greenhouse gases, a range of emission-generating activities, a range of impact categories, and local as well as global air pollution) (p. 378), such that no existing IAM could be considered a full-scale model by their definition.

However, some models do include more of the boxes in Figure 1 than others. It is the boxes at either end that tend not to be included. Some models (e.g. PAGE, FUND, and DICE) omit the first box, and start with exogenously specified emissions (if they are simulation models), or end with optimal tax levels (if they are optimization models). Others omit the last box and end their analysis with physical impacts (e.g. IMAGE 2, ProCAM).

Chapter 6 by Mendelsohn in this volume describes the components of this simple schematic in some detail.

The linear view in Figure 1 is too simple to contain some of the models, particularly those that incorporate adaptation and feedbacks. Figure 2 shows the effort by Parson and Fisher-Vanden (1997) to incorporate a richer view.

This bears a striking resemblance to the pressure–state–impact–response framework used by the OECD for environmental information in general (OECD, 1991). It also helpfully places policies at the heart of the enterprise.

(d) *Complex or Simple*

Simple IAMs may represent the whole of the global climate system, or the impact of climate change, in just a few lines of computer code. DICE and PAGE are at this extreme.

The damage function in DICE at time t is simply

$$D(t) = 0.0133(T(t)/3)^2$$

where $D(t)$ is the fractional loss of global output, and $T(t)$ is the rise in global temperature beyond the pre-industrial average (Roughgarden, 1997).

Figure 1
Vertical Integration: Simple End-to-end Form

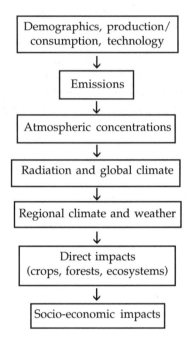

Figure 2
Vertical Integration: Fully Linked Form

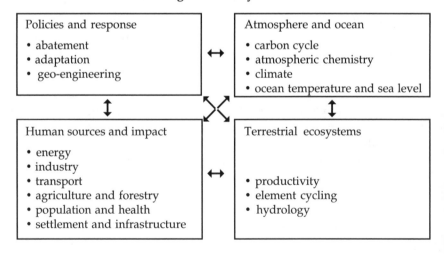

In PAGE, the entire carbon cycle is represented by

$$RE(t) = STAY*CEA(t-1)*(1-e^{-t/RES}) + RE(t-1)*e^{-t/RES} + E(t)*AIR*e^{-t/2RES}$$

where RE is the emissions of CO_2 that remain in the atmosphere at time t, STAY is the equilibrium partitioning of CO_2 between atmosphere and oceans, CEA is the cumulative emissions of CO_2, RES is the half-life of atmospheric residence of CO_2, E is the emissions of CO_2, and AIR is the proportion of those emissions that get into the atmosphere (Plambeck et al., 1997).

Contrast these with complex IAMs which may have detailed two-dimensional climate models (e.g. MIT), or model the effect on ecosystems at a half-degree grid square or river basin level (e.g. IMAGE 2).

There is an ongoing debate about the relative merits of complex and simple IAMs, with Kolstad (1998) claiming that 'small is usually better' (p. 279), while Edmonds (1998) feels that 'ultimately the simple models and high level of aggregation must give way' (p. 296) as policy questions become more specific.

However, Edmonds (1998) concedes that 'the current suite of predominantly simple IAMs have been particularly powerful in shaping understanding of the climate issue' (p. 295) and also makes the point that we should 'work from the problem to the model, not the other way round. . . . Where the modeler stops on the scale of disaggregation of any particular problem should, in principle, depend on the problem' (p. 295). This correctly brings the focus back to the insights that are being sought.

(e) Small or Large Groups

Many existing IAMs have been constructed by lone researchers or small groups, often over an extended period (e.g. DICE, FUND, ICAM, and PAGE). Others have the weight of large groups behind them, with funds from government or industry (e.g. IMAGE, MIT, ProCAM, and TARGETS). There is a positive correlation between the complexity of the model and the size of the group that has produced it, although there is no reason why this should be so. The trade-off in model construction is always between transparency, completeness, complexity, the representation of uncertainty, and the ability to optimize. Larger groups could have put their effort into any of these areas; they seem historically to have concentrated on complexity.

4. Capabilities

Parson and Fisher-Vanden (1997) divide existing models into three groups according to their intended purpose (p. 605).

(a) *Models that Emphasize Emission Dynamics and Optimization*

The main members of this group are DICE (and its progeny), CETA, and MERGE. DICE and CETA attempt to compute dynamically optimal emissions. To achieve this, they need to make some radical simplifications. Either the globe, or each region, is represented by a single representative producer-consumer, all costs and damages are represented in money terms, with damages expressed as a simple function of global temperature change, and adaptation is not included as a policy option.

MERGE has been used more often to calculate cost-effective ways of meeting specified environmental constraints, such as limits on CO_2 concentration. It has a detailed representation of the energy sector, including the vintages of energy producing and consuming plant. Its most noteworthy result is that trajectories in which global emissions climb for the next few decades and then decline, reduce present value abatement costs by as much as a half compared to trajectories requiring immediate cutbacks to meet the same targets. 'The lower costs reflect four factors—technological change, avoiding premature capital retirement, exploiting natural carbon absorption, and discounting' (Parson and Fisher-Vanden, 1997, p. 608).

(b) *Models that Emphasize Spatial Detail*

These include IMAGE, MIT, and ProCAM. Typically, they produce maps showing the effect of different energy policies or emissions trajectories on ecosystems and land use. The motivation for such models is well described by Weyant (1998): 'at some point policymakers will want to know if an increment of GDP loss is the result of fewer recreational amenities in Southern California or more deaths from Monsoon-driven flooding in Asia or climate-driven increases in malaria incidence in Africa' (p. 288).

However, Weyant (1998) feels that existing detailed models have tended to stray from the primary purpose of IAMs: 'Decision relevance has often been subjugated to process understanding. In other words, science has been pursued in and of itself without considering the likely policy relevance of that science' (p. 289).

(c) *Models that Emphasize Uncertainty*

These models include PAGE, ICAM, FUND, and SLICE. Two dominant approaches to uncertainty have been taken. One involves 'evaluating adaptive decision strategies that can respond to progressive resolution of uncertainty over time' (Parson and Fisher-Vanden, 1997, p. 609). These models are based on decision analytic theory, and normally consider only a few key uncertainties. They can calculate the value of improved information, at least in theory; in practice the simple representation of uncertainty resolution makes such calculations suspect.

The second main approach involves 'stochastic simulation with sampling over distributions of many uncertain inputs. Such sampling generates probability distributions of outputs' (Parson and Fisher-Vanden, 1997, p. 609). It can also allow the inputs that have the biggest effect upon the uncertainty in the outputs to be found. The next section gives an example of this approach applied to finding the social cost of a range of greenhouse gases.

5. The Social Cost of Greenhouse Gases from one IAM

The social cost of a greenhouse gas is the increase in future impacts, discounted to the present day, that occurs if current emissions of the gas are increased by 1 tonne. As other chapters, particularly that by David Pearce, show, the calculation of social costs is a major policy concern at present. In the UK, two Department for Environment Food and Rural Affairs (Defra) economists have proposed a value of £70 per tonne of carbon (tC) (in year 2000 prices) for the social cost of carbon, with upper and lower values of £35 and £140 per tonne (Clarkson and Deyes, 2002). Their work recognizes that an IAM is needed to make these estimates (Clarkson and Deyes, 2002, section 3.4).

As an illustration of the insights that can flow from the use of an IAM, this section briefly summarizes the social-cost results from a new version of the PAGE model, PAGE2002, which has been developed and used to calculate the marginal impacts of CO_2, methane (CH_4), and sulphur hexafluoride (SF_6) emissions. Full details of this work, which was funded by the UK Office of Gas and Electricity Markets (Ofgem), can be found in Hope (2003).

The PAGE2002 model uses relatively simple equations to capture complex climatic and economic phenomena. This is justified because the results approximate those of the most complex climate simulations, and because all aspects of climate change are subject to profound uncertainty. To express the model results in terms of a single 'best guess' could be dangerously misleading. Instead, a range of possible outcomes should inform policy. PAGE2002 builds up probability distributions of results by representing 31 key inputs to the marginal impact calculations by probability distributions. The main structural changes in PAGE2002 compared to PAGE95 are the introduction of a third greenhouse gas and the incorporation of possible future large-scale discontinuities, such as the disintegration of the West Antarctic Ice Sheet, identified by the IPCC third assessment report as a serious reason for concern (IPCC, WGII, 2001b, p. 5).

In this investigation, PAGE2002 is run with global emissions of greenhouse gases from Scenario A2 of the IPCC (IPCC, WGI, 2001a, p. 64). This scenario represents a heterogeneous world, with an underlying theme of self-reliance and preservation of local identities. As with all the IPCC illustrative scenarios, it assumes no active intervention to control emissions.

The PAGE2002 mean global temperature results track the IPCC climate results very well, as Figure 3 shows. The range of results from the PAGE2002 model is larger than the range reported in the IPCC TAR. This is to be expected, as the IPCC results are simply the highest and lowest best-guess results from the seven General Circulation Models considered by the IPCC, and not a true probability distribution. As the IPCC states, 'This is not the extreme range of possibilities, for two reasons. First, forcing uncertainties have not been considered. Second, some AOGCMs have effective climate sensitivities outside the range considered' (IPCC, WGI, 2001, p. 555). The PAGE2002 results do include uncertainties in forcing, particularly for sulphates, and the full range of climate sensitivities up to 5°C for a doubling of CO_2.

PAGE2002 gives the mean climate-change impacts of scenario A2 over the next two centuries from 2000 to 2200 as US$26 trillion in year 2000 dollars, discounted back to 2000 at a pure time preference rate of 3 per cent per year. The 5 per cent and 95 per cent points on the distribution are US$6 trillion and US$67 trillion.

The social cost of each of the three gases, CO_2, CH_4, and SF_6, is calculated by reducing the emissions of the gas by a small amount in the first analysis year, 2001, and finding the difference in impacts that this creates. The structure of the PAGE2002 model allows a probability distribution for the difference in impacts, and so the social cost, to be calculated.

Table 3 shows the social-cost results. The mean value for CO_2 is US$19 tC (or about US$5 per tonne of CO_2), for methane it is US$105 per tonne, and for SF_6, US$200,000 per tonne. Using the mean values, each tonne of methane has 21 times the impact of a tonne of CO_2, and each tonne of SF_6 has about 40,000 times the impact of a tonne of

Figure 3
Global Mean Temperature Change by Year

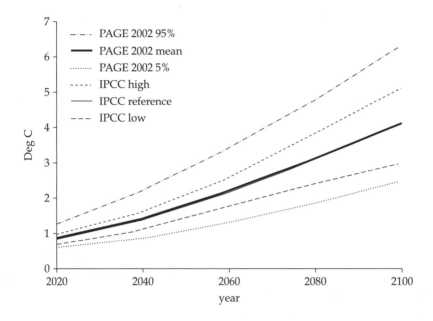

Source: PAGE2002 model runs and IPCC, WGI (2001*a*).

CO_2. For each gas, the range between the 5 per cent and 95 per cent points is about an order of magnitude. For comparison, the IPCC gives 100-year global warming potentials (GWPs) on a mass basis of 23 for methane and 22,200 for SF_6 (IPCC, WGI, 2001*a*, p. 388).

GWPs have at least three obvious drawbacks: they are very sensitive to the arbitrary time horizon chosen. They do not allow impacts that occur soon to be valued more highly than those that occur in the distant future, and they are relative, rather than absolute, measures. Knowing the GWP of a gas does not necessarily help very much in deciding how much effort, if any, should be devoted to reducing the emissions of it.

By contrast, the social cost calculated here is an absolute measure. It does not require the assumption of an arbitrary time horizon. It allows near-term impacts to be valued more highly. It can also be compared with estimated costs for abating emissions of the gas.

Market prices are about US$160 per tonne for methane and about US$25,000 per tonne for SF_6. The climate-change impacts of methane are a significant proportion of its market price. So a pipeline replacement to decrease losses could be justified if the net present cost were less than about US$265 per tonne saved in 2000 US dollars—made up of not just

Table 3
Social Costs by Gas
(2000–2200, US$(2000) per tonne)

	5%	mean	95%
C as CO_2	4	19	51
CH_4	25	105	263
SF_6	45,000	200,000	450,000

Source: PAGE2002 model runs.

US$160 from having the gas available to sell, but also US$105 from the reduction in climate-change impacts.

For SF_6 the climate-change impacts are much larger than the market price. The economics of schemes to reduce the leakage of SF_6 are transformed once the climate-change impacts are properly counted.

The social costs given in this section have been calculated for only a single IPCC scenario, A2. Although earlier work has shown the results to be fairly insensitive to the scenario used, it would probably be worthwhile to repeat the calculations at least for one other of the IPCC scenarios, scenario B2. This is not because the different emissions in scenario B2 would change the results, so much as because of the different GDP and population-growth assumptions, which imply different discount rates, which are known to affect the results strongly (Hope, 2004).

Figure 4 shows the most important influences on the social cost of a tonne of SF_6. The largest correlation, +0.732, is with the equilibrium warming for a doubling of CO_2 concentration. The sign of the correlation coefficient shows that a larger value for the input gives a larger value for the social cost, as we would expect.

All of the influences in Figure 4 are of the correct sign. That the top four influences divide into two scientific and two economic parameters is a strong argument for the building of IAMs such as PAGE2002. Models that are exclusively scientific, or exclusively economic, would omit important parts of the climate-change problem which still contain profound uncertainties.

6. The Limitations of IAMs

'At the broadest level, IA modelling faces two challenges: managing its relationship to research and disciplinary knowledge and managing its relationship to other assessment processes and to policy-making' Parson and Fisher-Vanden, 1997, p. 618). These challenges mirror the

Figure 4
Correlations with Social Cost of SF$_6$

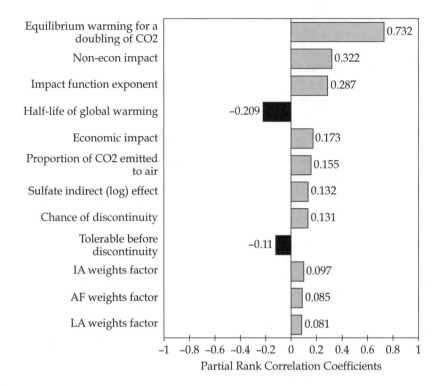

Partial Rank Correlation Coefficients

definition of an IAM that was provided in the first section. In particular the timescale required to construct and operate the models requires early warning from the policy community about the emergence of new critical issues.

Several specific limitations of the current generation of IAMs need special mention.

(a) *Representing and Valuing Impacts*

This limitation has several parts. Projecting climate at a regional scale stretches the capabilities of climate models. Translating changes in regional climate to physical impacts is in its infancy. The valuation of any physical impacts (such as ecosystem damage, or effects on human health) also requires assumptions that are controversial (how to value the loss of a life in developing countries was probably the most contentious issue in the second assessment report of the IPCC) (Weyant et al., 1996, p. 391). As Kolstad (1998) points out,

> Better measures of the impacts of climate change are important to IAMs but must come out of disciplinary studies . . . the problem of valuation in integrated assessment is not with the models but with the underlying basic sciences such as biology, ecology and economics. (p. 279)

The challenge for IAMs is to represent what is known about impacts, including the uncertainty in our knowledge, in the way that is most useful for policy, and to update that representation as knowledge changes over the years.

(b) *Low Probability but Catastrophic Events*

Many IAMs still concentrate on expected conditions. Even those models that take particular care to represent uncertainty (e.g. PAGE, ICAM) have difficulty with catastrophes that lie at the extreme tails of the probability distribution. 'Lack of data, lack of understanding of the relevant processes, and analytical intractability have prevented such events from receiving adequate attention in the integrated assessments that have been performed to date' (Weyant *et al.*, 1996, p. 391).

Here the problem is not entirely with the underlying disciplines; it would be possible for ecologists to give us some idea of the possible effects of, say, a 10°C rise in temperature over the next century. 'Not only do we need a better grasp of what catastrophes might befall us, we need to develop better methods for representing catastrophes within integrated assessment models' (Kolstad, 1998, p. 279). Recent versions of RICE (Nordhaus and Boyer, 2000, ch. 4) and PAGE (Hope, 2003) have gone some way towards incorporating catastrophes in their impact calculations.

(c) *Developing Countries*

With modelling groups dominated by the USA and Western Europe, it may not be surprising that costs and impacts in the OECD have received most attention, but it would be wrong to characterize this entirely as cultural myopia. There are several other reasons why it is difficult to model climate change in the developing countries: lack of data, inequity across different sections of society, the rapidity of growth of their population and economies over the timescale of IAMs, and the presence of more pressing concerns than climate change (Weyant *et al.*, 1996, p. 391).

(d) *Adaptation*

'The area of adaptation has remained largely untouched in integrated assessment models' (Kolstad, 1998, p. 280). Early models of damage assumed no adaptation (the 'dumb farmer' assumption), and this has now been largely corrected. But, even now, few IAMs consider adaptation as a policy option, either in addition to, or instead of, emission cutbacks.

(e) *Non-cooperation*

'Considering the problems of initiating and enforcing agreements with large numbers of parties, actions and treaties involving small numbers of countries must be considered a possibility' (Kolstad, 1998, p. 282). IAMs have not made much effort to date to analyse second-best solutions such as this.

(f) *Technical Change*

As with adaptation, there are two ways in which technical change can be included in IAMs. One is as an inevitable trend that needs to be incorporated in projections of emissions and costs. Several models attempt to do this, for example by assuming rates of autonomous energy efficiency improvement (e.g. MERGE 2.0). Another is to include R&D as a policy option that can be adjusted. This is much rarer. As with impacts, part of the reason is the lack of a good disciplinary understanding of the processes by which R&D spending leads to technical change. Indeed, Grubb and Walker concluded that 'there appears to be no discernible relationship between the allocation of government energy R&D expenditure . . . and the technologies that now appear most likely to have a significant impact' (Grubb and Walker, 1992, p. 240).

(g) *Links to Other Issues*

Typically, IAMs of climate change have treated the issue in isolation. One consequence has been high estimates of the costs of cutting back emissions, as the beneficial effects of recycling carbon-tax revenues through the economy have been neglected (Barker, 1998). Obvious links are those to other environmental issues, such as local air pollution and biodiversity (as covered in, for example, TARGETS), and to population control and fiscal policies. There may be problems with the relative timing of any concerted efforts to coordinate policies across environmental and other issues, as they are often dealt with by separate parts of government.

7. Advice to Policy-makers

As Edmonds (1998) reminds us, 'In the early stages of the discussion the principal question at hand is, "Does this question belong on the policy agenda at all?"' (p. 296). By and large, IAMs, and particularly the more simple ones, have done a good job of addressing this question. Approximate estimates of impacts and costs of cutbacks, particularly with uncertainties attached, were enough to show that the stakes could be high. Indeed, Edmonds (1998) goes so far as to state, 'What is truly remarkable is the degree of impact IAMs have had on framing the policy discussions' (p. 299). However, this may not be so surprising if the IAMs give a respectable academic veneer to the results that powerful actors want. To guard against this, Schneider (1997a) recommends 'transparency and accessibility, and that all values and assumptions that might be hidden in the analytic complexity of IAMs are purposefully made explicit to users' (p. 246).

Beyond this, Parson and Fisher-Vanden (1997) argue that 'contributions of IA models should be evaluated by several criteria: not just the persuasiveness and novelty of the insights, but their robustness, their specificity, and the extent to which the IA model was needed to obtain them.' (p. 614).

The insights from IAMs to date that might pass this test are the following.

(a) Need for Widespread Abatement

'OECD abatement alone cannot sustain reasonable limits on atmospheric concentrations' (Parson and Fisher-Vanden, 1997, p. 616). This appears to be a completely robust result, but perhaps does not require an IAM to demonstrate it. Only the top three boxes in Figure 1 are involved.

(b) The Value of Flexibility

'Providing flexible instruments could lower the costs of achieving various mitigation goals by an order of magnitude' (Edmonds, 1998, p. 299). This flexibility has two aspects: *when* and *where*. In particular, it is valuable to be able to cut emissions *where* that cutback can be made most cheaply (Manne and Richels, 1997). This result has not been contradicted by any IAM modelling team (but see Barker (1998) for a contrary view, arguing that, with tax reform, cut-backs can be obtained cheaply or free even in the European Union (EU)), but it is far from the reality of present negotiations, which place no obligations upon developing countries. This model result is fuelling the interest in tradable permits, joint implementation, and so on. Quantifying the benefits from flexible mechanisms is now one of the main driving forces for IAMs, particularly in the USA.

As for *when* flexibility, stabilization of CO_2 concentrations at, for instance, 550 parts per million (ppm) can be achieved either by starting to cut back emissions immediately, as in the scenario from WGI of the IPCC (1995), or by delaying cutbacks and then cutting back more, as in the scenario proposed by Wigley, Richels, and Edmonds (WRE) (1996). IAM calculations have shown that the costs of cutbacks could be 7×10^{12} lower in the WRE scenario (if there is no flexibility as to where the emission cutbacks are made), or 3×10^{12} lower (if there is flexibility) (Manne and Richels, 1997). As well as the obvious contribution from discounting, the costs are lower because less capital needs to be prematurely retired, there is more time for appropriate R&D, and emissions that occur early are partially removed by natural processes.

But the WRE scenario could lead to higher temperatures than the WGI scenario for much of the next two centuries. Although the difference in temperature is slight, IAM calculations have shown that the impacts from the WRE scenario could be $1.4 trillion higher than from WGI (ignoring sulphates), or between $0 and $2 trillion higher if sulphates are assumed to be proportional to CO_2 (Tol, 1998; Hope, 1999).

As Mendelsohn's chapter 6 in this volume confirms, there is also no consensus about the justification for continuing to discount costs at current rates of around 5 per cent per year into the indefinite future (Cline, 1992), nor about the right date at which to terminate the analysis. So the debate about the desirability of delaying controls on CO_2 is far from over. Plambeck and Hope (1996) caution that

> policy makers are advised to carefully consider the treatment of uncertainty as well as assumptions about adaptation to climate change, non-linearity in damage as a function of temperature rise, secondary benefits to CO_2 abatement, and the discount rate. . . . These assumptions, often hidden in the small print or not reported at all, have a profound effect. (p. 792)

(c) *Small Initial Amounts of Abatement*

'Optimal emission-control rates are small' (Edmonds, 1998, p. 298), particularly in the near term. This conclusion appears directly from the simple optimization models, such as DICE, and from models such as MERGE that show delays of a few decades in controlling emissions are not too harmful, and may even be beneficial, even if we later learn that stringent reductions are needed (Parson and Fisher-Vanden, 1997, p. 615).

This result depends upon a whole series of other results concerning the smallness of climate impacts in advanced economies, the continuation of autonomous trends in energy efficiency, the high cost of cutting emissions, the high value of information that will be obtained by waiting, and the continuation of discount rates close to those observed today rather than much lower ones.

Of these other results, it is probably only the first that enjoys anything like a consensus among modellers (and even then the consensus does not extend to other stakeholders). Schneider (1997a) speaks for many researchers when he says that 'in the actual economy neither the cost of non-conventional energy supply nor the rate of energy efficiency improvements (EEI) are fully "autonomous" . . . on the contrary . . . EEI should not only be autonomous, but also endogenous to the system' (p. 236). Barker (1998) finds that additional excise duties to cut CO_2 emissions in the EU by 10 per cent by 2010 show *increases* in employment and GDP in all member states (except for a small drop in GDP in the Netherlands) compared to the base case (Barker, 1998, p. 1090). Even the IPCC does not expect rapid resolution of uncertainty: 'Although progress has been made, considerable gaps in knowledge remain regarding exposure, sensitivity, adaptability, and vulnerability of physical, ecological and social systems to climate change.' (IPCC, WGII, 2001b, p. 73). Cline (1992) is far from alone in questioning the validity of present-day discount rates for long-term climate policy.

Taken together, for an activity that is still in its infancy, the list of achievements of IAMs is impressive. 'Considering the relatively short history of integrated assessment of climate, a surprising amount of knowledge has emerged' (Kolstad, 1998, p. 282). As the uncertainty in the results captured by the PAGE model has shown, policy-makers cannot expect IAMs to be a panacea, producing precise results that banish uncertainty and the need for judgement to be exercised. However, as IAMs mature, they will become more and more useful for representing the range of social costs, and other relevant quantities, that it is reasonable to consider when forming and implementing policy choices.

Annex 1: Brief Descriptions of Prominent IAMs of Climate Change, Taken Largely from Parson and Fisher-Vanden (1997)

CETA extends the Global 2100 macroeconomic-energy model by adding simple models of the carbon cycle and global-average temperature change, and a damage function. Energy CO_2 emissions are modelled by embedding an energy sector with substantial technical detail within the production function, while other emissions follow fixed scenarios similar to that of the IPCC. Doubled-CO_2 sensitivity is tuned to 3°C, while damage estimates are calibrated to 2 per cent GNP loss from 3°C equilibrium temperature change. The model is driven by a single global consumer-producer who maximizes the present value of utility of consumption, net of climate-change damages, over the period from the present to the year 2200.

In DICE, a single producer-consumer chooses between current consumption, investment, and reducing greenhouse emissions, to maximize the present value of utility. An abatement cost function, with no energy-sector detail, is fitted statistically to a collection of point estimates from prior studies, such that reducing emissions by half from their unconstrained level at any time costs about 1 per cent of output. A fixed fraction of each period's carbon emissions adds to atmospheric concentrations, while realized temperature change is represented by a three-box model. Climate damage is a quadratic function of realized temperature, in which a 3°C rise reduces output by 1.3 per cent.

RICE and SLICE are regionally disaggregated and stochastic forms of DICE respectively.

FUND is a nine-region model that combines exogenous emission scenarios with moderately detailed endogenous abatement costs and climate damages, including quantified, highly illustrative impacts in particular sectors, defined as functions of temperature change and income.

ICAM derives regional emissions from exogenous assumptions by a demographic and economic accounting framework. Simple linear atmospheric models yield concentrations and changes in radiative forcing, while regional impact functions combine direct dependence on regional climatic variables with explicit representation of a few specific impacts.

IMAGE2 contains three linked systems, representing energy and emissions, the terrestrial environment and land cover, and the atmosphere and oceans. Emissions are projected for 13 regions by a bottom-up technologically detailed model. Land cover, soil type, element fluxes and direct ecosystem impacts are represented on a global half-degree grid. The globally parameterized atmospheric chemistry model and climate-ocean model calculate annual average temperature and precipitation changes for 10-degree latitude bands, plus ocean circulation and transport of heat and CO_2.

MERGE combines a detailed energy-economy model with simple carbon and climate models and a damage function. It uses Global 2200, a five-region dynamic general equilibrium model with a detailed energy sector. A single agent in each region makes consumption and savings/investment decisions to maximize the present value of utility of consumption. A simple impulse-response function represents the carbon cycle, while CH_4 and nitrous oxide (N_2O) have fixed atmospheric lifetimes. Radiative forcing functions and a lagged adjustment model for realized global temperature are drawn from the IPCC. Simple regional damage functions separate market and non-market damages. Both are quadratic in temperature, and non-market damages also depend on regional income.

In the MIT model, multiple emissions are modelled by a dynamic computable general equilibrium model that includes 13 sectors and 12 world regions. Two-dimensional, land-ocean resolving linked chemistry and climate models represent the atmosphere and calculate average temperature, precipitation, cloudiness, and humidity for 23 latitude bands. Ecosystems are represented by a process-based model that calculates net primary production and nitrogen cycling at half-degree resolution as functions of changed climate, CO_2 concentration, and nutrient deposition.

In PAGE, the policy decision variables are the level of greenhouse gas emissions over time and the degree of adaptation to climate change in eight world regions. PAGE estimates the costs of enacting the policy as well as the resulting impacts. More than 30 key input parameters are represented as probability distributions.

ProCAM contains substantial technical detail in the energy sectors and vintaged capital stocks. Land-use emissions are estimated by models that allocate regional land among an unmanaged state and several competing uses, based on prices of biomass energy and agricultural products. Temperature and sea-level changes are projected at half-degree detail over selected high-resolution windows, and five-degree elsewhere. Impacts are projected for unmanaged ecosystems, and using detailed agricultural crop and hydrology models for managed ecosystems.

TARGETS is a broad, horizontally integrated model of sustainable development that links multiple environmental, social, and economic issues. It uses heuristic representations of uncertainty inspired by the three social types of cultural theory.

Part Two: The Social Cost of Carbon

5

The Social Cost of Carbon

DAVID PEARCE*

1. Introduction

The 1997 Kyoto Protocol to the 1992 UN Framework Convention on Climate Change (UNFCCC) sets targets for the industrialized countries to reduce their emissions of greenhouse gases by the period 2008–12. Analysis of the Protocol, the refusal of the USA to sign it, and the subsequent revisions to the Protocol in later Conferences of Parties, suggest strongly that the Protocol will secure little or no change in rates of global warming (see the chapter by Böhringer in this volume). Accordingly, if global warming is to be tackled, 'Kyoto 2', '3', etc. need to be developed very soon. Debate surrounds the reasons for the highly probable failure of Kyoto to be environmentally effective (for an excellent discussion see Barrett, 2003a), but the low participation rate in the agreement can in part be explained by individual countries' assessments of the costs and benefit to them of compliance with the targets. Certainly, the USA's stance can be explained by (a) a perception that the domestic costs of compliance are high, (b) recent work suggesting that the benefits of control are very low for the USA (see Mendelsohn and Neumann, 1999), and (c) the realization that future agreements will require significant side-payments to developing countries to bring them 'on board' with the Protocols. The new Bush Administration is unlikely to ratify the Kyoto Protocol and the US position on climate change, therefore, depends considerably on potential political changes within the USA and the success of other countries in meeting the Kyoto targets without significant economic disruption. Very recent appraisals

* Department of Economics and CSERGE, University College London, and Environmental Science and Technology, Imperial College London. This is an updated and revised version of Pearce (2003b). I am indebted to Richard Tol of the University of Hamburg, Rob Mendelsohn of Yale University, and Chris Hope of Cambridge University for comments on the earlier version. Any remaining errors are entirely my responsibility, as are the views expressed here.

of the impact of climate change on the USA confirm the possibility that, on balance, it may be beneficial in the short run, but detrimental in the long run (Smith, 2004; Jorgenson *et al.*, 2004). The climate of economic opinion may therefore be shifting towards a more pro-active stance in the USA. None the less, country-focused cost–benefit analysis is sufficient to explain the contrast between Kyoto and the Montreal Protocol on ozone depleting substances. In the latter case, benefits are huge, and domestic costs and side payments very low (Barrett, 2003a).

Central to cost–benefit analysis are estimates of the total and marginal damage to the world as a whole, and to major players, from greenhouse-gas emissions. The benefits of control are approximated by the fraction of damage that can be avoided by taking preventive measures, although benefits may exceed the amount of avoided damages because of ancillary benefits. Ancillary benefits include any reductions in non-greenhouse emissions, e.g. jointly produced particulates, acidic pollutants, etc. (OECD, 2000). This chapter surveys what is known about the damage from greenhouse gases, focusing on carbon dioxide (CO_2) as the main gas. The purpose is to highlight legitimate differences of view about carbon damage, and to show that, while a monetized damage figure cannot, and should not, be avoided, analysis of the consequences of choosing a specific figure is of the utmost policy importance. Once selected, a value for the marginal damage of carbon must be applied consistently across all policy areas. The problems of this consequentialist approach are discussed in the context of the UK government's initial decision to opt for a 'high' shadow price of carbon, at £70 per tonne of carbon (henceforth, tC). At the time of writing, this shadow price is under review and an interim range of values from £35 to £140/tC is being used. It is important to recognize that, while the discussion is framed within the context of UK climate-change policy, there are more general lessons to be learned about (a) the interpretation of warming damage estimates in integrated assessment models, and (b) the need to assess the implications of selecting one shadow price (for any environmental impact) rather than another.

2. Monetizing the Damage from Greenhouse Gases

The social cost of carbon refers to the estimate of the monetary value of world-wide damage done by anthropogenic CO_2 emissions. More precisely, the 'social cost of carbon' is defined as the monetary value of the global damage done by emitting one more tonne of carbon at some point of time. The usual time reference is the current period, but the resulting 'marginal damage cost' can be expected to rise for future emissions owing to (a) the fact that greenhouse gases cumulate in the atmosphere and (b) rising relative valuations of warming damage as real incomes rise. Damage is a function of the cumulated stock, so one extra tonne in the future will have a higher associated damage than an extra tonne released now. Additionally, as incomes grow, so the monetary value of damage is likely to grow owing to an associated higher willingness to pay to avoid warming damage. For ease of exposition we focus on the marginal damage done by emitting one tonne of carbon (or carbon equivalent) now, leaving aside the fact that future marginal damages will rise. None the less, a more thorough analysis needs to scrutinize the escalation factors adopted in the various studies: more than occasionally, *ad hoc* assumptions have been made about the rate at willingness to pay for avoided damage.

As is well known, CO_2 is the oxidized form of carbon, and is the major greenhouse gas implicated in projections of global warming. The social cost is the damage done by CO_2 emissions compared to a baseline context in which those emissions do not increase. But it does not follow from this that the correct or socially desirable level of emissions is such that this social cost is zero. There are two reasons for this. First, greenhouse gases have long residence times in the atmosphere, so that climate damage today and in the near future is the result mainly of past, irreversible emissions. Since nothing can be done about those emissions, the relevant 'policy window' relates to the difference between projected levels of warming from 'doing nothing' and the level of warming that will occur anyway owing to time lags in the climate system. Second, the socially optimal level of any pollutant or hazard is rarely zero. This is because reducing pollution is not costless. It makes sense to reduce pollution so long as the benefit of doing so exceeds the costs. But as soon as a further incremental ('marginal') reduction in pollution incurs greater costs than benefits, that is the time to declare the policy measures optimal and not go any further. As we shall see, while simple to state, this cost–benefit rule is immensely complicated to formulate in practice in the global warming context.

It is not necessary for this estimate of social cost to be precise. Few magnitudes in economics or in policy analysis are precise. Acting on reasonable estimates is better than acting on no estimate, because the latter course of action necessarily implies a social cost. If there is uncertainty about a social-cost estimate, that uncertainty does not magically disappear by not adopting the social-cost estimate. Indeed, as Thomas (1963) pointed out 40 years ago, it is not logically possible to avoid monetary valuation in the all-pervading contexts where policies cost money. If a policy costs $X then adopting the policy implies benefits must be at least $X, and not adopting it implies that benefits are less than $X. Despite the cost–benefit logic, a substantial part of the policy-oriented literature on warming control either ignores or explicitly rejects the commensurability of costs and benefits without an appreciation of Thomas's argument. A further argument for not being too obsessed with damage uncertainty has been advanced by Rabl *et al.* (2004). Working with a range of empirical abatement cost functions for CO_2, they show that a doubling of marginal damage costs induces an error of only 30 per cent in the cost of control. Put another way, optimal cost–benefit emission levels are not very sensitive to a doubling of damage estimates.

For a cost–benefit approach it is, of course, also necessary to have some idea of the costs of control, e.g. through energy conservation, slowing deforestation, switching to low- and non-carbon energy technologies, and so on. Curiously, looking at what it costs an economy to adopt warming-control policies tends to be widely accepted in the policy-oriented literature. What many people want is to avoid monetizing *benefits*. They prefer to set a target based on some principle or other, and then minimize the costs of achieving the target. This is cost-effectiveness, not cost–benefit analysis. But cost-effectiveness cannot answer the question: *how much* should we abate? It can only answer the question: which of several competing policies should be chosen, *given* that we must choose one or other of those policies. The focus, therefore, shifts to the criteria for setting the target.

Opponents of monetization argue that the way economists measure cost and benefit produces an inequity. A cost is any loss of wellbeing and a benefit is any gain in wellbeing. Those losses and gains are measured through the notion of willingness to pay (WTP) to avoid a loss or WTP to secure a gain. They might equally well be measured by willingness to accept compensation (WTA) to tolerate the loss or forgo the benefit. WTP and, less so, WTA are self-evidently influenced by wealth and income. Other things being equal, WTP will vary directly with income. Hence richer people get a bigger 'vote' than poor people. The 'unequal votes' argument appears especially powerful in the context of global warming, since, as climate-damage models show (e.g. Tol 2002*a*,*b*), those who stand to lose most relative to their income levels are the poorest in the world. Markets work by allocating resources according to WTP, so opposition to the standard economic approach tends to be associated with a wider opposition to markets generally as a means of allocating resources in society. Not all of these critics make this connection. If they did, they might, however, argue that global warming is 'something special', i.e. it is all right to have market-determination of resource allocation for most things, but not for global warming control. This is an argument for 'ring fencing' global warming from other policy areas, and we return to it later. The essential point is that how 'equity' is treated affects the size of the social cost estimate, as we shall see.

While the argument for rejecting market allocation of resources is based on equity concerns, it actually produces its own problem of equity. Unless global warming itself lowers future average incomes in poor countries—a prospect that some genuinely believe will be the case—action taken now will be for the benefit of communities who will be richer than the poorest people today. No global warming model projects future incomes to be less than incomes today. Since action has an opportunity cost, it follows that the sacrifice of resources today could be at the expense of transfers of income to poor people today. If so, the poor today may bear sacrifices in terms of forgone benefits in order to benefit their richer descendants. As Schelling (1992, 1998) has argued, one reason for the higher economic sensitivity to damage in poor countries is that poor countries are more dependent on climate-sensitive economic activity than are rich countries. It may pay, there-fore, to divert funds allocated to preventing climate change to improv-ing economic development in poor countries so as to reduce their vulnerability to climate stress. This would have the added benefit of improving the wellbeing of the poor now. The relevant comparison is that of costs to poor people now from forgone development with benefits to their descendants in the future. While the Kyoto Protocol makes some provision for funding adaptation to climate change, the dominant theme of the Protocol is prevention through emission reduc-tion.

Second, monetization as a measure of human preferences implies that those whose preferences should count are those who are living and present. Those yet to come—the future generations—cannot vote and hence appear to have no say. Yet it is they who will suffer the effects of warming, and at least some responsibility for that warming rests with the current generation. By definition, then, counting only current preferences disenfranchises future generations and must surely under-state the 'true' social cost of carbon. Once again, these are telling points but they are not as obviously destructive of the cost–benefit approach as they first appear. There is nothing in economics that says that any individual today is motivated solely by self-interest and that they are indifferent to other humans now or in the future, or even that they are indifferent to non-human wellbeing. If self-interest alone motivates choices, it would be hard to explain savings behaviour and charitable donations, for example. Future generations are not *necessarily* disen-franchised by the cost–benefit approach. It depends on what motivates preferences now. None the less, it is true that individuals will not feel the same way for persons to come in 10,000 years' time as for persons to come in 100 years' time. There will be 'time discounting', an issue we return to. But even if future generations are no richer than we are, and even without discounting, it is unclear that reducing savings today to combat global warming is a better option than keeping savings high so as to leave a larger capital stock to future generations. This is Schelling's cost–benefit point again.

Ekins (2000) criticizes Schelling for 'missing the point' because the 'arguments for development aid are quite different from those relating to whether rich country lifestyles should cost poor country lives'. But they are not at all different. Aid is a transfer from rich to poor. Spending money on warming control does not benefit the poor now, and, by virtue of opportunity cost, is equivalent to not giving aid now. If the distinction is meant to be a moral one, not giving aid costs poor country lives now. Global warming costs poor people lives in the future, but those poor people are probably better off than poor people today. The idea that a deliberate commission of harm is morally different to the equally deliberate failure to do good when the agent knows that doing good is feasible, cannot be sustained.

A more philosophical critique is that of Spash (1994) who argues that (a) future generations have 'rights' to a stable global environment and (b) the harm from warming cannot be 'undone' by doing good through leaving them higher capital stocks. The non-compensability of harm is usually illustrated by saying that one cannot offset a murder by then doing good. However, it is hard to imagine any policy that would pass a test of 'do no harm' to unrepresented individuals. The brute fact of human existence necessarily implies imposing costs on future individuals, including costs of forgone lives. Moreover, much of the justice system, domestic and international, is based on the idea that harm can, indeed, be offset by good deeds. The 'do no harm' principle, therefore, tends to imply an illusory world in which there are no trade-offs. Further, it is philosophically unclear that non-existent future generations have 'rights' to anything since the possession of rights is predicated on the existence of the individuals in question (Pasek and Beckerman, 2001).

The third objection to monetization is that it implies inappropriate fine-tuning in a context where damages are likely to be catastrophic, akin to past massive extinction periods. If the scenario is for the end of the world (as we know it) in the near future, it would obviously make little sense to talk about costs and benefits. The costs of damage would be extremely high at the margin. Indeed, cost–benefit analysis requires that the variance of the net benefits from climate-change control is finite (Tol, 2003a). If total catastrophe is feasible, then the variance would be infinite. The only rational action would appear to be to stop global warming immediately. But this is an empirical question, not a certainty by any means. No one appears to argue that catastrophe consists of the destruction of the entire human race. Rather, the kinds of events that are discussed are the melting of the West Antarctic Ice Sheet or reversal of the gulf stream. Thus, it seems more correct to refer to extremely high marginal damages occurring with some unknown probability, rather than marginal damages being infinite. Even if catastrophe were a certainty, *when* it happens matters. If it happens in 10,000 years that is quite different to it happening in 100 years, unless we believe that all lives are 'equal' regardless of when they occur (which is, however, what some people believe; see, for example, Broome (1992)). However, efforts to understand and estimate the costs of catastrophic events are clearly justified and some recent contributions are reviewed later – see, for example, Downing *et al.* (1996), Gjerde *et al.* (1999), and Nordhaus and Boyer (2000). The appropriate action to avoid catastrophe still has to be informed by some notion of what it costs to avoid it, what the likelihood is of it occurring, when it occurs, and the degree of risk aversion. Costs and benefits still need to be compared.

The final objection to monetization is that it is not necessary in a context where the goal is one of *sustainable development*. Two competing interpretations of the meaning of sustainable development largely explain the differences in approach. An economic definition of sustainable development is framed in terms of rising *per capita* levels of wellbeing through time. This definition says nothing about the time-horizon, but that might be inferred from analysis of preferences such that the 'end of time' is the future time where current concern for the future declines to zero. This reflects the point made earlier, namely that most people would not express a concern for humans 10,000 years from now, but might for humans 100 years from now. Clearly, this view is inconsistent with the notion that future generations have 'rights' to a stable or, at least, less warm environment than would otherwise be the case. An alternative interpretation is that sustainable development is about ensuring humans are present on Earth indefinitely. For example, Ekins (2000) says, 'The basic meaning of sustainability is the capacity for continuance [*sic*] more or less indefinitely into the future.' Just as the economic definition is hazy on the range of time over which *per capita* wellbeing should rise, so this non-economic definition says nothing about *per capita* wellbeing. It seems better to brand this notion 'survivability' rather than sustainability. The maximand becomes the survival time of humans on Earth. One obvious difficulty is that this maximand is consistent with each generation going to subsistence level in order to insure against threats to the existence of later generations.

The result is akin to that arising from assuming that one should not discount the future, i.e. that the discount rate is zero (Olson and Bailey, 1981). The notion that one should not discount the future is a further example of the confusion embodied in non-economic approaches. Not discounting is formally equivalent to discounting at 0 per cent. Ekins (2000) criticizes economists for not knowing what 'the' discount rate is, but appears not to appreciate that discounting cannot be rejected. In any event, zero discounting produces the 'immiseration' result noted by Olsen and Bailey (1981). In this sense, Ekins is consistent: setting survivability as a goal produces N-1 generations with subsistence wellbeing, where N is the number of generations to come.

The conclusion of this discussion must be that costs and benefits always have to be compared, and this should be done explicitly rather than by rejecting the approach and then adopting it under another guise.

3. Modelling the Social Cost of Carbon

The available quantitative estimates of the social cost of carbon emissions adopt models of varying degrees of sophistication. The essential linkages in all models are from emissions to atmospheric concentration, from concentrations to temperature change, and from temperature change to damage. The last link also involves an intermediate stage going from temperature change to sea-level rise. Highly simplified, the underlying form of most of the models is as follows. We work in discrete time for simplicity. This exposition relies initially on Nordhaus (1994a) with some of the notation changed.

First, total damage done, V, from the emission of 1 tonne of greenhouse gas (say, carbon) will be equal to the present value of all future incremental damages, $\partial D/\partial E$, since the carbon resides in the atmosphere for a long period. Hence, with t denoting time, we have:

$$V = \sum_0^T \frac{\partial D_t}{\partial E_t} \cdot (1+s)^{-t}. \tag{1}$$

In equation (1) s is the social discount rate. It is important to understand that equation (1) is an expression for the marginal damage cost of carbon. This records the change in the present value of all future damages from releasing one extra tonne of carbon in the present period. As noted earlier, since greenhouse gases are cumulative, the marginal damage figure will tend to increase with time. Population and income growth, as shown in equation (6), will also cause marginal damage cost to rise.

Second, atmospheric concentrations (C) of carbon are linked to emissions (E) via:

$$C_t = (1 - \frac{1}{L}) \cdot C_{t-1} + \beta \cdot E_t \tag{2}$$

where L is the residence time of carbon in the atmosphere and β is a factor that convert emissions (tonnes) into concentrations (parts per million). The first expression on the right-hand side captures the decay process, i.e. the rate at which carbon is removed from the atmosphere, e.g. by oceans.

Third, concentrations (C) give rise to radiative forcing (F) according to:

$$F_t = F_{t-1} + g \cdot \ln \left(\frac{C_t}{C_{t-1}} \right). \tag{3}$$

Fourth, the link between temperature change and changes in carbon concentrations in the atmosphere constitutes the climate-change section of the model. Climate-change models are complex, but the essence is captured in two equations:

$$T_t^U = T_{t-1}^U + \frac{1}{R^U} \left[F_t - \lambda T_{t-1}^U - \frac{R^L}{\theta} (T_{t-1}^U - T_{t-1}^L) \right] \tag{4}$$

$$T_t^L = T_{t-1}^L + \frac{1}{R^L} \left[\frac{R^L}{\theta} (T_{t-1}^U - T_{t-1}^L) \right]. \tag{5}$$

T is temperature, U refers to the upper ocean layer and L to the lower ocean layer, R refers to the thermal capacity of the ocean layers, F is radiative forcing, θ is the transfer rate between upper and lower ocean layers, and λ is a parameter showing how much temperature changes for a given increase in radiative forcing. Equation (5) tries to capture the process whereby radiative forcing heats up the atmosphere, which then heats up the upper ocean which then heats up the lower ocean.

Following Fankhauser (1995), the final basic equation links annual damage, D, to temperature, T:

$$D_t = k_t \left(\frac{T_t^U}{\Lambda} \right)^{\gamma} \cdot (1 + \phi)^{t^* - t^\wedge}. \tag{6}$$

The parameter Λ is the amount of warming (in °C) associated with a doubling of CO_2 concentrations (by convention, doubling is always relative to pre-industrial levels); t^* is the year in which that doubling is expected to occur, usually taken to be 2050. If temperature rises by 1 per cent, damage, D, rises by γ per cent, i.e. γ links temperature and damage. ϕ is a parameter that makes impacts greater if they occur before t^* and lower if they occur after t^* — an attempt to account for damage being related to speed of change. If the temperature rise associated with $2xCO_2$ is 2.5°C, then $\Lambda=2.5$. If the temperature rise that actually occurs is 2.5°C, and if $t^* = \hat{t}$, then $D_t= k_t$ where k_t is the estimated damage done by $2xCO_2$. This figure is estimated from 'bottom up' approaches, whereby sectoral damage is estimated region by region (or, in the early studies, for the USA alone). Damage will rise with time owing to population growth and income expansion according to:

$$\frac{k_t}{k_{t-1}} = (1+\omega \cdot y_t + p_t) \tag{7}$$

where y is the rate of growth of income *per capita*, p is the rate of growth of population, and ω is the income elasticity of willingness to pay to avoid damage. It is readily seen that the values of these three parameters can substantially influence estimates of future damage. For example, Fankhauser (1995) adopts a value of $\omega = 1.0$, whereas subsequent literature (Pearce, 2005) suggests that it is more likely to be 0.3–0.4. For a rate of income growth of, say, 2 per cent, $\omega.y$ will be 2 per cent if $\omega = 1$, but only 0.6 per cent if $\omega = 0.3$. As noted earlier, this potential bias in integrated assessment models appears to have gone unnoticed.

Even with such a comparatively simple model, it is easy to see that differing estimates of the social cost of carbon are likely to emerge. The example of the assumed value of ω shows this. But there is also considerable debate about the choice of discount rate, and even the parameters in the climate section of the model. It should occasion no surprise that social cost estimates will vary. The key parameters in such models are usually treated as being random so that the actual figures reported by the models tend to be ranges.

To see how the model works, we borrow the numbers in Fankhauser (1995): $\Lambda = 2.5°$, $t^* = 2050$, $\gamma =$ range 1–3, with best guess 1.3, ϕ is random with best guess of 0.006, k_t is the damage done from $2xCO_2$ warming, assumed to occur in 2050 and is \$270 billion. This is estimated from a 'bottom up' procedure of aggregating individual damages. Ignoring income and population growth, in any period t, annual damage is given by

$$D_t = \$270.10^9.(T_t/2.5)^{1.3}(1.006)^{t^*-t}.$$

For the $2xCO_2$ year, for example, $T_t=2.5$ and $t^*=t$, so the last expression is equal to 1, as is the second expression. D_t is thus \$270 billion. Suppose temperature is predicted to rise by 0.1°C per decade, then

$$D_{+10} = \$270.10^9.(2.6/2.5)^{1.3}.(1.006)^{10} = \$301.3 \text{ billion. And so on.}$$

Table 1
Aggregate Social Cost of Global Warming (% of world GNP)

Benchmark temperature increase for 2xCO$_2$ (Λ)	Pearce et al. 1996	Mendelsohn et al. 1996		Nordhaus and Boyer 2000	Tol 2002a
	2.5°C	1.5°C	2.5°C	2.5°C	1.0°C
DCs	n.a	+0.12	+0.03	−0.5 to +0.4	
LDCs	n.a	+0.05	−0.17	−0.2 to −4.9	
World	−1.5 to −2.0	+0.10		−1.5	+2.3

Note: + indicates a benefit, − a cost (damage). DCs are developed countries and LDCs less developed countries.
Source: Cited studies and Tol et al. (2000).

4. Estimates of 2xCO$_2$ Damage (k_t)

While the policy focus of the social cost of carbon is on the estimates of marginal damage cost, it is useful to look at the various measures of aggregate world social cost. In integrated assessment (mixed climate and economic models) this aggregate is benchmarked on a scenario in which pre-industrial CO$_2$ concentrations are doubled. Table 1 assembles the available estimates. The studies shown are recent and are compared to the 'first generation' of models which were surveyed in the IPCC Second Assessment (Pearce et al., 1996). The important feature of the post-1996 studies is that some of them make allowance for adaptation to climate change, and some include catastrophes. The role of adaptation can be illustrated by the 'dumb farmer syndrome'. Damage occurs to, say, crops and in the no-adaptation case the farmer simply suffers a loss of output and profits. In the adaptation case, efforts are undertaken to switch into climate-resistant crops. Climate change with adaptation is self-evidently far more realistic, but the scope for adaptation is also likely to be less in the developing world than the developed world. Hence, even under adaptation models, the poor are likely to lose more than the rich. This is borne out by the models (details are not shown here — see, for example, Nordhaus and Boyer, 2000). The main model involving adaptation is that of Mendelsohn et al. (1996) (see also Mendelsohn and Neumann, 1999). It can be seen on this model that, on balance, the world actually gains from CO$_2$ doubling.

The main model accounting for catastrophes is that of Nordhaus and Boyer (2000). The importance of catastrophes in their work is that they account for two-thirds of the world damages (1.5 per cent GNP loss compared to 0.5°C without catastrophes). Tol's recent work suggests the world might gain significantly at around 2 per cent of GNP. Overall, then, the recent work suggests a range of damages, the lower bound of which is consistent with the first generation models surveyed by Pearce *et al.* (1996) and the upper bound of which is a significant gain in world GNP. These aggregate figures mask the differential impacts on developed and developing countries, so that an equity problem remains even if there are net gains overall.

5. Estimates of the Marginal Social Cost of Carbon

Not all studies reporting warming-damage costs, report marginal social costs. Table 2 brings together the various estimates. The basis of the table is the set of estimates gathered in Clarkson and Deyes (2002), but other studies have been added. Most studies calculate the present value of future losses at 1990 prices and using 1990 as the base year. Clarkson and Deyes correct the estimates for 2000 prices and 2000 as the base year. The effect of both adjustments is to make the estimates higher than they appear in the literature. The studies not in the Clarkson–Deyes document are marked *. Comparison is difficult because of (a) the differing methodologies in the studies and (b) variations in the underlying assumptions about climate sensitivity and economic parameters. All estimates are especially sensitive to the discount rate. In Table 2, variations in the discount rate are given for the 'pure time preference rate' (the rate at which wellbeing is discounted), ρ, and the overall social time preference rate, s. The relationship between the two is given by $s = \rho + \mu.g$, where μ is the elasticity of the marginal utility of income function, and g is the expected growth rate in *per capita* consumption. Methodologies differ according to whether they are (a) based on a cost–benefit model (CBA), in which case the marginal social cost of carbon is the marginal damage done at the optimal level of abatement, (b) based on a 'marginal cost' (MC) approach, in which case incremental damage is measured relative to a small increase in emissions now. As Clarkson and Deyes (2002) note, the MC approach should yield higher estimates than the CBA approach. One other methodology is shown here. Schauer's study (Schauer, 1995) uses 'expert' valuations based on either getting experts to say what they think the most likely parameter values are, or getting them to estimate directly the marginal social cost. The usefulness of expert valuations is open to some question if those consulted have little or no experience in thinking about monetized damage.

What can be gleaned from Table 2? One problem in comparing studies concerns the discount rate. Values are reported for the pure time preference rate in some studies and for the overall discount rate

Table 2
Estimates of the Marginal Social Cost of Carbon $tC (no equity weights)

Study	Estimate $tC — base year prices: 2000			
	1991–2000	2001–10	2011–20	2021–30
Nordhaus (1991)				
MC, ρ = 1	9.9			
MC, ρ = (0,4)	3.0–194.9			
Nordhaus (1994a)				
CBA, ρ =3, best guess	7.2	9.2	11.6	12.8
CBA, ρ =3, expected value	16.2	24.3	24.3	–
Nordhaus and Boyer (2000)*				
CBA, optimal carbon tax, s=3	6.4	9.1	11.9	15.0
Fankhauser (1995)				
MC, ρ =(0,0.5,3)	27.4	30.8	34.2	37.5
MC, ρ =0	65.6	–	–	84.5
MC, ρ =3	7.3	–	–	11.1
Cline (1992)				
CBA, s = 0–10	7.8–167.5	10.3–208.0	13.2–251.2	15.9–298.5
Peck and Teisberg (1993)*				
CBA, ρ =3	13.5–16.2	16.2–18.9	18.9–24.3	24.3–29.7
Maddison (1994)				
MC, ρ = 5	8.0	10.9	15.0	19.9
CBA, ρ =5	8.2	11.3	15.5	20.5
Tol (1999) (FUND 1.6)				
MC, s = 5	14.9	17.5	20.2	24.3
Roughgarden and Schneider (1999)*				
DICE model: lower bound =				
k value in Nordhaus, upper				
bound = k value in Tol	6.7–14.9	8.1–17.5	10.8–21.6	13.5–28.4
Schauer (1995)*				
Expert, parameters	11.20			
Expert, direct	144.0			
Tol and Downing (2000)				
MC, ρ = 0		19.7		
MC, ρ = 1		3.5		
MC, ρ = 3		–6.8		
Plambeck and Hope (1996)* PAGE model				
ρ = 2	26.0–120.0			
ρ = 3	13.0–61.0			
Eyre et al. (1997)[a]	1995–2004	2005–14		
MC, s = 1	109–110	119–120		
MC, s = 3	42–53	49–63		
MC, s = 5	20–37	25–47		

Notes: [a] The range of values in the Eyre et al. study derives from two different models, FUND 1.6 and OF (Open Framework). See the text for a discussion of these figures. The values in Tol and Downing are the *unweighted* estimates for FUND 2.0, whereas Clarkson and Deyes (see below) report only the weighted results.
Sources: Clarkson and Deyes (2002) and own estimates based on the cited literature.

in others. Assuming income growth of 2 per cent p.a. and an elasticity of marginal utility of income of –1, a pure time preference rate of 1 per cent would correspond to a social discount rate of 3 per cent, and so on. On this assumption, the recent estimates clearly fall into two categories. The Nordhaus–Boyer, Tol (1999), Roughgarden and Schneider, and Tol and Downing studies all produce near-term estimates in the bracket $4–9/tC for a discount rate of 3 per cent , and –$7 to +$15 for a discount rate of 5 per cent. Tol and Downing's estimate for a 2 per cent discount rate is $20/tC. To some extent there is overlap: the Roughgarden and Schneider study uses Tol's estimates as an input. But Tol and Downing use a quite different model to Tol (1999). The second category is the Eyre *et al.* study which produces around $40–50/tC for s=3 and $20–37/tC for s = 5. The basic difference between the Eyre study and the Tol-Downing study is that the latter incorporates adaptive behaviour. As noted above, it is a serious weakness of an integrated model if it lacks adaptation — see also Mendelsohn (1999). Plambeck and Hope (1996) is one of the few earlier studies to consider adaptation and non-adaptation within a single model. Without adaptation, marginal social costs are $32/tC; with adaptation they are $21/tC. The Eyre *et al.* study uses as one of its models 'FUND 1.6' which was developed by Tol. The Tol and Downing study, however, uses an update (FUND 2.0), which reflects the more recent literature on adaptation. Accordingly, the Tol-Downing figures are likely to be more reliable. The other major study, and one which has the virtue also of including catastrophes, is Nordhaus–Boyer. Since Nordhaus–Boyer is a CBA study and Tol-Downing work is based on MC, we would expect the Tol-Downing estimates to lie above those of Nordhaus–Boyer on this criterion, but perhaps below it because of the greater sensitivity to catastrophe in the Nordhaus–Boyer model. In fact the Tol–Downing range encompasses the entire range in Nordhaus–Boyer. The upper bound of Tol–Downing reflects a pure time preference of 0 per cent, and this is inconsistent with the Olson and Bailey (1981) argument that time preference must be positive. However, it is consistent with positive discounting for income growth. Note that the lower bound of Tol–Downing is negative, i.e. there are net global benefits. The value of $3.5/tC for $\rho = 1$ can be compared to the Nordhaus–Boyer estimate for s= 3 of $9.1. Since s = 3 is a reasonable representation of a social discount rate, the probable range of marginal (unweighted) damages is in the region of $4–9/tC.

6. The UK Government and the Social Cost of Carbon

The UK government, via Defra, the Department for Environment Food and Rural Affairs, released a document early in 2002 on the social cost of carbon (Clarkson and Deyes, 2002). This is a workmanlike and well-researched document. Interestingly, it was not released as a Defra publication but as a Government Economic Service Working Paper. It does not therefore appear with any of the other publications on climate-change policy, but in a format likely to be accessed only by diligent researchers. It carries a disclaimer to the effect that the views in the document are those of the authors and not necessarily those of Defra. However, a later document from Defra gives official guidance for 'Whitehall' on the use of the £70/tC figure that emerges from the Clarkson–Deyes paper—see Defra (2002*a*). At the time of writing, the figure of £70/tC is under review.

While the literature surveyed in Clarkson–Deyes is generally well documented (the main exception is the Nordhaus–Boyer work, which is significant and is not mentioned), the conclusion is starkly at odds with that reached here at the end of the last section. Our conclusion was that an unweighted 'price' of $4–9/tC, or, roughly, £3–6/tC is probably about right. The conclusion in Clarkson–Deyes is that the right price is £70/tC, 4–23 times as high.

There are two basic explanations for the difference in these estimates. First, Clarkson–Deyes opt for the Eyre *et al.* study as being 'more sophisticated'. Second, they then double the figures for equity weighting.

Clarkson–Deyes opt for the figures in the Eyre *et al.* (1997) study which they revise as follows. Two adjustments are made to the original figures: (a) an adjustment for inflation to convert 1990 prices into 2000 prices. This is implicitly put at 28 per cent in the early text but cited as 35 per cent in Table 1 of Clarkson–Deyes and elsewhere in the text; and (b) an adjustment for the base year of emissions. Table 3 shows the original Eyre *et al.* figures (both *without* equity weighting) and the Clarkson–Deyes figures. Clarkson and Deyes appear to have been slightly influenced by the fact that Eyre *et al.* is based on FUND 1.6 and is considered as peer-reviewed, but FUND 2.0, underlying the Tol-Downing paper has not been peer reviewed. Events have overtaken this remark, however, as FUND 2.0 has been peer-reviewed and the results are published, see Tol (2002*a,b*). The Eyre *et al.* study has not in fact been published other than as a working paper for the 'ExternE' programme, an EU programme that monetizes pollution impacts from energy and transport. But models based on FUND 1.6 have been published by Tol. Tol has since produced yet another update: FUND 2.4 (Tol, 2002*c*).

Assuming the inflation adjustment is 35 per cent for converting 1990 prices to 2000 prices, then all the original figures in the Eyre *et al.* study need to be multiplied by 1.35. The remaining element is then the

Table 3
Comparison of Eyre *et al.* and Clarkson–Deyes Revisions (FUND 1.6 model only) (unweighted, 2000 prices)

	$s = 1\%$	$s = 3\%$	$s = 5\%$
Emission date 1995–2004			
Original Eyre *et al.* figure $/tC, assumed to be discounted to 1990	73	23	9
Clarkson–Deyes figure $/tC, assumed emission date 2000	109	42	20
Emission date 2005–14			
Original Eyre *et al.* figure $/tC	72	20	7
Clarkson–Deyes figure $/tC, assumed emission date 2010	119	49	25

Sources: Eyre *et al.* (1997) and Clarkson and Deyes (2002).

adjustment for changing the baseline period for emissions. Whereas the other studies use 1991–2000 as the base year for emissions, the Eyre *et al.* study uses 1995–2004, an apparent difference of four years. One would therefore expect the upwards adjustment to be $(1+s)^4$ for the base year and $(1+s)^{14}$ for the next period. The Eyre *et al.* study uses 1990 as the base year (Tol, personal communication) and *not* the reported period of emissions. If so, an adjustment of 10 years is required, i.e. $(1+s)^{10}$. This is consistent with the Clarkson–Deyes estimates.

The choice of the Eyre *et al.* study is more problematic, for the reasons outlined earlier. Including adaptation in the models is important, even on the basis of common sense. But FUND 1.6, the model underlying the Eyre *et al.* figures excludes adaptation and FUND 2.0, which underlies the Tol–Downing figures includes it. Clarkson and Deyes cite Tol *et al.* (2000) as suggesting that FUND 2.0 may be 'optimistic, perhaps too optimistic'. However, Tol and Downing (2000) also remark that 'FUND 1.6 . . . may be too pessimistic'.

7. Equity Weighting

The second major adjustment in the Clarkson–Deyes study is for equity weighting. It was noted earlier that, expressed as a proportion of *per capita* incomes, damage from global warming is higher in the developing world than in the developed world. An obvious issue of equity arises since $1 of damage to a poor person should attract a higher weight than $1 of damage to a rich person. In the original survey of damage estimates for the Intergovernmental Panel on Climate Change (IPCC), Pearce *et al.* (1996) noted that damage estimates were based on willingness to pay, and they showed how equity weights could be introduced. Subsequent and somewhat manipulated criticism of the absence of *actual* equity-weighted estimates in the IPCC report produced a sequence of revised estimates using various forms of equity weighting (Fankhauser *et al.*, 1997, 1998; Tol *et al.*, 1996, 1999). One obvious problem with equity-weighting is that any number of social welfare functions (SWFs) can be postulated, each producing different weightings and hence different overall climate-damage figures and different marginal social-cost estimates. However, just like 'not discounting', 'not equity weighting' implies a value of an equity weight equal to unity, i.e. $1 of damage to a poor person is treated as if it is the same as $1 of loss to a rich person. Hence there is no procedure that avoids explicit or implicit equity weighting and it seems better to consider 'reasonable' SWFs and see what they imply for climate damage.

Two broad classes of SWF are (a) the utilitarian SWF and (b) the 'Rawlsian' SWF. (For more discussion of other SWFs and the choice of weighting factors, see Tol, 2001; Azar, 1999; and Azar and Sterner, 1996). Applied to global warming damage, these are given by

$$D_{WORLD} = \sum_{i}^{n} D_i \cdot \left[\frac{\overline{Y}}{Y_i} \right]^{\varepsilon} \tag{7}$$

and

$$D_{WORLD} = D_P \cdot \left[\frac{\overline{Y}}{Y_P} \right]^{\varepsilon}. \tag{8}$$

In equations (7) and (8), Y is income, Y-bar is average world *per-capita* income, Y_i is income of the *i*th person, P refers to poor people, D is damage, and ε is the elasticity of the marginal utility of income schedule, a measure of 'inequality aversion'. In (7) damage to all individuals counts, but anyone below the average world *per-capita* income secures a weight greater than unity, and anyone above secures a weight below unity, the size of the weight varying with the degree of inequality aversion. In (8) only damage to poor people counts, all other damage is given a weight of zero. One paradox in using a Rawls-type welfare function is that global damages are less than if no weights are used at all, implying a lower marginal social cost of carbon and less global action. See Fankhauser *et al.* (1997, 1998) and Tol *et al.* (2003) for a discussion.

Generally, SWFs of the form shown in (7) have been the ones used in illustrating the effects of equity weighting on global warming damage. It can be seen that what matters is then the distribution of the initial level of damage between rich and poor regions, the income disparity between rich and poor, and the value of ε. Since, by and large, there is little dispute about real income data, variations in the estimates of global damage will, therefore, derive from the values chosen for D_R/D_P and ε.

To illustrate how the SWF is estimated, we rewrite it as:

$$D_{WORLD} = D_R \cdot \left[\frac{\bar{Y}}{Y_R}\right]^\varepsilon + D_P \cdot \left[\frac{\bar{Y}}{Y_P}\right]^\varepsilon \qquad (9)$$

where R = rich and P = poor. Crude estimates of the relevant magnitudes are then D_R = \$216 billion and D_P = \$106 billion, for 2 x CO_2 (Fankhauser, 1995); Y_R = \$10,000, and Y_P = \$1,110; and Y-bar = \$3,333. Substituting in (9) produces estimates of world damage of

unweighted	\$ 322 billion
weighted, ε = 0.5	\$ 307 billion
weighted, ε = 0.8	\$ 343 billion
weighted, ε = 1	\$ 390 billion
weighted, ε = 1.5	\$ 600 billion

Despite the rough-and-ready nature of the exercise, these numbers are consistent with those produced in Fankhauser *et al.* (1997, 1998). In that paper, ε = 0.5 makes hardly any difference to the unweighted damage estimate, and ε = 1 produces a 25 per cent increase on the unweighted damages. Only if ε > 1 do the aggregate damages increase markedly. In contrast, Tol's (1995) estimates of total damage increase by nearly 70 per cent on the unweighted damages for ε = 1. The reason for this is that Tol has a larger share of world damages accruing to the developing world. The value of ε obviously matters. The value of ε in Eyre *et al.* is unity, and Clarkson and Deyes also opt for a value of unity, based on a survey of some of the literature.

Two issues now arise. First, is ε = 1 the correct estimate of ε? Second, even if ε = 1 what does it imply for a multiplication factor for the marginal social cost of carbon? As noted above, the answer to the second question depends on how estimates of aggregate damage are distributed between rich and poor countries.

8. The Value of ε

Clarkson and Deyes (2002) opt for a value of ε = 1. In their review of the previous literature, Pearce and Ulph (1999) observe that the apparent consensus in the literature on the value of ε such that 0.5 < ε < 1.5 is based on a faulty reading of the literature. Details are not provided here, and the reader is referred to Pearce and Ulph (1999). However, one of the mistaken pieces of literature is that of Kula (1987), to which Clarkson and Deyes refer in support of their view that ε = 1. Clarkson and Deyes's second source of values for ε is an excellent survey paper by Cowell and Gardiner (1999). This survey suggests that work on savings behaviour implies a value of ε 'just below or just above one' (p. 31); that work on implied values of ε taken from UK tax schedules implies a range 1.2–1.4; and that experimental work produces values of around 4. Cowell and Gardiner conclude that 'a reasonable range seems to be from 0.5 . . . to 4' (p. 33). The selected value in Pearce and Ulph (1999), based on the same savings models as are surveyed in Cowell and Gardiner (1999), is 0.8. Values below unity should, therefore, be entertained seriously. Values such as 4, however, imply a quite dramatic degree of inequality aversion and it is difficult to take such estimates seriously for policy purposes. To see this, consider two nations, rich and poor, with utility functions of the form:

$$U_i = \frac{Y_i^{1-\varepsilon}}{1-\varepsilon} \qquad i = R, P. \tag{10}$$

The ratio of the two *marginal* utilities is given by:

$$\left[\frac{Y_P}{Y_R}\right]^{\varepsilon}. \tag{11}$$

Suppose $Y_R = 10Y_P$ as is the case for international real income comparisons between OECD countries and others. The range of social values is shown in Table 4, corresponding to various values of ε.

What this tells us is that at ε = 4, the social value of extra income to R is effectively zero. At ε = 1, a marginal unit of income to the poor is valued ten times the marginal gain to the rich. At ε = 2, the relative

Table 4
Effects of Inequality Aversion

ε =	0.5	0.8	1.0	1.2	1.5	2.0	4.0
Loss to R as a fraction of gain to P	0.31	0.16	0.10	0.06	0.03	0.01	~0

valuation is 100 times. On this 'thought experiment' basis, then, values even of $\varepsilon = 2$ do not seem reasonable. A value of $\varepsilon = 1$ does seem feasible. Overall, looking at the implied values of ε in savings behaviour and at the thought experiment above, values of ε in the range 0.5–1.2 seem reasonable.

9. From Unweighted Social Cost Estimates to Weighted Cost Estimates

Clarkson and Deyes (2002) suggest that equity weighting with $\varepsilon = 1$ roughly doubles the unweighted estimates. As noted earlier, however, this depends on the distribution of absolute damages between rich and poor. Hence, the difference made by equity weighting to unweighted estimates of marginal social cost is model-dependent. Moreover, the multiplication factor varies with the discount rate, as one would expect. Table 5 reports the results for FUND 1.6, FUND 2.0, and OF ('Open Framework'), which is also used in both Eyre *et al.* (1997) and Tol and Downing (2000). Results are shown only for near-term emissions.

The estimates of damage also vary according to the methodology used for valuing statistical lives lost. The value-of-statistical-life (VSL) approach values a statistical life at the WTP for risk reduction divided by the size of the risk. This produces VSL estimates of several millions of dollars. The value-of-a-life-year (VLY) approach seeks to avoid one of the problems with the VSL approach, namely that WTP appears to be very high for relatively small savings in life years. Hence WTP for a saved life-year appears more appropriate. However, the VLY approach adopted in Tol and Downing (2000) is that of the ExternE programme and it has been noted elsewhere that there is no economic rationale for this procedure (Pearce, 1998*b*). None the less, we report the estimates here.

Table 5 suggests that the 'equity multiplier' varies with the model, the discount rate, and with the use of VSL or VLY. But all multipliers are contained within the bracket 0.9–3.6, embracing the Clarkson–Deyes 'rule of thumb' of doubling the estimates. This range also applies if FUND 2.0 is the preferred model.

10. Discounting

The sensitivity of social-cost estimates to the discount rate is well established. However, there is a further issue concerning the discount rate which is not addressed in any of the integrated assessment models,

Table 5
The Effects of Equity Weighting on the Marginal Social Cost of Carbon

	$s = 2$	$s = 3$	$s = 5$
FUND 1.6			
VSL unweighted	38.9	26.1	12.3
VSL weighted	109.5	73.8	37.0
Equity multiplier	2.8	2.8	3.0
FUND 2.0			
VSL unweighted	19.7	3.5	−6.8
VSL weighted	27.5	12.5	1.3
Equity multiplier	1.4	3.6	n.a.
VLY unweighted	6.1	5.1	4.1
VLY weighted	15.1	8.9	3.8
Equity multiplier	2.5	1.7	0.9
Open Framework			
Unweighted	74.5	45.8	16.3
Weighted	104.0	64.0	22.8
Equity multiplier	1.4	1.4	1.4

Source: Adapted from Tol and Downing (2000).

nor in the Clarkson–Deyes paper. They all assume a constant rate of discount, i.e. one that does not vary with time. Recent work suggests, however, that discount rates for long-term issues such as global warming *decline* with time (Weitzman, 1998, 1999; Gollier, 2002, forthcoming; Newell and Pizer, 2000, 2001). The essence of these approaches is that either or both future discount rates and economic growth rates are uncertain. Uncertainty about the discount rate drives the results obtained in Weitzman (1998) and Newell and Pizer (2000, 2001), and uncertainty about future economic growth drives the results obtained in Gollier (2002). The argument can be illustrated by looking at uncertainty about the discount rate. What is uncertain is the *discount factor* (i.e. $1/(1+r)^t$) since this is the temporal weight attached to future periods in terms of today's preferences. Suppose the discount rate and, hence, the discount factor is not known with certainty and is a random variable. Suppose it takes the values 1 ... 6 per cent each with a probability of 0.167. Table 6 shows the relevant values.

While the weighted average (expected value) of the discount rate stays the same in all periods (3.5 per cent), the discount factor obviously varies with time. The value of the implicit discount rate, s^*, is given by the equation:

$$\frac{1}{(1+s^*)^t} = \frac{\sum DF_{t,i}}{n} \ldots\ldots i = n \tag{12}$$

Table 6
Values of the Discount Factor and the Certainty Equivalent Discount Rate

s	DF_{10}	DF_{50}	DF_{100}	DF_{200}
1	0.9053	0.6080	0.3697	0.1376
2	0.8203	0.3715	0.1380	0.0191
3	0.7441	0.2281	0.0520	0.0027
4	0.6756	0.1407	0.0198	0.0004
5	0.6139	0.0872	0.0076	0.0000
6	0.5584	0.0543	0.0029	0.0000
Sum	4.1376	1.4898	0.5900	0.1589
Sum/6	0.7196	0.2483	0.0983	0.0265
s*	3.34%	2.82%	2.34%	1.83%

Notes: DF_{10} = discount factor for year 10, etc. s* is the value of s that solves the equation shown in the text.

where n = the number of possible discount rates, DF is the discount factor and t is time. Table 6 shows that the 'certainty equivalent' discount rate goes down over time even though the average discount rate stays the same for each period.

Uncertainty about the future value of the discount factor is thus sufficient to generate a time-varying discount rate. Just what the time-path of this rate is varies according to the model chosen for simulating the effects of the uncertainty. Newell and Pizer (2001) work with the Nordhaus–Boyer 'DICE' model of climate change and show that the marginal social cost of carbon in the model needs to be multiplied further by the following factors:

$$s = 2\%: 1.07–1.56$$
$$s = 4\%: 1.14–1.82$$
$$s = 7\%: 1.21–1.95$$

where the ranges reflect two different approaches to simulating future uncertainty based on long-run historic interest rates in the USA. While Newell and Pizer do not consider equity weighting, the multiplication procedure is just as applicable to equity-weighted damages as it is to unweighted damages. This suggests that there are two potentially major adjustments to unweighted social-cost estimates, one for equity across current generations and one for time-varying discount rates.

11. Catastrophes Again

It was noted earlier that some integrated assessment models have attempted to include catastrophic events — such as runaway greenhouse effects owing to tundra methane release, changes in thermohaline circulation (THC), and very rapid sea-level rise. By and large, however, the approaches have aggregated these events into a single event, with fairly simplistic integration into the underlying economic model. In Nordhaus and Boyer (2000), for example, the impact of catastrophes is simulated by assuming high rates of relative risk aversion, variable rates of income loss by world region, and temperature-dependent probabilities of catastrophic risk. For the USA, for example, extreme and catastrophic events account for nearly 90 per cent of the total damages in the Nordhaus–Boyer model, and two-thirds of global damage. Catastrophe thus gets built into the models through a long tail in the probability distribution of damages. But the extent to which catastrophes can be built into integrated assessment models in this way is open to question (Wright and Erickson, 2003). Catastrophes cannot be lumped together in this way: some appear more likely than others and some appear to be nearer term than others. Other models adopt thresholds which 'kick in' at some predetermined rate of warming and which then result in rapid escalations of damages. Yet others, e.g. Keller *et al.* (2000) impose a catastrophe constraint, in their case no collapse of the THC, and work out what the money damage would have to be in order to prevent the collapse. The result, around 0.9 per cent of world GNP, will strike most as modest, i.e. by spending 0.9 per cent of world GNP this event could be avoided through emissions reduction. The Keller *et al.* model is, however, still deterministic in the sense that decision-makers are assumed to be able to foretell the point at which THC collapse would ensue, given the physical parameters of warming. In practice, scientific knowledge is far from this state. Climate systems are non-linear and complex and still very imperfectly understood. As yet, integrated assessment models have not addressed these issues in a satisfactory way.

12. Conclusions on the Marginal Social Cost of Carbon

We conclude that the 'base case' estimate of the marginal social cost of carbon is $4–9/tC without equity weighting and using a constant discount rate. This may *understate* damage due to the omission of very major catastrophes and due to the omission of 'socially contingent' damages, e.g. the costs of any induced mass human migration.

However, the range may *overstate* damage because the integrated assessment models generally exclude any amenity benefits from global warming. That the amenity benefits may be significant is evidenced by the contributions in Maddison (2001a). For example, Mendelsohn (2001a) finds that warming generates potential benefits to the US economy of some 0.5 per cent of its GNP. Frijters and van Praag (2001) find some benefits to Russian households, Maddison (2001b) finds beneficial amenity effects in the UK, while Maddison (2001c) finds evidence of a small net cost in India. While Clarkson and Deyes (2002) stress the likelihood of understatement of costs, they make no mention of potential amenity benefits.

Assuming $\varepsilon = 1$, and applying the lowest equity weight to the highest discount rate, and the highest weights to the lowest discount rate, equity weighting changes the marginal social cost estimate from $4–9/tC to $3.6–22.5/tC. In UK sterling, this is around £2.4–15/tC, compared to the Clarkson–Deyes estimate of £70. Thus, the choice of model matters enormously. Choosing a model with high baseline unweighted marginal social cost automatically produces a very high equity-weighted estimate. Moreover, this range makes no allowance for values of ε less than and greater than unity. So, it would be easy to expand the range in terms of both the lower and upper bounds.

The effect of allowing for time-varying discount rates is to raise both sets of estimates by perhaps 80 per cent again, taking the upper bound of the Newell–Pizer estimates (which they prefer). This would make the Clarkson–Deyes estimates around £126/tC, and the estimates suggested here about £4.3–27/tC.

These estimates have been quoted without ranges, which is obviously not correct. The purpose here has been to illustrate the step-by-step procedures for estimating a social cost of carbon without getting too lost in the figures. More seriously, the brief discussion of catastrophe raises the important issue of whether the simple mechanisms so far used to build catastrophe into integrated assessment models adequately capture the immensely complex mix of geophysical, economic, and social uncertainty. It seems fairly clear they do not.

How does this assessment fit with the only available meta-analysis of marginal damage estimates? Tol (2004) finds 103 estimates of marginal damage. At a pure time preference rate of 3 per cent, corresponding to, say, 5 per cent social discount rate (assuming $e=1$ and $y = 2$), the mean estimate of marginal damage is $16/tC or about £9/tC. At a pure time preference rate of 1 per cent, and a social discount rate of 3 per cent, which corresponds closely to the UK 'official' social discount rate of 3.5 per cent, marginal damage is $51/tC or £28/tC. Tol's personal judgement is: 'climate change impacts may be very uncertain but it is unlikely that marginal damage costs of CO_2 exceed \$50/tC (about £28/tC) and are likely to be substantially smaller than that' (Tol, 2004).

Tol's meta-analysis thus conforms reasonably well with the outcome of the sequence of judgments made above. However, Tol does not test for time-varying discount rates — his time preference rates are constant over time. If the approximate 80 per cent adjustment suggested above is applied, Tol's upper limit would be \$90/tC or £50/tC.

13. Some Policy Implications of the Social Cost of Carbon Estimates

The previous sections discuss the £70/tC figure in the context of the models from which the estimate was derived. Clearly, there is always room for debate over the choice of models, but the suggestion here is that the £70/tC figure is too high, subject to all the caveats about uncertainty. Indeed, even the lower end of the interim range adopted by Defra in 2004 (£35–140/tC) appears too high. There is, however, a second way of analysing the correctness or otherwise of the £70/tC estimate. The Defra (2002a) guidance on the £70/tC figure very correctly points out that, whatever the figure is, it should be used consistently across government departments. Hence, a second approach to analysing the correctness of the estimate is to see what it would imply in some selected policy areas. If those implications are, in some sense, unacceptable, then the figure should be treated with caution. However, before looking at some of the policy implications, arguments for 'ring fencing' the £70/tC figure need some discussion. The argument here is that £70/tC is the 'right' figure to use in the context of global warming but that this has no implications for any other policy. As noted above, the Defra (2002a) guidance acknowledges the generality of the shadow price, i.e. it should be used in all relevant policy applications. But the Clarkson–Deyes paper takes a different view, arguing that equity weighting is central to the £70/tC figure, but that equity weighting need not apply outside the global-warming context.

Equity weighting has a firm rationale in what might be termed unreconstructed utilitarianism. On this approach, what matters are 'utils' rather than magnitudes reflecting willingness to pay. Hence, some form of equity weighting is justified on moral utilitarian grounds. Other moral judgements will produce different sets of weights. Economics has nothing to say about which welfare function should be chosen. Indeed, it is not easy to think of a meta-ethical principle that would justify one function rather than another. None the less, those functions illustrated earlier tend to be the ones that have influenced the climate-change literature.

But once equity weighting is adopted, it has to be adopted consistently. One virtue of policy-appraisal procedures is that they provide a framework for at least guiding policy measures so that they allocate resources *across* government expenditures in a consistent manner. On this basis, it is not logical to argue that equity weighting applies to global-warming control but not to any other form of government policy. Clarkson–Deyes come too close to arguing that global-warming control is generically different to other policies:

> The fact that the developed world is responsible for the majority of the damage inflicted makes this issue different to foreign aid and other similar policies. Equity weighting goes some way to incorporating the full impact of our emissions on others into our policy making, which is in line with the polluter pays principle. (p. 52)

But, as noted earlier, trying morally to ring-fence global-warming control from all other policies is indefensible. *Not* giving foreign aid imposes a potentially substantial cost on the developing world and that is an act of deliberate policy. Indeed, comparisons of foreign-aid expenditures with, say, expenditure on domestic health services produces an uncomfortable result. Taking all UK expenditure on the National Health Service as being potentially 'life saving' and all foreign aid as being potentially life saving in the developing world, the implied value of a UK life is 25 times that of a developing-country life. The ratio is simply the ratio of the two levels of expenditure. The same calculation for the USA shows that the USA values lives in developing countries at 1/100th of a life in the USA. What countries actually do need not, of course, correspond to what they ought to do. But the comparison reflects on the contrast between actual and publicly declared morality. Not only do humans time discount, they spatially discount as well, and, in the latter case, by very substantial rates of discount.

Using resources to combat global warming is at the potential expense of foreign aid and other transfers. The World Bank estimates that OECD country policies of industrial and agricultural protection cost the developing world over $100 billion per annum *now*, twice the annual flow of official aid (World Bank, 2002). It is hard to see any empirical or moral distinction between action that damages the immediate wellbeing of the poor — and does so quite consciously — and global-warming damage from rich-country emissions that will affect mainly future generations. Equity weighting in which the weights are not unity is not, therefore, an option for one area of policy and not for others. Yet, once that is accepted, the implications for appraisal procedures are substantial. Interestingly, and for the first time, UK Treasury appraisal guidance quite explicitly recommends equity weighting (HM Treasury, 2003, ch. 4 and Annex 6). However, it is unclear from the text if the full implications have been recognized. First, one of the criteria for deciding whether to equity weight is 'whether there is an explicit distributional rationale to the proposal under consideration' (p. 49). This would obviously fit foreign-aid decisions, but it is not clear that the Treasury Guidance is meant to extend to this budget-level decision. It ought clearly to affect any decision about state aid to agriculture and industry, both of which have formidable implications for the wellbeing of poor nations. Second, the Treasury text reads as if the decisions to be appraised with equity weights are those that are confined to UK geographical boundaries, i.e. the relevant weights are to be applied to the social distribution of income within the UK. The issue of spatial discounting is, therefore, neatly sidestepped.

(a) Does UK Climate Policy Pass a Cost–Benefit Test?

The UK is a member of the European Union and the European Union has ratified the Kyoto Protocol. This process of ratification makes the targets legally binding within the Union, regardless of what else happens to the Protocol. The burden-sharing agreement within the EU (revised at the subsequent Conferences of Parties) gives the UK a legally binding target of 88.8 per cent of 1990 emissions for all greenhouse gases. Hence, it could be argued that the relevant cost figure is not the marginal social cost of damage, but the marginal abatement cost at this level of emission reduction. The targets have been agreed and hence the *implied* total social cost of carbon must be above whatever the total abatement cost is, and the marginal social cost must be above the marginal abatement cost.

There are several powerful reasons for not adopting this argument. First, it comes close to falling into the trap noted at the beginning — namely, that whatever governments agree to do is, in some sense, the 'right' thing. The purpose of appraisal procedures such as cost–benefit analysis is to cast light on those decisions and to check whether they meet reasonable criteria for justifying policy. Otherwise, there would be no point in policy analysis: simply saying that the political process produces the 'right' answer is Panglossian — whatever happens happens for the best. Second, the UK government espouses cost–benefit analysis. Indeed, HM Treasury issues guidance on policy appraisal that makes it quite clear that cost–benefit analysis *should* be used to guide policy, while accepting that net benefit gains are not the only criterion

Table 7
The Kyoto Protocol and UK Costs and Benefits

	Marginal control cost	Marginal avoided damage	Marginal ancillary benefit	Marginal total benefit	Cost–benefit passed?
Kyoto	£ 45/tC	£70/tC	£35–50	£105–120	yes
		£16/tC	£35–50	£ 51–66	yes
CO₂ target	£100/tC	£70/tC	£35–50	£105–120	yes
		£16/tC	£35–50	£ 51–66	no

for good policy (HM Treasury, 2003). Third, the Kyoto Protocol has to be the first in a sequence of Protocols or amendments—as noted, the Protocol itself does little or nothing to reduce rates of warming. While it might be expedient to allow ratification of one agreement that fails a cost–benefit test, it would seem distinctly unwise to allow ratification of future agreements if they systematically fail a cost–benefit test. As Clarkson and Deyes (2002) note, abatement costs are likely to rise through time, so that the cost burden on UK citizens will rise.

Does the UK's commitment to the Kyoto Protocol pass a cost–benefit test? Table 7 brings together the estimates and assumes that ancillary benefits from control are some £35/tC. Table 7 suggests that the UK has signed up to a treaty that passes a cost–benefit test, but only if ancillary benefits are significant. Some studies find these ancillary benefits to be negligible. On the basis of avoided damage alone, the cost–benefit test is met if and only if the 'official' figure of £70/tC marginal damage is accepted.

Time-varying discount rates obviously affect the outcome. As noted earlier, these would probably raise the marginal avoided damage figure (only) by around 80 per cent.

Similarly, the marginal cost of control, set here at £45/tC based on an estimate quoted by Defra, may be an overestimate. It is assumed to reflect abatement technologies within the UK, and excludes the potential for buying emission reduction credits through the Kyoto 'flexibility mechanisms'. A notable possibility is the potential purchase of Russian 'hot air' which would very probably sell at far lower prices. ('Hot air' refers to the fact that Russia has emission targets above their actual emissions in 2010 and can hence sell the difference, even though this has no effect on emission reductions.) Equally, it is hard to envisage the United Kingdom purchasing hot air while maintaining a credible political image on environmental improvement. Even without hot-air trading, it is well known that trading *per se* lowers abatement costs, as does the use of policy measures such as taxes, the revenues from which are used to reduce other 'distortionary' taxes. For a review showing that estimates of marginal abatement costs vary enormously, see Hourcade and Shukla (2001).

Overall, UK climate policy may or may not pass a cost–benefit test, depending on the climate-damage model chosen, the role of ancillary benefits, the treatment of the discount rate, and the stance the UK takes with respect to emission trading. Public documents that produce social-cost estimates below estimated abatement costs have the potential for being politically embarrassing, but it is just as arguable that the emphasis that positive net benefit estimates give to emissions reduction may be at the cost of better directed policies, e.g. by investing in adaptation, especially in the developing world. The Defra guidance on the social cost of carbon (Defra, 2002a) comes close to suggesting that the £70/tC figure is a convenient justification for the UK's climate-change policy to achieve its (modified) Kyoto target: 'In addition, the figure is likely to be at least roughly consistent with the level of effort that will be needed to meet our international commitments on climate change' (Defra, 2002a, para. 10).

(b) *Energy Policy: A Carbon Tax*

Any carbon tax should, on cost–benefit grounds, be equal to the marginal damage from global warming at the point where marginal damage equals marginal control cost: the 'Pigovian' solution. Alternatively, if benefit estimation is not pursued, the tax should equal the marginal control cost at the target level of emission reduction. The UK does not have a pure carbon tax, but does have two taxes that are considered to be climate-related taxes. These are the Climate Change Levy (CCL) and the Fuel Duty Escalator (FDE).

The CCL is a tax on fossil fuels and electricity. While explicitly introduced as a climate-control tax, political considerations dictated that it would not vary directly with the carbon content of fuels. In other words, it is not, as it should be, a carbon tax. The 2000 Budget confirmed the following tax rates—there are several discounts and exemptions so that the effective tax rate is not easy to calculate. Here we have taken the pre-allowance tax rates:

> Coal: 0.15 pence kWh
> Gas: 0.15 pence kWh
> Electricity: 0.43 pence kWh

These rates can be converted into carbon taxes as follows:

Coal	£16/tC
Gas	£30/tC
Electricity	£31/tC

Clearly, if the CCL was a carbon tax, the tax rate per tonne of carbon would be the same. None the less, what we have is a range of £16–£31/tC. This range can be compared to the £70/tC marginal damage figure. If marginal damages do not change with control effort – a reasonable first-cut assumption – then the correct 'Pigovian' tax rate is also £70/tC, two to four times the implicit carbon tax in the CCL. The £70/tC figure would, therefore, justify a substantial increase in the CCL, even allowing for the fact that the CCL is a long way from being a proper carbon tax.

The second form of carbon tax is the FDE. It was introduced in 1993, by the then Conservative government, as a perpetual increase in the real price of petroleum fuels. It was also explicitly introduced as a climate-related tax, although in later years the message as to the purpose of the tax became very confused (Pearce, 2001). It was abandoned as an automatically rising tax in late 2000 after the 'fuel tax protests'. Taking the escalator between 1993 and 1999, the nominal increase in FDE amounted to some 21p/litre for gasoline and about 25p/litre for diesel (that is, the increase in fuel duty over and above 1993 levels; the 1993 levels were not environmentally motivated). In real terms – the relevant basis for the environmental component of the FDE – this was about 17p/litre and 21p/litre respectively. But a £70/tC marginal damage tax corresponds to a tax per litre of 4.4p for gasoline and about 5p/litre for diesel (gasoline has 855 kgC per tonne, with 1,345 litres per tonne, i.e. 0.63 kgC per litre; for diesel the figures are 857 kgC per tonne, 1,190 litres per tonne, and hence 0.72 kgC per litre).

If the FDE was intended to be solely a carbon tax, then the tax rate went well beyond what would be justified by the £70/tC damage figure, by a factor of five, and even further beyond what would be justified by the lower marginal damage figures suggested here. However, as noted above, the precise purpose of the tax became blurred over the years. Tax rates beyond 4–5p/litre could be justified by including other pollutants – as was implied in some public pronouncements.

(c) *Energy Policy: Choice of Fuel*

It should also be obvious that the number chosen for the marginal social cost of carbon should also affect the design of energy policy. Consider the issue of the future of nuclear power in the UK. British Energy has

Table 8
Carbon-emission Factors for Competing Fuel Cycles in the UK

Fuel cycle	Grams CO_2/ kWh	Grams C/ kWh	Carbon damage p/kWh at £15/tC	Carbon damage p/kWh at £70/tC
Coal	955–987	260–269	0.39–0.40	1.82–1.87
Oil	818	223	0.33	1.54
Orimulsion	905	247	0.37	1.73
Natural gas	446	122	0.18	0.84
Nuclear	4	1	0.00	0.00

Source: Emissions only from Bates (1995).

not found it possible to compete in the electricity market in the wake of falling electricity prices. This is because nuclear electricity *private* costs are greater than, say, gas-fired electricity. But nuclear power could have a *social* cost less than its competitors once due allowance is made for the value of carbon. Nuclear power emits substantially less CO_2 over its life cycle than do fossil fuel energy sources. Table 8 shows emission factors for different fuel cycles. The implication is that, at the £70/tC social-cost figure, nuclear power carries with it a 'carbon credit' of around 0.8p/kWh relative to natural gas, and over 1.5p/kWh relative to other fossil fuels. While these differentials are unlikely to make nuclear competitive in social-cost terms compared to gas, they are very likely to tip the balance relative to other fossil fuels. If we adopt the maximum lower figure for the social cost of carbon suggested here, £15/tC, then the nuclear carbon credit is only 0.2p/kWh relative to gas, and 0.3–0.4p/kWh relative to other fossil fuels. These differentials are unlikely to tip the balance between nuclear and its competitors. But enough has been said to show that the value of the marginal social cost of carbon matters significantly for the debate about the future of nuclear power in the UK. The 'official' value for carbon implies that that future is far more assured than if the lower values suggested here are used A full analysis would also account for other greenhouse gases, such as methane, and also for conventional pollutants, such as particulate matter and nitrogen oxides. Time-varying discount rates would also affect the social cost of nuclear power (OXERA, 2002).

(d) *Energy Policy: Renewables*

Policy on the introduction of renewable energy in the UK is driven by the 'Renewables Obligation', a requirement that electricity generators supply 10 per cent of their electricity from certified renewable sources by 2010. Proof of supply is via a renewables obligation certificate (ROC).

Failure to meet the target involves generators buying ROCs from those who have over-complied, or paying a 'buy out' fee of 3p/kWh. Since renewables have private costs greater than current fuels, the Renewables Obligation comes at a resource cost, while the benefit is primarily (but not exclusively) in terms of the avoided carbon emissions. Accordingly, the Renewables Obligation has an implicit price. This has been put at £310/tC (*Utilities Journal*, 2001). Clearly, if the marginal damage from carbon is £70/tC, renewables policy fails a cost–benefit test, since it is costing £310/tC to secure a benefit of £70/tC. The difference, some £240/tC, is unlikely to be made up by other avoided pollutants.

(e) *Forestry Policy*

Growing trees sequester CO_2. Afforestation in the UK is widely regarded as being unprofitable in terms of commercial timber, but social arguments have been widely used to justify some forest expansion. The main non-timber benefits considered are recreational use and carbon sequestration. Brainard *et al.* (2003) estimate that the value of carbon sequestered in English woodland is some £770m p.a., using a social discount rate of 3.5 per cent. However, the Brainard *et al.* estimate is based on a shadow price of carbon of £6.7/tC (with 1 per cent p.a. increases). If £70/tC is the right shadow price of carbon, this annual value needs to be multiplied by a factor of ten, making annual sequestration worth some £7.7 billion. CJC Consulting *et al.* (2003) estimate the average English per-hectare value of sequestration at the £6.7 figure as £1,380. The £70/tC figure would raise this to £15,200 for broadleaves and £13,450 for conifers. As CJC Consulting *et al.* note: 'Here, the gains from planting are so large that rapid afforestation is called for' (p. 64).

In short, the £70/tC figure would totally transform the economics of forestry in the UK.

(f) *Green Accounting and the Social Cost of Carbon*

What value is chosen for the social cost of carbon also affects any attempt to modify the national economic accounts for environmental damage. Conventional accounting measures gross and net national product (GNP, NNP) but fails to deduct from these measures any environmental damage. There is now a substantial literature that makes these adjustments — see, for example, Atkinson *et al.* (1997). The essential result is given by the identity:

$$gNNP = GNP - d_M - d_E$$

where gNNP denotes 'green' net national product, d_M is depreciation on conventional 'man-made' capital assets, and d_E is depreciation on environmental capital. d_E would then be measured by the value of the economic rents from depleted natural resources and the value of pollution damage. Focusing *solely* on carbon emissions and using the £70/tC figure for marginal social cost of carbon, produces the following results for the UK:

GNP in 2000 at 2000 prices = £890 billion
CO_2 emissions in 2000 = 145m tonnes C = £10,150m = £10.15 billion

The £70/tC figure amounts to total damage equal to 1.1 per cent of GNP, compared to just 0.2 per cent if the lower value for carbon is used. Green accounting need not be confined to nations. Damage estimates can also be used to adjust corporate accounts. Note that the correct adjustment involves damage estimates, not control cost estimates as is commonly and erroneously done in some 'corporate sustainability' accounts. Atkinson (2000) reports adjusted accounts for UK electricity generator, Powergen. These suggest that, once pollution damage is subtracted from operating profits, the resulting measure of 'genuine savings' shows net losses from 1992 to 1995, but a modest net gain in 1996. Effectively, Powergen was not 'sustainable' in social terms. Atkinson's value of carbon is £12/tC, so if this is raised to £70/tC, Powergen would be even less sustainable in the first few years and almost certainly for 1996 as well (Atkinson does not report emission figures). Once again, adopting a specific damage estimate requires that the implications be scrutinized. The £70/tC figure could have formidable implications for corporate accounting.

14. Conclusions

The central conclusions from this discussion are:

(i) while the figures are necessarily uncertain, it is possible to estimate the aggregate and marginal social cost of greenhouse-gas emissions, also bearing in mind that errors of even 100 per cent may not matter very much for policy purposes;

(ii) the marginal social-cost estimates have a role to play in appraising climate-change policy, and especially in determining whether 'too much' or 'too little' abatement is being considered;

(iii) marginal social-cost estimates are model-dependent. Recent models suggest quite wide ranges of estimates;

(iv) few early models incorporate adaptive behaviour, most being based on the 'dumb farmer syndrome'. Yet adaptation is clearly going to be an integral part of dealing with climate change;

(v)   those generally more recent models that have adaptive behaviour show marked reductions in social-cost estimates relative to those without such behaviour. While adaptive models may be 'too optimistic', it is equally likely that non-adaptive models have been 'too pessimistic';

(vi) recent models suggest a range for the marginal social cost of carbon, without equity weighting, of £3–6/tC. Equity weighting, using a marginal utility of income elasticity of unity, raises this range to £3–15/tC;

(vii) there is increasing evidence that the correct approach to discounting in the global-warming context is to use a time-varying discount rate. Borrowing estimates from recent US work, the £3–15/tC range should be multiplied by around 1.8 to give a range of £4–27/tC;

(viii) the treatment of catastrophic events in the various integrated assessment models remains, as the authors of those models know full well, unsatisfactory. This issue has to be one of the driving forces for the future work in this area;

(ix) the UK government originally opted for a central estimate of the marginal social cost of carbon of £70/tC. The difference between this figure and the ones derived above reveals the sensitivity of the estimates to the model chosen. The chosen model in this case largely excludes adaptation;

(x)   at the lower set of estimates, UK policy in joining the EU in ratifying the Kyoto Protocol may not pass a cost–benefit test, and future Protocols or Amendments would be even less likely to pass a cost–benefit test. On the 'unofficial' UK government estimate of social cost, however, Kyoto would pass a cost–benefit test but the domestic 'target' of 20 per cent reduction in CO_2 would not. Thus, even this figure raises serious doubts about whether a second and third Protocol would meet the cost–benefit criterion. However, if time-varying discount rates are adopted, UK policy would pass a cost–benefit test both in terms of Kyoto and the 20 per cent carbon reduction target. Much also depends on whether control costs are being accurately portrayed here;

(xi) the negative results for climate policy do not imply 'doing nothing' but rather point the way for (a) a reappraisal of the balance between investing in emissions reduction and investing in adaptation, especially in developing countries, and (b) research work on uncertainty and major adverse events;

(xii) equity weighting has a strong utilitarian rationale to it, but the choice of the utility of income elasticity is more open than UK government documents suggest. More importantly, once equity weighting is accepted, as it appears to be in new UK Treasury appraisal guidance, it has to be applied consistently across all policies with distributive impacts within the UK *and* beyond. It is not defensible to argue that global warming is 'special' because the damage is the responsibility of the rich countries. Responsibility arguments are just as valid in other contexts such as aid and trade protection. Efforts to 'ring fence' global warming as if it is wholly separate from other policy concerns, and hence deserving of 'special' treatment, are illicit;

(xiii) a second approach to assessing the 'reasonableness' of a social-cost figure is to investigate the policy implications. If energy policy was rationally decided on the basis of overall private plus external costs, the £70/tC figure would have major implications for nuclear power relative to other fossil fuels, and there would be a sizeable but probably undecisive credit compared to natural gas. Prevailing 'carbon taxes' would need either to be increased (the CCL) or acknowledged as too high (the FDE). Renewables policy in the UK fails a cost–benefit test even at the 'high' estimate of £70/tC, but such a figure would give the green light to extensive afforestation, a complete reversal of forestry policy in the UK. As far as green accounting is concerned, the £70/tC figure also produces a fairly dramatic adjustment to GNP of over 1 per cent, ignoring all other pollutants. The £70/tC figure is also like to have potentially dramatic effects on the 'sustainability' of some corporations.

What does seem to be clear is that the choice of shadow price for carbon, whatever it is, brings to light the serious inconsistencies in government policy of energy, climate control, and forestry. Getting the number right matters.

The Social Costs of Greenhouse Gases: Their Values and Policy Implications

ROBERT MENDELSOHN*

1. Introduction

If greenhouse gases (principally carbon dioxide (CO_2), methane (CH_4), and nitrogen oxides (NOX)), continue to accumulate in the earth's atmosphere, future temperatures are expected to increase (Houghton *et al.*, 2001). These changes in climate, in turn, will cause both market and non-market impacts on humans across the planet (McCarthy *et al.*, 2001). Society faces a complex task of balancing abatement costs against the damages that these gases cause over very long time periods. The social cost of greenhouse gases is the present value of the net damages caused by an additional ton of emissions. Intuitively, it is the marginal damage of emissions. By determining the value of the social cost, society can design globally efficient programmes to control greenhouse gases. In this paper, we focus on the social cost of carbon (SCC), the social cost of adding another ton of CO_2.[1]

Greenhouse gases mix readily in the atmosphere so that emissions anywhere in the planet effectively make the same contribution to concentrations. The consequences of greenhouse-gas emissions are therefore global, not local. There is only one value for the SCC for the entire planet at each moment in time. Whether an emission is made in Fiji, Great Britain, or Russia, there is a single value of SCC. In contrast, the damages caused by most pollutants are more localized and depend greatly on where the pollution is emitted.

There are several important intertemporal features about the stream of impacts caused by an additional ton of greenhouse gases. First, each

* School of Forestry and Environmental Studies, Yale University. I would like to thank Chris Hope and William Nordhaus for their very helpful comments on earlier drafts.

[1] Although we discuss only the social cost of CO_2, the principles can be readily applied to the other greenhouse gases as well.

ton is expected to remain in the atmosphere for a long period and the earth takes a long time to return to equilibrium, so the impacts are expected to last a very long time. The SCC must look far into the future to count all the damages caused by an emission today. Second, to make mitigation decisions, society must balance far-future consequences against near-term abatement costs. The difference in timing must be taken into account. Analysts use a discount rate in order to compare far-future with current costs. The discount rate is the value of time. By discounting the damages back to the moment that mitigation is considered, the long stream of impacts can be balanced against the marginal cost of mitigation (the cost of preventing the emission from occurring). Third, there are long delays between emissions and consequences (Houghton *et al.*, 2001). The oceans carry much of the heat in the system and the oceans warm slowly. Fourth, the impact of an additional ton of emission changes as greenhouse gases accumulate in the atmosphere. Globally, the harmful effects gradually increase as temperatures increase and the beneficial effects diminish (Mendelsohn and Williams, 2004). The SCC rises over time as the concentration of greenhouse gases rises.

In order to measure the SCC, analysts must organize vast amounts of information across many disciplines into a cohesive integrated assessment model (see ch. 4 by Hope in this volume). This is a difficult task and cannot be done perfectly. Consequently, the measurements of SCC are uncertain. The uncertainty is partly due to the underlying complexity of the natural science and the fact that many components are not thoroughly understood (Houghton *et al.*, 2001). However, another important source of uncertainty lies in our inability to measure the response of climate-sensitive sectors (McCarthy *et al.*, 2001). It is sometimes hard to do controlled experiments on sensitive sectors because they are too expensive (examining whole ecosystems) or there are moral constraints (human health experiments). The adaptations that sectors make to adversity have also proven to be difficult to capture. One of the intriguing questions facing policy-makers is whether to adjust the SCC because of this uncertainty (see ch. 3 by Ingham and Ulph in this volume).

Finally, it is important to note that the measurement of the SCC requires values. The consequences of global warming must ultimately be valued in units comparable with abatement costs (pounds or US dollars). That means that changes in agricultural production, water supplies, health risks, recreation, etc., must all be valued in monetary terms. Except for globally traded goods, the value of most of these goods and services will vary across locations and, often, people. The values that should be used in this case are the values of the people who are actually affected. There is a temptation in constructing the SCC to substitute other values for the values of the victims. Unfortunately, this has led to a great deal of contention and misunderstanding in the literature (Schneider, 1997*a*).

This paper begins with a brief review of the theory behind controlling greenhouse gases. The theory highlights the central role that the SCC plays in mitigation policy and provides a precise definition of it. What affects the SCC and why the SCC is a dynamic concept is also discussed in this section. In the third section, we illustrate an integrated assessment model that follows the logical steps between cause and effect and how each step depends upon a particular branch of science to lead to our understanding. In section 4, we discuss measuring the resulting outcomes. We rely heavily on the Intergovernmental Panel on Climate Change (IPCC; see Houghton *et al.*, 2001) for overviews of the natural science. The section, instead, emphasizes the empirical evidence linking climate change and final impacts. Aggregate impacts and the resulting values for the SCC are presented. This section also discusses how those values are likely to change over time. The paper concludes with a discussion of the policy implications of both the theory and the measurements of SCC.

2. Theory

The most basic principle in managing environmental pollution is that society wants to minimize the sum of the environmental damages and mitigation costs. With a long-lived problem such as greenhouse gases, this requires society to take a long-run view. Society must minimize the present value of the mitigation costs and the present value of the damages. The seminal paper to capture this basic principle in the greenhouse context was done by Nordhaus (1991). In this section, we rely on the paper by Falk and Mendelsohn (1993), largely because of its simplicity.

The most basic principle is to choose a path of carbon control that minimizes the sum of the abatement costs $C(Q(t))$ and environmental damages $D(S(t))$:

$$Min \int_0^\infty C(Q(t))\exp(-\gamma t)dt + \int_0^\infty D(S(t))\exp(-\gamma t)dt, \tag{1}$$

$$\text{where } S(t) = S(t-1) + Q(t) - \lambda\, S(t)\, ,$$

and $Q(t)$ is global emissions of greenhouse gases, t is time, γ is the social discount rate, $S(t)$ is the stock of greenhouse gases in the atmosphere, and λ is the decay rate of the stock. The first line in equation (1) reflects the costs to society discounted back to the present. The second line describes how the stock changes over time. It increases with emissions but it also has a decay effect that tends to push the stock back towards its natural equilibrium. As long as emissions are greater than the decay, the stock increases over time.

There are many greenhouse gases: carbon, methane, nitrous oxides, and a set of compounds named halocarbons. Each gas has a different expected lifetime $(1/\lambda)$ in the environment and a different effect on temperature (radiative forcing) (Houghton et al., 2001). The stock is an indexed sum of the greenhouse gases in the atmosphere at any moment in time weighted by radiative forcing. However, for illustrative purposes, we are going to proceed as though there is only CO_2.

In order to solve this problem, one needs to differentiate equation (1) with respect to an emission of each greenhouse gas and compute the first-order conditions:

$$MC(Q(t)) = \int_{t0}^{\infty} MD(S(t))dS(t)/dQ(to)\exp(-\gamma t)dt \qquad (2)$$

$$SCC(t0) = \int_{t0}^{\infty} MD(S(t))dS(t)/dQ(to)\exp(-\gamma t)dt. \qquad (3)$$

Equation (2) states that the marginal cost of abatement in each year should be equated with the present value of the damages caused by that ton. The marginal damage of an emission at time $t(0)$ is the present value of all the added damages caused by that ton into the future. Because that ton will decay into the future, the marginal effect of a ton on the stock will also decay as time proceeds. Starting at the moment of emission, $t(0)$, one must calculate the stream of marginal damages caused by that original ton. This stream depends upon how much of that ton is still in the atmosphere in each future time period $t(i)$ and the radiative forcing of the gas. The SCC is a forward-looking calculation that presumes the analyst knows the future stream of concentrations and marginal impacts.

The discount rate and the decay rate are both important. In the case of carbon, the decay rate is quite small (0.005) (implying a life expectancy of atmospheric carbon of 200 years) whereas the discount rate can be quite large (4 per cent) (Houghton et al., 2001). There is, however, a substantial debate in the literature concerning what value to use for the social discount rate (Arrow et al., 1996). The important point is that one cannot choose a separate discount rate for greenhouse gases from all other social problems. The discount rate is the price of time, not the value of greenhouse gases. Whatever rate is chosen must be consistent with other public investments and tax policy. Attempts to use very low discount rates of 1 per cent and, especially, 0 per cent are hard to justify. If the mitigation costs compete with private investment for savings, the opportunity cost of the funds is the market interest rate (4 per cent), what they would otherwise have earned society (see Arrow *et al.*, 1996).

The left-hand term in equation (2) is the marginal cost of mitigation, the cost of preventing emissions. The model implies that the globally efficient mitigation policy would equate the marginal cost of carbon across the planet with SCC. Given any specific carbon target, equilibrating the marginal cost of carbon across all opportunities will achieve that target at the least cost to society. If any one country spends far more on controlling carbon than the rest of the globe, it will be effectively wasting resources that could have been far more effectively used elsewhere. Similarly, if any country fails to engage in mitigation that costs less than the SCC, the country will have underinvested in mitigation. Because carbon benefits are enjoyed by every country, but abatement is generally financed entirely by each country, it is in each country's self-interest to underinvest in global warming (and all other global public goods).

As shown in equation (3) the SCC is the present value of all the future net damages from a ton of emission in period $t(0)$. The SCC requires the analyst to compute damages far into the future. These damages are conditional on a number of assumptions about what the future holds, including population growth, economic growth, and sectoral shifts.

Equation (2) highlights another important principle. The SCC is tied to the stock of carbon in the atmosphere at the moment of emission. It reflects the additional consequences of making the stock slightly larger. The SCC is consequently dynamic. As the stock of carbon in the atmosphere increases, the marginal damage is expected to rise. Over time, the SCC should increase. That, in turn, implies a dynamic control strategy that begins with only low-cost mitigation but gradually includes more and more expensive control options over time.

It is a common mistake made by some global-warming observers to confuse the consequences of current emissions with the damages caused by future emissions. Future emissions will likely have a high SCC if global warming unfolds in a harmful direction. That does not imply that current emissions also have a high SCC. Current emissions should be evaluated on the basis of what they alone cause to happen. The SCC today should not be averaged with future SCCs for policy purposes. The SCC in each time period guides mitigation policy in that period alone.

3. Integrated Assessment

It is one thing to write a general formula for controlling a cumulative pollutant, it is quite another to organize all the science required to measure the value of social cost. Integrated assessment puts the myriad relevant sciences in logical sequence (see Hope, ch. 4). The purpose of the modelling is to follow cause and effect. The first model to put together this vast array of information for greenhouse gases was Nordhaus (1991). Subsequently, there has been a host of economic integrated assessment models for greenhouse gases that capture ever more detail and new science (for example: Peck and Teisberg, 1993; Nordhaus, 1994a; Manne et al., 1995; Plambeck and Hope, 1996; Tol, 1995, 1999; Nordhaus and Boyer, 2000).

Figure 1 displays a simple schematic that links the major components of an integrated assessment model for greenhouse gases. The model moves through causal mechanisms from emission control through to final damages. The schematic highlights six key steps: emissions, ambient concentrations, climate and ocean changes, ecosystem changes, social impacts, and valuation. Each of these steps requires the service of at least one discipline, and often more than one.

All of the steps listed in Figure 1 must be carried forward through time. As the theory dictates, the problem requires long-term modelling. It is not correct to match current costs with current damages. Current costs must be linked with a long stream of future marginal damages. The model consequently must be solved far into the future. Every step of the model is consequently burdened with predicting events across, at least, several decades, and possibly centuries. As events occur further and further into the future, they become more uncertain. However, it is not possible to determine even near-term policies without having some idea what the consequences of current emissions are for many decades into the future. Partly because of the long lags between emissions and climate changes (30 years), and partly because of the long schedule of damages once climate changes (200 years), it is critical to forecast what current emissions do to future impacts. Although we clearly will learn more about global warming over time, it is very likely that global warming policy will always be shrouded in uncertainty about the distant future.

The first step of the integrated assessment model in Figure 1 determines the level of emissions in each period and mitigation costs. Forecasting future emissions and mitigation costs has been the focus of many economic and engineering studies (see Metz et al., 2001). Forecasting emissions is not straightforward because it depends upon future economic growth and energy use. The difficulty of forecasting far into

Figure 1
Integrated Assessment Schematic

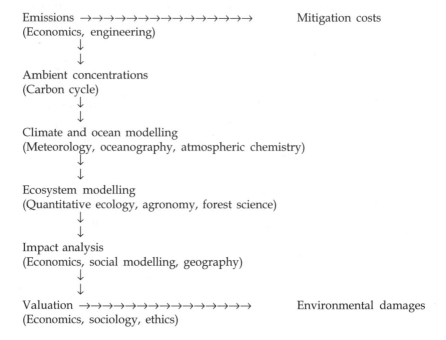

Emissions →→→→→→→→→→→→→→→→→→→→→→   Mitigation costs
(Economics, engineering)
                ↓
                ↓
Ambient concentrations
(Carbon cycle)
                ↓
                ↓
Climate and ocean modelling
(Meteorology, oceanography, atmospheric chemistry)
                ↓
                ↓
Ecosystem modelling
(Quantitative ecology, agronomy, forest science)
                ↓
                ↓
Impact analysis
(Economics, social modelling, geography)
                ↓
                ↓
Valuation →→→→→→→→→→→→→→→→→→→→→→   Environmental damages
(Economics, sociology, ethics)

the future has led to a wide range of cost estimates (see Metz *et al.*, 2001). The actual cost, of course, depends upon how aggressively policy tries to reduce emissions. One general conclusion of the literature is that it will be expensive to engage in extensive mitigation that will keep concentrations from rising far above current levels (Metz *et al.*, 2001). The question about how deeply to control carbon emissions is not an academic exercise but rather a very central concern in greenhouse-gas policy and an important social investment decision.

The second step in the model determines how concentrations change with emissions. What happens to natural sinks and sources? Studying this problem has been the focus of both atmospheric scientists who have made many detailed measurements of greenhouse gases (see Houghton *et al.*, 2001) as well as ecologists who have built ever more detailed carbon-cycle models (see Prentice *et al.*, 2001). The models and measurements reveal that greenhouse gases are building up in the atmosphere, though not quite as fast as society is adding emissions. The measurements suggest that sinks in the carbon system are absorbing some of the additional emissions. One of the large uncertainties in the integrated assessment model concerns how these sinks might behave in the future and whether some sinks could become sources as the planet warms.

The third step of the model captures how the oceans and climate change together. This has been the singular focus of a large number of oceanographers and climate scientists (Houghton *et al.*, 2001). They have very carefully measured historical records as well as projected what might happen into the future. There is growing evidence that greenhouse-gas emissions have already warmed the planet 0.5°C (Houghton *et al.*, 2001). However, of much greater concern, is what will happen if emissions continue unabated. The most recent projections suggest that, if nothing is done to control emissions, the planet would warm by 1.4°C to 5.8°C by 2100 (Houghton *et al.*, 2001). There is a very wide range of possible climate outcomes from a very mild to a relatively severe scenario. Unfortunately, the 2001 IPCC report made no attempt to identify how likely each outcome might be. This has handicapped careful estimation of the SCC because it is not clear whether the high end of the temperature range is likely or a low probability event. It is further not clear what the expected value of the temperature change is supposed to be. Hopefully, the next IPCC report will address this serious shortcoming in the presentation of the science.

The fourth step of the model captures changes in ecosystems including changes in forests and crops. Ecologists predict that biomes will move towards the poles as a result of warming (see Prentice *et al.*, 2001). The speed of this change, however, is not clear. One scenario implies rapid change as fires and insect outbreaks obliterate the southern (northern) edge of each biome in the northern (southern) hemisphere. Biomes to the south will gradually move into this disrupted space leading to a relatively quick transition. Alternatively, old biomes could hold on for decades as new seedlings only gradually replace existing species. This process could take decades and leave pockets of remnant species for centuries. Along with predicting that biomes will move, the modellers also predict changes in bioproductivity (Prentice *et al.*, 2001). The changes in bioproductivity and the changes in the biomes must be modelled together as they are simultaneous and interactive. Agronomists have also measured changes in crop productivity that might occur with warming.

Another important topic covered in this step is the impact of carbon fertilization. Through both laboratory and open-field experiments, it has been determined that CO_2 acts as a fertilizer to almost all plant species. The carbon fertilization effect appears to be logarithmic, which implies that it will be positive but diminishing. On average, crop yields are expected to increase 30 per cent with a doubling of CO_2, although this will vary dramatically across crops (Reilly *et al.*, 1996). The magnitude of this effect for crops may be much less for trees in natural conditions as they may be limited by the availability of other nutrients.

However, with crops, farmers already add fertilizer so that the nutrient constraint is not generally binding.

The fifth step measures the social impact of all the changes in both market and non-market sectors. The market impacts include changes in agriculture, timber, water, energy, and coastal resources (see Watson *et al.*, 1996; McCarthy *et al.*, 2001). The non-market effects include the changes in biomes and bioproductivity which lead to changes in wildlife habitat, the human health effects from air pollution, water pollution, heat stress, and vector borne diseases, and the amenity values of weather (see Watson *et al.*, 1996; McCarthy *et al.*, 2001).

Impacts can be measured in physical terms, such as loss of bushels of corn, or potential new cases of diseases, but ultimately they need to be converted to the same units of value as mitigation costs (Pearce, 2003b). The final step in the model captures what values local people assign to the changes that they experience. These values need not be the same across the planet. Goods and services that are not traded generally will have different values. For example, corn is traded worldwide so that there is a global price of corn. However, water is hard to move from basin to basin. There should be a basin-wide price for water but that price will vary across basins. Life (health) is not traded at all. There is every reason to believe that the value of life is different even across people in the same location. The key is that the analysis should use the values of the people who actually experience the effects. Valuation is clearly a contentious but critical step in the integrated assessment model.

Some scientists, model builders, may have the impression that they can substitute their own values in this last stage (see criticism by Schneider, 1997a). However, it is not the values of the scientists that are required but rather the values of the victims. Valuation must rely on proven methods to elicit values from the directly affected individuals. In the case of market impacts, economics has already developed many powerful valuation methods. However, the non-market impacts are much more difficult to value. The valuation of non-market impacts is one of the most poorly developed sections of the integrated assessment model. Non-market impacts are changes in goods and services that are not traded in markets. These goods and services are often public goods, shared by many individuals at a time. For example, wilderness can be enjoyed by many people simultaneously to hunt, hike, camp, or just view. In many circumstances, people are not required to pay to enjoy these services because the land or at least access to the land may be owned by the government. The absence of a fee, however, does not imply the service has no value. There simply is not a market for it. The valuation of non-market services requires more than simply observing prices because, in the absence of markets, there are no prices. Some other valuation method must be employed. Valuation efforts have increased dramatically in the last two decades to capture many non-market services, including recreation sites and human health. However, few studies have addressed non-market services peculiar to global warming, such as shifting ecosystems. Further, valuation studies have not been done across the globe and so the values of most people on earth have never been measured.

Another important valuation issue surrounds adaptation. Victims will tend to react to adverse conditions by avoiding damages when possible. For example, farmers will adjust their crops as climate changes, countries will build sea walls if the ocean rises, and dam operators will adjust water management if run-off changes. The early climate-change literature struggled to include adaptation. Analysts often underestimated adjustments that victims might make to reduce negative impacts and seize new opportunities. They consequently overestimated the net damages from climate change (see the comprehensive review of early literature by Pearce *et al.*, 1996). Subsequent research, however, has revealed that adaptation could be substantial for an environmental change that occurs gradually over many decades (Mendelsohn and Neumann, 1999; Mendelsohn, 2001*b*). Even hard-to-change resources such as forests can gradually be moulded over many decades to new conditions. Adaptation changes the results. Temperature still has a hill-shaped relationship with respect to many sectors, but the climate sensitivity can be reduced with adaptation. The harmfulness of impacts tends to fall. Unfortunately, few of the non-market studies have yet to include adaptation. For example, the health impact studies have yet to include a public health response to warming, and the ecological studies have yet to include any management responses.

A complete integrated assessment model provides a link between emissions and damages. In the next section of the paper, we discuss the results in the literature. Not only are the values expected to change as greenhouse gases accumulate, but it is also apparent that the values have changed as research has revealed new insights. Specifically, we focus on what new social science research is finding.

4. Estimates of the Social Cost of Carbon

In order to measure the SCC, each of the steps outlined in the integrated assessment model above must be estimated over the next century and beyond. There is simply too much information to review this empirical data in detail in this paper. We rely heavily on the IPCC to describe what is expected in each step (Houghton *et al.*, 2001). The IPCC entertains two scenarios where emissions will fall and concentrations will rise to only 540 parts per million (ppm), but these scenarios entail a substantial amount of abatement forced by government action. In order to get a sense of what will happen if no controls are implemented, we focus on the remaining scenarios. In the uncontrolled case, emissions are expected to rise over the next century (from the current 8 gigaton (Gt)/year) to between 12 and 27 Gt/year, CO_2 concentrations will rise (from the current 350 ppm) to between 650 and 970 ppm, and temperatures will increase between 2.0 and 5.8°C by 2100.

We give short shrift to the natural scientific details that have led to the conclusions above, in order to focus our attention carefully on the link between climate change and the resulting welfare impacts on mankind. The very earliest impact studies in the 1980s examined individual sectors in individual countries under very limited circumstances. These studies were hard to compare and to use as a basis of measuring national impacts. The first comprehensive national study was done by the United States Environmental Protection Agency, which examined all vulnerable sectors in the United States (Smith and Tirpak, 1990). Although this comprehensive evaluation did not quantify the welfare impacts of climate change, the study provided sufficient quantitative information for analysts subsequently to make the first valuations of aggregate impacts (Nordhaus, 1991; Cline, 1992). Using extrapolation, impacts were predicted in all regions of the world (Fankhauser, 1995; Tol, 1995). The estimates of the impacts from climate change for the United States are summarized in Table 1. The doubling of CO_2 was expected to cause annual damages of between 1 and 1.5 per cent of GDP in the USA and between 1.6 and 2.7 per cent in developing countries. This result became the standard used by the impact literature once published by the IPCC (Pearce *et al.*, 1996).[2]

However, there are many reasons to believe that the impact results estimated in the Second Assessment Report are not accurate. First, the early impact studies examined the effect of doubling CO_2 on a 1990 economy. They made no effort to forecast how the economy or population might change over time. The studies consequently overestimated the size of the damages relative to GDP, since climate-sensitive sectors such as agriculture are expected to grow more slowly than the rest of the economy. Adjusting for this error alone would reduce impacts as a fraction of GDP substantially.

---

[2] Unfortunately, the most recent summary of impacts by the IPCC (McCarthy *et al.*, 2001) moved to qualitative analysis and so did not provide updated quantitative estimates.

Table 1
Initial Estimates of Aggregate Climate Damages for the United States
(1990 US$ billion/year)

Sector	Nordhaus	Cline	Fankhauser	Tol
Agriculture	1.1	17.5	8.4	10.0
Timber	—	3.3	0.7	—
Energy[a]	1.1	9.9	7.9	—
Sea-level rise	12.1	7.0	9.0	8.5
Water supply	—	7.0	15.6	—
Total market	14.3	44.7	41.6	18.5
Mortality	—	5.8	11.4	37.4
Migration	—	0.5	0.6	1.0
Hurricanes	—	0.8	0.2	0.3
Leisure/amenity	—	1.7	—	12.0
Water pollution	—	—	—	—
Urban infrastructure	—	0.1	—	—
Air pollution	—	3.5	7.3	—
Species loss	—	4.0	8.4	5.0
Total non-market	41.2	16.4	27.9	55.7
Total	55.5	61.1	69.5	74.2

Note: [a] Energy costs include electricity, other heating, and mobile air conditioning.
Source: Pearce et al., 1996.

Perhaps the most serious error in the early studies is that they assumed that damages were a strictly increasing function of climate change. Warming was assumed to be strictly harmful (see Table 1). A very important insight of more recent empirical studies is that climate-sensitive sectors tend to have a hill-shaped relationship with temperature (Mendelsohn and Schlesinger, 1999). Each sector has an optimal temperature (which varies by sector). Any change to either the cooling side or the warming side of this optimum causes a reduction in value. This hill-shaped response function implies that the impacts of warming will not be the same across the planet. Places that are currently cool will climb the hill with warming whereas places that are too warm will fall down the hill. There will consequently be both benefits and damages from global warming.

The new sets of studies make one final improvement. They do a much better job of including adaptation. Although many earlier studies included some adaptation, they generally did not capture the full potential of adaptive behaviour. The new studies expect farmers to shift crops, sea walls to be built over time, foresters gradually to adjust their stocks of trees, and water to be reallocated when these activities are

Table 2
New Estimates of Climate Impacts on the United States Economy in 2060
(1998 US$ billion/year)

Sector	Climate scenario			
	No precipitation change		15% precipitation increase	
	2.5°C	5.0°C	2.5°C	5.0°C
Agriculture	25.5	14.1	26.1	17.0
	(17 to 33)	(–7 to 24)	(16 to 36)	(–7 to 27)
Timber	1.5	1.5	6.9	7.8
	(1 to 2)	(1 to 2)	(6 to 8)	(6 to 10)
Energy	–5.3	–21.3	–8.3	–26.9
	(–10 to –1)	(–32 to –15)	(–14 to –3)	(–37 to –17)
Coastal[1]	–0.2	–0.4	–0.2	–0.4
	(–0.4 to –0.1)	(–1 to –0.2)	(–0.4 to –0.1)	(–1 to –0.2)
Water	–4.8	–11.3	0.6	–5.4
	(–9 to –2)	(–5 to –25)	(–5 to +5)	(–15 to 5)
Total	16.7	–19.9	25.1	–7.8
	(3 to 29)	(–49 to –2)	(10 to 38)	(–41 to 11)
% 2060 GDP	0.08	–0.09	0.12	–0.04

Note:[1] The sea-level rise estimates assume that higher temperatures lead to more sea-level rise. Note that a positive value implies benefits.
Source: Mendelsohn and Neumann (1999).

profitable. Many of these adaptations will be privately done. There is every reason to expect these will be undertaken as they are in the best interest of the firms and people who will do them. However, some adaptations are public. They will benefit many people at once. These adaptations require the coordination of many users, such as the building of sea walls or building of dams. These adaptations will also require government involvement and it is not certain that governments will respond efficiently to these new demands. Some of this new literature, which assumes efficient government response, may consequently be over-optimistic (Mendelsohn, 2000).

Table 2 provides estimates of what climate change might do to the United States given these new research findings. Four scenarios are presented: mild and severe temperature changes coupled with no increases and a 15 per cent increase in precipitation. It is quite clear that the climate scenario matters. The two scenarios examining a 2.5°C warming suggest net economic benefits to the United States. With the severe 5°C warming, however, the impacts do turn harmful for the USA. Overall, though, the net impacts in Table 2 as a percentage of GDP are an order of magnitude smaller than in Table 1.

Table 3
Aggregate Global Net Impacts From Climate Change in 2100

| Climate model | Climate response function | | | |
| | Experimental | | Cross-sectional | |
	Total	%GDP	Total	%GDP
PCM (2.5°C)	220.4	0.11	63.8	0.03
CSIRO (3.7°C)	–69.7	–0.03	–22.8	–0.01
CCC (5.2°C)	–302.2	–0.14	–17.3	–0.01

Notes: Impacts are measured in US$ billions/year. A negative value implies a damage.

In a comparative analysis using many Atmosphere–Ocean General Circulation Models (AOGCMs), Mendelsohn and Williams (2004) forecasted the dynamic impacts to each country around the world from warming over the next century. The estimates rely on the American studies to interpolate impacts to the mid- to high latitudes (Mendelsohn and Neumann, 1999; Mendelsohn, 2001b) and an Indian study for the low-latitude countries (Mendelsohn et al., 2001). Separate impacts are estimated for each country, based on the climate changes predicted in each country, the climate response function, and numerous background factors, such as cropland, coasts, GDP, and population. The results in Table 3 report the outcomes in 2100 for three climate models: PCM (Washington et al., 2000), CSIRO (Gordon and Farrell, 1997), and CGCM1 (Boer et al., 2000). The three climate forecasts include sulphates and they reflect some of the best predictions of warming currently available. These three models were carefully selected to provide a range of realistic outcomes by the end of the century from a warming of 2.5°C to 5.2°C. Table 3 shows that different climate projections lead to a wide range of impacts by 2100. Overall, the net global impacts in 2100 from uncontrolled climate change are surprisingly small. As the benefits in mid- to high-latitude countries offset the damages in low-latitude countries, the range of net effects for the globe are between –0.14 per cent and 0.11 per cent of GDP. These global net estimates are an order of magnitude smaller than the earlier IPCC estimates. Further, depending on how climate change unfolds, the net impacts include the possibility that warming will be beneficial for the next century.

Extreme events, such as climate variance, shutdown of the thermohaline circulation, and the collapse of the West Antarctic Ice Sheet, are not included in Table 3. Some authors argue that speculative examples of these events could be included in integrated assessment models (Downing et al., 1996; Ulph and Ulph, 1997; Nordhaus and Boyer, 2000).

Other authors argue that these effects may have infinite value, for example, if they cause the destruction of life on the planet (Tol, 2003). Finally, other authors argue that these effects are likely to be small (Ingham and Ulph, ch. 3 in this volume). Further, the natural science evidence linking catastrophic events to warming in this century is inconclusive. Most of the theories suggesting such a link depend on centuries of warming. Whether or not to include highly speculative catastrophic events in integrated assessment models is not clear.

Table 3 also does not include non-market effects. Given the high values placed on non-market effects in the early literature (see Table 1), non-market impacts should be taken seriously. Unfortunately, quantitative estimates of many non-market effects remain as elusive today as when the Second Assessment Report was being prepared, though there are some recent studies that provide some new insights into non-market effects. Several non-market studies have found that warming might be beneficial to at least some sectors. For example, several outdoor recreation studies have found that warming increases summer recreation and that these benefits outweigh reductions in winter recreation (Pendleton and Mendelsohn, 1998; Loomis and Crespi, 1999; Mendelsohn and Markowski, 1999). Hedonic wage studies in both Europe and the United States suggest that people prefer warmer climates (Maddison, 2001a). At least with moderate warming, there may be large non-market benefits accruing to people living in mid- and high-latitude countries. Of course, these benefits might not extend to people living in the low latitudes so that the global impact is ambiguous.

The non-market studies are also notorious for leaving out adaptation. Although it may be expensive to manipulate the natural ecosystems of the entire world to facilitate new equilibrium ecosystem outcomes, it is reasonable to imagine that special programmes could be developed to focus on endangered species. There is every reason to believe that a concerted effort could substantially limit the number of valuable endangered species lost to warming. Health studies have also conspicuously omitted adaptations. Despite the fact that these studies have been conducted in Schools of Public Health, there is absolutely no public-health response built into the model estimates. Instead, the research focuses on potential cases of disease and mortality. Including potential cases as actual mortality suggests that health is an important component in damages (Tol and Downing, 2000). However, it is likely that control programmes can limit potential cases from becoming actual cases. American cities in warm climates have avoided losing elderly to heat stress. Developed countries have controlled vector-borne diseases such as malaria from actually causing any deaths. These public health responses would severely reduce the mortality figures implicit in the

Fankhauser (1995), Tol (1995), and Tol and Downing (2000) estimates. There are many reasons to believe that the original estimates of non-market impacts are overestimated by a factor of 10, just like the market impacts.

Taking the impact estimates in Table 2, many authors have relied on a host of integrated assessment models to compute the SCC (see Pearce, 2003b). The estimate of SCC from this literature for this decade ranges from $3 to $195 per ton. However, if we remove estimates that rely on unrealistic discount rates below 2 per cent, we obtain a narrower range of $7–27 with one outlier, which we discuss below (Eyre *et al.*, 1997). Although some of these optimal control results may have been calculated using up-to-date empirical evidence, we argue they most of the higher-end estimates rely on out-of-date impact studies. The new wave of empirical impact studies (see collections in Mendelsohn and Neumann, 1999, and Mendelsohn, 2001b) suggest values that may be an order of magnitude smaller. The SCC for this decade may well be closer to $1–7 per ton. Of course, these values are likely to rise over the next 30 years, but it is very likely that the SCC will remain below $10 for the next three decades.

The Eyre *et al.* (1997) study and the derivative results in Clarkson and Deyes (2002) lie well outside the range considered reasonable in this paper.[3] There are several reasons, as mentioned by Pearce (2003b), why these two studies have probably overestimated damages. First, they give too much credence to scenarios based on very low discount rates. Second, they tend to rely on impact estimates from the early literature that are turning out to be overly pessimistic. Third, they have doubled damages when they occur in poor countries. Several authors have advocated weighting damages to poor countries (Azar, 1999; Tol, 2001) because a disproportionate burden of the damages falls on poor countries. However, doubling the estimated damages of poor countries only distorts the actual damages that the poor countries endure. This leads to slightly more mitigation being done worldwide. In the meantime, the poor countries receive no compensation. If people are concerned about poor countries, the world should consider a serious compensation programme to low-latitude countries. Doubling estimated damages to poor countries leads to inefficient mitigation programmes and no compensation, and should be abandoned.

---

[3] Note that if a country unilaterally adopts an unusually high value for SCC, it will effectively be over-investing into the global commons. It is ironic that the British government is considering such over-investment in the global commons when the political economy theory suggests that the problem most countries will face is under-investment.

Because concentrations of carbon are expected to rise over time and damages will increase with concentrations, there is every reason to believe that the expected value of the SCC will rise over the century. For example, RICE predicts that the SCC will increase from about $5 today to about $65 at the end of the century (Nordhaus and Boyer, 2000). The exact shape of this path, however, becomes more uncertain towards the end of the century. Exactly how the earth's systems will interact with higher concentrations of greenhouse gases is less clear. What sectors will do as climate changes more dramatically is not easily measured. New technologies may change the role of mitigation in reducing emissions. We also do not know how the economy and global population will change. Projections of the SCC in the distant future are highly uncertain.

5. Policy Conclusion

This study has examined the social cost of carbon and explained why the concept is so important to carbon policy. The chapter begins with a description of the economic theory of carbon control. The theory suggests that the SCC should equal the present value of the future stream of global damages caused by a ton of emissions at a particular moment. The SCC should serve as a global target for the marginal cost of mitigation. Countries concerned about the global commons should design mitigation policies that equate the marginal cost of abatement with the SCC. Symmetrically, firms and people should be exempt from any control regulation that exceeds the SCC. It is consequently an extremely important number and not one to be taken lightly.

The theory also suggests that the SCC is the same for all countries. Because emissions are readily mixed in the global atmosphere, it makes no difference where the emission occurs. The emission will cause the same damage and so has the same SCC. Second, the SCC is dynamic and is expected to rise over time. Each SCC value is tied to a particular moment in time and one must be careful not to average SCC values over the century. Third, the SCC is forward looking and requires insights far into the future.

The paper makes it clear that estimating the SCC is difficult. It requires an immense body of scientific literature to be organized in a structured logical sequence to determine the consequences of carbon emissions. This body of information must extend across the entire globe and look far into the future. Partially because it is so difficult, the SCC will also always be uncertain. Natural scientists have only partial understanding of all of the earth's systems. Social scientists know even less about how different sectors will respond to climate change. The places we probably need to understand the most, the high- and low-latitude countries, we understand the least. Peering into what will happen far into the future is hazy at best. However, just because the SCC is uncertain, does not necessarily mean that near-term mitigation should be increased. As Ingham and Ulph comprehensively discuss in this book, policy-makers may well want to use the expected value of the SCC to make decisions.

Despite these problems, the literature has steadfastly moved forward and calculated bold SCC estimates. Starting with the seminal research of Nordhaus (1991), a host of models has subsequently been built to measure the SCC. Pearce *et al.* (1996) led a noble effort to summarize this literature for the Second Assessment Report. A comparable value is notably missing in the Third Assessment Report. A range of values between $7 and $27 per ton has recently been gathered (Pearce, 2003*b*).

This paper argues that even these most recent values of the SCC are probably too high. Climate-sensitive sectors, such as agriculture, will likely shrink relative to GDP over time. Hill-shaped response functions in most sectors suggest that warming will be beneficial as well as harmful, especially for mild warming. Including adaptation more fully has reduced impacts even further. In net, the global damages from warming appear to be about an order of magnitude smaller than was previously thought. Although a great deal of uncertainty still remains about these estimates, the expected value of damages from near-term emissions is considerably smaller. These results imply that the SCC is currently closer to $1–7 per ton. Although it will rise over time as carbon accumulates, there is every reason to expect that the SCC will remain below $10 per ton for the next 30 years.

Viewed from another perspective, the low SCC suggested in this paper is a blessing for policy-makers responsible for carbon control. The results suggest that there is time for efficient programmes to be designed for the future. Crash programmes that impose very high burdens can be avoided. Negotiators have time to work out international agreements. Countries have time to experiment with alternative control approaches. There is time to find effective long-term solutions before SCC values rise to the point where more stringent controls are needed.

7

The Marginal Damage Costs of Carbon-dioxide Emissions

RICHARD S. J. TOL*

1. Introduction

Estimates of the marginal damage costs of carbon-dioxide (CO_2) emissions are a welcome input into policy advice. Never a prescription, marginal-damage-cost estimates provide guidance to the intensity of a policy, and provides transparency and consistency, and hence accountability to policy choices. To put it differently, marginal-damage-cost estimates reduce the arbitrariness of policy goals. In theory, the marginal damage costs should be equal to the tax on carbon, to the price of tradable permits, or to the marginal costs of emission reduction. In practice, the carbon tax (etc.) should not be too far from the estimated marginal damage costs because otherwise environmental and economic objectives would be too far out of step with each other. In that sense, an estimate of the marginal damage costs provides a yardstick for climate policy. At the same time, it allows for the coordination of climate, energy, transport, and other policies. This is important for economic efficiency, but also for accountability. Why would CO_2 emissions from cars be treated differently from power plants emissions? Finally, in explicitly choosing a number, a government is forced to justify its policy and make public its deliberations on why it considers climate change to be a problem of a certain seriousness, but not more serious nor less serious.

* Hamburg, Vrije, and Carnegie Mellon Universities.

UK Defra, the US National Science Foundation through the Center for Integrated Study of the Human Dimensions of Global Change (SBR-9521914), and the Michael Otto Foundation for Environmental Protection provided welcome financial support. An earlier version of this paper was presented at the International Workshop on the Social Costs of Carbon, London, 7 July 2003. Many there gave valuable comments. Any errors and all opinions are mine.

The marginal damage costs of CO_2 emissions are defined as the net present value of the difference in monetized climate-change impacts induced by an infinitesimally small change in current emissions of CO_2. Estimates of the marginal damage costs, therefore, suffer from all the drawbacks from which estimates of the welfare effects of climate change suffer, that is, uncertainties about future emissions, uncertainties about climate change, uncertainties about climate-change impacts, incompleteness of impact estimates, uncertainties about adaptation, uncertainties in valuation, uncertainties in future vulnerabilities, problems of extrapolating impact and value estimates from one place and time to other places and times, and problems of aggregation across different sectors and countries. Marginal-damage-cost estimates depend strongly on the choice of discount rate, because they reflect the additional *future* damage costs owing to small changes in *current* emissions. Estimates of the marginal damage costs are also particularly sensitive to uncertainties in the carbon cycle. Marginal damage costs are typically approximated by normalized incremental damage costs—that is, with the difference between two almost identical emissions scenarios. The uncertainties about the total impact of climate change are perfectly correlated between the two emissions scenarios; the uncertainties about the carbon cycle, on the other hand, determine how far apart the scenarios are.

Because of all these uncertainties and complexities, some have argued—spoken rather than written (van den Bergh, 2004, is an exception)—that the marginal damage costs of CO_2 emissions are unknown, perhaps even unknowable. I do not share that view. Although the exact marginal damage cost is unknown at the present time, it is certainly possible to put upper and lower limits on the estimated marginal damage costs, and even to come up with some sort of best guess. Furthermore, it is possible to analyse the structure of marginal-damage-cost estimates, so that we know which assumptions and value judgements lead to higher estimates, and which to lower ones. This implies that there is room for political judgement, but not unlimited room.

The next section discusses the uncertainty about the marginal damage costs of CO_2. Section 3 continues with aggregation over time, better known as discounting. Section 4 discusses aggregation over spaces. Section 5 investigates the relationship between development and vulnerability. Section 6 continues this investigation by looking at the trade-off between development and vulnerability. Section 7 concludes.

Figure 1
The Uncertainty about the Marginal Damage Costs of Carbon-dioxide Emissions

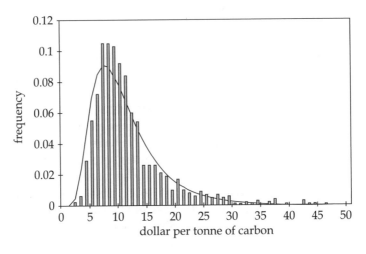

Notes: The figure displays the results of a 1,000 runs Monte Carlo analysis (bars) and a fitted lognormal distribution (line). Emissions are in the period 1995–2004. The consumption discount rate is 3 per cent.
Source: Tol (1999).

2. Uncertainty

Figure 1 (from Tol, 1999) illustrates the parametric uncertainty about the marginal damage costs of CO_2. Note that the uncertainty is right-skewed, that is, negative surprises are more likely than positive surprises of equal size. This is because many of the uncertainties about the natural system are asymmetric; for instance, the best-guess climate sensitivity is a global warming of 2.5°C for a doubling of the atmospheric concentration of CO_2, with an uncertainty range of 1.5–4.5°C. Another reason is that many dose-response relationships are more than linear; for example, warming that is twice as rapid does more than twice as much damage. The right-skewed uncertainty implies that the expected value of the marginal damage costs exceeds the best guess. For welfare analysis, the expected value matters more than the best guess, and studies that have compared the two are unanimous in concluding that the expected value is larger than the best guess. See Tol (2003a) for a further discussion.

The uncertainty as described in Figure 1 is based on a single study, using a single model based on a single set of estimates. The uncertainty in Figure 1 is the parametric uncertainty within a single mind-set.

Figure 1 thus underestimates the true uncertainties, as it does not include alternative yet valid views on the controversial assumptions that need to be made in order to estimate the marginal damage costs of CO_2. A more appropriate way of estimating the uncertainty about the marginal damage costs of CO_2 emissions is to look at all available estimates in a meta-analysis. In Tol (2003b), I collect 103 estimates from 28 studies. As one would expect, the estimates vary considerably; the highest estimate is \$1,666/tonne carbon (tC), the lowest –\$7/tC. The reasons behind this wide range are differences in scenarios, impact estimates, aggregation, and discounting. Another, perhaps surprising, reason is that there are differences in methods. Some estimate the marginal damage costs along a business-as-usual scenario, while others use an optimal control path; more worryingly, some authors use average costs as an approximation for marginal damage costs. Some studies report a confidence interval, others a complete probability density function (PDF); for those studies that do not estimate the uncertainty (unfortunately, this is the majority), I imputed a PDF. The individual PDFs combine to form a joint PDF, based on vote-counting with various alternative ways of weighting the marginal-damage-cost estimates for quality and appropriateness.

Figure 2 shows the joint PDF. The characteristics of the PDF depend on the weighting of the votes. If all estimates count equally, the best-guess estimate is \$1.5/tC, the expectation is \$129/tC, and the 90th percentile \$220/tC. However, if only peer-reviewed studies are included, the expectation falls to \$50/tC and the 90th percentile to \$125/tC. Clearly, the higher marginal-damage-cost estimates have not been peer-reviewed, either because the peer-review process is biased or, perhaps more likely, because higher estimates are of lower quality. Interestingly, the best-guess estimate increases to \$5/tC; one paper in the grey literature claims that the marginal damage costs of CO_2 is \$1–2/tC. Figure 3 shows the alternative PDFs.

3. Aggregation Over Time

Figure 3 also illustrates another important sensitivity. A large part of the uncertainty about the marginal damage costs is due to the choice of discount rate.[1] The 90 per cent is \$165/tC for all studies, but only \$35/tC for those studies with a 3 per cent discount rate, rising to \$125/tC for a 1 per cent discount rate, and to \$755/tC for a 0 per cent discount rate

---

[1] I use the word 'discount rate' as the utility discount rate, or the pure rate of time preference; in order to get the consumption discount rate, add the consumption elasticity of marginal utility times the growth rate of consumption.

Figure 2
The Probability Density Functions of 88 Estimates of the Marginal Damage Costs of Carbon-dioxide Emissions (grey) and the Combined Probability Density Function (black)

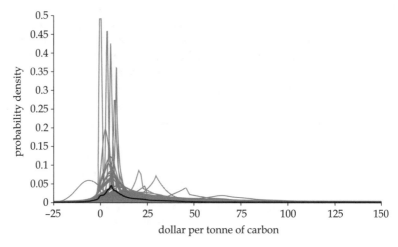

Source: Tol (2003*b*).

or lower. The discussion on the choice of discount rate has been lively, but to me the bottom line is that a government should use the same discount rate for all its projects, and that the government discount rate should not deviate too much from the preferred social discount rate of its citizens. These two rules seem to preclude very low discount rates, and thus high marginal damage costs.

Figure 4 further demonstrates the sensitivity of marginal-damage-cost estimates to discounting, turning once again to a single set of estimates, due to Tol and Heinzow (2003). A low discount rate reflects care for posterity, the crucial component of sustainable development; if we do not care for posterity, we should not care about climate change. However, day-to-day decisions on investments in companies, infrastructure, education, and pensions reveal a higher discount rate than is compatible with sustainability. Using a low discount rate for climate change, but a high discount rate for other policies would violate the internal consistency and accountability principles laid out in the introduction. Overhauling all policies because of climate change would be infeasible, and may not be desirable. Recently, theory has advanced to combine higher discount rates in the short run with lower discount rates in the longer run. Some authors derive this from observations (Henderson and Bateman, 1995; Heal, 1997). Others derive declining discount rates from uncertainty or heterogeneity. Intuitively, if one

Figure 3
The Combined Cumulative Probability Function for All Studies (grey— both panels), for All Peer-reviewed Studies (black—top panel), and for Studies Using a 3, 1, and 0 per cent Utility Discount Rate (black—bottom panel)

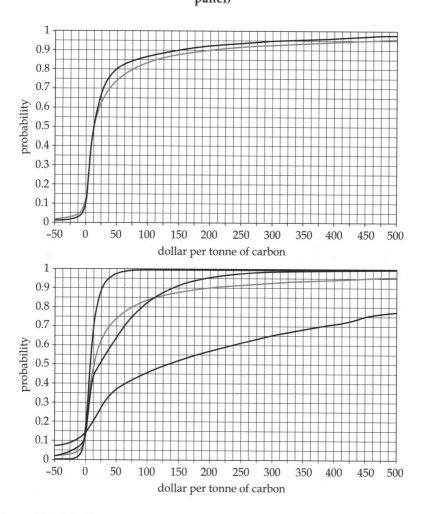

Source: Tol (2003*b*).

takes the average of alternative, exponential discount factors, then the discount factors based on lower discount rates become more and more dominant as time progresses. This is equivalent to using a discount rate that falls over time.[2]

[2] A peculiar implication is that a social planner should suffer from time illusion, even if the people he or she represents are time consistent.

Figure 4
The Sensitivity of the Marginal Damage Costs of Carbon-dioxide
Emissions to Discounting

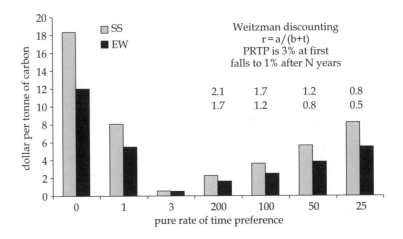

Notes: The three bars to the left use exponential discounting with a discount rate of 0, 1, and 3 per cent per year, respectively. The four bars to the right use Weitzman discounting; the utility discount rate starts at 3 per cent per year and falls to 1 per cent after 200, 100, 50, and 25 years, respectively; the numbers above the bars show the equivalent exponential discount rate after 50 and 100 years. The grey bars show the results for simple summation (SS); the black bars use equity weighting (EW).
Source: Tol and Heinzow (2003).

Besides conventional exponential discounting, Figure 4 includes Weitzman's (2001) γ-discounting as well. This form of discounting reconciles high discount rates for decisions with short time horizons with low discount rates for decisions with long time horizons, based on arguments of uncertainty. The estimates of the marginal damage costs under Weitzman discounting lie somewhere in between the cost estimates for a 3 per cent discount rate (the anchoring point for the short run) and a 1 per cent discount rate (the anchoring point for the long run) depending on how far into the future one puts the anchor for the long run. This is as expected.

4. Aggregration over Countries

Aggregation of impacts over countries with different *per capita* income is another 'ethical parameter' which is important in the estimation of the marginal damage costs of CO_2 emissions. Although it is tempting to add up the dollar estimates of country impacts, this would be inconsistent with the views that cost–benefit analysis is approximate welfare analysis, and that money is a measure of preferences rather than a source of utility. In its simplest form, 'equity weighting' corrects for the fact that a dollar is worth more to a poor man than to a rich man. However, equity weighting can also be used to reflect a desire for reallocating wealth. In the meta-analysis, the mean of the studies that use 'equity weighting' is $101/tC, while the mean of the other studies is only $90/tC. With equity weighting, one puts a higher weight on the impacts to countries with below-average *per capita* income. As such countries are generally more vulnerable, equity weighting tends to increase impact estimates. It is a common misconception, however, that this is necessarily the case, a point already made in the first papers on equity weighting in climate change (Fankhauser *et al.*, 1997, 1998).

Figure 4 has marginal-damage-cost estimates both with and without equity weighting. The equity weighted estimates are *lower*, contrary to expectations. The explanation is found in Figure 5, which shows the results of a sensitivity analysis of health-impact valuation. Health impacts are important, but they are ambiguous. Besides negative impacts owing to expanding malaria, dengue fever, and heat stress, there are positive impacts owing to declining schistosomiasis and cold stress. Whether health impacts are positive or negative on balance, depends on time, location, and valuation. Figure 5 varies the valuation of health impacts. There are two basic ways to value a premature death. If one values a premature death on the basis of the value of a statistical life, then all premature deaths are equal. That is, it does not matter whether a 7 year old or a 77 year old dies, the loss to society is the same. This reflects current medical practice and, albeit weakly, the people's behaviour. The alternative way to value premature deaths is to use the value of a life-year lost. That is, the death of someone who could expect to live another 10 years is twice as bad as the death of someone with a life expectancy of 5 years. Although at odds with observations, this method is preferred by the ExternE network, which encompasses the European establishment on energy and transport externalities.

If health is valued on the basis of the value of a statistical life, cardiovascular and respiratory diseases dominate, and these on balance become less severe owing to climate change. The higher the value, the lower the marginal damage cost; this is less pronounced when using equity weights, as the bulk of the avoided cold deaths are in temperate and rich regions. However, cardiovascular and respiratory diseases are diseases of the elderly. If one values health impacts on the basis the value of a life-year lost, the above effect becomes less pronounced. The income elasticity of the willingness to pay for avoiding mortality risks is also important, and again ambiguous. As the valuation of health risks

Figure 5

The Sensitivity of Estimates of the Marginal Damage Costs of Carbon-dioxide Emissions to Variations in Health Valuation

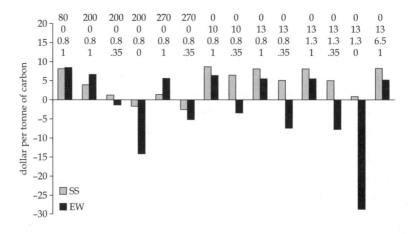

Notes: The first number gives the value of a statistical life, the second number the value of a life-year lost, the third the value of a life-year diseased, and the fourth the income elasticity of the willingness to pay to avoid health risks. The grey bars are based on simple summation, the black on equity weights.

Source: After Tol and Heinzow (2003).

is based on studies in the OECD, this elasticity is used to extrapolate health values both through space and through time. A lower elasticity, therefore, implies higher values in developing countries, but also lower values in the future. As positive health impacts dominate in the short run, lower elasticities imply lower marginal-damage-cost estimates; this effect is much stronger with equity weighting.

5. Development and Vulnerability

It is clear from the discussion above that underdevelopment and vulnerability to climate change are closely correlated. This is generally acknowledged. However, this also implies that vulnerability to climate change will considerably change in the future, which is often over-looked, at least in quantitative analyses. Figure 6 shows the results of a sensitivity analysis to the parameters that govern vulnerability change. The speed of penetration of air conditioning turns out to be the most important determinant of vulnerability, or at least when one measures vulnerability as relative monetary impact. Figure 6 also shows the sensitivity of the marginal damage costs to the sensitivity of

Figure 6
The Sensitivity of the Marginal Damage Costs of Carbon-dioxide Emissions to Development

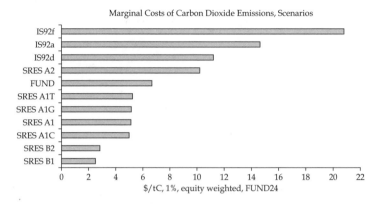

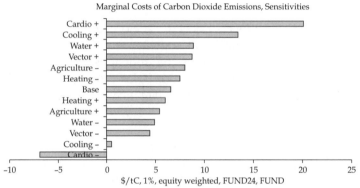

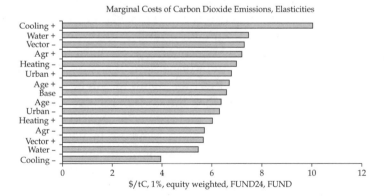

Notes: In the top panel, development scenarios are varied; in the middle panel, the climate sensitivities of impact sectors are varied; in the bottom panel, the income elasticities of these impact sectors are varied.
Source: Tol and Heinzow (2003).

Figure 7
**Market Damages (right axis, upper lines) and Warming (left axis, lower
lines) According to Three Alternative Scenarios**

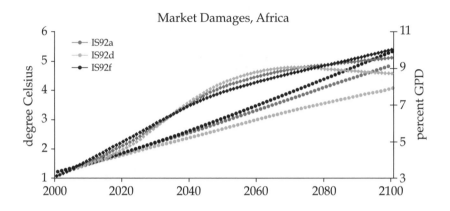

Market Damages, Africa

the sectors that are most subject to socio-economic development.
Again, air conditioning stands out, together with health care and water
resources. Finally, Figure 6 shows the dependence of marginal-damage-cost estimates on the scenario. Scenarios differ in their emissions,
but also in population sizes and *per-capita* income. Generally speaking,
scenarios with lower emissions lead to lower marginal-damage-cost
estimates.

Figure 7 shows that this is true only in general terms. Figure 7
displays the aggregate costs of climate change to Africa for three
scenarios, viz. IS92a, IS92d, and IS92f. At first, impacts are highest
under IS92f and lowest under IS92d, corresponding to the emissions
levels. Then, however, impacts reverse, with IS92f the lowest and IS92d
the highest. The reason is agriculture and human health. IS92f has
higher emissions but also higher economic growth, so that health care
improves and agriculture dwindles relatively fast. Still later, the
situation reverses again, and IS92f has again the highest impacts. The
reason is that the IS92d has reached the stage of relative invulnerability
of health and agriculture as well, and the IS92f scenario sees a lot more
air conditioning. Obviously, the exact numbers in Figure 7 are very
uncertain, but the qualitative insights are not: vulnerability is complex.
The simple picture painted by early climate-change impact studies is not
very realistic, and may lead to misleading results.

For instance, it is unlikely that the future marginal damage costs of
CO_2 emissions have a simple relation to the current marginal damage
costs—as has been proposed by some. Figure 8 shows marginal-
damage-cost estimates in future periods. Indeed, marginal damage

Figure 8
Estimates of the Marginal Damage Costs of Carbon-dioxide Emissions at Various Points in Time, for Three Alternative Utility Discount Rates and With and Without Equity Weighting

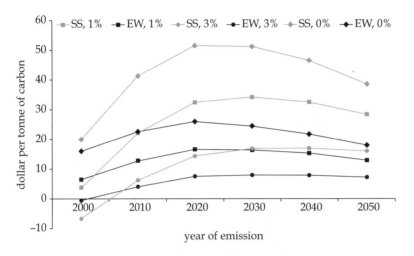

costs may go up as well as down as time progresses, and do so slower and faster depending on the discount rate, aggregation method, and (results not shown) scenario.

6. Development versus Abatement

The fact that marginal-damage-cost estimates depend on projections of future vulnerability has long been known, although the quantification is of more recent date.

One implication was formulated by Schelling (1992, 1995). If vulnerability to climate change is a result of underdevelopment, should money be spent on development aid rather than emission reduction? Tol (2002c) seeks to answer this question from the narrow perspective of the reduction of climate-change impacts. Figure 9 shows the results for Africa. Let us assume that emission abatement costs $1/tC, and that that money can be spent on development aid instead. Both emission reduction and development aid reduce climate-change impacts. Figure 9 shows the ratio of the two reductions under a range of parameter choices and scenarios. In almost all cases, development aid is more effective in reducing impacts than is emission reduction. If emission abatement costs $20/tC, a more realistic estimate, the numbers of Figure 9 should be multiplied by 20—and development aid overwhelmingly

Figure 9
The Sensitivity of the Marginal Damage Costs of Carbon-dioxide Emissions Relative to the Returns on Development Aid (measured in reduced climate-change impacts)

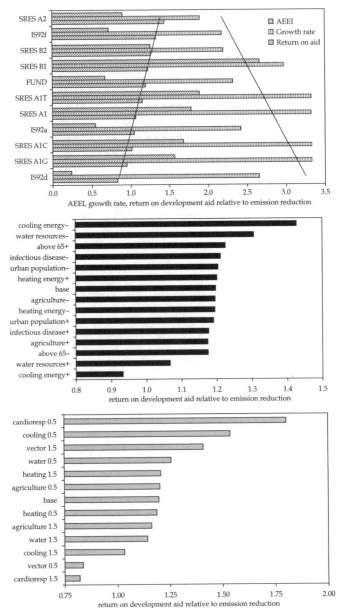

Notes: In the top panel, development scenarios are varied; in the middle panel, the climate sensitivities of impact sectors are varied; in the bottom panel, the income elasticities of these impact sectors are varied.
Source: Tol (2002).

dominates emission reduction. However, if only 5 per cent of development aid is effective in stimulating economic growth, the numbers should be divided by 20 again. For other regions, the situation is more mixed (results not shown). Latin America is in almost the same position as Africa, but the developing countries of Asia are largely undecided or seem to prefer emission reduction. Schelling's conjecture can be confirmed, but only for the least developed and stagnant developing countries.

7. Conclusion

In sum, estimates of the marginal damage costs of CO_2 are uncertain, but not so uncertain that any number goes. For every reason to increase the current best guesses, there is a reason to reduce the estimates. However, caution is warranted as the uncertainty seems right-skewed. High marginal-damage-cost estimates are typically based on strong ethical positions, which are often at odds with the accepted moral standards, and may be logically flawed. A marginal damage cost of CO_2 of some $15/tC seems justified; marginal-damage-costs estimates of $50/tC or more cannot be defended with our current knowledge. A substantial part of the marginal damage costs is due to impacts in developing countries. Regulating CO_2 emissions up to the full Pigou tax would constitute an act of altruism, which may be misplaced as the beneficiaries would prefer the money to be invested otherwise.

Although the current literature on the economic impacts of climate change in general and the marginal damage costs of CO_2 is considerably richer than it was 10 years ago—which allows us to distinguish more confidently between robust findings and less robust ones—much remains to be done. The science of climate change and its impacts are far from perfect. Perhaps most urgently, the impact on water resources is still not well under control. The economics of climate-change impact are also still at an early stage. Particularly, the valuation of ecosystem change and species extinction remains a formidable challenge. Some impacts have been omitted altogether, such as the effects of climate change on amenity and tourism. Large-scale disruptions of the climate system, such as a collapse of the West Antarctic Ice Sheet or the thermohaline circulation, are omitted too, although first assessments of the impacts of a shutdown of the thermohaline circulation do not point at dramatic impacts (Link and Tol, forthcoming). Interactions between climate-change impacts and their higher-order implications are another missing area. On all of these issues, progress is being made and, over time, the enhanced knowledge will be used for new estimates of the

Figure 10
Estimates of the Marginal Damage Costs of CO_2 as a Function of the Date
of Publication of the Estimate

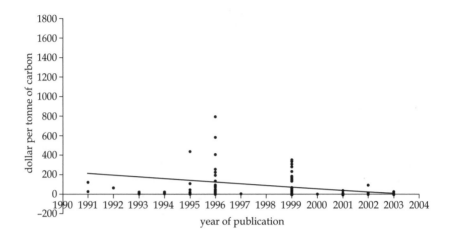

Source: Data are from Tol (2003*b*).

marginal damage costs of CO_2. Progress would be faster, however, if more of the considerable amounts of funds for climate-change research would be devoted to the economics of the impacts of climate change.

Some of the missing issues are clearly negative. An example is the 5–6 metre sea-level rise resulting from a collapse of the West Antarctic Ice Sheet. This may happen, but the chance is small, and if it does happen, it will be in a remote future. The effect on the marginal damage costs is likely to be small. Other missing impacts, such as amenity and tourism, are positive for some and negative for others; adding these would probably increase the disparity of impact estimates, but not increase the total or marginal damage-cost estimate by a lot. Current policy, however, should be based on current knowledge. The current estimate of the marginal damage costs of CO_2 is uncertain, but this uncertainty is limited. What is more, the marginal-damage-cost esti-mates have decreased over time (cf. Figure 10). Although one cannot extrapolate this trend, it does not suggest that current estimates understate the marginal damage costs.

Part Three: Tradable Permits and Carbon Taxes

8

The Tradable-permits Approach to Protecting the Commons: Lessons for Climate Change

TOM TIETENBERG*

1. Introduction

(a) *Background*

The atmosphere is but one of many commons and climate change is but one example of over-exploitation of the commons. An approach employed increasingly for coping with the problem of rationing access to the commons involves the use of tradable permits. Applications of this approach have spread to many different types of resources and many different countries. A recent survey found nine applications in air-pollution control, 75 in fisheries, three in managing water resources, five in controlling water pollution, and five in land-use control (OECD, 1999, Appendix 1, pp. 18–19). And that survey failed to include many current applications, including those that have sprung up in response to the Kyoto Protocol.

The logic behind this rather remarkable transition is quite simple. One of the insights derived from the empirical literature is that traditional command-and-control regulatory measures, which depend upon government agencies to define both the goals and the means of meeting them, are, in many cases, insufficiently protective of the value of the resources.

A principal theorem of environmental economics demonstrates that, under specific conditions, an appropriately defined tradable-permit system can minimize the cost of reaching a predefined environmental target (Baumol and Oates, 1971). In a perfectly competitive market,

* Colby College, Maine.

This paper draws upon previous studies completed for the National Research Council in the United States and the OECD in Paris. The author is indebted to Nick Johnstone of the OECD for helpful comments on a previous draft and to Dieter Helm, David Pearce, and three anonymous referees for very useful comments.

permits will flow towards their highest-valued use. Those that would receive lower value from using the permits (owing to lower abatement costs, for example) have an incentive to trade them to someone who would value them more. The trade benefits both parties. The seller reaps more from the sale than s/he could from using the permit and the buyer gets more value from the permit than s/he pays for it.

A rather remarkable corollary (Montgomery, 1972) holds that this theorem is true regardless of how the permits are initially allocated among competing claimants, including whether they are auctioned off or allocated free of charge. Furthermore, when permits are allocated free of charge, *any* particular initial allocation rule can still support a cost-effective allocation. Again, the logic behind this result is rather straightforward. Whatever the initial allocation, the transferability of the permits allows them ultimately to flow to their highest-valued uses. Since those uses do not depend on the initial allocation, all initial allocations result in the same outcome and that outcome is cost-effective.

The potential significance of this corollary is huge. It implies that with tradable permits the resource manager can use the initial allocation to solve other goals (such as political feasibility or equity) without sacrificing cost-effectiveness. In Alaskan fisheries, for example, some of the quota has been allocated to communities (rather than individuals) to attempt to protect community interests (Ginter, 1995).

As compelling as this theoretical case may seem, these approaches have been controversial. Consider just three examples from the US experience. In air-pollution control, a legal challenge was brought in Los Angeles during June 1997 by the Los Angeles-based Communities for a Better Environment. (Tietenberg, 1995). In fisheries, a legal challenge was brought against the halibut/sablefish tradable-permits system in Alaska (Black, 1997) and Congress imposed a moratorium on the further use of a tradable-permits approach in US fisheries (National Research Council Committee to Review Individual Fishing Quotas, henceforth NRCC, 1999). Though both legal cases were ultimately thrown out and the moratorium has been lifted, these situations demonstrate the controversies that can lie just beneath the surface.

(b) *Policy Context and Overview*

The 1992 United Nations Framework Convention on Climate Change (UNFCCC) recognized the principle of global cost-effectiveness of emission reduction and thus opened the way for tradable permits. As it did not fix a binding emission target for any country, the need to invest in emission reduction either at home or abroad was not pressing.

In December 1997, though, industrial countries and countries with economies in transition agreed to legally binding emission targets at the Kyoto Conference and negotiated a legal framework as a protocol to the UNFCCC—the Kyoto Protocol. The Kyoto Protocol took effect in February 2005.

Together, Annex I countries must reduce their emissions of six greenhouse gases by at least 5 per cent below 1990 levels over the commitment period, 2008–12. The six greenhouse gases listed in Annex A are: CO_2, methane, nitrous oxide, hydro-fluorocarbons (HFCs), perfluorocarbons (PFCs), and sulphur hexafluoride.

The Kyoto Protocol authorizes three cooperative implementation mechanisms that involve tradable permits. These include emission trading, joint implementation, and the Clean Development Mechanism (CDM).

- 'Emissions trading' allows trading of 'assigned amounts' (national quotas established by the Kyoto Protocol) among Annex I nations (countries listed in Annex I of the UNFCCC of the Kyoto Protocol), primarily the industrialized nations and the economies in transition).
- Under 'joint implementation', Annex I parties can receive emissions-reduction credit when they help to finance specific projects that reduce net emissions in another Annex I party country.
- The CDM enables Annex I Parties to finance emission-reduction projects in the countries of non-Annex I parties and receive certified emission reductions (CERs) for doing so.

These programmes have, in turn, spawned others. The European Parliament passed a bill capping European industry's CO_2 output and letting firms trade the allowed emissions. From January 2005 many plants in the oil-refining, smelting, steel, cement, ceramics, glass, and paper sectors will need special permits to emit CO_2. Individual countries, such as the United Kingdom and Denmark, have created their own national trading programmes.

Individual companies are even involved. BP, an energy company, has established company-wide goals and a trading programme to help individual units within the company to meet those goals. Despite the fact that the United States has not signed the Kyoto Protocol, many American companies, states, and municipalities have accepted voluntary caps on CO_2 and methane emissions and are using trading to facilitate meeting those goals. The Chicago Climate Exchange has been set up to facilitate these trades. The unprecedented scope of these climate-change trading programmes breaks new ground in terms of geographic coverage, the number of participants, and the types of polluting gases covered.

This chapter attempts to draw together what we have learned about tradable permits in practice that might offer some insights to the climate-change implementation process as it unfolds. It reviews the experience with three main applications of tradable-permit systems — air-pollution control, water supply, and fisheries management — as well as some unique programmes, such as the US programme to mitigate the loss of wetlands and the programme in the Netherlands to control the damage from water pollution owing to manure spreading. The purpose of this review is to exploit the large variation in implementation experience that can be gleaned from this rich variety of applications. This experience provides the basis for formulating some general lessons about the effectiveness of these systems in practice and their application to the general problem of climate change.

2. A Review of *Ex-post* Evaluations of Tradable-permit Systems

This assessment of the outcomes of these systems focuses on three major categories of effects. The first is implementation feasibility. A proposed policy regime cannot perform its function if it cannot be implemented or if its main protective mechanisms are so weakened by the implementation process that it is rendered ineffective. What matters to policy-makers is not how a policy regime works in principle, but how it works in practice. The second category seeks to answer the question 'How much environmental protection did it offer not only to the targeted resource, but also to other resources that might have been affected either positively or negatively by its implementation?' Finally, what were the economic effects on those who either directly or indirectly use the resource?

(a) *Implementation Feasibility*

Until recently, the historic record on tradable permits seemed to indicate that resorting to a tradable-permits approach usually only occurred after other, more familiar, approaches had been tried and failed. In essence, the adjustment costs of implementing a new system with which policy administrators have little personal experience are typically perceived as so large that they can only be justified when the benefits have risen sufficiently to justify the transition (Libecap, 1990).

For example, most fisheries that have turned to these policies have done so only after a host of alternative input and output controls have failed to stem the destructive pressure being placed upon the fishery. A similar story can be told for air-pollution control. The offset air-pollution control policy, introduced in the USA during the 1970s, owes its birth to an inability to find any other policy capable of reconciling the desire to allow economic growth with the desire to improve the quality of the air.

It is also clear from the historical record that not every attempt to introduce a tradable-permit approach has been successful. In air-pollution control, attempts to establish a tradable-permits approaches have failed in Poland (Zylicz, 1999) and Germany (Scharer, 1999). The initial attempts to introduce a sulphur-dioxide (SO_2) trading system also failed in the United Kingdom (Sorrell, 1999), although recent attempts to establish a CO_2 programme there have succeeded. Programmes in water-pollution control have generally not been very successful (Hahn and Hester, 1989).

On the other hand, it does appear that the introduction of new tradable-permit programmes becomes easier with familiarity. In the USA, following the very successful lead phase-out programme, new supporters appeared and made it possible to pass the sulphur-allowance programme. The introduction of the various flexibility mechanisms into the Kyoto Protocol was facilitated by the successful experience with the US sulphur-allowance programme, among others. And the recent introduction of tradable-permits systems in several European countries and the EU itself was precipitated by the opportunities provided by the Kyoto Protocol.

It also seems quite clear that, to date at least, using a grandfathering approach to the initial allocation has been a necessary ingredient in building the political support necessary to implement the approach. Existing users frequently have the power to block implementation, while potential future users do not. This has made it politically expedient to allocate a substantial part of the economic rent that these resources offer to existing users as the price of securing their support. While this strategy reduces the adjustment costs to existing users, it generally raises them for new users.

One tendency that seems to arise in some new applications of this concept is to place severe restrictions on its operation as a way to quell administrative fears about possible undesirable, unforeseen outcomes. As Shabman (2003) points out, this is precisely the case with the US wetlands credit programme. In some cases, and the wetland programme may well be the foremost example, these restrictions are so severe that they cripple the programme, thereby preventing its ultimate evolution to a smoothly operating system. Although with increased familiarity (and comfort) initially imposed restrictions tend to disappear over time, they can severely diminish the early accomplishments of the programmes.

(b) *Environmental Effects*

One common belief about tradable-permit programmes is that their environmental effects are determined purely by the imposition of the aggregate limit, an act that is considered to lie outside the system. Hence, it is believed, the main purpose of the system is to protect the economic value of the resource, not the resource itself.

That is an oversimplification for several reasons. First, whether it is politically possible to set an aggregate limit at all may be a function of the policy intended to achieve it. Second, both the magnitude of that limit and its evolution over time may be related to the policy. Third, the choice of policy regime may affect the level of monitoring and enforcement and non-compliance can undermine the achievements of the limit. Fourth, the policy may trigger environmental effects that are not covered by the limit.

(i) Setting the limit

In general, the evidence seems to suggest that, by lowering compliance costs, tradable-permit programmes facilitate the setting of more stringent caps. In air-trading programmes, the lower costs offered by trading were used in initial negotiations to secure more stringent pollution-control targets (acid-rain and lead phase-out programmes) or earlier deadlines (lead phase-out programme). The air-quality effects from more stringent limits were reinforced by the use of adjusted offset ratios for trades in non-attainment areas. (Offset ratios were required to be greater than 1.0, implying a portion of each acquisition would go for improved air quality.) In addition, environmental groups have been allowed to purchase and retire allowances (acid-rain programme). Retired allowances represent pollution that is authorized, but not emitted.

In fisheries, the institution of individual transferable quotas (ITQs) has sometimes, but not always, resulted in lower (more protective) total allowable catches (TACs). In the Netherlands, for example, the plaice quota was cut in half over time (Davidse, 1999).

(ii) Meeting and enforcing the limit

In theory, the flexibility offered by tradable-permit programmes makes it easier to reach the limit, suggesting the possibility that the limit may be met more often under a tradable-permits system than under the systems that preceded it. In most fisheries, this expectation seems to have been borne out. In the Alaskan halibut and sablefish fisheries, for example, while exceeding the TAC was common before the imposition of an ITQ system, the frequency of excedences dropped significantly after the introduction of the ITQ (NRCC, 1999).

Regardless of how well any tradable-permit system is designed, non-compliance can prevent the attainment of its economic, social, and environmental objectives. Non-compliance not only makes it more difficult to reach stated goals, it sometimes makes it more difficult to know whether the goals are being met.[1]

Although it is true that any management regime raises monitoring and enforcement issues, tradable-permit regimes raise some special issues. One of the most desirable aspects of tradable permits for resource users — their ability to raise income levels for participants — is a two-edged sword because it also raises incentives for non-compliance. In the absence of an effective enforcement system, higher profitability could promote a greater likelihood of illegal activity. Insufficient monitoring and enforcement could also result in failure to keep a tradable-permit system within its environmental limit.[2]

Technology has played an important role in expanding the degree to which monitoring and enforcement needs of a tradable-permits programme can be met at reasonable cost. In the US sulphur-allowance programme (Kruger et al., 1999), both the collection and dissemination of the information derived from the continuous emissions monitors is now handled via the web. Special software has been developed to take individual inputs and to generate information both for the public and for Environmental Protection Agency enforcement activities. According to Kruger et al., the development of this technology has increased administrative efficiency, lowered transactions costs, and provided greater environmental accountability.

The enhanced profitability that accompanies a tradable-permit system can provide a convenient source of financing for monitoring and

---

[1] In fisheries, for example, stock assessments sometimes depend on the size and composition of the catch. If the composition of the landed harvest is unrepresentative of the actual harvest owing to illegal discards, this can bias the stock assessment and the total allowable catch that depends upon it. Not only would true mortality rates be much higher than apparent mortality rates, but the age and size distribution of landed catch would be different from the size distribution of the initial harvest (prior to discards). This is known in fisheries as 'data fouling'.

[2] For example, prior to 1988, the expected positive effects of ITQs did not materialize in the Dutch cutter fisheries, owing to inadequate enforcement. Fleet capacity increased further, the race for fish continued, and the quotas had to be supplemented by input controls, such as a limit on days at sea (NRCC, 1999, p. 176).

enforcement.[3] Sometimes the rent involved in transferable-permit programmes is used to finance superior enforcement systems. In the sulphur-allowance programme, for example, the environmental community demanded (and received) a requirement that continuous emissions-monitoring be installed (and financed) by every covered utility. Coupling this with the rather stringent penalty system has meant 100 per cent compliance. In the Danish system (Pedersen, 2003), which does not rely on continuous emissions-monitoring, the electricity producers pay an administration fee of 0.079 DKK per ton of CO_2 allowance to the Danish Energy Authority to cover the administration costs (verification of CO_2 emissions; control, hearing, and distribution of allowances; operating the registry; monitoring of trading; development of the scheme; etc.).

The rents generated by ITQs have also provided the government with a source of revenue to cover the costs of enforcement and administration. In many of the fisheries in Australia, Canada, Iceland, and New Zealand, industry pays for administration and enforcement with fees levied on quota owners.

A successful enforcement programme also requires a carefully constructed set of sanctions for non-compliance. In the sulphur-allowance programme, generally considered the most successful tradable-permit programme, those found in non-compliance must not only pay a substantial financial penalty, they must also forfeit a sufficient number of future allowances to compensate for the overage. It is also possible to allow only those in compliance to transfer permits. Any egregious violations can lead to forfeiture of the right to participate in the programme.

It is not true, however, that the steepest penalties are the best penalties. Penalties should be commensurate with the danger posed by non-compliance. Penalties that are unrealistically high may not be imposed. Unrealistically high penalties are also likely to consume excessive enforcement resources as those served with penalties seek redress through the appeals process.

One quite different and rather unexpected finding that emerges from *ex-post* evaluation of tradable-permit systems is the degree to which the number of errors in pre-existing emission registries are

---

[3] Not only has the recovery of monitoring and enforcement costs become standard practice in some fisheries (New Zealand, for example), but funding at least some monitoring and enforcement activity out of rents generated by the fishery has already been included as a provision in the most recent amendments to the US Magnuson–Stevens Fishery Conservation and Management Act. The sulphur-allowance programme mandates continuous emissions-monitoring financed by the emitting sources.

brought to light by the need to create accurate registries for tradable-permit schemes (Montero, 2002*a*; Montero *et al.*, 2002; Hartridge, 2003; Pedersen, 2003; Wossink, 2003). Although inadequate inventories plague all quantity-based approaches, tradable permits seem particularly effective at bringing deficiencies to light and providing incentives for the deficiencies to be eliminated.

(iii) Direct effects on the resource

Air-pollution programmes have typically had a very positive effect on reducing emissions. The US programmes to phase out lead and to reduce ozone-depleting gases were designed to eliminate, not merely reduce, pollutants. Both the US programme to control sulphur and RECLAIM (the programme designed to control emissions of oxides of nitrogen (NOx) and oxides of sulphur (SOx) in the greater Los Angeles area) involve substantial reductions in emissions over time.

In the fisheries, what have been the effects on biomass? One specific problem in any quota-based fishery is discards caused by highgrading. Highgrading involves discarding low-valued fish to make room in the quota for higher-valued fish. The discarded fish commonly die. Do the protective aspects of the programme outweigh the potential for highgrading?

The evidence on the overall effect on the fishery has been mixed. On the one hand some rather spectacular successes have been recorded. In the Chilean squat lobster fishery, for example, the exploitable biomass rebounded from a low of about 15,500 tons (prior to ITQs) to a level in 1998 of between 80,000 and 100,000 tons (Bernal and Aliaga, 1999). The herring fishery in Iceland experienced a similar rebound (Runolfsson, 1999).

On the other hand, one review of 37 ITQ or IQ (individual quota) fisheries, found that 24 experienced at least some temporary declines in stocks after instituting the programmes. These were largely attributed to a combination of inadequate information on which to set sufficiently conservative TACs and illegal fishing activity resulting from ineffective enforcement. Interestingly, 20 of the 24 fisheries experiencing declines had additional command-and-control regulations such as closed areas, size/selectivity regulations, trip limits, vessel restrictions, etc. (OECD, 1997, p. 82). These additional regulations were apparently also ineffective in protecting the resource; the problems plaguing ITQs plague more traditional approaches as well.

(iv) Effects on other resources

The resource controlled by the permit programme is frequently not the only resource affected. In water applications, one significant problem has been the protection of non-consumptive uses of water (Young, 2003). In the USA, for example, historically some states have only protected private entitlements to water if water was diverted from the stream and consumed. The entitlements for water left in the stream to promote recreational uses could be confiscated by authorities as they did not meet the definition of a beneficial use. Recent changes in policy and some supportive legal determinations have afforded more protections to these environmental uses of water.

According to Shabman (2003), the wetlands permitting programme has failed to stem the degradation of wetlands. Some reviews have found that the ecological functions, especially for wildlife and habitat, of avoided wetlands and on-site wetlands offsets are compromised by polluted runoff and adverse changes in hydrologic regimes. In some cases, ecological failure resulted from poor construction techniques. In other cases, a promised offsetting restoration project may not have been undertaken at all. In general, the failure to prevent these compromises to the programme can apparently be traced back to limited agency resources available for enforcement.

Leakage provides another possible source of external effects. Leakage occurs when pressure on the regulated resource is diverted to an unregulated, or less regulated, resource, as when fishermen move their boats to another fishery or polluters move their polluting factory to a country with lower environmental standards.

In air-pollution control, several effects transcend the normal boundaries of the programme. In the climate-change programme, for example, it is widely recognized (Ekins, 1996) that the control of greenhouse gases will result in substantial reductions of other air pollutants associated with the combustion of fossil fuels.

In fisheries, two main effects on non-targeted species have been the discard of fish for which no quota is held (bycatch discards) and habitat destruction.

- Bycatch is a problem in many fisheries, regardless of the means of control. The evidence from fisheries on how the introduction of ITQs affects bycatch is apparently mixed. Two reviews found that bycatch may either increase or decrease in ITQ fisheries depending on the fishery (OECD, 1997, p. 83; NRCC, 1999, p. 177).
- Habitat damage occurs when the fishing gear causes damage to the seabed or geological formations that provide habitat for species dwelling on or near the ocean floor. Tradable permits could, in principle, increase or decrease the amount of habitat damage by affecting both the type of gear used and the timing and location of its use. Evidence about this relationship is

extremely limited, but it is certainly true that limiting the size of the harvest does not automatically protect the ecosystem that sustains it.

(c) Economic Effects

Ex-post studies that purportedly tackle the question of economic efficiency typically examine some or all of three rather different concepts: Pareto optimality, cost effectiveness, or market effectiveness. Since these are, in fact, quite different concepts, studies relying on them could come to quite different conclusions, even if they are examining the same programme.

Pareto optimality, or its typical operational formulation, maximizing net benefits, examines whether or not the policy derives all the net benefits from the resource use that are possible. Naturally, this requires a comparison of the costs of the programme with all the benefits achieved, including the value of reduced pollution or conserved resources. Conducting this kind of evaluation is time- and information-intensive and they are apparently rare.

A more common evaluation approach relies on cost-effectiveness, particularly for *ex-ante* studies. This approach typically takes a predefined environmental target as given (such as an emissions cap or a TAC) and examines whether the programme minimizes the cost of reaching that target.[4] Another form is to compare the cost of reaching the target with the programme to the cost of reaching the target with the next most likely alternative. This approach, of course, compares the programme not to an optimal benchmark, but rather to the most pragmatic benchmark.

While the evidence on environmental consequences is mixed (especially for fisheries), the evidence on the economic consequences is clearer. In the presence of adequate enforcement, tradable permits do normally appear to increase the value of the resource (in the case of water and fisheries) or lower the cost of compliance (in the case of emissions reduction).

In air-pollution control, considerable savings in meeting the pollution-control targets have been found (Hahn and Hester, 1989; Tietenberg 1990; Ellerman, 2003; Harrison, 2003). For water, it involves the increase in value brought about by transferring the resources from

---

[4] The demonstration that the traditional regulatory policy was not value-maximizing has two mirror-image implications. It either implies that the same environmental goals could be achieved at lower cost or that better environmental quality could be achieved at the same cost. In air-pollution control, while the earlier programmes were designed to exploit the first implication, later programmes attempted to produce better air quality and lower cost.

lower-valued to higher-valued uses (Easter *et al.*, 1998; Young, 2003). In fisheries, a substantial increase not only results from the higher profitability due to more appropriately scaled capital investments (resulting from the reduction in over-capitalization), but also from the fact that ITQs frequently make it possible to sell a more valuable product at higher prices (fresh fish rather than frozen fish; NRCC, 1999). One review of 22 fisheries found that the introduction of ITQs increased wealth in all 22 (OECD, 1997, p. 83).

In both water and air pollution the transition following the introduction of transferable permits was not from an open-access resource to tradable permits, but rather from a less flexible control regime to a more flexible one. The transition has apparently been accomplished with few adverse employment consequences, though sufficient data to do a comprehensive evaluation on that particular question do not exist (Goodstein, 1996; Berman and Bui, 2001).

The employment consequences for fisheries have been more severe. In fisheries with reasonable enforcement, the introduction of ITQs has usually been accompanied by a considerable reduction in the amount of fishing effort. Normally, this means not only fewer boats, but also less employment. The evidence also suggests, however, that the workers who remain in the industry work more hours during the year and earn more money (NRCC, 1999, p. 101).

The introduction of ITQs in fisheries has also had implications for crew, processors, and communities. Traditionally, in many fisheries, crew are co-venturers in the fishing enterprise, sharing in both the risk and reward. In some cases the move to ITQs has shifted the risk and ultimately shifted the compensation system from a profit-sharing to a wage system. Though this has not generally lowered incomes, it has changed the culture of fishing (McCay *et al.*, 1989; McCay and Creed, 1990).

Secondary industries can be affected by the introduction of tradable permits in a number of ways. Consider, for example, the effects on fish processors. First, the processing sector is typically as overcapitalized as the harvesting sector. Since the introduction of ITQs typically extends the fishing season and spreads out the processing needs of the industry, less processing capacity is needed. In addition, the more leisurely pace of harvesting reduces the bargaining power of processors versus fishers. In some remote areas, such as Alaska, a considerable amount of this processing capital may lose value owing to its immobility (Matulich *et al.*, 1996; Matulich and Sever, 1999).

Communities can be, and in some cases have been, adversely affected when quota held by local resource users is transferred to resource users who operate out of other communities. Techniques developed to mitigate these effects, however, seem to have been at least moderately successful (NRCC, 1999, p. 206).

Generally, market power has not been a significant issue in most permit markets, despite some tendencies toward the concentration of quota. In part this is due to accumulation limits that have been placed on quota holders and the fact that these are typically not markets in which accumulation of quota yields significant monopoly-type powers. In fisheries some concern has been expressed (Palsson, 1998) that the introduction of ITQs will mean the demise of the smaller fishers as they are bought out by larger operations. The evidence does not seem support this concern (NRCC, 1999, p. 84).

Although hard evidence on the point is scarce, a substantial amount of anecdotal evidence is emerging about how tradable-permit programmes can change the way environmental risk is treated within firms (Hartridge, 2003; McLean, 2003). This evidence suggests that environmental management used to be relegated to the tail end of the decision-making process. Historically, the environmental risk manager was not involved in the most fundamental decisions about product design, production processes, selection of inputs, etc. Rather s/he was simply confronted with the decisions already made and told to keep the firm out of trouble. This particular organizational assignment of responsibilities inhibits the exploitation of one potentially important avenue of risk reduction — pollution prevention.

Because tradable permits put both a cap and a price on environmental risks, corporate financial people tend to get involved. Furthermore, as the costs of compliance rise in general, environmental costs become worthy of more general scrutiny. Reducing environmental risk can become an important component of the bottom line. Given its anecdotal nature, the evidence on the extent of organizational changes that might be initiated by tradable permits should be treated more as a hypothesis to be tested than a firm result, but its potential importance is large.

Economic theory treats markets as if they emerge spontaneously and universally as needed. In practice, the applications examined in this review point out that participants frequently require some experience with the programme before they fully understand (and behave effectively) in the market for permits. This finding seems potentially important for the implementation of the Kyoto Protocol's CDM.

3. Lessons for Programme Design

As new tradable-permit programmes are being defined to meet the obligations of the Kyoto Protocol at both the national and the EU levels, examining the lessons from previous applications might prevent repeating the mistakes of the past or the need to reinvent the wheel. What have these lessons been?

(a) *The Baseline Issue*

In general, tradable-permit programmes fit into one of two categories: credit programmes or cap-and-trade programmes. Air-pollution control systems and water have examples of both types. Fisheries tradable-permit programmes are all of the cap-and-trade variety.

- Credit trading, the approach taken in the US Emissions Trading Programme (the earliest programme), allows emission reductions above and beyond baseline legal requirements to be certified as tradable credits (Tietenberg, 1985). The baseline for credits in that programme was provided by traditional technology-based standards.
- In a cap-and-trade programme a total resource access limit (the cap) is defined and then allocated among users. Compliance is established by simply comparing actual use with the assigned firm-specific cap as adjusted by any acquired or sold permits.

Establishing the baseline for credit programmes in the absence of an existing permitting system can be very difficult. The basic requirement in the Kyoto Protocol is 'additionality'. In other words, to become tradable credits the reductions must be surplus to what would have been done otherwise. Deciding whether created entitlements are 'surplus' requires the existence of a baseline against which the reductions can be measured. When emissions are reduced below this baseline, the amount of the reduction that is 'excess' can be certified as surplus.

Defining procedures that assure that the baselines do not allow unjustified credits is no small task. A pilot programme for Activities Implemented Jointly, which was established at the first Conference of the Parties in 1995, is useful for demonstrating the difficulties of assuring 'additionality'. Results under this programme indicate that a greenhouse-gas credit-trading programme that requires a showing of additionality can involve very high transaction costs and introduce considerable *ex-ante* uncertainty about the actual reductions that could be achieved (Rentz, 1996, 1998; Jepma, 2003).

Many credit-based programmes keep a large element of the previous regulatory structure in place. For example, some programmes require regulatory pre-approval for all transfers (i.e. wetlands credits and water trading). In addition, other specific design features, such as the opt-in in the sulphur-allowance programme (Ellerman, 2003) and the use of relative targets in the UK Emissions Trading System (Hartridge, 2003), also add administrative complexity.

Theory would lead us to believe that cap-and-trade systems would be much more likely to achieve the efficiency and environmental goals and the evidence emerging from *ex-post* evaluations seems to support that conclusion (Shabman *et al.*, 2002). This is of considerable potential importance in climate-change policy since only one of the three Kyoto programmes (Emissions Trading) is a cap-and-trade programme.

(b) *The Legal Nature of the Entitlement*

Although the popular literature frequently refers to the tradable-permit approach as 'privatizing the resource' (Spulber and Sabbaghi, 1993; Anderson, 1995), in most cases it does not actually do that. Rather, it privatizes the right to access the resource to a pre-specified degree.

Economists have consistently argued that tradable permits should be treated as secure property rights to protect the incentive to invest in the resource. Confiscation of rights or simply insecure rights could undermine the entire process.

The environmental community, on the other hand, has just as consistently argued that the air, water, and fish belong to the people and, as a matter of ethics, they should not become private property (Kelman, 1981). In this view, no end could justify the transfer of a community right into a private one (McCay, 1998).

The practical resolution of this conflict in most US tradable-permit settings has been to attempt to give 'adequate' (as opposed to complete) security to the permit holders, while making it clear that permits are not property rights.[5] For example, according to the Title of the US Clean Air Act dealing with the sulphur-allowance programme: 'An allowance under this title is a limited authorization to emit sulfur dioxide. . . . Such allowance does not constitute a property right' (104 Stat 2591).

In practice, this means that, although administrators are expected to refrain from arbitrarily confiscating rights (as sometimes happened with banked credits in the early US Emissions Trading programme), they do not, however, give up their ability to adopt a more stringent cap as the need arises. In particular, they would not be expected to pay compensation for withdrawing a portion of the authorization to emit, as they would if allowances were accorded full property-right status. It is a somewhat uneasy compromise, but it seems to have worked.

---

[5] One prominent exception is the New Zealand ITQ system. It grants full property rights in perpetuity (NRCC, 1999, p. 97).

(c) *Adaptive Management*

One of the initial fears about tradable-permit systems was that they would be excessively rigid, particularly in the light of the need to provide adequate security to permit holders. Policy rigidity was seen as possibly preventing the system from responding either to changes in the resource base or to better information. And this rigidity could be particularly damaging in biological systems by undermining their resilience. Resilient systems are those that can adapt to changing circumstances (Hollings, 1978).

Existing tradable-permit systems have responded to this challenge in different ways, depending on the type of resource being covered. In air-pollution control the need for adaptive management is typically less immediate and the right is typically defined in terms of tons of emissions. In biological systems, such as fisheries, the rights are typically defined as a share of the TAC. In this way the resource managers can change the TAC in response to changing biological conditions without triggering legal recourse by the right holder. Some fisheries and water-allocation systems have actually defined two related rights (Young, 1999, 2003). The first conveys the share of the cap, while the second conveys the right to withdraw a specified amount in a particular year. Separating the two rights allows a user to sell the current access right (perhaps due to an illness or malfunctioning equipment) without giving up the right of future access embodied in the share right. Though share rights have not been used in air-pollution control, they have been proposed (Muller, 1994).

Water has a different kind of adaptive management need. Considerable uncertainty among users is created by the fact that the amount of water can vary significantly from year to year, implying that caps are likely to vary from year to year. Since different users have quite different capacities for responding to shortfalls, the system for allocating this water needs to be flexible enough to respond to this variability, or the water could be seriously misallocated.

(d) *Caps and Safety Valves*

Even if the apparent 'schedule' of targets is equivalent to those under direct regulation, in the face of 'shocks' the cap is binding in a way that may not be the case for other policies, such as environmental taxation. This has been particularly true in RECLAIM (Harrison, 2003), the Australian water case (Young, 2003), and New Zealand fisheries (Kerr, 2003).

- RECLAIM participants experienced a very large unanticipated demand for power that could only be accommodated by older, more-polluting plants. Permit prices soared in a way that was never anticipated.

- In the New Zealand fisheries case (Kerr, 2003), a lack of understanding of the biology of the orange roughy led to a cap that permitted unsustainable harvests.
- In the Australian water case (Young, 2003), excessive withdrawal would trigger substantial increases in salinity.

The experience with the price shocks in the RECLAIM case shows how to handle unexpected, and sometimes rather large, changes in circumstances that can cause the cost of achieving the cap to skyrocket. The general prescription is to allow a 'safety valve' in the form of a predefined penalty that can be imposed on all emissions over the cap in lieu of meeting the cap. This penalty can be different from the normal sanction imposed for non-compliance during more normal situations. In effect this penalty would set a maximum price that would have to be incurred in pursuit of environmental goals (Roberts and Spence, 1976; Pizer, 1999a; Harrison, 2003). RECLAIM rules specified that, if permit prices went over some threshold, the programme would be suspended until they figured out what to do. An alternative (substantial) fee per ton was imposed in the interim with the revenue used to secure additional emission reductions (Harrison, 2003).

(e) *Initial Allocation Method*

The initial allocation of entitlements is perhaps the most controversial aspect of a tradable-permits system. Four possible methods for allocating initial entitlements are:

- random access (lotteries);
- first come, first served;
- administrative rules based upon eligibility criteria; and
- auctions.

All four of these have been used in one context or another. Both lotteries and auctions are frequently used in allocating hunting permits for big game. Lotteries are more common in allocating permits among residents, while auctions are more common for allocating permits to non-residents. First come, first served was historically common for water, especially when it was abundant. The most common method, however, for the applications discussed here, is allocating access rights based upon historic use.

Though an infinite number of possible distribution rules exist, 'grandfathering' tends to predominate.[6] Grandfathering refers to an

---

[6] In the EU carbon-trading programme the rules allow 5 per cent of the allowances to be auctioned off by 2005 and up to 10 per cent after 2008.

approach that bases the initial allocation on historic use and existing sources get allocations of rights at no charge. They only have to purchase any additional permits they may need over and above the initial allocation (as opposed to purchasing *all* permits in an auction market).

Grandfathering has its advantages and disadvantages. Recent work examining how the presence of pre-existing distortions in the tax system affects the efficiency of the chosen instrument suggests that the ability to recycle the revenue (rather than give it to users) can enhance the cost-effectiveness of the system by a large amount. That work, of course, supports the use of taxes or auctioned permits rather than 'grandfathered' permits (Goulder *et al.*, 1999).

How revenues are distributed, however, also affects the attractiveness of alternative approaches to environmental protection from the point of view of the various stakeholders. To the extent that stakeholders can influence policy choice, 'grandfathering' may have increased the feasibility of implementation of transferable permit systems (Svendsen, 1999). Interestingly, the empirical evidence suggests that the amount of the revenue needed to hold users harmless during the change is only a fraction of the total revenue available from auctioning — not the whole amount (Bovenberg and Goulder, 2001). Allocating all permits free of charge is therefore not inevitable in principle, even if political feasibility considerations are important.

A second consideration involves the treatment of new firms. Although reserving some free permits for new firms is possible, this option is rarely exercised in practice. As a result, under the free distribution scheme new firms typically have to purchase all permits, while existing firms get an initial allocation free. Thus, the free distribution system imposes a bias against new users in the sense that their financial burden is greater than that of an otherwise identical existing user. In air-pollution control this 'new user' bias has retarded the introduction of new facilities and new technologies by reducing the cost advantage of building new facilities that embody the latest innovations[7] (Maloney and Brady, 1988; Nelson *et al.*, 1993).

A third consideration involves how a grandfathered process may promote inefficient strategic behaviour. When the initial allocation is based upon historic use and users are aware of this aspect in advance, an incentive to inflate historic use (to qualify for a larger initial allocation) is created (Berland *et al.*, 2001). This strategic behaviour can

---

[7] The 'new source bias' is, of course, not unique to tradable-permit systems. It applies to any system of regulation that imposes more stringent requirements on new sources than existing ones.

intensify the degradation of the resource before the control mechanism is set in place.

Some tendency to over-allocate quota in the initial years has been evident, presumably in many cases to enhance the political feasibility of programme adoption.

- The evaluation of the Dutch phosphate quota programme, for example, shows that initial quota was over-allocated 10–25 per cent (Wossink, 2003).
- Initial allocations were also high in the initial years of the RECLAIM programme (Harrison, 2003).

In the climate-change case, a primary concern has been about 'hot air'. (Hot air is the part of an Annex I country's assigned amount that is likely to be surplus to its needs without any additional efforts to reduce emissions.) Hot air resulted from the initial allocation because assigned amounts are defined in terms of 1990 emission levels and, for some countries (most notably Russia and the Ukraine), economic contraction has resulted in substantially lower emissions levels. Hence, these countries would have surplus permits to sell, resulting in the need for less emissions reduction from new sources.

Other initial allocation issues involve determining both the eligibility to receive permits and the governance process for deciding the proper allocation. In fisheries the decision to allocate permits to boat owners has triggered harsh reactions among both crew and processors.

Finally, some systems allow agents other than those included in the initial allocation to participate through an 'opt-in' procedure. This is a prominent feature of the sulphur-allowance programme, but it can be plagued by adverse-selection problems (Montero, 1999, 2000).

Traditional theory suggests that tradable permits offer a costless trade-off between efficiency and equity, since, regardless of the initial allocation, the ability to trade assures that permits flow to their highest-valued uses. This implies that the initial allocation can be used to pursue fairness goals without increasing compliance costs.

In practice, implementation considerations almost always allocate permits to historic users, whether or not that is the most equitable allocation. This failure to use the initial allocation to protect equity concerns has caused other means to be introduced to protect equity considerations (such as restrictions of transfers). These additional restrictions tend to raise transactions costs and to limit the cost-effectiveness of the programme. In practice, therefore, tradable-permits systems have not avoided the trade-off between efficiency and equity so common elsewhere in policy circles.

(f) *Transferability Rules*

While the largest source of controversy about tradable permits seems to attach to the manner in which the permits are initially allocated, another significant source of controversy is attached to the rules that govern transferability. According to supporters, transferability not only serves to assure that rights flow to their highest-valued use, but it also provides a user-financed form of compensation for those who voluntarily decide to use the resource no longer. Therefore, restrictions on transferability only serve to reduce the efficiency of the system. According to critics, allowing the rights to be transferable produces a number of socially unacceptable outcomes, including the concentration of rights, the destruction of community interests, and the degrading of the environment.

Making the rights transferable does allow the opportunity for some groups to accumulate permits. The concentration of permits in the hands of a few could either reduce the efficiency of the tradable-permits system (Hahn, 1984; Anderson, 1991; Van Egteren and Weber, 1996), or it could be used as leverage to gain economic power in other markets (Misiolek and Elder, 1989; Sartzetakis, 1997). Although it has not played much of a role in air-pollution control, concentration has been a factor in fisheries (Palsson, 1998).

Typically, the problem in fisheries is *not* that the concentration is so high that it triggers antitrust concerns (Adelaja *et al.*, 1998), but rather that it allows small fishing enterprises to be bought out by larger fishing enterprises. Smaller fishing enterprises are seen by some observers as having a special value to society that should be protected (Palsson, 1998).

Protections against 'unreasonable' concentration of quota are now common. One typical strategy involves putting a limit on the amount of quota that can be accumulated by any one holder. In New Zealand fisheries, for example, these range from 20 to 35 per cent, depending upon the species (NRCC, 1999, pp. 90–1), while in Iceland the limits are 10 per cent for cod and 20 per cent for other species (NRCC, 1999, p. 102).

Another coping strategy involves trying to mitigate the potential anticompetitive effects of hoarding. The US sulphur-allowance programme does this in two main ways. First, it sets aside a supply of allowances that could be sold at a predetermined (high) price if hoarders refused to sell to new entrants.[8] Second, it introduced a zero-

---

[8] This set-aside has not been used because sufficient allowances have been available through normal channels. That does not necessarily mean the set-aside was not useful, however, because it may have alleviated concerns that could have otherwise blocked the implementation of the programme.

revenue auction that, among its other features, requires permit holders to put approximately 3 per cent of their allowances up for sale in a public auction once a year. The revenue is returned to the sellers rather than retained by the government. Hence, the name 'zero-revenue auction' (Svendsen and Christensen, 1999).

Another approach involves directly restricting transfers that are perceived to violate the public interest. In the Alaskan halibut and sablefish ITQ programme, for example, several size categories of vessels were defined. The initial allocation was based upon the catch record within each vessel class and transfer of quota between catcher vessel classes was prohibited (NRCC, 1999, p. 310). Further restrictions required the owner of the quota to be on board when the catch was landed. This represented an attempt to prevent the transfer of ownership of the rights to 'absentee landlords'.

A second concern relates to the potentially adverse economic impacts of permit transfers on some communities. Those holders who transfer permits will not necessarily protect the interests of communities that have depended on their commerce in the past. For example, in fisheries a transfer from one quota holder to another might well cause the fish to be landed in another community. In air-pollution control, owners of a factory might shut down its operation in one community and rebuild in another community, taking their permits with them.

One common response to this problem in fisheries involves allocating quota directly to communities. The 1992 Bering Sea Community Development Quota Program, which was designed to benefit remote villages containing significant native populations in Alaska, allocated 7.5 per cent of the walleye pollock quota to these communities (Ginter, 1995). In New Zealand, the Treaty of Waitangi (Fisheries Claims) Settlement Act of 1992 effectively transferred ownership of almost 40 per cent of the New Zealand ITQ to the Maori people (Annala, 1996). For these allocations, the community retains control over the transfers and this control gives it the power to protect community interests. In Iceland, this kind of control is gained through a provision that if quota is to be leased or sold to a vessel operating in a different place, the assent of the municipal government and the local fishermen's union must be obtained (NRCC, 1999, p. 83).

A final concern with transferability relates to possible external effects of the transfer. The theory presumes that the commodity being traded is homogeneous. With homogeneity, transfers increase net benefits by allowing permits to flow to their highest-valued use. In practice, without homogeneity, that is not necessarily so if the transfers confer external benefits or costs on third parties.

When the location of the resource use matters, spatial issues can arise because the transfer could alter the location of use. Spatial issues can be dealt with within the tradable-permit scheme, but those choices typically make transfers more difficult. Both the RECLAIM programme (Harrison, 2003) and the Nutrient Quota System in the Netherlands (Wossink, 2003) place restrictions on the spatial area within which the permits may be traded. The US Wetlands Program requires regulatory pre-approval of trades. In the sulphur-allowance programme (Ellerman, 2003), no regulatory restrictions are placed on permit trades, but permit users do have to assure that any permit use does not result in a violation of the National Ambient Air Quality Standards.

(g) *The Temporal Dimension*

Standard cost-effectiveness theory suggests that a cost-minimizing tradable-permit system must have full temporal fungibility, implying that allowances can be both borrowed and banked (Rubin, 1996). Banking allows a user to store its permits for future use. Borrowing allows a permit holder to use permits earlier than their stipulated date.

Tradable-permit schemes differ considerably in how they treat banking and/or the role of forward markets. No existing system that I am aware of is fully temporally fungible. Older pollution-control programmes have had a more limited approach. The emissions-trading programme allowed banking, but not borrowing. The lead phase-out programme originally allowed neither, but part way through the programme it allowed banking. The sulphur-allowance programme has banking, but not borrowing, and RECLAIM has very limited banking and borrowing owing to the use of an overlapping time frame for compliance.

How important is temporal flexibility? The message that emerges from this review is that this temporal flexibility can be quite important. Ellerman (2003) discusses the considerable role that both banking and forward markets have played in the US sulphur-allowance programme. Harrison (2003) reports that, during the tremendous pressure placed on the market by the power problems in California, even the limited temporal flexibility in RECLAIM allowed the excess emissions to be reduced by more than a factor of three — from about 19 per cent to 6 per cent. Pedersen (2003) also notes the importance of temporal flexibility for investment in the Danish greenhouse-gas programme.

Interestingly, what will happen after the initial commitment period in the Kyoto Protocol is up in 2012 has not been defined. This means that those who are investing in greenhouse-gas-emissions reductions face a great deal of uncertainty about the value of those reductions after 2012 and that uncertainty presumably has a detrimental effect on incentives to invest in abatement.

4. The Lessons for Climate Change

What can be gleaned from this necessarily brief survey of the theory and implementation experience with tradable permits that might be useful in thinking about their application to climate change?

What does the historical implementation evidence suggest? Though this review has uncovered several success stories for the application of tradable permits, it has also uncovered some failures. Though tradable-permit systems can be, and often are, cost-effective, they are not always so. In some cases they may even be more expensive than traditional policy instruments, if the preconditions for the successful operation of this system are not present.

What lessons seem to emerge for the climate-change case?

- The climate-change permit programme will inevitably move tradable-permits programmes on to new ground. The number and types of participants will necessarily be much larger than ever before experienced. The Kyoto Protocol envisions controlling six greenhouse gases under the rubric of a single programme. Experience with multi-pollutant programmes is rare. The implication is that, while past experience is no doubt helpful, it is unlikely to be definitive.
- Cap-and-trade programmes have in general proved superior to credit-trading systems in terms of both economic and environmental results. Reasons for this have to do with the higher transaction costs and regulatory barriers typically associated with credit programmes.
- Some previous programmatic failures have been due to inadequate monitoring and enforcement. Although it is probably true that monitoring carbon emissions indirectly via fuel use is relatively effective, other monitoring issues could still be important in the climate-change case. Not only do some countries have substantially less capability for reliable monitoring, but also some sources of greenhouse gases (land-use changes and carbon sequestration, for example) are inherently less easy to monitor reliably. Furthermore, the European Union trading scheme excludes non-CO_2 greenhouse gases on grounds of inadequate monitoring (despite protests by several members states that monitoring protocols are adequate). Reliable monitoring in the climate-change case is by no means a foregone conclusion.

- Enforcement at the international level relies heavily on the effectiveness of national enforcement. National enforcement capabilities vary widely across countries. Weak national enforcement systems would provide a significant opportunity for non-compliance in those countries, jeopardizing the achievement of the climate-change goals. Although these weaknesses in international enforcement apply to other means of controlling greenhouse gases as well as to permits, a tradable-permit system could intensify the problem. Countries with poor enforcement systems could end up selling permits to those with good enforcement systems, in effect substituting ineffectively for effectively enforced permits.

- The spatial externalities that plague fisheries and water allocation seem less important for the climate-change effects of CO_2 since the emission location of CO_2 does not matter. However, CO_2 is only one of the greenhouse gases and the other gases could impose spatial externalities. In addition, the leakage problem, where production facilities move to avoid the regulations, does seem a potentially serious problem. Leakage problems could arise either within countries (if certain sized plants or certain sectors are exempt) or between signatory and non-signatory countries, particularly if greenhouse-gas controls result in considerably higher energy costs in signatory countries.

- The evidence suggests that setting the cap is a crucial step in the process. Given the level of scientific uncertainty associated with some dimensions of the climate-change problem, the appropriate level of the cap for commitment periods that follow the first is by no means a foregone conclusion. Lack of consensus about the appropriate level of the cap can undermine the determination to reach it.

- A tradable-permits system depends upon the ability of emitters to recognize and to seize cost-effective opportunities to reduce carbon. While some emitters, particularly large emitters in the industrialized countries, could probably live up to that expectation, it is not at all clear that all emitters in developing countries have the requisite knowledge of the spectrum of emission-reducing choices. To some extent, the CDM mechanism diminishes the disadvantage of this asymmetry by allowing industrialized nations to identify and propose promising projects in developing countries.

- The evidence suggests that while the security of a full property right is not essential for the promotion of investments in greenhouse-gas reduction, some adequate level of security is. In terms of the Kyoto Protocol, the lack of any definition of what obligations and responsibilities will accrue to nations and companies after 2012 could become a major impediment to the smooth transition to a new greenhouse-gas regime.

- It is common for tradable programmes to evolve considerably over their lifetime. Generally, the evolution moves from a more to a less restrictive environment as participants (both public and private) become more familiar with the system. We have also seen, however, in both the US wetlands and Dutch nutrient programmes, that it is possible to add so many restrictions to the initial system that it prevents the evolution. A balance must be struck.

- Banking of allowances allows sources significant additional flexibility in compliance investment and decision-making. Heavy use of banking in both the US sulphur-allowance and lead credit-trading programmes have led to early reductions and substantially lower overall costs of compliance. Banking is especially significant for industries in which major capital expenditures must be made, as it allows individual sources flexibility in the timing of such major investments.

- In existing programmes, the private market has supplied an adequate to high number of allowances or credits, so that market-power issues have not been a problem. Several mechanisms can be and have been implemented in past programmes to address concerns about market power, should they arise.

We have also derived some specific lessons for programme design.

- One enforcement principle that has become firmly established in fisheries could be usefully established for climate change as well — the presumption that the administrative cost associated with monitoring, enforcing, and administering the system will be borne by permit holders rather than by general taxpayers. These costs could be financed with a fee levied on each permit.

- Monitoring in the Kyoto Protocol will inevitably involve some degree of self-reporting. Systems of self-reporting do offer many risks of deception, although analysts may overstate the extent to which purposefully deceptive self-reporting occurs. Creating layers of veracity checks should strengthen the integrity of the allowance- and emissions-monitoring systems. At the initial stages of the permit system, veracity checks of government self-reporting will be needed, but as the system matures more extensive checks on emission sources at the domestic level will be needed. National governments could provide many (or most) of the domestic checks, provided that those checks are themselves reviewed occasionally at the international level. It remains to be seen how intrusive the international monitoring system for greenhouse gases will be, but this review suggests it is an essential element.

- Enforcement could be enhanced by allowing trading only among eligible parties and by defining 'eligibility' to include only those countries that have approved domestic enforcement systems and were in compliance in the previous commitment period.

- Transparency can be an important aspect of both monitoring and enforcement and the smooth functioning of the market.

  Transparency of prices can facilitate the smooth working of the market. Providing price information is important to reduce the uncertainty of trading and create public confidence in the trading programme. Price information could be required to be revealed in reporting requirements for emissions trades, or through alternative systems, such as holding regular public auctions.

  Transparency of compliance behaviour should be promoted through wide public availability of collected data. Quality assurance is easier if data are widely available; veracity-checking is facilitated by the availability of multiple sources of information; and the involvement of private monitors is frequently heavily dependent upon the existence of a rich database. There will be reluctance to reveal some information because of privacy and industrial secrets, but free flow of information should be the norm. One model for tracking trading activity is provided by the US Allowance Tracking System used in the Acid Rain Program. This publicly open allowance registry system helps to create a transparent and self-enforcing compliance system, and has contributed to high compliance records in the programmes. It has also made a considerable amount of data available to external, objective programme evaluators.

- The mischief caused by not having defined the reduction obligations for at least one future commitment period (after 2012) could be considerable.

  Knowing future ground rules would reduce uncertainty about the value of emission-reduction investments.

  Once the future assigned amount is specified, assigned-amount adjustments could provide a reasonable means of protecting the goals of the climate-change convention while encouraging compliance. This approach, which has been applied in the US sulphur-allowance programme, subtracts any overages (and possibly a penalty) from the assigned amounts in the next commitment period.

- Permit systems can be (and should be) designed to deal with the price-spike problem. Safety-valve mechanisms involving a maximum price on permits (perhaps coupled with the requirement to offset overages in any year with reductions in future allocations) could eliminate the severe economic damage that could result from a dramatic, if temporary, change in circumstances, such as occurred in the California electricity deregulation case. The California case also points out the importance of having some temporal flexibility built into the programme as a hedge against temporary price spikes.

- Credit programmes, such as the CDM and joint implementation, must face the need to define a reliable 'additionality' baseline that does not pose a significant barrier to the creation and certification of tradable credits. History suggests that this is no small task.

Two important expectations flowing from the economic theory have proved to be an inaccurate characterization of reality.

The first example comes from the theoretical expectation that transferable-permit programmes do not affect conservation of the resource because the cap handles that and setting the cap is considered to be outside the system. Hence, it is believed, the main purpose of the system is to protect the economic value of the resource, not the resource itself. In fact, the stringency of the cap as well as the level of compliance with the cap may both be affected by the policy instrument choice.

The second theoretical expectation that falls in the light of implementation experience involves the trade-off between efficiency and equity in a tradable-permits system. Traditional theory suggests that tradable permits offer a costless trade-off between efficiency and equity, since, regardless of the initial allocation, the ability to trade assures that permits flow to their highest-valued uses. This implies that the initial allocation could be used to pursue equity goals without lowering the value of the resource. In practice, implementation considerations almost always result in permits being allocated to historic uses, whether or not that is the most equitable allocation. This failure to use the initial allocation to protect equity concerns has caused other means to be introduced to protect equity considerations (such as restrictions of transfers). The additional restrictions generally do raise compliance costs. In practice, therefore, tradable-permits systems have not avoided the trade-off between efficiency and equity so common elsewhere in policy circles.

This evidence seems to suggest that tradable permits are no panacea, but they do have their niche. Climate change may well turn out to be the most important niche.

9

Carbon Trading in the Policy Mix

STEVEN SORRELL AND JOS SIJM*

1. Introduction

Climate policy is relatively immature but growing rapidly in scale, scope, and complexity. In particular, the Kyoto mechanisms have created a unique international framework for market-based regulation which is stimulating the development of greenhouse-gas emissions trading schemes at the regional, national, and international level. The EU Emissions Trading Scheme (EU ETS) is the most significant of these developments and will cover some 45 per cent of EU carbon-dioxide (CO_2) emissions from 2005 onwards (CEC, 2003a).[1]

As climate policy develops, so the number of policy instruments grows, together with the potential for interaction between these instruments. This interaction can be complementary and mutually reinforcing, but there is also the risk that different policy instruments

* SPRU (Science and Technology Policy Research), University of Sussex, and Energy Research Centre of the Netherlands (ECN), respectively. This research was supported by the European Commission under the project *Interaction in EU Climate Policy (EVK2-2000-00613)*. The authors would like to thank their colleagues on the INTERACT project, particularly Adrian Smith of SPRU, and the many individuals from government and industry who gave up their valuable time to attend workshops and provide interviews.

[1] The EU ETS is a harmonized, EU-wide 'cap-and-trade' scheme for CO_2 emissions. Participants include electricity generators, oil refineries, and energy-intensive manufacturing installations in sectors such as iron and steel, minerals, and paper. Phase 1 of the EU ETS runs from 2005 to 2008, while Phase 2 coincides with the first commitment period of the Kyoto Protocol (2008–12). The size of the aggregate cap (total number of allowances) in Phase 1 has yet to be finalized. Each participating member state is developing national allocation plans (NAPs), which define the number of allowances to allocate to national participants. These must be consistent with the allocation criteria set out in Annex III of the Directive and are subject to approval by the European Commission. The sum of these national caps will establish the overall EU cap.

will interfere with one another and undermine the objectives and credibility of each. Furthermore, the unprecedented scope of the climate problem means that climate policy also interacts with a range of other instruments in the areas of energy, environment, transport, trade, fiscal, technology, agricultural, and social policy. These interactions are likely to have a determinate impact on the success of climate policy in general and on the development of emissions-trading schemes in particular. But despite this, the topic of policy interaction remains under-researched. With a few notable exceptions (Smith, 1999; Johnstone, 2002; Egenhofer, 2002), the majority of the economics literature confines itself to the study of individual instruments in isolation.

The political-science literature engages with the problem of policy interaction rather more successfully. Majone (1989) describes the problem of policy congestion where: 'solutions beget new problems in the form of policy overlaps, jurisdictional conflicts and unanticipated consequences.' Wildavsky (1979) considers this interaction to be a prime cause of much policy development, with the solution of these internally generated problems becoming as important as responding to external changes. A study by Glachant (2000), on the implementation of EU environmental directives found that the pervasiveness of interactions meant that a simple link between policy and outcome could not be found. Instead, the research question was recast as 'how can the implementation of a particular regulation cope efficiently with policy interactions?' Similarly, Gunningham and Gabrosky's (1998) detailed study of the operation of environmental regulation in the chemical and agricultural sectors concluded that approaches to environmental regulation based on single policy instruments were misguided. A better strategy was to harness the strengths of individual instruments while compensating for their weaknesses by the use of additional and complementary instruments within a broader policy mix. This includes the use of multiple instruments to achieve a single objective ('killing one bird with two stones' (Johnstone, 2002)), as well as the use of multiple instruments to achieve multiple objectives (as exemplified by government regulation of the energy industry) (Helm, 2003).

This chapter aims to contribute to the literature on policy interaction by examining the conditions under which a cap-and-trade[2] emissions

---

[2] In a cap-and-trade emissions trading scheme for CO_2 emissions, a fixed number of allowances are allocated each year to the participating sources. Each participant must surrender one allowance for every tonne of CO_2 emitted. Participants who face high abatement costs can continue to pollute by buying additional allowances, while participants who face low abatement costs can take abatement action and sell their surplus allowances for a profit. In this way, each participant can minimize its overall abatement costs. The scheme places an overall 'cap' on the annual quantity of CO_2 emissions equal to the number of allowances distributed, and the trading mechanism should allow this cap to be achieved at the lowest possible cost.

trading scheme (ETS) for CO_2 emissions may usefully coexist with other climate-policy instruments.[3] Three types of coexisting instruments are explored, namely: carbon/energy taxes; support mechanisms for renewable electricity; and non-price instruments to overcome barriers to energy efficiency. The chapter argues that each of these instrument combinations may be acceptable, provided they contribute to either improving the static or dynamic efficiency of the ETS, or delivering other valued policy objectives. But successful combinations require transparency in policy objectives, anticipation of potential conflicts and careful design. In practice, the incremental evolution and 'lock-in' of individual instruments can militate against such successful combinations.

The chapter is in five parts. Section 2 explores some of the issues related to policy interaction with a cap-and-trade ETS, including the distinction between directly and indirectly affected target groups, the cost incidence of an ETS, the different types of policy interaction, and the implications of an emissions cap. Section 3 applies these ideas to the three combinations of instruments identified above and seeks to identify the conditions under which such combinations may be justified. Section 4 provides a brief overview of how these types of interaction may be triggered by the introduction of the EU ETS in the UK. Section 5 concludes.

2. Policy Interaction and Carbon Emissions Trading Schemes

(a) *Direct and Indirect Impacts of a Policy Instrument*

It is rare for policy innovations such as an ETS wholly to displace existing instruments. Instead, an ETS is likely to operate in parallel with existing instruments and to interact with them in a variety of ways. In exploring these interactions, a useful distinction is between *directly* and *indirectly* affected target groups — where a target group is defined as the collection of economic actors influenced in some way by a policy (Sorrell *et al.*, 2003). A directly affected target group has obligations and incentives imposed upon it directly by a policy instrument, while an indirectly affected target group is influenced in some way by the behavioural changes that are made by the directly affected group. Of particular interest is the extent to which the additional costs imposed by a policy instrument on the business sector are indirectly borne by

[3] The discussion in this chapter is confined to the trading of CO_2 emissions. In practice, such trading schemes may also include other greenhouse gases, which in turn may be influenced by a broader range of environmental regulations.

consumers, suppliers, and shareholders. So, for example, electricity generators participating in an ETS may either increase wholesale electricity prices (pass to consumers), reduce the consumption or unit price paid for supply inputs (pass to suppliers), or reduce dividends and capital gains (pass to shareholders) (Cramton and Kerr, 1998). In each case, the extent to which costs can be passed on will depend upon the market situation of the firm and the elasticities of demand and supply in each market. It will also depend upon the timeframe under consideration and the extent to which companies have the opportunity to change behaviour and invest.

Indirect effects permeate throughout the economy and require analysis within a general equilibrium framework. But if the electricity generators are participating in the ETS, the indirect impact on electricity consumers becomes of particular interest. This is because, first, the economic implications of carbon controls on electricity generation are potentially very large and, second, electricity consumers are typically subject to a wide range of other policies that will interact with the ETS.

The direct/indirect distinction is also relevant to the design of an ETS for CO_2 emissions. There is a basic choice between a *downstream* ETS, in which fossil-fuel users surrender allowances for their emissions, and an *upstream* scheme, in which fossil-fuel producers surrender allowances for the carbon content of the fuel. Within a downstream scheme, there is a second choice between the *direct* treatment of electricity emissions, where electricity generators surrender allowances, and an *indirect* treatment, where electricity consumers (or a subset of consumers) surrender allowances in proportion to the carbon content of delivered electricity. Each option has pros and cons and each has different implications for incentives and abatement options. For example, electricity generators have full and direct control over the carbon intensity of electricity generation, through investment and operational decisions, but they have only indirect and partial control over electricity demand through electricity prices. In contrast, electricity consumers have full and direct control over their electricity demand, but have no control over the carbon intensity of electricity generation unless some form of 'carbon labelling' of electricity is available.[4] Similarly, while an upstream scheme ensures an economy-wide cap on fossil-fuel emissions and a single price for carbon throughout the

---

[4] This is due to be introduced into Europe during 2004 as a result of Directive 2003/54/EC on the liberalization of the European electricity market. This requires 'disclosure' to consumers of the sources and environmental impacts of the electricity they are purchasing and hence should empower consumers to switch to lower-carbon sources (Boardman *et al.*, 2003).

economy, a downstream scheme will be confined to a subset of emission sources and may lead to carbon being priced differently between sectors and fuels.

(b) *The Indirect Impacts of an ETS*

A fundamental choice in the design of an ETS is between the auctioning or free allocation of allowances (or some combination of the two). While this choice may lead to different costs for ETS participants, there should be no difference in the costs passed on in product prices. This important result rests on a number of assumptions including:

- the majority of firms in a particular product market are covered by the allowance programme;
- firms are profit maximizing and decisions about entry and exit are not affected by financing constraints;
- there is no market power in either the product or allowance market; and
- product prices are not subject to economic regulation.

With allowance auctioning, firms incur costs for abatement plus the allowances purchased in the auction which are used to cover residual emissions. Both are real accounting costs. With free allocation, firms only incur abatement costs, including the net cost of any acquisition of allowances. But the freely allocated allowances have an *opportunity cost*, in that they could be sold on the allowance market. This opportunity cost should be treated identically to real accounting costs in a firm's pricing decisions (Harrison and Radov, 2002). Viewing the situation another way, the wealth provided by freely allocated allowances represents a lump-sum profit which should not influence product-pricing decisions since, in theory, these are based upon marginal costs.

The difference between auctioning and free allocation lies in the capture of the economic rent, rather than the cost increases for consumers. With free allocation, the rent is captured by the participating firms, thereby increasing their market value. With auctioning, the rent is captured by the government and may be used in a variety of ways throughout the economy, including compensating affected groups and reducing other forms of taxation. But the price impacts for consumers should be identical in both cases.

Whether this result holds in practice will depend upon the validity of the assumptions behind the economic model. For example, agency problems may move firms away from profit-maximizing behaviour or an individual firm may be able to exercise market power. In the US Acid Rain Program, the participating electricity generators were subject to utility regulation, which distorted product pricing by valuing allow-

Table 1
Estimates of the Impact of the EU ETS on UK Electricity Prices
(% increase)

	€5/tCO$_2$	€16/tCO$_2$
Wholesale	14.8	53.0
Industrial	8.9	32.1
Domestic	4.1	14.8

Note: Low gas price scenario (15p/therm)
Source: ILEX (2003).

ances at historic cost (zero) rather than opportunity cost (Bohi and Burtraw, 1992). This problem should not apply in Europe as electricity generation is liberalized, but vertically integrated electricity companies may be reluctant to increase retail prices if this increases the risk of losing customers to a competing supplier. Table 1 shows some estimates of the potential impact of the EU ETS on electricity prices in the UK.

It may be possible to compensate consumers for these price increases by separating the *allocation* of allowances from the *compliance obligations* for emissions. For example, allowances could be allocated to electricity consumers, while electricity generators remained responsible for compliance. Here, the generators would need to purchase allowances from consumers, with the revenue transfers compensating for any increase in electricity prices. In practice, a combination of transaction costs, lobbying by ETS participants, and legal restrictions on who can receive allowances may limit the feasibility of this alternative. This is the case with the EU ETS, which restricts the allocation of allowances to participants in the scheme. While it would be possible to allocate allowances to EU ETS participants to compensate them for increases in electricity prices, the same compensation could not be extended to non-participants.

(c) A Typology of Policy Interaction

The distinction between directly and indirectly affected target groups leads naturally to a distinction between *direct* and *indirect* policy interaction. In addition, with an ETS there is the additional possibility of *trading* interaction. Each of these is introduced below.

- *Direct interaction* is where the target groups directly affected by two policies overlap in some way. For example, some or all of the participants in a carbon ETS may already be subject to CO$_2$ emission limits or to a carbon tax on fuel use.

- *Indirect interaction* occurs when a target group is indirectly affected by one policy and either directly or indirectly affected by a second. So, for example, there is indirect interaction between a downstream ETS that includes the electricity generators and a tax on electricity at the point of consumption. Here, electricity consumers are indirectly affected by the ETS and directly affected by the tax. Similarly, there is indirect interaction between this type of ETS and obligations upon electricity suppliers to purchase renewable electricity, since both will lead to higher prices for electricity consumers and lower emissions from electricity generators.

- *Trading interaction* is where two policies influence one another by the exchange of an environmental trading commodity. For example, allowances from a trading scheme in one country may be exchangeable for allowances from a trading scheme in a second. Any such links would need to be governed by transfer and exchange rules, which in combination would define the *fungibility* of the different commodities. Trading interactions between the Kyoto mechanisms and national and international trading schemes are becoming a critical issue as the Kyoto regime develops and have important implications for abatement costs and environmental integrity (Haites and Mullins, 2001). In addition, the parallel development of schemes such as tradable green credits for renewable electricity opens up the possibility of linking schemes where the tradable commodities have different denominations (e.g. megawatt hours (MWh) and tonnes of CO_2 (tCO_2), respectively) (Morthorst, 2001; Sorrell, 2003*a*). This is possible because the tradable commodities in such schemes represent, in part, displaced carbon emissions and hence can be converted to tCO_2 by means of a suitable exchange rate.

Each type of interaction may have implications for abatement costs, administrative costs, environmental effectiveness, equity, and political feasibility. Furthermore, each type of interaction may lead to differential treatment, with some target groups being affected by both instruments and some by only one. Hence, the extent to which such interactions can be judged as beneficial, neutral, or counterproductive requires a careful examination of the nature and consequences of the interaction and an evaluation of those consequences within a multicriteria framework. This should lead to a judgement as to whether the combination of instruments is useful, redundant, or positively harmful.

(i) Double regulation and double counting

In most OECD countries, the existing climate-policy mix contains a series of examples of the above categories of interaction. If an ETS is introduced into this mix, the number of interactions can be expected to multiply. If both the ETS and the existing instruments have significant economic impacts, the affected target groups may complain of *double regulation*, where they perceive themselves as paying twice for reducing carbon emissions (Sorrell, 2002). The validity of such perceptions will depend upon the objectives of each instrument, the clarity, transparency, and legitimacy of these objectives, and the degree of overlap between them. For example, two instruments may each have the objective of reducing carbon emissions, but if they are targeted at two different market failures (e.g. carbon externalities and asymmetric information) their coexistence may be considered acceptable.

In the fluid post-Kyoto policy mix, it is also possible that more than one type of carbon-trading scheme will coexist, or that a carbon ETS will coexist with trading schemes for other commodities, such as renewable electricity. In these circumstances, there may also be problems with *double counting* of carbon emissions, where the compliance obligations for the same emissions are either given to two separate parties, or given to the same party under two separate terms (Sorrell, 2002). These disputes may occur whether or not there is trading interaction between the two instruments and may have two consequences:

- *double coverage:* where two separate carbon allowances or carbon credits are surrendered for a 1-tonne increase in physical emissions; and
- *double crediting:* where two separate carbon allowances or carbon credits are generated from a 1-tonne decrease in physical emissions.

A cross-border example of double coverage would be the export of electricity from country A, which has an ETS with direct accountability (electricity generators hold allowances), to country B, which has an ETS with indirect accountability (electricity consumers hold allowances). Both the seller of the electricity (generators) in country A and the purchaser of the electricity (consumers) in country B would need to surrender allowances to cover the emissions associated with this electricity, which means the emissions would be covered twice by two separate trading schemes. A primary motivation for introducing a harmonized ETS throughout the EU was to avoid such problems (Zapfel and Vainio, 2001).

In some cases double counting will offset the double coverage and there will be no threat to environmental integrity. But in other cases, the integrity of one or both schemes may be undermined. For example, the UK ETS originally included proposals for the generation of carbon credits from projects that improved electricity efficiency (Begg *et al.*, 2002). But if the UK electricity generators subsequently joined the EU ETS, this would have led to double crediting without any compensating double coverage. Very similar problems have been encountered in the development of the 'Linking Directive', which allows credits from Joint Implementation projects to be imported into the EU ETS (CEC, 2003*b*).

(d) *Policy Interaction under a Cap*

A defining feature of a cap-and-trade ETS is that, assuming adequate enforcement and full compliance, there is certainty that total emissions will be less than or equal to the aggregate cap. A second feature of a cap-and-trade scheme is that, under a standard set of assumptions regarding the competitive operation of the allowance market, the trading scheme will allow the target to be met at least cost. In the equilibrium, marginal abatement costs will be equalized across sources and equal to the allowance price.

As Sijm (2003) has argued, these idealized features of an ETS have important implications for policy interaction. Coupled with comparable assumptions regarding the idealized operation of the relevant product markets, they imply that the use of a second instrument that directly or indirectly interacts with the ETS will increase the overall costs of meeting the emissions cap, while at the same time having zero environmental impact — i.e. providing no additional emissions reductions. The aggregate abatement costs of ETS participants may be either increased (e.g. by a carbon tax) or reduced (e.g. by a subsidy scheme) by the second instrument, but in all cases the aggregate social costs of meeting the cap will be increased and participant emissions will continue to be less than or equal to the cap. This result applies both to instruments which directly affect CO_2 emissions from ETS participants, such as a carbon tax on fuel use, and to instruments which indirectly affect those emissions, such as a tax on electricity consumption of both participants and non-participants (Sijm, 2003).

To illustrate this, assume that the second instrument is a negotiated agreement (NA) that sets emission limits on a subset of ETS participants in terms of emissions per unit of output. It is straightforward to demonstrate that, where the NA limits are binding, they increase the marginal abatement costs of affected ETS participants by a factor λ, which is a measure of the change in costs for a marginal change in the NA emission limit (Sorrell, 2002, pp. 112–15). As a consequence of this double regulation the affected participants are likely to reduce emissions further than they would under the ETS alone, which means that they are likely either to sell more allowances or purchase fewer allowances. The consequent reduction in allowance prices will make it easier for other ETS participants that are not affected by the NA to comply with their ETS obligations. Aggregate emissions will not have changed, since any 'freed-up' allowances will simply be used by other participants to cover increases in emissions. But aggregate abatement costs will have increased, since the distribution of abatement actions across participants will have departed from the cost-minimizing optimum (Sijm, 2003). Also, the differential treatment of participants may have introduced distortions to competition, with the participants subject to the 'double regulation' effectively subsidizing competitor participants that are not.[5] If *all* ETS participants are subject to the NA targets, the primary effect will be to increase overall abatement costs and lower the allowance price. If the emission limits from the NAs are sufficiently stringent, aggregate emissions will be reduced below the cap, the ETS will become redundant and the price of allowances will fall to zero.

Very similar conclusions apply to instruments that indirectly affect ETS participants, such as an electricity tax. In this case, reductions in electricity demand will substitute for lower cost abatement by ETS participants (e.g. fuel switching), while overall emissions will be unchanged. Again, a very stringent electricity tax could reduce electricity consumption sufficiently that aggregate emissions are reduced below the cap and the ETS becomes redundant. However, if the electricity generators form only a subset of ETS participants, this is unlikely.

In practice, allowance and product markets may only approximate the theoretical ideal. Market failures will pervade both markets, and the political bargaining that led to the ETS cap is unlikely to provide an adequate reflection of the 'social optimum' for carbon externalities (to the extent that such a concept is meaningful for global climate change). In addition, governments have objectives which go beyond efficiency, such as the promotion of social equity. In these circumstances, there *may* be legitimate grounds for introducing or maintaining other climate-policy instruments that directly or indirectly interact with the ETS. These include:

- improving the static efficiency of the ETS by overcoming market failures other than CO_2 externalities;
- improving the dynamic efficiency of the ETS by overcoming market failures in the area of technology innovation and diffusion;

[5] This only applies to those competitors which are buyers of allowances. If they are sellers, the value of their sales will be reduced.

- delivering social objectives other than efficiency, such as equity and political feasibility; and
- compensating for deficiencies in the ETS design (Sijm, 2003; Johnstone, 2002).

However, the fact that positive combinations between an ETS and other instruments are theoretically possible does not mean that such combinations will result when an ETS is introduced into an existing policy mix. Furthermore, when an ETS is in place, aggregate emission reductions will be set solely by the ETS cap. Instruments that target emissions covered by the ETS cap will contribute nothing further to emission reductions – unless they are sufficiently stringent that they make the ETS redundant. This means that, once the ETS is in place, the justification for maintaining such instruments must rely upon one of the above rationales, rather than the contribution of the instrument to overall emission reductions (Sijm, 2003).

It is important to note that the same conclusion does not follow for instruments that do not directly or indirectly interact with the ETS. These will contribute emission reductions independently of and in addition to the ETS cap. So, for example, if the ETS is a downstream scheme that includes the electricity generators, emissions from household electricity consumption will be covered by the cap while emissions from household fuel consumption will not. Hence, policies that affect the former will directly or indirectly interact with the ETS, while policies that affect the latter will not. Conversely, if the EU ETS is an upstream scheme, the cap will cover *all* fossil-fuel emissions and all policies that affect these emissions will interact with the ETS. Since none of these policies will contribute anything further to overall emission reductions, the justification for maintaining them must rely solely on one of the above categories.

The following sections use these insights to discuss possible justifications for combining a cap-and-trade ETS for CO_2 emissions with:

- carbon/energy taxes;
- policies to support renewable electricity; and
- policies for promoting energy efficiency.

3. Interactions Between Carbon ETSs and Selected Climate-policy Instruments

(a) *Carbon Trading and Carbon/Energy Taxation*

Most OECD countries use some form of carbon/energy taxation. Unless these taxes are removed when a carbon ETS is introduced, or exemptions introduced for target groups directly and indirectly affected by the ETS, policy interaction becomes inevitable.

Carbon/energy taxation of the fuel used by a participant in a downstream ETS will distort the *substitution* objectives of each instrument. Marginal emissions will be priced twice for ETS participants, at different implicit or explicit rates, but only once for non-participants. Similarly, the coexistence of carbon/energy taxation of electricity with the participation of electricity generators in the ETS will distort the incentives to substitute between fuel and electricity consumption. In practice, the majority of existing tax regimes do not price carbon consistently between sectors and fuels (Newbery, 2001) and introducing a downstream ETS in this context is likely to distort the substitution incentives still further.[6]

Despite these distortions, there may be circumstances where the retention of the carbon/energy tax provides compensating benefits. This may particularly be the case when allowances are freely allocated to ETS participants rather than auctioned. Free allocation violates the polluter-pays principle in that participants only pay for the marginal damage of CO_2 emissions, while inframarginal emissions remain unpriced. This is in contrast to the use of allowance auctions which impose costs for all emissions. Free allocation may also undermine the incentives for technical innovation to reduce emissions. This topic is a subject of a substantial literature, with most studies arguing that auctioning provides greater incentives for innovation than free allocation (Downing and White, 1986; Millman and Prince, 1989; Jung et al., 1996).

Free allocation also means that the ETS can contribute nothing to the government's fiscal objectives. No revenue is being raised and the economic rent from allowance distribution is distributed wholly to shareholders. This is in contrast to an auction scheme, where allowance revenue can be used to compensate affected groups or to reduce other forms of taxation. Numerous studies have demonstrated how the recycling of auction or tax revenue to reduce other forms of taxation can provide a net welfare benefit (de Mooji, 1999; Bovenberg, 1999; Pezzey, 2002). While the extent of this 'double dividend' is contested, the efficiency benefits of auctioning compared to free allocation are not.

---

[6] For example, the UK Climate Change Levy (CCL), which applies to the business and public sectors, corresponds approximately to a £8.15/tCO_2 tax for natural gas, a £4.55/tCO_2 tax for coal and a £9.35/tCO_2 tax for the primary fuel input to electricity generation. Oil products are excluded on the grounds that these are already subject to excise duties, which in turn correspond to an equivalent carbon tax of £8.90/tCO_2 for heavy fuel oil and £11.60/tCO_2 for gasoil.

Despite the theoretical benefits of auctioning, free allocation is the norm and is likely to remain so for the foreseeable future. Political opposition to large-scale rent transfers undermines the feasibility of auctioning in the same manner as it constrains carbon/energy taxes to sub-optimal levels and/or necessitates the use of extensive tax exemptions. In these circumstances, the retention of existing carbon/energy taxes after an ETS is introduced may be seen as a pragmatic, second-best alternative to the use of allowance auctions. If applied directly to ETS participants, it will: (a) ensure that a portion of inframarginal emissions are priced—albeit at a different rate to marginal emissions; (b) increase the incentives for technical innovation—although this will be balanced by the reduction in the value of allowance holdings that a tax creates; and (c) provide a means to recover some of the windfall rent from allowance allocation. If applied either directly to participants or indirectly to consumers, it will ensure that the revenues from the carbon/energy tax are maintained (Johnstone, 2002).

In practice, the last benefit is likely to be particularly important. Existing carbon/energy taxes have generally been established in the face of vigorous opposition, sometimes as part of a broader programme of environmental tax reform. Having established such a tax, a government will be reluctant to relinquish the income benefits simply to rationalize the substitution incentives of the policy mix. Carbon/energy tax revenues are commonly used to offset other forms of taxation, fund R&D programmes or provide subsidies and tax allowances for the adoption of low-carbon technologies. If the tax is removed, this revenue must either be recovered from other sources or the relevant programmes abandoned.

(i) Carbon/energy taxation as a 'back-up'

The relative merits of retaining or abandoning the coexisting tax will depend upon its marginal rate relative to the anticipated allowance price in the ETS, and the consequent expectations regarding the economic impacts of the double regulation on affected groups. Tax exemptions or reductions for ETS participants may provide one mechanism to reduce these impacts, with the full rate of the tax continuing to be applied to non-participants. Alternatively, if allowance prices are anticipated to be low, there may be an argument for retaining the carbon/energy tax as a 'back-up' to ensure a minimum level of abatement by ETS participants.

In the first instance, allowance prices will be determined by the size of the cap relative to the aggregate marginal abatement cost curve. But an important complication with a carbon ETS is the possibility of trading interaction with other schemes or with the Kyoto mechanisms. A combination of the refusal of the USA to ratify the Kyoto Protocol, the surplus 'hot air' in the assigned amounts to Russia and the Ukraine, and the generous provisions for crediting carbon sequestration by 'sinks' has created the possibility of very low carbon prices after 2008 (Den Elzen and de Moor, 2003). In this context, any interface between a carbon ETS and the international carbon market could have the effect of reducing the ETS allowance price and substituting the purchase of fungible carbon commodities from outside the ETS for abatement by ETS participants. The debate over 'supplementarity' demonstrates that this is an ongoing concern for many EU countries, several of which give priority to emission reductions within their own borders. While one method of incentivizing such abatement would be to restrict trading links, this option may not always be available. For example, the Linking Directive establishes relatively unrestricted links between the EU ETS and the project-based Kyoto mechanisms, despite the reservations of environmental groups and some participating member states (CEC, 2003b; Climate Action Network, 2003).

If existing carbon/energy taxes are maintained as an alternative means of ensuring 'supplementarity', the net result will be to increase abatement costs within the domestic ETS, reduce emissions from ETS participants, and either increase allowance sales to or reduce allowance purchases from the linked trading scheme. If both the domestic and linked ETS are of the cap-and-trade form, the aggregate emissions within the two schemes will remain unchanged. Conversely, if the linked ETS uses relative rather than absolute targets, or if credits from project mechanisms are used, the environmental integrity of an overall cap will be lost.

A possible rationale for giving priority to domestic abatement would be to put a country 'on course' for achieving much greater reductions in CO_2 over the next half century. This objective relies on a set of explicit or implicit arguments regarding:

- the uncertainty and potential severity of climate threats;
- the appropriate global targets for CO_2 emissions over the medium to long term;
- the appropriate contribution of different countries towards those targets;
- the importance of domestic action by developed countries to encourage the subsequent participation of developing countries in the Kyoto Protocol;
- the need to ensure a transition away from long-lived, CO_2-intensive capital stocks and infrastructure; and

- the consequent threat of high adjustment costs in the future should that transition be delayed (Grubb, 1997; RCEP, 2000).

While each of these arguments can be contested, the 'pathways' objective has become explicit in the climate policy of some OECD countries. For example, the UK has a 'goal' of reducing CO_2 emissions to 20 per cent below 1990 levels by 2010 (DETR, 2000) (a target which goes beyond requirements under the EU burden-sharing agreement) and has recently expressed a commitment to 'put the UK on a path' to reducing CO_2 emissions by some 60 per cent below current levels by 2050 (DTI, 2003a).

These domestic targets have led to an acrimonious debate over whether the allocation to UK participants in the EU ETS should be consistent with the 20 per cent goal or with the UK's burden-sharing target. But the former would not necessarily succeed in reducing *domestic* UK emissions because participants could simply purchase allowances from other member states. Although the overall EU cap would be tightened by the UK's actions, the overall size of that cap will depend upon the allocation decisions of other member states—and early indications suggest that these will be more generous than the UK (Betz *et al.*, 2004). In contrast, the coexistence of the EU ETS with a carbon/energy tax would achieve greater emissions reductions in the UK (but not in the EU) at the expense of higher abatement costs and potential damage to the competitiveness of UK industry.

In sum, the direct or indirect interaction of a carbon/energy tax with an ETS may potentially be justified through the polluter-pays principle, the increased incentives for innovation, the capture of windfall rent from allowance allocation, the maintenance of fiscal revenue, or the perceived need for a 'back-up' regulation to ensure a minimum level of abatement by groups directly or indirectly affected by the ETS. It is a matter of judgement as to whether these benefits offset the distortions in substitution incentives that such double regulation creates.

(b) *Carbon Trading and Policies to Promote Renewable Electricity*

Many OECD countries use one or more instruments to support the diffusion of renewable electricity sources. These instruments may be price based, such as a guaranteed purchase price for renewable electricity; quantity based, such as an obligation upon electricity suppliers to purchase a certain percentage of electricity from renewable sources; or a hybrid, in which the price risk of a quantity scheme is mitigated by placing a ceiling on the total costs of achieving the renewables target (Roberts and Spence, 1976; Menantau *et al.*, 2003). Each effectively combines a financial subsidy to renewable generators (generally paid for by electricity consumers rather than taxpayers) with a long-term take-or-pay contract to reduce investment risk in an increasingly liberalized electricity market (Helm, 2002). The equivalent abatement costs of such mechanisms are typically high compared to competing options. For example, the price ceiling in the UK Renewables Obligation (a hybrid scheme) corresponds to maximum abatement cost of approximately €100/tCO$_2$, which is 20 times higher than current allowance prices in the UK ETS. While a comparable quantity of renewables deployment could be achieved through an ETS, the cap would need to be much more stringent than is required to meet existing targets under the Kyoto Protocol.

As with a tax, the coexistence of a support scheme for renewable electricity with a carbon ETS will raise overall abatement costs while contributing nothing to aggregate emission reductions. However, there may be legitimate grounds for supporting renewables, independent of their contribution to carbon abatement over the short term. For example, it is well established that private markets will under-invest in R&D as a consequence of both the uncertainty and intangibility of R&D outcomes and the inability of innovators fully to appropriate the social returns of such investment (Stoneman and Vickers, 1988). Also, the development of new technologies is characterized by learning-by-doing, where performance improves and costs fall as production experience is accumulated (Ibenholt, 2002). Learning creates an additional source of positive externality, as the act of investment benefits future investors, but the benefit is not paid for by the market (Arrow, 1962). These arguments point to a general role for government in both funding R&D and in steering innovation in desired directions (Grubb, 1997; Gross and Foxon, 2002). This can be achieved in a variety of ways, but it is generally recognized that policies need to avoid 'picking winners' (Hall, 2002). Quantity-based support schemes are designed to provide aggregate targets for renewables deployment while not specifying the contribution from individual technologies, but they still require the government to define those technologies that qualify as 'renewable'.

Two other arguments may legitimate government support for renewables deployment. First, the increasing returns to adoption as a result of learning-by-doing may combine with other factors to both *lock-in* dominant technologies and *lock-out* viable alternatives (Arthur, 1989). These other factors include scale economies in production, the inertia of long-lived capital stock, and the network economies associated with the relations between technologies, infrastructures, interdependent industries, suppliers, users, public and private institutions (e.g. trade associations, universities, etc.), and public expectations

(Unruh, 2000). As with the 'pathways' objective, this evolutionary perspective on technical change implies that a failure to invest in the development of low-carbon technologies such as renewables could lead to lock-in to a high emissions path. In turn, this creates the risk that the cost of switching to alternative technologies could become prohibitive, particularly if climate impacts turn out to be more severe than antici-pated. In contrast, targeted policy support for promising low-carbon technologies can mitigate economic and environmental uncertainty by either creating options that would otherwise not exist, or bringing them forward in time (Foxon, 2004). This may in turn reduce the carbon price required to achieve long-term emission targets and increase the likeli-hood of effective international agreement on climate change.

The expectation that global targets on carbon emissions will tighten also creates the possibility that early support for renewable technolo-gies may drive down unit prices sufficiently to form the basis for viable industries with significant export potential. An example of this 'early mover advantage' is German support for wind power, which saw investment costs decreasing from €4,500/kWh in 1992 to below €1,000/kWh in 2002 and enabled German firms to capture much of the world market (Haas, 2002). However, in the absence of a viable domestic industry, such support would merely subsidize technology imports.

A further rationale for supporting renewables relates to the possi-bility of improving security of supply through the promotion of *diversity* in generation sources. This argument has a long history within energy policy, but has rarely been subject to serious scrutiny. A notable exception is Stirling (1994), who distinguished between variety (number of options), balance (extent of reliance on individual options), and disparity (difference between options), and developed a systematic approach to optimizing portfolio diversity taking into account multicriteria appraisals of the performance of different options and the willingness to pay for diversity implicit in previous government sup-port for nuclear power. A robust conclusion from this analysis is that a 'diversity optimal' generation mix would have a higher contribution from renewables than at present (e.g. up to 30 per cent) and that, under a range of scenarios, renewables investment at the margin was a more effective route to increasing diversity than investment in nuclear power. Security of supply has recently re-emerged as a concern within energy policy, but the extent to which it justifies policy intervention is contested (NERA, 2003). Furthermore, diversity represents only one dimension of security of supply, and existing support mechanisms may lead to a high reliance on a single renewable technology (wind) with intermittent output.

In sum, both technology market failures and supply security objectives could potentially provide a rationale for supporting the diffusion of renewable technologies. These rationales are less well-established than environmental externalities as a basis for government intervention and there is a lack of consensus over either the extent of intervention that is appropriate or the particular instruments that should be used. But if such instruments are to coexist with a cap-and-trade ETS, these rationales become more important. This is because aggregate emission reductions will be set solely by the ETS cap, and the renewables policy will simply shift abatement to technologies which impose significantly higher costs in the short term. The question then becomes whether the perceived, long-term benefits of renewables are considered sufficient to offset these short-term costs.

(c) *Carbon Trading and Policies to Promote Energy Efficiency*

Most OECD countries utilize a range of policies to promote energy efficiency, including information programmes, labelling schemes, tax allowances, subsidies, regulatory standards, and market-transformation programmes. These are typically justified as a means to overcome non-price 'barriers' to energy efficiency that prevent individuals and organizations from investing in highly cost-effective efficiency improvements. Economists have been more sceptical of such approaches and consider that only a subset of these barriers can be considered as market failures that justify public intervention (Jaffe and Stavins, 1994; Sutherland, 2000). For example, if efficiency investments are associated with real but 'hidden' costs, such as disruptions to production, this creates a barrier but does not justify intervention. Nevertheless, a wide range of failures in energy service markets have been identified, including imperfect information on efficiency opportunities, and asymmetric information between contracting parties leading to problems of split incentives, adverse selection and moral hazard (Sorrell *et al.*, 2004). A standard example is landlord–tenant relationships in the housing market, where neither party has the incentive to invest in energy efficiency. Similarly, asymmetric information between buyers and sellers prevents house prices reflecting the discounted value of efficiency investments.

Following Arrow (1969), it is perhaps more useful to consider these market failures in a relative rather than absolute sense using: 'a broader category, that of transaction costs, which in general impede and in particular cases completely block the formation of markets'. Transaction costs are a feature of all contractual relationships and are shaped by both the nature of the transaction and the associated legal, organizational, and institutional arrangements (Williamson, 1985). Combined with the behavioural assumptions of bounded rationality and opportunism, transaction costs can provide a valuable insight into the nature of barriers to energy efficiency (Sorrell *et al.*, 2004). For example, transaction costs help explain why landlords and tenants do not enter into shared-savings contracts to share the benefits of efficiency investments. Similarly, the bounded rationality of economic agents, coupled with the nature of energy efficiency as a credence good helps explain why purchase decisions are biased towards equipment with low capital cost, but high running costs. In manufacturing, the asymmetric information between senior management and individual departments helps explain the use of capital budgeting procedures that prevent all but the most cost-effective energy-efficiency projects from going ahead (Ross, 1986). And in the construction industry, opportunism and asymmetric information help explain why subcontractors substitute cheaper and less efficient building services equipment, leading to higher running costs for the client (Sorrell, 2003*b*).

Proponents of energy efficiency argue that public intervention can overcome barriers such as these through reducing transaction costs, economizing on bounded rationality, aligning the incentives of different groups in the direction of improved efficiency, and safeguarding against opportunism (Golove and Eto, 1996). Furthermore, they argue that such measures can be more effective than relatively small increases in energy prices and can deliver net social benefits (Krause, 1996). Economists are more sceptical of such claims and question whether many existing energy-efficiency policies are, in fact, cost effective (Joskow and Marron, 1992; Sutherland, 2000).

This is a long-standing debate within energy policy and there is an extensive literature on both the economic potential for energy efficiency (IPCC, 2001*c*) and the win–win opportunities within individual organizations (Lovins and Lovins, 1997). But, owing in part to measurement difficulties, evaluations of the costs and benefits of individual policy instruments are much harder to find. Nevertheless, some evidence suggests that common types of energy-efficiency programme can be highly cost effective. For example, the Levine *et al.* (1994) study of US appliance standards found a total benefit-to-cost ratio of more than 2.5 (at a discount rate of 6 per cent), excluding environmental externalities. The Eto *et al.* (1994) study of US utility lighting programmes found the weighted average cost of electricity saved was $0.039/kWh. And an assessment of a UK scheme to promote household energy efficiency found a benefit-to-cost ratio of 2.3, considering energy savings alone, or 3.0 if the benefits of improved comfort to low-income households were included (EST, 2001*b*).

If the proponents of energy efficiency are correct, the coexistence of such instruments with an ETS will lead to an improvement in static efficiency and a reduction in overall abatement costs. If they are not correct, the coexistence of such instruments will increase overall costs. Ultimately, this is an empirical question, the answer to which will depend upon the specific market, technology, and policy under examination. It may be expected that such policies will be more effective for sectors such as households and small business which have both a low energy price elasticity and a substantial economic potential for efficiency improvement. While these sectors are unlikely to participate directly in a carbon ETS, they may be indirectly affected by increases in fuel or electricity prices. But allowance prices would need to be very high to have a significant impact on energy efficiency in these sectors, and the resulting impacts are likely to be regressive without explicit compensation (Johnson *et al.*, 1990).

In addition to overcoming a variety of market failures, many energy-efficiency policies have social objectives. This is particularly true in the UK, where a combination of income inequality and a poor quality housing stock leads to several million households living in 'fuel poverty'. Efficiency investments in these households are commonly taken up in improved levels of energy service, such as warmer homes, rather than reduced consumption. While the CO_2 benefits of such investments are close to zero, quality of life is improved and savings may be made in areas such as health care. In view of this, the energy-efficiency obligations imposed on UK electricity and gas suppliers require that at least 50 per cent of investment be in low-income households.

Policies to promote energy efficiency may also be justified in terms of employment benefits and the mitigation of non-CO_2 externalities of energy supply such as acid rain, nuclear waste, and the visual impacts of wind farms. But these rationales appear less convincing. While jobs are frequently created in priority sectors, locations, and skill groups, research suggests that the cost effectiveness of this employment creation is relatively low (UKACE, 2000). Similarly, non-CO_2 externalities are increasingly reflected in energy prices through regulations such as the EU Large Combustion Plant Directive.

In sum, the use of additional policies to promote energy efficiency among target groups directly or indirectly affected by a carbon ETS may be justified through their contribution to overcoming a range of market and organizational barriers to energy efficiency, or to delivering non-efficiency objectives such as improved social equity. Taken together, these appear to provide a good case for the continuation of such policies. However, since the costs and benefits of such instruments are disputed, each case will need to be judged on its merits.

4. Interaction Between the EU ETS and UK Climate Policy

The introduction of the EU ETS into a crowded 'policy space' within each member state is likely to bring these issues of policy interaction to the fore. The issues discussed within the previous three sections are likely to be faced by the majority of member states, together with related issues such as the future of negotiated agreements with energy-intensive industry. The complex, elaborate, and interdependent mix of climate policies developed in the UK provides a particularly rich example of the challenges to be faced. This mix includes:

- a downstream, revenue-neutral energy tax for business and the public sector;
- negotiated agreements for energy-intensive industry which give participants exemption from 80 per cent of the energy tax;
- an elaborate greenhouse-gas trading scheme (UK ETS), developed in collaboration with industry;
- the UK implementation of the EU Integrated Pollution Prevention and Control (IPPC) Directive, which includes provisions on energy efficiency;
- a tradable green credit scheme, in which obligations to purchase renewable electricity are imposed upon electricity suppliers; and
- a tradable white credit scheme, in which obligations to invest in household energy efficiency are imposed upon electricity suppliers, with priority given to low-income households.

These instruments are closely interlinked. For example, the negotiated agreements provide exemption from the energy tax as well as forming part of the trading scheme. Similarly, there is (in principle) trading interaction between the carbon trading scheme and the instruments for promoting renewable electricity and household energy efficiency. The carbon trading scheme itself includes: a voluntary cap-and-trade scheme, with participation incentivized by direct subsidy; a 'baseline and credit' trading scheme for the negotiated agreement participants; and a proposed scheme for emission-reduction projects. Table 2 lists all these instruments and indicates the nature of their interaction with the EU ETS.

The interactions summarized in Table 2 lead to a series of examples of double regulation and double counting (Sorrell, 2003c). Unless resolved, these interactions could lead to substantial economic impacts

Table 2
The Nature of the Potential Interaction between Selected UK Policy
Instruments and the EU ETS

Category	Name	Direct	Indirect	Trading
Carbon/energy taxes	Climate Change Levy	✓	✓	
Negotiated agreements	Climate Change Agreements	✓	✓	✓
Emissions trading	UK ETS – cap-and-trade scheme	✓	✓	✓
Emissions trading	UK ETS – project scheme	✓	✓	✓
Industrial pollution control	IPPC Directive	✓	✓	
Support for renewables	Renewables Obligation		✓	✓
Promotion of energy efficiency	Energy Efficiency Commitment		✓	✓

for the affected groups, and/or threaten the overall environmental integrity of the policy mix. For example:

- Organizations eligible for the energy tax will also face electricity price increases as a consequence of the generators participating in the EU ETS (Table 1). Modelling work conducted for the UK government (ILEX, 2003) suggests that an EU ETS allowance price of €7/tCO$_2$ could increase average electricity prices by some £3.90/MWh, which compares to an energy tax on delivered electricity of £4.30/MWh.

- The proposed UK project scheme would allow projects to be awarded carbon credits for improving downstream electricity efficiency. But this action also 'frees up' allowances held by the electricity generators participating in the EU ETS. If the credits are subsequently traded into the EU ETS, the cap will be breached and the environmental integrity of the scheme will be undermined.

To avoid these problems, the existing UK policy mix will need to be rationalized. But such changes are likely to create administrative costs for both government and industry. They are also likely to encounter resistance from a range of sources – particularly since none of the above instruments is more than 4 years old.

In the UK, as elsewhere, policy instruments resist replacement even when a more viable alternative is available. This inertia may derive from a number of sources. For example: a legislative framework will have been established which may be difficult to change; regulatory institutions will have been established, or responsibilities assigned to existing institutions; procedures and standards will have been established for functions such as monitoring, reporting, and verification; a network of private organizations will have become involved in implementation; and the target groups themselves will have invested substantial time and money in gaining familiarity with the policy instruments and putting the appropriate procedures in place. All these activities are separate from investment in abatement, but each will cultivate vested interests and encourage resistance to change. As a result of this 'institutional lock in' (Pierson, 2000), there is a strong possibility that many of these instruments will continue after the ETS has been introduced, whether or not this is helpful to overall government objectives.

In the case of the UK, the government is reviewing the policy mix in the light of the EU ETS and has already made some small changes — such as exempting EU ETS participants from the energy tax on fuel use. But a major overhaul of the policy mix appears unlikely, at least not before 2008. This means that policy interaction could have a determinate impact on the success of the EU ETS in the UK.

5. Summary and Conclusions

Policy interaction has been neglected within the economics literature but is of central importance in determining the success of individual instruments and of the overall policy mix. This is particularly true within climate policy, where the introduction of a carbon ETS into an already overcrowded 'policy space' poses a particularly difficult challenge.

In theory, cap-and-trade schemes should provide assurance of meeting an overall emissions target at least cost. It follows that, if we assume a perfect economy with no market failures, instruments that directly or indirectly interact with a carbon ETS will raise overall abatement costs while providing no additional contribution to emission reductions. Hence, once a cap is in place, the rationale for introducing or retaining such instruments must rely upon either their contribution to overcoming market failures other than carbon externalities, or in delivering social objectives other than efficiency. Their contribution to emission reductions can no longer form part of their rationale.

This chapter has explored the rationales for the coexistence of a carbon ETS with carbon/energy taxation, support mechanisms for renewable electricity and non-price instruments to overcome barriers to energy efficiency. In each case, there are possible justifications which fall into one of the above categories and which may have validity (Table 3). But these are disputed and raise both theoretical issues regarding the legitimacy of government intervention and empirical issues regarding the design of individual instruments. In many cases there will be

Table 3
Possible Rationales for the Coexistence of Policies with a
Cap-and-trade ETS

Policy	Possible rationales for coexistence	Primary theoretical basis
Carbon/energy taxes	Internalizing negative externalities of inframarginal emissions. Increasing incentive for innovation. Capturing windfall rent from allowance allocation Maintaining fiscal revenue. Ensuring a minimum level of abatement from participants.	Welfare economics
Support for renewables	Positive externalities of innovation. Mitigating economic and environmental risk through the creation of options. Improving supply security through greater diversity in generation sources.	Evolutionary economics Innovation theory
Promotion of energy efficiency	Overcoming non-price barriers to energy efficiency, resulting from information asymmetries, transaction costs and bounded rationality. Improving social equity.	Economics of information New institutional economics

trade-offs between long-term and/or non-efficiency objectives and short-term increases in abatement costs. If the policy mix is to gain legitimacy, these objectives and trade-offs need to be explicit.

The fact that positive combinations between an ETS and other instruments are theoretically possible does not mean that such combinations will result in practice While the introduction of a carbon ETS should provide an opportunity to rationalize the policy mix, this may not always be taken. Governments may be reluctant to abandon tried and tested instruments in favour of an unfamiliar alternative, and the inertia of existing instruments may make them difficult to displace. The net result may be a mix of overlapping, interacting and conflicting instruments that lack any overall coherence. In short, a policy mix may easily become a policy mess.

10

Fiscal Interactions and the Case for Carbon Taxes over Grandfathered Carbon Permits

IAN W. H. PARRY*

I. Introduction

Economists have long recognized that the welfare effects of environmental and other regulatory policies depend on how they interact with distortions in other markets of the economy (e.g. Lipsey and Lancaster, 1956; Harberger, 1974). One market that is particularly large (around three-quarters of GDP), and badly distorted at the margin, is the labour market, where income, payroll, and other taxes combine to drive a large wedge between the gross wage paid by firms and the net wage received by households. Yet, prior to the 1990s, there had been very little analysis of how interactions with the labour market might change the welfare effect of environmental policies, and regulatory policies more generally.

In the early 1990s, economists, grappling with ways to combat the emerging possibility of global warming, began to emphasize that large welfare gains could be realized from using the revenues from carbon taxes to reduce taxes that distort factor markets (e.g. Pearce, 1991; Repetto *et al.*, 1992; Nordhaus, 1993*b*; Oates, 1993). It was suggested that carbon taxes could yield a 'double dividend' by reducing emissions and the costs of pre-existing tax distortions at the same time. The idea that 'revenue recycling' might keep the overall economic costs of carbon taxes small, or even negative, was particularly appealing as it suggests that the policy is worthwhile, despite considerable controversy over the benefits from slowing atmospheric accumulation of greenhouse gases.

* Resources for the Future.

I am grateful to David Pearce, Dieter Helm, Larry Goulder, Bob Shackleton, and two referees for helpful comments.

However, a second wave of papers pointed out another important linkage between emissions taxes and the broader tax system, working in the opposite direction to the revenue-recycling effect (e.g. Bovenberg and de Mooij, 1994; Parry, 1995; Oates, 1995; Bovenberg and Goulder, 1996). By increasing energy prices, carbon taxes drive up product prices throughout the economy, as energy is an input in most production sectors; this leads to a slight reduction in real household wages and labour supply. In general, the efficiency loss from this reduction in labour supply, or 'tax-interaction effect', exceeds the benefits from the revenue-recycling effect, implying that carbon tax swaps increase rather than decrease the costs of labour taxes. This finding is not surprising because, as explained below, it is entirely consistent with the familiar result in public finance that the efficiency costs of narrow taxes (ignoring externalities) tend to exceed those of broad taxes on labour income.

More striking are the implications for other emissions-control instruments (e.g. Goulder *et al.*, 1997, 1999; Parry *et al.*, 1999; Fullerton and Metcalf, 2001). When carbon emissions are reduced by a system of tradable permits, and the permits are grandfathered (i.e. given out to existing firms for free), the government forgoes the potential efficiency gains from the revenue-recycling effect. Yet the policy still causes the costly tax-interaction effect as it increases energy prices by the same amount as an equivalent carbon tax. Consequently, there is a potentially strong case on efficiency grounds for preferring emissions taxes (or auctioned emissions permits) to grandfathered permits, so long as they are revenue neutral. This case is even stronger when we allow for additional deadweight losses from the US tax system arising because certain types of spending (e.g. homeowner mortgage interest, employer-provided medical insurance) are tax-exempt or deductible while other spending is not (see below).

These findings raise concerns about the momentum for tradable-permit approaches in countries that remain pledged to achieving emissions targets embodied in the 1997 Kyoto Protocol, and in the United States, which pioneered the tradable-permit approach.[1] Policy-makers should be open-minded about the possibility of abandoning this approach in favour of internationally harmonized carbon taxes. To be sure, there are many other factors, besides fiscal issues, that are relevant to the choice among policy approaches, though, as we discuss later, many of them seem to favour a tax-based rather than a quantity-based approach.

---

[1] The European trading system introduced in January 2005 allows countries to auction only a small fraction of permits.

One caveat is that we focus mainly on an analysis that is applicable to the United States, which has a competitive labour market—fiscal interactions are more subtle in countries where the labour market contains significant institutional distortions which lead to 'sticky' real wages and involuntary unemployment (e.g. Bovenberg and van der Ploeg, 1994a; Schöb, 2003, section 3). The next section explains how fiscal interactions affect the costs of carbon policies in a transparent, though highly simplified, framework. Section 3 discusses complicating factors, including income-tax deductions, pre-existing energy taxes, and taxes on capital. Section 4 comments on broader issues that are relevant to the choice between taxes and permits. Section 5 concludes and discusses caveats to the analysis.

2. Basic Theoretical Framework

This section presents a heuristic analysis, simplified as follows: labour is the only primary factor; the pre-existing tax system distorts only the labour market; and all markets are competitive with constant returns production. We provide formulas for adjusting, approximately, the costs of carbon policies to account for fiscal interactions (for derivations see Parry, 1995, 2002; Goulder *et al.*, 1999; Parry *et al.*, 1999).

(a) *Traditional Analysis*

Consider the top panel in Figure 1, which represents the economy-wide market for fossil fuels, denoted X. D^X is the demand curve, and S^X is the supply curve drawn as perfectly elastic because of constant returns. In the absence of policy intervention the competitive output level is X_0, where the marginal value of fossil fuels in production (the height of D^X) equals the per-unit cost of producing fossil fuels (the height of S^X).

For expositional purposes, we assume that carbon emissions are proportional to aggregate fossil fuel use; initial emissions are $E_0 = eX_0$ where e is an exogenous emissions factor.[2] Suppose a tax of t per unit of emissions is introduced, equivalent to te per unit of fossil fuels. Output falls to X_1 in Figure 1 as firms and households adopt energy saving technologies, motorists drive less and demand more fuel-efficient vehicles, etc. The resulting efficiency cost, which we call the *primary cost*,

---

[2] Emissions factors differ across individual fuels so that the substitution of gas for coal in, for example, power generation, reduces emissions. Models that allow for emissions reduction through fuel substitution, and also end-of-pipe abatement technologies (which are currently not applicable to carbon), produce analogous formulas to those below.

Figure 1
Primary Abatement Costs

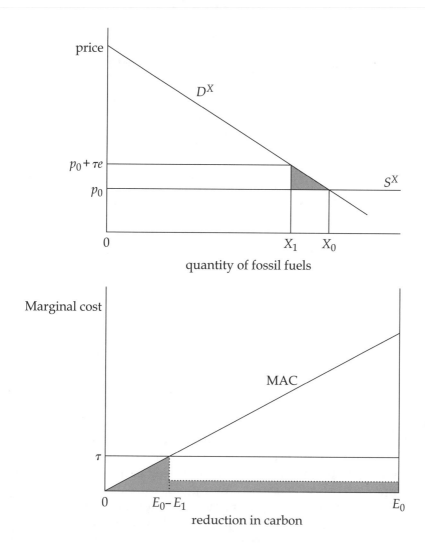

is shown by the shaded triangle, equal to forgone benefits from fossil fuel production net of reduced production costs. The primary cost is also represented by the shaded triangle in the lower panel of Figure 1; here MAC denotes the marginal abatement cost curve for reducing emissions, where the height of MAC equals the difference between D^X and S^X in the top panel, divided by e. Assuming D^X is linear over the relevant range, the primary cost (PC) is:

Figure 2
Tax Distortions in the Labour Market

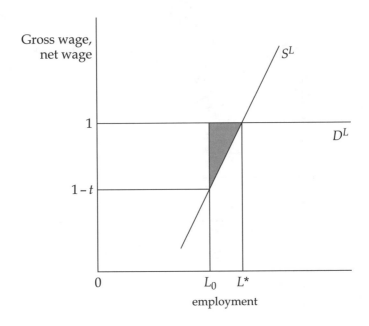

$$PC = \frac{\tau}{2}(E_0 - E_1). \qquad (1)$$

Suppose, for example, that reducing annual US carbon emissions by 10 per cent below current levels, which are roughly 1,500m tons, requires a carbon tax of $20 per ton (see Weyant and Hill (1999) and Council of Economic Advisors (1998) for a discussion of estimates); in this case, from (1) the primary cost would be $1.5 billion.

Prior to the 1990s, economists focused only on primary costs when assessing the costs of emissions-control policies. However, in the early 1990s they began to emphasize the large revenue potential from carbon taxes; in our example, revenues would be $tE_1 = \$27$ billion (= 20 x 0.9 x 1,500m). What happens if these revenues are used to cut labour income taxes?

(b) *Labour Market*

Figure 2 shows the labour market for the whole economy, which constitutes around three-quarters of GDP. D^L is the aggregate demand for labour by firms where the height of this curve is the value marginal product of labour; the curve is perfectly elastic due to constant returns (this may be a reasonable long-run approximation—see Hamermesh, 1986, p. 467).

S^L is the aggregate supply of labour from households; it is upward sloping because higher wages encourage secondary workers to join the labour force, older workers to postpone retirement, and existing workers to take out a second job, increase overtime, etc. The height of S^L is the marginal opportunity cost of forgone non-market time: someone well to the left of L_0 in Figure 2 has a low opportunity cost to working (e.g. a single person who would be bored at home) while someone to the right of L^* has a high opportunity cost (e.g. the partner of a working spouse who would rather stay home with the children).

The socially optimal level of employment is L^*, where the marginal social benefit and marginal social cost of labour would be equated. However, various taxes, including federal and state income taxes and payroll taxes, combine to create a tax wedge of around 35–40 per cent for the average US worker;[3] denoting this tax by t, equilibrium employment is at L_0, with a wedge of t between the gross wage (normalized to one) and net wage. There is a deadweight loss indicated by the shaded triangle, because employment $L^* - L_0$ is forgone, for which the marginal social benefit would have exceeded the marginal social cost. The difference between L_0 and L^* may not be large in practice—indeed empirical evidence suggests that labour supply is only moderately sensitive to taxes. However, small changes in labour supply can still lead to significant welfare effects, given the large size of the labour market and the large wedge between the gross and net wage.

A number of studies have estimated the *marginal excess burden* of labour taxation (e.g. Stuart, 1984; Ballard *et al.*, 1985; Browning, 1987; Snow and Warren, 1996); this is the efficiency cost from the increase in labour tax required to raise an extra dollar of revenue. Leaving some complications aside (e.g. tax deductions, heterogeneous agents, non-proportional tax increases) a simple formula for the marginal excess burden of labour taxation (denoted M) when the dollar is recycled in transfers to households is (e.g. Mayshar, 1991; Snow and Warren, 1996):

$$M = \frac{\dfrac{t}{1-t}\varepsilon^c}{1 - \dfrac{t}{1-t}\varepsilon^u} \tag{2}$$

[3] Most of the labour-supply elasticity for the United States is driven by participation decisions, particularly of married females, rather than changes in hours of existing workers. Therefore, the relevant tax wedge reflects a combination of average and marginal rates (e.g. Kleven and Kreiner, 2003).

where e^u and e^c denote the uncompensated and compensated labour-supply elasticities respectively.[4] For illustration we assume $e^u = 0.2$ and $e^c = 0.35$, based on an average across US studies and professional opinion (see Blundell and MaCurdy, 1991, Tables 1 and 2; Fuchs et al., 1998); using $t = 0.38$ implies M is approximately 0.25. However, there is considerable uncertainty over labour-supply elasticities—a plausible range for M might be around 0.1 to 0.5 (Browning, 1987)—though the implications of different assumptions can easily be seen in the formulas below.[5]

(c) Revenue-recycling Effect

The revenue-recycling effect is the efficiency gain from recycling carbon tax revenues in other tax reductions (relative to returning them lump sum). It equals the revenue recycled multiplied by the marginal excess burden:

$$RR = M\tau E_1. \tag{3}$$

The revenue-recycling effect (RR) is shown by the shaded rectangle in the lower panel of Figure 1. In our numerical example it equals $6.75 billion (= 0.25 × $27 billion), or 4.5 times the primary cost. More generally, using (1) and (3), the revenue-recycling effect relative to the primary cost is $2M(1 - z)/z$, where $z = (E_0 - E_1)/E_0$ is the proportionate emissions reduction. Thus, the relative importance of the revenue-recycling effect diminishes with the level of abatement: it is 117 per cent and 33 per cent of primary costs at emissions reductions of 30 per cent and 60 per cent, respectively. This is easily seen from the lower panel in Figure 1 by comparing the shaded triangle and rectangle at small and large amounts of abatement.

Based on the reasoning so far, a number of people have suggested that there might be a 'double dividend' from carbon and other environmental taxes, owing to the reduction in emissions and in the costs of pre-existing taxes; indeed, it was argued that the overall costs of environmental taxes could be negative (e.g. Terkla, 1984; Lee and Misiolek, 1986; Pearce, 1991; Repetto et al., 1992; Nordhaus, 1993b; Oates, 1993).

---

[4] The formula depends on both compensated and uncompensated elasticities because households are only partially compensated for the tax increase; the reduction in their wages is Ldt, but the government receives $Ldt + tdL/dt < Ldt$ in revenue.

[5] Marginal excess burden estimates for other countries tend to be larger due to higher labour tax rates (e.g. Kleven and Kreiner, 2003).

(d) *The Tax-interaction Effect*

However, a second wave of papers revealed that there is another linkage with the labour market that undermines the double-dividend argument (e.g. Bovenberg and de Mooij, 1994; Bovenberg and van der Ploeg, 1994*b*; Parry, 1995, 1997; Bovenberg and Goulder, 2002). A carbon tax increases the price of electricity, gasoline, and other energy goods; in turn, this drives up the prices of products in general, as they require energy inputs in production. The general increase in the price level reduces real household wages, which should slightly reduce employment given econometric evidence that lower real household wages leads to lower labour-force participation and work effort. This leads to an efficiency loss of $t\Delta L$, where ΔL is the (small) reduction in labour supply (this is the addition to the deadweight-loss triangle in Figure 2 from a slight shift in of the labour supply curve). And labour tax revenues fall by $t\Delta L$; to maintain revenues labour taxes must be increased slightly, resulting in an efficiency cost of $Mt\Delta L$. The combined loss from these two effects, $(1 + M)t\Delta L$, is referred to as the *tax-interaction effect*.

Assuming linearity and (for the moment) that final output produced with fossil fuels is an average substitute for leisure, the tax-interaction effect (TI) can be expressed (e.g. Parry, 2002) as:

$$TI = M\tau \left\{ E_0 - \frac{(E_0 - E_1)}{2} \right\}.$$ (4)

Comparing (3) and (4), the tax-interaction effect exceeds the revenue-recycling effect for all levels of emissions reduction; that is, the net effect of the carbon tax is to increase rather than decrease the efficiency costs of pre-existing labour taxes, and there is no double dividend.[6]

[6] Several different notions of the double-dividend hypothesis have appeared in the literature (e.g. Goulder, 1995). The weak form of the hypothesis asserts that using revenues to cut distortionary taxes rather than returning them in lump-sum transfers increases efficiency; an intermediate form asserts that the tax-interaction effect exceeds the revenue-recycling effect; a strong form asserts that the revenue-recycling effect offsets both the primary cost and the tax-interaction effect so that the cost of the environmental tax is negative. The above results reject the latter two definitions but not the weak double dividend, which is clearly valid so long as the reduced tax has a positive marginal excess burden.

The intuition for the failure of the strong double dividend is straightforward. In the absence of non-labour income, a shift from a labour tax to a uniform tax on all consumption goods has no effect on the household's real wage and labour supply (assuming no money illusion). A further tax shift on to energy goods leaves this basic result unchanged, but adds an additional inter-commodity distortion. For further discussion of the double dividend see, for example, Goulder (1995), Smith (1998), Bovenberg and Goulder (2002), and Schöb (2003).

Suppose this was not the case, then—at least for small amounts of abatement—the overall costs of the carbon tax swap would be negative, implying that even with no environmental benefits it is always optimal to raise at least some revenues from carbon taxes.[7] But this contradicts an extensive literature on optimal tax theory (e.g. Diamond and Mirrlees, 1971; Sandmo, 1975; Atkinson and Stiglitz, 1980; Ng, 1980) which implies that, leaving aside certain special cases, narrow taxes on sector-specific inputs or outputs involve higher efficiency costs per dollar of revenue than economy-wide labour taxes. The above analysis could only be consistent with this literature if the tax-interaction effect exceeds the revenue-recycling effect.

More generally, it can be shown that the tax-interaction effect is smaller (larger) if consumption goods produced by polluting industries are relatively weak (strong) substitutes for leisure (e.g. Parry, 1995; Bovenberg and Goulder, 2002). There is a lack of solid empirical evidence on this issue. However, given that energy is used pervasively in production sectors throughout the economy, a logical starting assumption is that aggregate output affected by a carbon tax is an average substitute for leisure.

From (1), (3), and (4), the ratio of the total cost of the emissions tax with fiscal interactions to the primary cost is:

$$\frac{PC - RR + TI}{PC} = 1 + M. \tag{5}$$

With $M = 0.25$, fiscal interactions raise the costs of carbon taxes by 25 per cent relative to primary costs.[8]

(e) *Tradable Permits*

Now suppose that fuel producers must have a permit for each ton of carbon content contained in their fuels, and that the government restricts the availability of permits so that emissions are reduced by $E_0 - E_1$ in Figure 1. Assuming competition, perfect certainty, and that

---

[7] This is because the primary cost is a second-order effect (a triangle) and converges to zero for an arbitrarily small amount of abatement; the welfare change in the labour market is first-order (a rectangle).

[8] Some, though not all, studies show a negligible effect of environmental regulations on employment at the industry level (e.g. Berman and Bui, 2001) and this has sometimes been interpreted to mean that we do not need to worry about the employment effects of carbon and other environmental policies. However, these findings do not tell us anything about the tax-interaction and revenue-recycling effects, which apply so long as economy-wide labour supply is responsive to changes in real net wages. And changes in economy-wide employment need not be large to generate welfare effects that can be substantial relative to primary costs, given the huge size of the labour market and that it is badly distorted at the margin.

permits are tradable across firms, the equilibrium permit price will be t. The primary abatement costs are the same as under the equivalent emissions tax. The tax interaction effect is also the same, because the policy has the same impact on driving up energy and final goods prices, and reducing the real household wage. This can be seen from the top panel in Figure 1, where the price of fossil fuels at X_1 is the same, regardless of whether fuels are reduced by a tax or the equivalent binding quota.

The crucial difference is that, if permits are given out free to firms, as they were in the case of the US sulphur-trading programme, they, rather than the government, receive the policy rents; that is, they receive a valuable asset (permits with a market price). A portion of the rents may indirectly go to the government—rents are reflected in higher firm profits that are taxed at the corporate level, and at the personal level when they are paid out in dividends or lead to capital gains. Denoting the rate of profits/rent taxation by q, and assuming that government revenues are used to cut labour taxes, freely allocated permits will produce an indirect revenue-recycling effect of:

$$RR^p = \theta M t E_1. \tag{6}$$

Following other studies (e.g. Goulder *et al.*, 1997) we adopt a value for θ of 0.4 for grandfathered permits; for auctioned permits, $\theta = 1$.

Using (1), (4), and (6) the total cost of grandfathered permits (with fiscal interactions) relative to the primary cost can be expressed as:

$$\frac{PC - RR^p + TI}{PC} = 1 + \frac{M\{(1-0.5z) - \theta(1-z)\}}{0.5z}. \tag{7}$$

Figure 3 plots the expressions in equations (5) and (7) for emissions reductions up to 40 per cent. The main point here is that fiscal interactions raise the cost of grandfathered permits by a much greater amount than they raise the cost of revenue-neutral carbon taxes (or auctioned permits), as the net loss from the tax-interaction and (indirect) revenue-recycling effect is much greater under grandfathered permits. In our example, the total costs of grandfathered permits are $6 billion at an emissions reduction of 10 per cent, or four times the primary costs.[9]

[9] The costs ratios in (5) and (7) do not depend on the share of fossil fuels in GDP, or the slope of the marginal abatement cost function, as these factors affect the primary cost, revenue-recycling, and tax-interaction effects all in the same proportion. This proportionality does not apply when linearity assumptions are relaxed; however, relatively simple numerical models that incorporate more general functional forms yield very similar relative costs to those in Figure 3 (e.g. Goulder *et al.* 1997, 1999; Parry *et al.* 1999).

Figure 3
Policy Costs with Fiscal Interactions Relative to Primary Costs

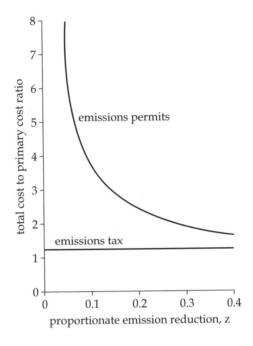

(f) *Welfare Effects*

There is much dispute about attaching a dollar figure to the benefits from slowing atmospheric greenhouse-gas accumulation—controversies rage over appropriate discount rates, how to value non-market effects, such as species extinction, the likelihood and extent of instabilities within the climate system, and how to account for the greater vulnerability of poor countries to climate change. The majority of studies put the benefits from reducing carbon at around $25 per ton or less, though some estimates that incorporate low discount rates and distributional weights are over $200/ton.[10]

Take a 'mainstream' estimate of $20 per ton, so that a $20 carbon tax, or permit-equivalent, would be optimal in the absence of fiscal interac-

---

[10] Most damage estimates are fairly moderate because the bulk of world GDP (manufacturing and services) is not especially sensitive to predicted changes in climate over the next century, and discounting greatly reduces the present value of long-range costs (e.g. Nordhaus, 1994a; Fankhauser, 1995). However, the marginal damage from emissions is likely to rise in the future as economic growth increases the real value of GDP at potential risk; for example, optimal carbon taxes in the RICE model rise from around $10/ton to $70/ton over the next century (Nordhaus and Boyer, 1999a, ch. 7). For reviews of the literature see Tol *et al.* (2000) and Pearce (this issue).

tions. Total benefits from reducing emissions by 150m tons are, therefore, $3 billion. If we ignored fiscal interactions we would compute a welfare gain (environmental benefits less primary costs) of $1.5 billion per annum (using (1)); with fiscal interactions the carbon tax still produces a welfare gain, of $1.13 billion, but grandfathered permits produce a welfare loss of $6 billion. Grandfathered permits can easily be welfare improving under higher benefit scenarios (when benefits per ton exceed $40); but the point here is that accounting for fiscal interactions may substantially affect the magnitude, and possibly even the sign, of the welfare effect of grandfathered permits (Parry et al., 1999).

Fiscal interactions do not always have such striking implications for the costs and social welfare effects of environmental policies. As shown in Figure 3, the cost of grandfathered permits with fiscal interactions relative to primary cost declines with the extent of abatement; the tax-interaction effect (net of the indirect revenue-recycling effect) increases in rough proportion with the extent of abatement, while the primary cost increases in rough proportion to the square of the abatement level. The United States is currently debating the Bush Administration's Clear Skies initiative, along with competing bills, that would reduce power-plant emissions of sulphur dioxide, nitrogen oxide, and mercury by around 70 per cent or more below no-abatement levels; the welfare gain from auctioning permits (relative to primary costs) would be less dramatic in these cases.

(g) Alternative Assumptions for Revenue Recycling

Although a number of revenue-neutral environmental tax packages have recently been implemented in European countries (see Hoerner and Bosquest, 2001, p. 3), there is no guarantee that new revenue sources would be used to lower other distortionary taxes, particularly if an environmental agency rather than the Treasury were responsible for the policy. If revenues were used for government deficit reduction, this would reduce future debt interest and repayment of principal, allowing future taxes to be reduced—there is still an efficiency gain, though it occurs in the future.

If revenues were used to expand public spending, the revenue-recycling effect is larger or smaller depending on whether the social benefits from increased spending exceed the social benefits forgone by not using the revenues to cut distortionary taxes. This would have to be assessed on a case-by-case basis; for example, it is often argued that environmental tax revenues should be used to subsidize the development of renewable energy sources. None the less, probably the biggest worry about carbon taxes is that the revenues may not be used productively.[11]

(h) *Other Policies for Reducing Carbon*

Despite ongoing pressure to implement a system of tradable carbon permits, the Bush Administration has so far favoured a more piecemeal approach that includes tax credits for energy-saving and alternative fuel technologies (e.g. Lyon, 2003). It is sometimes suggested that such subsidy policies might be quite costly because their financing implies higher taxes elsewhere in the economy. But again the argument neglects the tax-interaction effect: if subsidies lower (marginal) production costs and product prices, they will have a stimulating effect on labour supply at the margin though, most likely, the beneficial tax-interaction effect will not fully offset the efficiency costs of additional financing requirements (Parry, 1998).[12]

Pollution regulation in the United States traditionally took the form of command and control (CAC) approaches, such as technology mandates and uniform standards for emissions per unit of output across firms. These policies raise product prices and induce a costly tax-interaction effect, while raising no revenues for recycling. However, the tax-interaction effect can be weaker under CAC policies than under emissions taxes and tradable permits (Goulder *et al.*, 1999; Fullerton and Metcalf, 2001). Under the market-based policies, prices rise owing to (i) primary abatement costs and (ii) the tax paid on remaining emissions, or the scarcity rents created by permits. The latter effect is absent under CAC policies, though the former effect is larger, as CAC policies generally do not exploit the least-cost combination of options for emissions reductions within or across firms. None the less, the increase in cost owing to fiscal interactions can actually be greater under grandfathered permits than under CAC policies, particularly at modest levels of emissions abatement.

---

[11] Moreover, even though revenues from energy taxes implemented in the United Kingdom and Germany in the late 1990s were initially tied to reductions in labour taxes, labour taxes were subsequently raised in both countries. And much of the recent, substantial expansion of public spending in the UK seems to have leaked into public-sector pay rather than increased output, which may not be a good omen.

[12] Alternatively, firms might receive subsidies for reducing emissions. This policy is equivalent to a lump-sum subsidy to firms, plus a tax on emissions; in this case both the tax-interaction and revenue-financing effects cause efficiency losses (Parry, 1998).

3. Complicating Factors

(a) *Tax Deductions*

Motivated by recent studies in public finance, Parry and Bento (2000) extended the model outlined above to account for inter-commodity tax distortions. These distortions are important in the United States, where a significant sector of the economy is effectively subsidized through the tax system; for example, owner-occupied housing and employer-provided medical insurance receive large tax deductions/exemptions. In Parry and Bento (2000) the marginal excess burden of taxation—and hence the revenue-recycling effect—increases by around 60 per cent when tax deductions are included; this is because the deadweight losses from income taxes are greater when they distort the choice between tax-favoured and ordinary consumption, in addition to the labour market.

On the other hand, if emissions per unit of final output are the same for both the tax-favoured and non-tax-favoured sectors (which seems a reasonable rough approximation), a carbon tax will not affect their relative prices, and will have no effect on the tax-subsidy distortion. Consequently, the tax-interaction effect from the change in labour supply is similar to before (although the loss of labour tax revenues involves a higher efficiency cost).

Figure 4, which is based on Parry and Bento, illustrates the total costs of carbon taxes and grandfathered permits relative to primary costs when the efficiency gain per dollar of recycled carbon tax revenue is 0.4 rather than 0.25. The larger revenue-recycling effect substantially lowers the cost of carbon taxes for modest levels of abatement; overall costs are negative for emissions reductions below 16 per cent (i.e. the revenue-recycling effect exceeds primary costs plus the tax-interaction effect). And the cost differential between grandfathered permits and carbon taxes at modest abatement levels, which was already large, is even more striking; at a 10 per cent emissions reduction the carbon tax has a negative cost of $1.3 billion (or –88 per cent of primary costs); grandfathered permits have costs of $5.2 billion (344 per cent of primary costs).[13]

[13] These results should be viewed with caution. There is much dispute over the marginal excess burden in the presence of tax deductions (one estimate, by Feldstein (1999), exceeds unity); housing and healthcare markets contain a variety of non-tax distortions (regulations, externalities, and information asymmetries) that have been excluded from marginal excess burden estimates; and tax deductions may have less relevance for other countries such as the United Kingdom where tax relief for private medical insurance and home-ownership has been phased out.

Figure 4
Relative Policy Costs Accounting for Tax Deductions

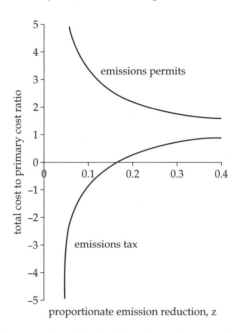

proportionate emission reduction, z

The possibility of a double dividend in this case is illustrative of a general theme: a double dividend is possible when (*a*) the pre-existing tax system is inefficient along some non-environmental dimension and (*b*) the environmental tax shift serves to reduce this non-environmental inefficiency. Of course, directly reforming the tax system would be a far better response to pre-existing inefficiencies, rather than indirectly mitigating them through carbon or other environmental tax swaps. None the less, there is considerable political opposition to direct tax reforms (i.e. removing tax subsidies for housing and medical insurance) in the United States.

(b) *Pre-existing Energy Taxes*

Gasoline taxes are another source of pre-existing tax distortions, though there are offsetting externalities associated with automobile use. We provide a quick illustration of how induced changes in gasoline consumption might affect the social costs of a carbon tax.

In the United States, annual gasoline consumption is about 130 billion gallons. A carbon tax of $20 per ton would increase the retail price of gasoline by about 5 cents per gallon, or about 3 per cent.[14]

---

[14] One gallon of gasoline contains 0.0024 tons of carbon (National Research Council, 2002, p. 85); gasoline prices have recently averaged about $1.50 per gallon (from www.eia.doe.gov).

Assuming a gasoline demand elasticity of −0.6 (e.g. Dahl and Sterner, 1991, Table 2), gasoline consumption would fall by about 2.5 billion gallons in response to the carbon tax. The welfare change from this fuel reduction (excluding carbon benefits) is:

$$(D - t_G)(-\Delta G) - Mt_G(-\Delta G). \tag{8}$$

D denotes the marginal external damage per gallon from gasoline consumption and t_G is the gasoline tax per gallon. The first component in (8) is the reduction in gasoline consumption $(-\Delta G)$ times the gap between the marginal external cost net of the gasoline tax. The second component is the welfare loss from the reduction in gasoline tax revenues, equal to the marginal excess burden times the revenue loss $(-t_G\Delta G)$. For the United States, Parry and Small (2004) put the external costs of local pollution, traffic congestion, and accidents at the equivalent of about $0.80 per gallon (though there is much dispute over the magnitude of these costs), while federal and state gasoline taxes amount to about $0.40 per gallon. Using these figures, and $M = 0.25$, there is a welfare gain from (8) of $0.75 billion, or half the primary cost. This back-of-the-envelope calculation therefore suggests that pre-existing gasoline taxes and externalities are important to consider in the context of carbon policies, though less so than pre-existing labour tax distortions.

(c) Capital Market Interactions

A number of studies in public finance have explored the efficiency costs of taxes on capital (i.e. dividend, capital gains, and capital income taxes) using dynamic models with endogenous capital accumulation (e.g. Chamley, 1981; Judd, 1987; Lucas, 1990). In these models the marginal excess burden for capital taxes usually exceeds those for labour taxes, implying that capital is overtaxed from an efficiency perspective, though by how much is sensitive to different assumptions.

Bovenberg and Goulder (1997) use a dynamic model, that incorporates a detailed treatment of the tax system and energy sector, to explore how capital-market interactions affect the costs of energy tax shifts. They show that the costs of energy taxes can either be higher or lower than those implied by models ignoring the capital market, depending on whether the tax shift expands or reduces inefficiencies associated with the over-taxation of capital. Their empirical analyses suggest that abatement policies tend to shift the burden of taxation off labour and on to capital since the energy sector is relatively capital intensive, at least when revenues are used to cut personal income taxes.

Thus, an analysis exclusively focused on labour may bias downwards estimates of overall abatement costs.[15]

4. Further Considerations in the Choice Between Taxes and Permits

(a) *Distributional Effects*

Another drawback of grandfathered permits is their adverse effect on the distribution of household income. The rents or profits created by grandfathered permits ultimately accrue to shareholders, either directly through dividends and capital gains, or indirectly through their holdings in retirement accounts. Stock ownership is highly skewed towards the better-off; the top income quintile in the United States owns approximately 60 per cent of stocks, while the bottom income quintile owns less than 2 per cent. Indeed, this windfall to the wealthy can more than compensate them for higher energy prices: Dinan and Rogers (2002) estimate that using grandfathered permits to reduce US carbon emissions by 15 per cent would reduce annual real income for the lowest income quintile by around $500 per household, while *increasing* that for the top income quintile by over $1,500 per household.[16] Emissions taxes (and auctioned permits) do not create windfall gains for shareholders. Instead, the government obtains revenues that can be recycled to households in distributionally neutral tax reductions, or reductions that favour the poor.[17]

---

[15] Other numerical investigations are broadly consistent with these findings (see Goulder, 1998, Table 3). One exception is Jorgenson and Wilcoxen (1996), who find that a carbon tax with revenues used to cut capital taxes has a negative cost. In their model the marginal excess burden of capital taxation is substantially higher than in other models, as they assume a relatively high capital-supply elasticity and perfect capital mobility across sectors.

One issue that has received little attention is the possibility that part of the burden of carbon taxes comes at the expense of rents earned by owners of non-renewable resources, rather than being passed on in higher product prices (e.g. Perroni and Whalley, 1998). My guess is that this issue is of minor importance for carbon taxes: coal reserves are very abundant, and the scarcity-rent component of oil prices appears to be small (e.g. Leiby *et al.*, 1997, pp. 18–19).

[16] Poor households suffer disproportionately, not only because they receive so little rent, but also because they have higher budget shares for energy-intensive goods (e.g. OECD, 1996, ch. 4).

[17] Tax reductions that favour the poor, such as higher personal allowances or expanded earned income tax credits, may have lower efficiency gains than proportionate reductions in marginal tax rates. In particular, cutting average tax rates stimulates labour supply through the participation decision only, while cutting marginal rates also encourages an increase in average hours worked (e.g. Pearson and Smith, 1991).

The choice between carbon taxes and permits also affects the distribution of policy costs among interest groups competing for political influence. The political process should favour grandfathered permits over pollution taxes, if affected firms have political clout (Buchanan and Tullock, 1975). None the less, at least for modest carbon taxes, fossil-fuel producers may only require limited compensation (through, for example, exempting a small fraction of infra-marginal emissions from the tax base) to prevent their equity values falling. This is because the supply curve for fossil fuels is flat relative to the demand curve, and only a small portion of the tax burden comes at the expense of producer surplus (Bovenberg and Goulder, 2001). This suggests that political feasibility does not have to be a major obstacle to the implementation of carbon taxes, though energy firms may still lobby for fully grandfathered permits over carbon taxes.

(b) Uncertainty over Control Costs

There remains substantial uncertainty over the (primary) costs of reducing carbon emissions. A familiar result from one-period models with uncertain abatement costs (e.g. Weitzman, 1974) is that emissions taxes yield higher expected welfare gains than permits when the marginal environmental benefit curve is flat relative to the marginal abatement cost curve, while the converse applies when marginal benefits are relatively steep. Taxes allow emissions to vary but place a cap on abatement costs—if abatement costs turn out to be high, firms can avoid abatement and pay more in taxes, while if abatement costs are low, firms can lower tax payments by doing more abatement. In contrast, under permits emissions must be reduced by a fixed amount; the emissions cap is not automatically relaxed if control costs turn out to be high, nor tightened if control costs are low.

Carbon dioxide is a stock pollutant—atmospheric accumulations of carbon dioxide decay at only about 1 per cent per year. Global carbon emissions in 1 year add less than 4 per cent to the atmospheric stock; therefore the marginal damage from global emissions in 1 year is essentially constant, even though climate-change damages are non-linear in the stock. Using a carefully calibrated dynamic model with abatement-cost uncertainty, Newell and Pizer (2003) estimate that the expected welfare gains from carbon taxes amount to *several times* those under emissions permits, under a wide range of scenarios.[18]

---

[18] Uncertainty over future government policy may also be an issue; however, there has been little analysis of whether emissions permits might be a more credible policy instrument than emissions taxes.

(c) *Other Issues*

At the international level, reaching agreement on baselines for allocating permit allowances across countries can be problematic. The 1997 Kyoto Protocol set targets for allowable emissions in 2008–12 based on countries' actual emissions in 1990. This penalizes countries such as South Korea and the United States where emissions have expanded rapidly in the intervening years owing to above-average economic growth, while 'letting off the hook' countries such as Germany and Britain, where emissions fell owing to the closure of uneconomic coal mines. It may prove difficult to agree on baseline adjustments in the future to account for diverging economic conditions across countries.

A different issue would arise under a carbon tax, imposed at the same rate across all countries participating in a climate-change treaty, regardless of prevailing economic conditions and emissions rates. The problem is that individual countries may undermine its effect by reducing fuel taxes or granting tax breaks and regulatory relief to industries most adversely affected. In principle, countries could agree on a convention for calculating effective carbon taxes, and how they change over time with changes in the broader taxation and regulation of the energy sector. However, changes in energy policy might be warranted on other grounds; for example, if the cordon pricing scheme recently introduced to reduce traffic congestion in London spreads to other urban centres in the United Kingdom, some relief for motorists through lower gasoline taxes would seem appropriate. For a more in-depth discussion of these, and other practical issues in the choice of carbon taxes and permits, see Nordhaus (2003).

5. Conclusion

A simple cost–benefit analysis suggests that grandfathered carbon permits might be welfare reducing under certain scenarios for environmental benefits, owing to their impact on compounding pre-existing tax distortions. In spite of this, there are many reasons why it may still be better to go ahead with a grandfathered permit scheme than to do nothing about carbon emissions. There is much dispute over marginal benefits from carbon-emissions mitigation and marginal benefits grow over time with expansion of the global economy; establishing a price for carbon emissions could boost the development of energy-efficient technologies, thereby substantially reducing the costs of future emissions abatement; once the programme is introduced it is conceivable that an increasing portion of the permits might be auctioned over time;

and, once in place, emissions targets could be quickly altered in response to emerging evidence on the seriousness of climate change.

None the less, on economic grounds there appears to be an almost overwhelming case for an internationally harmonized carbon tax—at least if taxes could be introduced in a revenue-neutral fashion in individual nations. The efficiency costs of moderate carbon taxes can be dramatically lower than those of equivalently scaled grandfathered permits, and for the United States costs might actually be negative. These economic arguments, in addition to the transparency of the carbon tax compared with the endless bargaining over inter-country permit allocations endemic in the Kyoto Protocol, suggest that a regime of harmonized taxes is more likely to achieve what is ultimately the most important objective—the establishment of a credible international emissions control regime that will stand the test of time.

11

Tradable Permits for Climate Change: Implications for Compliance, Monitoring, and Enforcement

NICK JOHNSTONE*

1. Introduction

With the Kyoto Protocol (which encouraged the use of 'flexible mechanisms' to meet emission-reduction commitments) and the European Union's Emissions Trading Directive (CEC, 2003*a*), tradable permits have taken centre stage as a means to address global warming. While the theoretical case for their economic efficiency and environmental effectiveness is well-established (OECD, 2004), the implications of their use for compliance, monitoring, and enforcement is less well understood. In this chapter, an effort is made to review their likely implications in these areas, drawing upon existing experience with the use of tradable permits in the area of climate change (which remains limited), and other air and water pollutants and natural resources (for which there is much more extensive experience).

Assessing the implications of tradable permits for compliance, monitoring, and enforcement must be undertaken relative to a policy counterfactual. In most cases, the most plausible policy alternative is likely to be direct regulations involving either performance standards or technology standards, and this is generally the assumption made in this chapter. All environmental policy instruments have implications for monitoring and enforcement, and thus the pertinent question is whether or not such implications are very different under tradable permits, relative to the most likely direct regulation policy alternatives.

This chapter indicates that for various reasons the compliance, monitoring, and enforcement costs are likely to be (but may not necessarily be) somewhat lower owing to their relative transparency and their benefits in terms of information revelation. Perhaps more significantly, the resources required are likely to differ in nature. And

* OECD Environment Directorate.

finally, the 'quality' of monitoring and enforcement may also be greater, complicating the assessment of relative monitoring and enforcement costs for different policy tools. However, it must be emphasized that the chapter focuses on 'cap-and-trade' schemes, rather than 'baseline-and-credit' schemes, for which the conclusions are likely to be very different with respect to all of these issues.

2. Evidence on Relative Levels of Compliance

One of the two most important purported benefits of tradable-permit systems relative to other environmental policies is their ability to meet given environmental objectives with relative certainty.[1] More specifically, under a cap-and-trade tradable-permit scheme the regulator will meet its environmental objective with certainty, even if there is uncertainty with respect to issues such as firm entry and exit (which undermine the achievement of environmental objectives under direct regulations) or abatement costs (which undermine the achievement of environmental objectives under environmental taxes).

However, this depends upon the levels of compliance associated with tradable-permit systems. If compliance is less than under alternative policy instruments, then 'environmental certainty' will be correspondingly less. Indeed, in the early days of the analysis of environmental-policy design and implementation, some argued that tradable-permit systems would be much easier to enforce than direct regulations (see Freeman et al., 1973). However, others (e.g. Drayton, 1978) argued the converse.

In general, the evidence has tended to support the first view, at least with respect to air and water pollution tradable-permit schemes.[2] While many such schemes have faced implementation problems or market inefficiencies — particularly in the area of water pollution — imperfect compliance and enforcement has been less of an issue. Relative to 'standard' levels of compliance with direct forms of regulation, which can vary widely but are often in the region of 80 per cent (Swift, 2001), levels of compliance are often much higher.

Indeed, the American sulphur-dioxide (SO_2) tradable-permit scheme stands out as one of the few (if not only) environmental policies in which there is verified compliance of very nearly 100 per cent. Through the use

[1] The other is, of course, efficient allocation of abatement efforts across emitting sources — an advantage they share with all other market-based instruments, such as Pigovian taxes.

[2] See Tietenberg and Johnstone (2004) for a discussion of the more ambiguous evidence which relates to tradable-quota schemes for fisheries.

of 'continuous emissions monitoring systems' which are linked electronically in real time to the regulatory authority the level of compliance is almost perfect (see www.epa.gov/airmarkets) (see Stranlund *et al.*, 2002; McLean, 2003; Kruger and Pizer, 2004). In effect, when Title IV of the Clean Air Act Amendments (which brought the programme into being) was introduced, the 'bar' for compliance was set much higher, with regulated facilities and regulatory authorities being required to meet standards for monitoring and enforcement which far exceeded the standards in the direct regulation system which preceded it.

This appears to have been due in part to the controversial and innovative nature of tradable-permit schemes in general. Interest groups 'demanded' far higher levels of assurance than had been demanded of previous regulations because they lacked confidence in the ability of tradable-permit schemes actually to deliver environmental certainty in the manner which was frequently stated. (See Tietenberg and Johnstone (2004) for a discussion of the 'endogeneity' of monitoring and enforcement with respect to environmental-policy instrument choice.)

While the SO_2 programme is clearly a significant success, other recent tradable-permit schemes have also proved to have remarkably high levels of compliance. For instance, despite the apparent flaws in Los Angeles County's RECLAIM programme, levels of compliance have been high (although not perfect). Owing to the more heterogeneous nature of sources, monitoring is not exclusively by means of continuous emissions-monitoring systems but has some smaller sources using 'estimated' emissions based upon different algorithms (see Stranlund *et al.*, 2002). However, it has been estimated that fewer than 10 per cent of facilities have been non-compliant (with excess emissions much less than that figure).

The north-eastern United States Ozone Transport Commission (OTC) NOx Budget Program has also had high compliance rates. According to the 2002 Compliance Report,[3] total emissions represented 92 per cent of allowances issued (and 68 per cent of allowances available if the effect of banking is included). Violations were few in number. Out of a total of over 200,000 allowances and over 1,100 sources, only six sources had either year 2002 (90 allowances) or year 2003 (78 allowances) penalty allowances deducted because they did not hold enough allowances in their compliance accounts to cover their emissions. In 2001, five sources had 57 allowances deducted, and in 2000 two sources had 18 allowances deducted.

There are, of course, exceptions. For instance the tradable-permit system established for particulate matter in Santiago, Chile, exhibited

[3] http://www.epa.gov/airmarkets/cmprpt/otc02/index.html

very high levels of non-compliance (see Montero *et al.*, 2002) at least in the early years of the programme. In 1995 (2 years after the introduction of the programme), actual emissions from regulated sources were 6,500 kg/day relative to a permit cap of 4,604.1 kg/day. By 1997 the level of emissions was below the cap, where it remained. The lack of effective enforcement and inadequate baseline emissions data have been blamed for the low level of compliance in the early years of the programme.

In addition, important enforcement failures have arisen in the area of fisheries, with individual transferable quota (ITQ) systems some-times being inadequately enforced (see Tietenberg and Johnstone, 2004). Part of the reason for high levels of non-compliance can be attributed to the incentives provided by some ITQ schemes themselves. By increasing the value of the resource, ITQ schemes also increase the benefits from exceeding the quota. In many cases, ITQ schemes have had to be supplanted by direct controls to guard against highgrading and bycatch discards.

In general, however, tradable-permit schemes do appear to compare favourably with other environmental policy measures in terms of compliance if sufficient resources are devoted to monitoring and enforcement.[4] Moreover, since tradable-permit schemes tend to be relatively transparent, leaving little room for discretion on the part of regulators, it is likely that relatively more resources can be devoted to monitoring and enforcement of the policy rather than dealing with the types of rent-seeking behaviour associated with many direct forms of regulation.[5] Indeed, it has been argued that this is one of the great benefits of tradable-permit schemes — allowing regulators to focus on meeting the environmental objective itself, and not the process by which it is achieved.

3. Tradable Permits, Concepts of Non-compliance, and Transparency of Enforcement

Part of the reason why tradable-permit systems may result in improved levels of compliance relative to direct regulation clearly has to do with the severity of sanction imposed and the probability of enforcement.

[4] However, this may only be true of cap-and-trade schemes. The compliance record of baseline-and-credit schemes is not well documented, and is likely to be much less favourable owing to the nature of such schemes. (See ENDS Report (2003) for a discussion of the UK emissions market.)

[5] However, once again a clear distinction between cap-and-trade and baseline-and-credit schemes must be made. If anything, under the latter type of scheme rent-seeking incentives are likely to increase (see Tietenberg and Johnstone, 2004).

Table 1
Penalties for Non-compliance under Different Tradable-permit Schemes[a]

Scheme	Penalty
L.A. RECLAIM	$500/day
US Acid Rain	$2,000/ton SO_2 (indexed on inflation)
Denmark CO2	$6/ton CO_2
US OTC NOx	3:1 offset in subsequent period
EU ETS	€40/t CO_2 in Phase I and €100/t CO_2 in Phase II (plus 1:1 offset in subsequent period)

Note: [a] As noted below, separate sanctions are often imposed for procedural violations such as fraudulent reporting.

Malik (1992) has emphasized that under direct regulations judges have often been reluctant to impose sufficiently dissuasive penalties since they see the standards as essentially arbitrary. He argues that this is less of a problem under tradable permits, since the level of abatement undertaken and permits held are decisions explicitly undertaken by the firm. As such, if a given firm is non-compliant, this can be interpreted as a conscious decision taken by the firm, and regulatory authorities are more likely to impose dissuasive penalties.

It is difficult to compare effective levels of enforcement across different types of policy instrument. However, as noted above, it may be that political considerations encourage greater monitoring and enforcement under tradable-permit schemes. In any event, it is clear that the level of sanctions are often more easily documented in the case of tradable-permit schemes. For instance, Table 1 provides figures on penalty levels for different programmes (see Boemare and Quirion, 2002).

However, perhaps a more significant consequence of their introduction than the level of enforcement, is that tradable-permit schemes can result in a fundamental change in the very notion of compliance and non-compliance. Ever since Becker's (1968) seminal article on the economics of compliance, administrative and juridical notions of non-compliance and economic notions of non-compliance have been conflated, at least in the minds of most economists. However, generally speaking, levels of compliance with environmental regulations are far higher than would be expected using simple profit-maximization rules, given the level of penalties and the probability of enforcement which usually prevail (see Cohen (1998) for a review). Among other reasons, the discretionary power of the regulator with respect to both the 'level' of the penalty and the 'probability' of enforcement have been forwarded as possible explanations for this apparent sub-optimal behaviour, with the regulated sector not being able to predict the behaviour of the regulatory authorities.

This discretionary power on the part of regulatory authorities, particularly with respect to the likely level of the penalty, is certainly endemic in direct regulations. In effect, violations of technology-based standards or other direct regulations are necessarily treated on a case-by-case basis and punished through administrative and criminal penalties which can vary widely. In addition, issues such as the cause, nature, and degree of non-compliance may be taken into account, adding additional potential for discretion on the part of regulatory authorities.

However, as noted above, under tradable-permit systems, non-compliance (or at least some elements of non-compliance) can be treated in a less discretionary and more transparent manner through the imposition of explicit financial penalties for facilities which do not surrender a sufficient number of permits to meet their emission levels. Indeed, with an annual reconciliation period, compliance becomes an *ex-post* market transaction, fully embedding penalties within a commercial calculus.[6] In effect, non-compliance becomes a normal 'cost of business', and one for which there is very little discretionary power for the regulator to determine the penalty *ex post*. Thus, it is arguably only with the more widespread use of tradable permits that punishments for non-compliance in the environmental sphere have been truly reduced to an economic calculus for the regulated sectors.

Stranlund *et al.* (2002) have argued that the 'certainty' associated with penalties under tradable-permit schemes can result in higher compliance levels, citing a comparison between the SO_2 and RECLAIM programmes and stating that the relatively unambiguous nature of penalties under the former results in high compliance levels. The reasons why compliance levels should be higher under conditions of greater certainty with respect to non-compliance costs are not clear. However, the transparency of the means by which sanctions are imposed under tradable-permit systems can certainly have important implications for economic efficiency. Since the sanctions associated with emissions in excess of permit holdings in tradable-permit schemes are likely to be much more predictable than judicial sanctions associated with non-compliance with direct regulations, this can allow firms to 'optimize' their compliance strategy, enabling them to approach their production possibilities frontier.

---

[6] In addition to a financial penalty for non-compliance other measures are often applied such as the requirement to surrender additional permits in subsequent periods. However, this is known in advance and with certainty. For instance, under the north-east NOx programme, three permits have to be surrendered in the subsequent period for every excess unit of excess emissions.

A graphic illustration of this is found in the American SO_2 regulatory framework. Under the direct regulation system which preceded the allowance trading programme firms often had 'back-up' scrubbers in place to ensure that emission limits would not be violated in the event that there was a malfunction with the main scrubber. Since the sanction for non-compliance in such cases could, in theory, be quite severe, firms had every incentive to ensure that such cases would not arise, even if this necessitated over-investment (from a social-welfare perspective) in abatement technologies. Conversely, under the tradable-permit scheme temporary excess emissions for unexpected reasons can be easily addressed *ex post* in the market for permits. Since there is always a reconciliation period in which firms can purchase permits (or sell permits) to resolve any discrepancies between anticipated and actual emission levels, this allows firms to approach their production possibilities frontier. Across all emitters, this can result in significant efficiency gains, with significant deadweight losses removed.

However, not all tradable-permit schemes apply simple and transparent sanctions for non-compliance. For instance, Stranlund *et al.* (2002) have emphasized the difference between the relatively predictable nature of sanctions under the SO_2 programme with more the 'case-by-case' approach adopted in the RECLAIM programme. In the UK tradable-permit scheme for 'packaging recovery notes', designed to increase recycling of household packaging waste, the regulatory authorities explicitly retained the right for judicial authorities to use discretion in determining sanctions, resulting in considerable uncertainty (see Johnstone, 2003*a*).

In addition, it must be emphasized that the use of fixed penalties for non-compliance comes at the cost of environmental uncertainty. With unknown marginal abatement costs and a fixed penalty serving as a permit price cap, emissions may be much greater than anticipated — the penalty serves as a 'safety valve'. Although, this may be welfare-enhancing (since marginal abatement costs and marginal emission damages will be closer than in the absence of an explicit penalty), it may be politically unpalatable. In order partially to mitigate this problem, it has been argued that it is important to link the penalty imposed to the prevailing permit price so that the 'cost' of non-compliance (the penalty) shifts relative to the actual cost of compliance (marginal abatement costs), and not the forecast cost of compliance (see Stranlund *et al.*, 2002).

And, finally, almost all tradable-permit schemes allow for some distinction between types of non-compliance which are more appropriately considered to be part of the judicial sphere (i.e. fraud and misrepresentation of permit holdings) and those which are more appropriately considered to be part of the commercial sphere (i.e. unanticipated increases in emissions, exceeding permit holdings).[7] As noted, in the latter case, sanctions can be expressed in transparent financial terms as a penalty. However, in the former case, sanctions for non-compliance are likely to be similar to those applied for other environmental policy tools — i.e. subject to legal resolution in the juridical system, and thus subject to some uncertainty. (See Kruger and Pizer (2004) for a discussion of this distinction in the case of the EU Emissions Trading Scheme (ETS).)

4. The Costs of Assessment, Monitoring, and Enforcement

There are various reasons to believe that the costs of assessment, monitoring, and enforcement are likely to be different for tradable-permit systems than other environmental-policy instruments. However, if this improved compliance comes at the cost of vastly increased monitoring and enforcement costs, this must be borne in mind. For instance, under the SO_2 programme the costs of continuous emissions monitoring systems are in the region of US$1m per facility. Under the Danish carbon-dioxide (CO_2) programme, the regulated sector (the electricity supply industry) pays a fee of 0.079 DKK/tCO_2 to cover the costs of verification, monitoring and administration (see Tietenberg and Johnstone, 2004).

However, these costs (borne by the regulated sectors) may be counterbalanced by other savings (realized by the regulatory authority). For instance, McLean (2003) has pointed out that many fewer person-hours are required to enforce the allowance trading programme for SO_2 than was the case for the previous direct regulation system. Moreover, the introduction of the Continuous Emission Monitoring System (CEMS) is certainly not a precondition for the introduction of a tradable-permit scheme, and many schemes have been effective with more rudimentary monitoring systems.

In other cases, monitoring and enforcement costs do appear to be high for reasons which are inherent in the tradable-permit scheme itself. For instance it has been estimated that 'verification' costs under the UK's ETS are €120m annually, or 5 per cent of the total costs of the policy (Kruger and Pizer, 2004). However, as with all baseline-and-credit schemes, this arises from the significant costs associated with verifying the credibility of the baseline and the reductions for which

[7] Stranlund et al. (2002) discuss this distinction, emphasizing that differentiated penalties for the two cases can result in increased economic efficiency.

credits will be received. Owing to the uncertainties and incentives associated with such programmes, and some of the incentives they give to participating firms, monitoring and enforcement costs are likely to be much higher relative to much simpler cap-and-trade schemes.

Irrespective of the precise scheme applied, emission inventories and resource stock assessments are pre-conditions for the introduction of effective tradable-permit schemes (see Stavins (2003) for a discussion). In the case of cap-and-trade tradable-permit systems for pollutants, or transferable-quota systems for resources, this is key to setting the cap itself. Similarly, if the programme takes the form of baseline-and-credit scheme, then it is important to have developed a reliable forecast of counterfactual pollution emissions or resource use that would arise in the absence of a policy intervention.

Generally, a strong theoretical case can be made for the use of auctioning of tradable permits rather than various gratis forms of allocation of permits. However, there may be some advantages associated with grandfathering permits in terms of monitoring and enforcement costs, particularly in cases where the regulatory authority has inadequate information concerning emission sources. Since most such gratis allocations are based upon historic emissions, as under 'pure' grandfathering, firms have incentives to reveal information about their historic level of pollution emissions or resource exploitation in the early stages of the introduction of the programme.

The importance of these rent-seeking incentives associated with grandfathered tradable-permit schemes in developing accurate emission inventories is revealed by the tradable-permit scheme implemented in Santiago for particulate matter (see Montero et al., 2002). Prior to the introduction of this scheme in the mid-1990s, the regulatory authorities possessed very little information on the level of emissions from the stationary sources which were to be affected. However, since firms which wished to be allocated permits gratis had to divulge their actual emission levels, the programme provided incentives for revealing valuable information to the regulatory authority.

Indeed, 85 facilities that had not been identified as potential sources prior to the introduction of the programme approached the regulator independently, claiming permits (Montero et al., 2002). Within six years, no 'undefined' sources were bringing themselves forward, indicating that the initial incentives were strong enough to generate a reasonable overview of emission sources relatively quickly, and certainly much more quickly and inexpensively than would have been the case under other policy measures, where the only incentives which can be provided are through threats, etc.

However, there can be other types of benefits for monitoring and enforcement costs from auctioned cap-and-trade schemes. For instance, under auctioned regimes (or even schemes under which at least some permits are auctioned) the use of programme rents can be used to finance monitoring and enforcement programmes. In some cases this can arise directly, as under the Canadian and Icelandic fishery ITQ regimes. Indeed, under the American Magnuson–Stevens Act, by law auction rents from the ITQ scheme must be used to finance monitoring and enforcement programmes (see Tietenberg and Johnstone, 2004).

More generally, tradable-permit systems generate information which can reduce the costs of monitoring and enforcement. In a sense, monitoring and enforcement can become integral elements of the programme itself, and not 'add-ons' as is the case under most environmental policies. Thus, the information generated when permits are traded and surrendered can generate valuable information. For instance, information on the spatial pattern of trade can provide valuable information for monitoring and enforcement agencies. Unfortunately, many tradable-permit schemes do not systematically collect and apply this readily available information.

Moreover, the information-generating benefits of tradable-permit/transferable-quota schemes can also play an on-going role in reducing monitoring and enforcement costs. In particular, if the scarcity of the resource stock is directly linked to the quota price, price trajectories can be used to provide information on the status of the resource stock or pollution concentrations. For instance, in the case of fisheries ITQs quota prices reflect resource scarcity directly. (See Arnason (2003) for a discussion of the case of fisheries.) This is unlikely to be relevant for most pollution-related schemes since permits would have to be denominated in terms of concentrations (rather than emissions) for analogous effects to arise.

And, finally, in the face of scarce public resources for monitoring and enforcement, the information can be used to optimize inspection programmes (see Harrington, 1988). Since permit holdings and use, as well as trade patterns, can provide valuable information to determine which firms should be targeted, this can result in a much more efficient monitoring and enforcement programme, with resources devoted toward the firms most likely to be non-compliant (see Keeler, 1991). However, as has been noted in the literature, other facility-specific information is much less valuable to the regulator under tradable-permit schemes than under direct regulation, since incentives for compliance and non-compliance will not vary with marginal abatement costs (see Stranlund and Chavez, 2000). In effect, under a tradable-permit scheme the regulator has no reason to suppose that a high-cost abater is more or less likely to be in compliance than a low-cost abater.

5. The Internalization and Demand for Monitoring and Enforcement

As has been noted above, owing to their controversial nature, the 'demand' for monitoring and enforcement may be greater under tradable-permit schemes than under direct regulation. Thus, when comparing the costs of monitoring and enforcement under the two alternatives it may be inappropriate to take the 'quality' of monitoring and enforcement as exogenous. Under the American SO_2 emissions trading programme and the Alaska ITQ for halibut fishery, the accuracy of monitoring is much greater than the direct regulation schemes which they supplanted, with continuous monitoring applied (see Tietenberg and Johnstone, 2004).

Political demand can also affect the efforts which go into ensuring the integrity of individual trades, particularly for baseline-and-credit schemes. For instance, relative to the system of 'in-lieu' fees (in which publicly managed conservation areas are funded by fee payments) which it supplanted, under the American Wetlands Credit Trading Program, considerably greater effort has gone into ensuring that the credits created protect the wetlands to be conserved (Shabman, 2004). The transition from a 'public' environmental policy instrument to a 'private' environmental policy instrument has increased demand for ensuring that transactions do not undermine the environmental integrity of the resource to be protected.

In some cases, 'demand' for improved monitoring and enforcement can arise from within the regulated sector itself. Most interestingly, under New Zealand's lobster ITQ scheme the regulated fleets even requested the use of programme rents for improved monitoring and enforcement of their own fleets (Tietenberg and Johnstone, 2004). The value of the resource rents generated with the introduction of the scheme were such that the regulated community had an incentive to ensure its environmental integrity, and thus their rents. In effect, the benefits of 'privatizing' the commons were such that those using the resource wanted to ensure that the property rights created were protected effectively.

Tradable permits can also result in a degree of internalization of monitoring and enforcement functions within the regulated firm itself. Evidence has shown that sub-optimal abatement strategies and unintended non-compliance are rarely deliberate, but instead are often a function of information barriers (and even organizational failures) within the firm—i.e. mistakes (see Harrington, 1988, and Cohen, 1998). Thus, non-compliance with environmental policies is usually inadvertent, rather than the outcome of a rational calculus of costs and benefits. However, the incentive structures put in place and the resources devoted toward ensuring compliance are the consequence of a conscious decision within the firm.

Thus, Cohen (1998) argues that different resource allocations and incentive structures within firms can go a long way toward explaining divergencies in compliance levels. Since tradable permits—as financial assets—are likely to encourage the management of environmental matters at a more 'senior' level within the firm than other policy measures (particularly direct regulation), this may well result in better internal incentive structures to ensure compliance. While there is little empirical evidence in this regard, it is interesting that with the introduction of some American tradable-permit schemes there was a shift in responsibility for environmental matters to more senior levels of management (Swift, 2001).

Moreover, in an OECD survey of just over 4,000 facilities in seven OECD countries (Japan, Germany, France, Hungary, Norway, Canada, and the United States), there is evidence that the use of tradable permits results in the designation of higher-level officials as responsible for environmental matters (Johnstone, 2003b). Table 2 gives data on the institutional location of the person responsible for environmental matters, distinguished by the perceived relative importance of tradable permits and technology-based standards on production practices. While the percentage of facilities in which 'nobody' is designated as being explicitly responsible for environmental matters is approximately the same for facilities in which the two instruments are seen as being 'very' important, there is a marked difference in the institutional location for those who do designate such an individual. In the case where tradable permits were seen as being very important, 27 per cent were in senior management and 20 per cent in a specialized environmental health and safety department. Conversely, for technology-based standards, the figures are 19 per cent and 31 per cent. In theory this more senior oversight should improve compliance.

And, finally, another form of delegation of monitoring and enforcement functions arises from the transparent nature of tradable-permit schemes, in which the broader public has much greater awareness of firms' compliance strategies than under direct regulation (see Malueg and Yates (2004) for a recent discussion). In such cases, local community organizations, financial markets, and environmental non-governmental organizations may use the information generated by the transparency

Table 2
Responsibility (%) for Environmental Matters and Policy Choice

| | Tradable permits | | | | Technology-based standards | | | |
| | Importance | | | | Importance | | | |
	N.a.	None	Moderate	Great	N.a.	None	Moderate	Great
Senior management	21.21	23.07	25.08	27.03	25.02	24.28	24.29	19.30
Production/ operations	11.13	12.12	10.38	12.68	4.69	9.24	14.63	16.69
Env., health & safety	12.55	21.00	18.71	19.96	3.77	10.62	23.44	31.38
Other location	17.10	17.18	20.04	19.96	21.07	28.55	13.85	11.96
Nobody	38.01	26.64	25.80	20.37	45.45	27.31	23.79	20.67

of permit schemes to bring pressure to bear on particular emitters. Arguably, the adverse 'reputation effects' of Illinois Power's decision to use permits as the primary means of compliance with the American Acid Rain Programme was instrumental in discouraging other firms to follow a similar strategy (see Johnstone, 2003a).

6. Conclusions and Implications for Climate Change

While it has long been known that tradable permits have potential benefits relative to other environmental policy instruments in terms of economic efficiency and environmental effectiveness, the implications of their use for compliance, monitoring, and enforcement are less well known. Since effective compliance, monitoring, and enforcement are key to the conversion of these potential benefits into actual welfare gains, it is important to assess the implications of their use in these areas more fully. This chapter has sought to do so in a preliminary fashion, drawing upon the relevant theoretical and empirical literature.

Tradable-permit schemes with inadequate resources devoted to monitoring and enforcement are unlikely to result in welfare improvements. However, it has been noted that compliance levels are generally satisfactory for tradable-permit schemes, and sometimes much higher than under direct forms of regulations—in some cases, such as the American Acid Rain programme, reaching almost 100 per cent. There are exceptions, of course, but these are often a consequence of scheme design, which imposes significant administrative burdens on the regulatory authority. In other cases (e.g. fisheries), effective enforcement may necessitate the application of direct regulations in combination · with a tradable-permit scheme.

One of the great advantages of tradable-permit schemes with respect to enforcement and compliance is that the transparency of the instrument allows for the application of relatively unambiguous sanctions for non-compliance. In an uncertain world this can result in significant efficiency gains since firms are able to approach their production-possibilities frontier through marginal decisions. Moreover, there are reasons to believe that the penalties applied may well be more dissuasive than is often the case under direct regulations, resulting in greater incentives for compliance.

Generally speaking, while the costs of monitoring and enforcement under tradable-permit schemes may in some cases be comparable to those for direct regulation, they are certainly no higher. However, because of their capacity to generate rents, they have the advantage (at least when auctioned) to allow for the introduction of mechanisms to finance such costs. Conversely, grandfathering of tradable permits may reduce initial assessment and monitoring costs by giving emitters an incentive to divulge information concerning their historic emissions in order to claim rights to the permits issued.

And finally, tradable-permit schemes may result in both increased demand for, and increased internalization of, compliance, monitoring, and enforcement. On the one hand, owing to their controversial nature it is clear that the 'bar' has often been set much higher with the introduction of tradable permits. This has resulted in much more comprehensive public compliance, monitoring, and enforcement regimes. On the other hand, the regulated sector also has incentives to monitor its emissions more accurately and ensure that the level of compliance is optimal. Since tradable-permits are financial assets, their holdings and use are more likely to managed in the core of the firm's business strategy.

However, little of this evidence is drawn from tradable-permit schemes for greenhouse gases. With the European Union's ETS entering into force in January 2005, it is interesting to conjecture as to whether these general conditions are likely to hold with the use of tradable permits to address climate change. The first thing to note is that, as an international scheme with delegated responsibility for enforcement, there were understandable concerns that there will be a 'race to the bottom'. In effect, the environmental integrity of the programme (and thus the credibility of the commodity traded) will be determined by the credibility of the least satisfactory enforcement regime. It is for this reason that the European Commission has devoted considerable attention to setting out guidelines for monitoring and reporting (CEC, 2004). However, some concerns remain (see Kruger and Pizer, 2004).

Second, it is important to underline that relative to other pollutants, CO_2 is a relatively easy pollutant to 'monitor'. Indeed, with the exception of some sectors (e.g. chemicals and cement), there is no need for direct monitoring at all. Since emissions have a fixed relationship with the carbon content of fuels, irrespective of combustion processes, enforcement can be achieved through monitoring of commercial fuel inputs. However, with the possible addition of other greenhouse gases in a later phase of the EU programme, compliance and enforcement costs will have to rise considerably if standards are not to fall, since methane, nitrous oxides (NOx), and other greenhouse gases do not have the same desirable characteristics as CO_2 with respect to monitoring costs. Indeed, the implications are analogous to those mentioned above: the system will only be as credible as the emission which is monitored least satisfactorily. NOx permits[8] will 'pollute' the market for CO_2 permits.

And finally, while most of these arguments made above may hold for well-designed cap-and-trade schemes, they are unlikely to be true of baseline-and-credit schemes. In particular, costs of monitoring and enforcement are unlikely to be lower than under direct regulation and may even be higher. Moreover, their record for meeting declared environmental objectives appears to be decidedly mixed. Perhaps most significantly, they continue to encourage the kind of rent-seeking behaviour that plagues many forms of direct regulation, with firms lobbying for the creation of 'credits', sometimes on the basis of emission reductions which are no better than what would have occurred in the absence of a policy intervention. This is significant for climate change since the so-called 'Linking Directive' (CEC, 2003b) risks combining existing baseline-and-credit schemes (the Clean Development Mechanism and the Joint Implementation Mechanism) with a pure cap-and-trade Emissions Trading Directive. The implications, once again, will be reflected in reduced credibility and environmental integrity.

---

[8] If tradable with CO_2 permits according to their relative global warming potential.

Part Four: Kyoto and After

12

The Kyoto Protocol: Success or Failure?

CHRISTOPH BÖHRINGER* AND MICHAEL FINUS**

1. Introduction

Climate change has emerged as one of the most important and complex issues facing the world over the next century. Concentration of so-called greenhouse-gas emissions has increased markedly during the past century owing to human activities such as fossil-fuel combustion which releases carbon dioxide (CO_2) into the atmosphere. Scientific evidence suggests that a continued increase in the greenhouse-gas concentration is likely to have significant effects on the climate. Despite large uncertainties about the concrete impacts on the ecosystem, a global consensus exists that global climate change constitutes a serious potential threat.

Concerns on climate change led more than 180 countries to sign the United Nations Framework Convention on Climate Change (UNFCCC) in Rio de Janeiro in 1992, which declares that serious action should be taken to reduce man-made greenhouse-gas emissions (UNFCCC, 1992). To this end, the Kyoto Protocol was signed in 1997 (UNFCCC, 1997). This treaty contains legally binding greenhouse-gas-emission targets for industrialized countries to be achieved in the target period 2008–12 (the so-called Kyoto commitment period). The proponents of the Kyoto Protocol celebrated it as a breakthrough in international climate policy because (i) it aimed at substantial emission reductions for industrialized countries *vis-à-vis* business-as-usual emissions, and (ii) it established a broad international mechanism for widening and deepening climate-protection activities in the future.

Opponents of the treaty rejected it as a 'deeply flawed agreement that manages to be both economically inefficient and politically imprac-tical' (McKibbin and Wilcoxen, 2002, p. 107). This scepticism seems to be

* Centre for European Economic Research (ZEW), Mannheim and University of Heidelberg; ** University of Hagen.

justified for several reasons. First, the abatement targets, as well as the timetable for emission reduction, neither reflect an optimum from a cost–benefit analysis (first-best solution) nor from a cost-efficiency analysis (second-best solution) perspective.[1] Second, developing countries that are projected to account for a larger share of anthropogenic greenhouse-gas emissions in the future refused to become part of the Kyoto Protocol. Moreover, the USA announced its withdrawal from the Kyoto Protocol in 2001, meaning that the largest current emitter of greenhouse-gas emissions is no longer subject to emission constraints. Third, in the aftermath of the US withdrawal, many countries renegotiated the Kyoto Protocol, leading to a substantial downgrading of original abatement targets. In particular, full tradability of emission entitlements conceded to former Eastern European countries in excess of their anticipated business-as-usual emissions (so-called *hot air*) renders the Kyoto Protocol hardly effective in terms of global emission reduction (see, for example, Buchner *et al.* (2002) or Springer (2003) for surveys of Kyoto assessment studies).

Against this background, we provide a critical assessment of the Kyoto Protocol's anticipated performance and discuss potential amendments to foster effectiveness and efficiency in subsequent commitment periods. In section 2, we first summarize the fundamental features of the climate-change problem and then present an overview of key issues of treaty design that have been proposed in the theoretical literature to foster the effectiveness and efficiency of international environmental agreements. In section 3, we lay out important provisions of the Kyoto Protocol, and provide a critical assessment of the associated economic and environmental impacts. In section 4, we propose amendments to the Kyoto Protocol that might improve upon the performance in 'post-Kyoto' commitment periods. In section 5, we summarize our main findings and conclusions.

2. Climate Protection — The Key Issues

(a) First-best Solution

Rational decision-making in climate policy requires balancing total costs of greenhouse-gas-emission abatement and total benefits of avoided undesirable consequences of global warming. A cost–benefit analysis (see, for example, Mishan (1975) and Pearce (1998*a*)) measures all negative and positive impacts of climate policies worldwide over all future periods in monetary terms. In order to make net benefits

---

[1] See section 2 for an explanation of these terms.

(benefits from global abatement minus costs of abatement) comparable across time, the total net benefit stream is discounted. It is then possible to determine (a) the globally optimal abatement level, (b) the optimal allocation of abatement levels to different countries, and (c) the optimal timing of abatement measures, by maximizing the *sum of discounted net benefits across all countries*. The globally optimal solution requires participation of all countries and implies *de-facto full cooperation*. It is characterized by two features. First, total abatement and total welfare is larger than in the absence of cooperation, i.e. a situation where each country maximizes only its *own discounted net benefits*. The reason is that — under cooperation — each country does not only take into account its own abatement costs and benefits but also benefits generated by its abatement for all remaining countries. To put it differently, countries take into consideration that their abatement efforts also generate positive externalities in other countries. Second, the allocation of abatement is cost-efficient. On the one hand, marginal abatement costs are equalized across countries at a given time. That is, abatement should be undertaken where it is cheapest (so-called 'where'-flexibility). On the other hand, marginal abatement costs are equalized across time with appropriate discounting. That is, abatement should be undertaken when it is cheapest and most effective (so called 'when'-flexibility), taking into account that abatement costs may decrease over time owing to technical progress, and that greenhouse gases accumulate in the atmosphere over time but decay (though slowly) with some natural rate (Wigley *et al.*, 1996).

In order to achieve the optimal pattern of emission control across countries and time, market-based instruments should be used. Typically, either an emission tax or emission permits are proposed to implement a first-best policy. A uniform emission tax ensures that marginal abatement costs are equalized across countries; sequential temporal adjustments of the tax rate ensure that discounted marginal abatement costs equalize across time. In general, the tax rates must be chosen to achieve the optimal trajectory of emissions (abatement). In the case of spatially and intertemporally tradable emission permits, marginal abatement costs will equalize across countries and time independent of the initial allocation of emission entitlements, provided the permit market is perfectly functioning. Thus, in a first-best world without uncertainty, both instruments are equivalent.

At first glance, the optimal solution to the greenhouse-gas problem seems straightforward. However, a closer look reveals severe obstacles. First, owing to large uncertainties about the costs and benefits of greenhouse-gas abatement, only second-best solutions can be pursued at best (see subsection (b) below). Second, central economic and political features associated with the issue of climate change cause severe incentive problems that make it difficult to implement even second-best solutions (see (c) below).

(b) *Second-best Solutions*

The first-best solution to climate change requires complete information, not only about the costs, but also about the benefits of abatement. The chain of causality — from greenhouse-gas emissions to ambient concentrations of greenhouse gases in the atmosphere, from temperature increase to physical effects such as climate change and sea-level rise — is very complex and hardly understood. Moreover, economists do not even agree on the methodology to be used for valuing potential climate-change impacts, such as the extinction of species. The large uncertainties in predicting global climate change, as well as quantifying and monetizing the associated biophysical impacts, explain much of the controversy on the desirable long-term level of greenhouse-gas concentrations in the atmosphere and the scope and timing of emission-mitigation measures.

These uncertainties, together with (partial) irreversibilities of greenhouse-gas accumulation in the atmosphere and the accumulation of capital investments, imply a trade-off between the risk of premature abatement action and the risk of delayed action. In the context of uncertainty, option theory typically replaces classical cost–benefit analysis in evaluating decisions (see, for example, Arrow and Fisher, 1974; Hanemann, 1989; as well as Dixit and Pindyck, 1994). The 'relative irreversibilities' between climate change and mitigation measures (including adaptation) will determine whether waiting until more information becomes available, or investing now in abatement, will be optimal. In practice, this leads to a sequential decision-making approach that is sufficiently flexible to incorporate new information on abatement costs as well as on benefits from abatement.

Presuming that uncertain future outcomes of climate change could be extreme and irreversible, risk aversion justifies the adoption of a precautionary approach rather than balancing costs and benefits based on an elaborate option-value approach (see, for example, Gollier *et al.*, 2000).[2] In this vein, the UNFCCC aims at establishing an ample margin of safety based on recommendations from natural science on 'tolerable' emission levels. The UNFCCC's stated goal is the 'stabilization of greenhouse gas concentrations in the atmosphere at a level that would

---

[2] Gollier *et al.* (2000) identify conditions such that scientific uncertainties justify immediate prevention measures. They also mention the precautionary principle as a safeguard against the opportunism of decision-makers in situations of asymmetric information or imperfect societal monitoring.

prevent dangerous anthropogenic interference with the climate system' (UNFCCC, 1992, Article 2). As pointed out by the Intergovernmental Panel on Climate Change (IPCC), which serves as the scientific advisory board to the UNFCCC, stabilizing concentrations at 'safe' levels would eventually mean reducing emissions by more than 50 per cent compared to 1990 in the distant future (IPCC, 1996).

Given some 'tolerable' emission levels, a rational climate policy should be based on a cost-efficiency analysis. That is, the allocation of abatement burdens should be chosen such as to minimize discounted total abatement costs for a given abatement target.[3] Obviously, global abatement policy may then no longer be optimal.

Apart from the problem of identifying cost-efficient abatement allocation, uncertainty may have important implications for the choice of the regulatory instrument. Under uncertainties of damages and abatement cost estimates, price instruments (such as a harmonized greenhouse-gas tax) and quantity instruments (such as tradable greenhouse-gas emission permits) are no longer equivalent in cost-efficiency terms. Under a quantitative limit, marginal costs are uncertain; under a price limit, emission reductions are uncertain. Weitzman (1974) showed that the tax is superior to permits if the marginal cost curve is steep relative to the marginal benefit curve (and vice versa). Several economists have used Weitzman's argument to make the case that taxes are likely to be more efficient than tradable permits in the case of greenhouse gases. The underlying presumption is that 'all evidence to date suggests that the [aggregate] marginal cost curve for reducing GHG emissions is very steep . . . [whereas] . . . the [stock] nature of climate change indicates that the [aggregate] marginal benefit curve for reducing emissions will be very flat.' (McKibbin and Wilcoxen, 2002, p. 118).

However, the presumption of a rather flat marginal damage function need not accurately reflect the expectations of most scientists about substantial non-linearities in the climate system with the possibility of catastrophic events (Higgins et al., 2002) and warrants caution with a rather simplistic view. Incorporating uncertainty, Roberts and Spence (1976) demonstrate that the combination of a quantity instrument with a price instrument can efficiently protect against the failings of each single instrument. Applied to climate-change policies, this means that a mixed system is likely to do better than either a pure quantity or price instrument. More specifically, a 'finite penalty' can provide an 'escape

---

[3] Cost-efficiency includes 'where-flexibility' and to some extent 'when-flexibility', depending on how much the emission trajectory is exogenously fixed.

valve' under a quantity regime, in case abatement costs turn out to be very high.

(c) *Third-best Solutions*

There are fundamental problems to achieving even second-best solutions within an international environmental agreement (IEA) aimed at combating global warming. The main problem is the lack of a supranational authority that could force countries into the implementation of globally efficient and effective climate policy.[4] That is, the participation in a global climate treaty must be voluntary, abatement targets as well as other institutional details must be agreed upon by consensus, and obligations must be implemented and controlled by the parties themselves.

First, a basic prerequisite for a self-enforcing IEA is profitability. That is, all participants must be better off with the IEA than in the non-cooperative status quo. Often first- or second-best solutions would violate this condition for at least some countries (though profitability at the aggregate level holds). For instance, a cost-efficient allocation of abatement burdens would require that developing countries with flat marginal abatement cost curves contribute more to joint abatement than industrialized countries with steep marginal abatement costs. If developing countries do not value the benefits from reduced climate damages very highly, then those countries may feel that they are worse off from joining an IEA. Paradoxically, the larger the asymmetries between countries in terms of abatement costs, the larger the gains are from implementing a cost-efficient abatement scheme. However, the larger these asymmetries are, the more likely it is that profitability is violated for some countries, given that countries also perceive the benefits from a joint abatement policy very differently.

Second, even if profitability were to hold for all parties, there would still be severe free-rider incentives—either to remain a non-signatory or to participate in the IEA but to violate its terms—that hamper cooperation (Finus, 2003b). In both cases, the rationale behind free-riding is to save abatement costs while benefiting from the abatement efforts of other countries. Although all countries could be better off if they behaved in a cooperative way, each country has an incentive to take a free ride. This may lead to the well-known 'tragedy of the commons'. Paradoxically, the free-rider incentives of non-participation and non-compliance are particularly strong for conditions under which cooperation would generate large global welfare gains, as is the case for

---

[4] This includes the imposition of fairness principles about how gains from cooperation should be shared.

global warming (Carraro and Siniscalco 1993; Barrett, 1994*a*, 2003; Finus 2002, 2003*a,b*).

(i)   The global character of the greenhouse-gas externality implies large gains *vis-à-vis* the non-cooperative solution. However, the larger the number of countries affected by emissions, the larger the free-rider incentive will be from a single-country perspective: environmental quality will deteriorate only marginally if a country defects from an IEA, whereas participation and compliance may impose substantial costs with only marginal improvements in environmental quality for a single country.

(ii) As pointed out above, the higher the degree of asymmetry between countries with respect to abatement costs, the larger the gains will be from a cost–efficient abatement policy. However, those asymmetries pose problems for participation and compliance: countries that benefit less from cooperation on average have an incentive either to remain non-signatories or to violate the terms of an agreement.

(iii) The more countries participate in an agreement, the more attractive it is for countries to participate in an agreement because their own abatement efforts are matched by other participants. Moreover, more participants means fewer free-riders and hence smaller leakage effects that contradict abatement efforts of cooperators.[5] However, the incentive to take a free-ride also sharply increases with participation owing to decreasing marginal benefits and increasing marginal abatement costs from joint abatement.

(iv) Starting from non-cooperative abatement levels and increasing abatement efforts towards optimal levels increases global welfare. However, as a tendency, the free-rider incentive also increases with the level of abatement, making it more difficult to control free-riding.

Third, even if profitability would be ensured and free-riding could be controlled, it is usually hard to agree on a particular treaty design by consensus. Critical issues are the level of abatement, the allocation of abatement burdens and the level, kind, as well as the net donors and recipients of transfers. The perception of a 'fair' allocation of abatement burdens may substantially differ from a cost-efficient one. Moreover, the tendency in international politics to agree on the lowest common

---

[5] 'Leakage effects' means the expansion of emissions of non-signatories as a reaction to the reduction of emissions by signatories. Leakage effects may occur, for instance, if a reduction of energy demand by treaty members leads to drop of the oil price that may encourage increased demand by non-treaty members. See, for an analysis, Bohm (1993), Felder and Rutherford (1993), and Golombek *et al.* (1995).

denominator frequently leads to total and individual abatement below optimal levels. Also the issue of transfers, that crucially determines how the gains from cooperation are allocated across countries, is a normative issue related to 'equity principles' (see, for example, Moulin, 1990, 1991, or Böhringer and Helm, 2001) and is hotly debated. Moreover, and to make things even worse, climate-change policy has an important public choice dimension (Congleton, 1992, 2001). Governments may not maximize the welfare of their citizens, but the probability of being re-elected. From a political economy point of view, the median voter's willingness to pay ultimately determines the outcome of international environmental negotiations. If voters are myopic and discount time to a large extent, the incentives for governments to agree on ambitious abatement targets may decline substantially. The reason is that major greenhouse gases, such as CO_2, are stock pollutants that remain in the atmosphere for several decades before they disappear owing to the natural rate of decay. Therefore, short-term abatement efforts will have an immediate impact on abatement costs, but will only generate benefits in the very long run.

All three fundamental problems make it difficult to implement an ambitious, cost-efficient, and self-enforcing IEA that enjoys a high participation rate. This is particularly true for the greenhouse-gas problem, but is also evident when considering other environmental problems of trans-boundary character (see Barrett (2003a) and Finus (2003b) for a discussion). Therefore, the main challenge to climate policy is to shape a treaty that overcomes or at least mitigates these problems. Principal guidelines may come from coalition theory, a field in game theory that analyses the incentive structures of countries to participate in an IEA and to comply with the terms of the agreement (for non-technical overviews, see, for example, Carraro and Siniscalco (1998); Folmer and de Zeeuw (2000); and Finus (2003a,b)). However, it will become evident from the discussion in the next section that there is no universal solution to fix the fundamental problems.

(d) Possible Measures to Improve Upon Third-best Solutions

(i) Transfers

Direct transfers are an obvious instrument to compensate the losers from cooperation, to increase participation in an IEA, and to encourage compliance. Possible direct compensation measures are monetary and in-kind transfers, where the latter comprise, for instance, technical assistance of developing countries by industrialized countries. Whereas monetary transfers directly target compensation, in-kind transfers do so only indirectly and hence the aim of compensation is often blurred and overlapped by other aims. Therefore, theoretically, efficiency of in-kind transfers is lower than of monetary transfers. However, the order of frequency of the application of these instruments is reversed in practice. Almost all IEAs have no provisions for monetary transfers, except the Montreal Protocol on the reduction of substances that deplete the ozone layer, signed in 1987, and the Convention on Biological Diversity, signed in 1992 in Rio de Janeiro. Though both treaties have established a fund, it covers only incremental costs of developing countries compared to the status quo, and suffers from missing contributions from donor countries. In contrast to monetary transfers, the number of IEAs including provisions for technical ex-change and assistance between industrialized and developing coun-tries is larger, though a closer reading reveals that obligations are usually very vague. Another option of indirect transfers has been chosen under the Kyoto Protocol that is discussed in section 3.

There may be several reasons for the resistance of governments to paying monetary transfers. First, transfers provide an incentive for governments strategically to misrepresent their preferences in order to extract larger compensation payments or to pay low transfers (Mäler, 1990). For instance, under the Montreal Protocol, if a developing country indicates non-compliance despite 'best intentions' to the Imple-mentation Council, it may receive additional financial assistance. Sec-ond, governments may fear that if they pay transfers, they are judged as weak bargainers which may weaken their position in future negotia-tions (Mäler, 1990). Third, there is a compliance problem *between* donor and recipient (Finus, 2002). Either the recipient may take the money but does not fulfil its promised abatement obligation, or the recipient fulfils its part of the deal but the donor does not pay promised transfers. Fourth, there is a compliance problem *within* the group of donor countries (Barrett, 1994b). Individual donors are better off if they take a free ride, though the group of donors as a whole benefits from transfers through higher participation and compliance. As shown in Barrett (1994b) and Finus (2002), both types of compliance problems can be mitigated in a dynamic setting where payments can be made conditional on past performance. Nevertheless, the compliance prob-lem of monetary transfers between donors and recipients is less severe for in-kind transfers which helps to explain the prominence of these. On the one hand, environmental projects, such as the construction of environmental power plants in developing countries by industrialized countries, cannot usually be used for other purposes. Thus, enforce-ment on the side of the recipients is *de facto* automatically ensured. On the other hand, recipient countries can wait until the project has been finalized before they have to fulfil their part of the deal. For instance, a power plant can only start operation after the plant has been built.

(ii) Issue Linkage

An alternative compensation measure is issue linkage, where concessions in one agreement are exchanged against concessions in another (see, for example, Folmer and van Mouche (2000) and Finus (2003b) for surveys). Thus, issue linkage may be used to ensure profitability. However, issue linkage may also be used to raise participation. Examples include links between an IEA (public good) and trade agreements as well as R&D agreements (both club goods). Countries are only allowed to join the club-good agreement if they also join the IEA. Since club-good agreements usually enjoy a higher stability, since the benefits are exclusive to members, linkage may raise participation in and success of the linked agreement (Carraro, 1997). Moreover, issue linkage may also encourage compliance with IEAs by threatening to exclude a violator from the benefits of the linked agreement (Folmer et al., 1993; Cesar and de Zeeuw, 1996). In reality, however, issue linkage faces a couple of problems.

First, in reality, membership will be mixed in different agreements and it will be difficult to exclude countries from a trade agreement or defence pact if they do not join an IEA. Second, in the context of many countries, negotiating package deals may be a time-consuming undertaking associated with large transaction costs. Thus, it is not surprising that most reported examples include bilateral links (Ragland, 1995; Bennett et al., 1998). For instance, Krutilla (1975) suggests that the Columbia River Treaty of 1961 between the USA and Canada which — viewed as a single issue was to the disadvantage of the USA — was built on concessions by Canada involving North American defence. In the context of multilateral agreements, only a wider interpretation allows us to detect issue linkage. One example is the Montreal Protocol, where the import and export of controlled substances with non-parties is banned (Article 4), or the efforts to include environmental issues in the World Trade Organization (WTO), which may be interpreted as a link between an IEA and a trade agreement. Also the provision of technical assistance and exchange under many protocols may be interpreted as a link between an IEA and an agreement to share the costs of R&D.

(iii) Abatement Schemes

Given the problems of implementing transfers or issue linkage mentioned above, a departure from cost-efficient and ambitious abatement schemes may be an option to raise participation and to mitigate the free-rider problem. For instance, under many 'old' IEAs uniform emission-reduction quotas have been negotiated, which implies that countries have to reduce their emissions by the same percentage compared to some base year. The list of examples is long and includes several protocols under the umbrella of the framework convention, LRTAP (Long Range Transboundary Air Pollution). For instance, the Helsinki Protocol suggested a 30 per cent reduction of sulphur emissions from 1980 levels by 1993. Moreover, the 'Protocol Concerning the Control of Emissions of Nitrogen Oxides or Their Transboundary Fluxes' signed in Sofia in 1988 called on countries *uniformly* to freeze their emissions at 1987 levels by 1995, and the 'Protocol Concerning the Control of Emissions of Volatile Organic Compounds or Their Fluxes', signed in Geneva in 1991, required parties to reduce 1988 emissions by 30 per cent by 1999. The Montreal Protocol and some amendments also started with uniform reduction targets, though subsequently differentiated obligations have been introduced.

Obviously, uniform abatement schemes imply efficiency losses. Nevertheless, in the context of severe free-rider incentives, there may be some rationale, explaining the frequent application of uniform schemes. First, Barrett (1992*a,b*) and Hoel (1992) suggest that uniform abatement obligations constitute some kind of focal point on which bargaining partners can agree relatively easily. Second, Endres (1996, 1997), Endres and Finus (1998, 1999, 2002), Eyckmans (1997), and Finus and Rundshagen (1998*a*) show that negotiating uniform emission-reduction quotas leads to a rather symmetric distribution of the gains from cooperation that does not violate profitability and makes it easier to enforce compliance. Moreover, the bargaining outcome when nego-tiating uniform emission-reduction quotas may well be superior to other regimes if one accounts for the fact that countries usually agree only on the lowest common denominator in international politics. Third, Finus and Rundshagen (1998*b*) show that uniform quotas may allow the stabilization of larger and more successful agreements since the interests of 'bottleneck countries' are better accounted for than under efficient policy regimes. Fourth, Altamirano-Cabrera and Finus (2004) find in an empirical setting on climate change that, in the context of permit trading, an initial allocation of permits based on uniform emission reductions may lead to larger and more successful stable coalitions than if the allocation is based on various equity rules, as for instance discussed in Rose *et al.* (1998). The reason is that many equity rules, though they may well be defended on moral grounds, lead to very large transfers from industrialized to developing countries. Hence, these equity rules introduce a new kind of asymmetry that jeopardizes participation of key industrialized countries, rendering cooperation not very successful and contradicting original intentions.

The level of abatement in most IEAs is also far below optimal levels as suggested by Murdoch and Sandler (1997a), analysing the Montreal Protocol, Murdoch and Sandler (1997b), investigating the Helsinki Protocol, and Finus and Tjøtta (2003), considering the Oslo Protocol, the successor protocol of the Helsinki Protocol on sulphur reduction. This departure from optimality should not be viewed as negatively as it may appear at first glance according to Barrett (2002) and Finus (2004). They suggest that, in the context of free-rider incentives, 'modesty may pay'. They show that in many instances a high participation but modest individual abatement targets may lead overall to better outcomes than a low participation associated with ambitious and optimal individual abatement targets.

(iv) Monitoring and Sanctions

Obvious measures to control free-riding are sanctions. However, empirical evidence tells us that either most IEAs have no provision for sanctions or they have hardly been used in the past. Probably, the only exception of sanctioning non-participation is Article 4 under the Montreal Protocol. For sanctioning non-compliance, most IEAs have only a provision for the establishment of an arbitration and dispute settlement committee if a party accuses another of violating the spirit of an agreement (Széll, 1995, p. 97; Marauhn, 1996, p. 696; and Werksman, 1997, p. 85). Owing to the voluntary character of the arbitration scheme, and since the provision contains no threat of punishment, it is not surprising that *there are no reported instances of application* (Sands, 1996, p. 48). Again, the ozone regime is an exception, where the parties first agreed on an indicative list of measures (Annex V) at their fourth meeting in Copenhagen in 1992, and then defined non-compliance at their sixth meeting in Nairobi in 1994. The measures include (a) assistance for the collection and the reporting of data, technical assistance, technology transfers, and financial assistance, (b) issuing cautions, and (c) suspension of specific rights and privileges including transfers of technology, financial mechanisms, and institutional arrangements. It is evident that only item (c) can be regarded as a sanction in the true sense. Moreover, these sanctions can only be used against developing countries since only these countries can claim assistance and enjoy specific rights and privileges (e.g. they are allowed a longer transition period until they have to meet the targets of the various protocol) under Article 5 of the ozone regime. However, any formal statement of non-compliance by the Implementation Committee has to be passed unanimously.[6] Another exemption is the Kyoto Protocol, where the parties agreed at the meeting in Marrakesh in 2001 on 'Consequences Applied by the Enforcement Branch' (Annex XV) that are discussed in section 3 in more detail.

The main problem of establishing sanctions in an IEA is that the design of effective sanctions faces credibility,[7] institutional, and technical problems in reality (Finus, 2002).

(i)   Sanctioning countries for not acceding to an IEA is at odds with the notion of voluntary participation.

(ii) Sanctions often have also a negative effect on those countries carrying out the punishment. Thus, harsh sanctions are not always credible and constitute themselves a public good that is subject to free-riding. Thus, only sanctions that leave the punishers not worse off during punishment are credible.

(iii) Sanctioning non-compliance is flawed by the fact that, under most treaties, signatories can withdraw from the agreement after giving notice 3 years (Kyoto Protocol, Article 27) or 4 years (Montreal Protocol, Article 19) in advance. Thus, sanctions cannot be too harsh and must provide the punished country with an incentive to go along with the punishment.

(iv) Sanctions may be in conflict with the regulations of other treaties (e.g. trade sanctions under the WTO).

(v)   Coordination of sanctions among signatories is often time consuming and costly. Thus, the regulations of sanctions must be simple and transparent.

Obviously, a basic prerequisite to sanction non-compliance is detection through monitoring. An optimal monitoring scheme should have frequent inspections by independent authorities with high-quality detection. In reality, however, most monitoring regimes are far from optimal. *First*, though scientists may identify the total amount of pollutants released into the atmosphere, it might be difficult for technical reasons to assign these emissions to single countries. There may remain some uncertainty about the exact amount of emissions each country releases. The problem is aggravated by the fact that non-compliance can only be punished if the breach can unambiguously be attributed to a party. *Second*, monitoring of most IEAs relies on self-reporting by countries which is usually rather patchy (GAO, 1992, pp. 3ff; Sands, 1996, p. 55; and Bothe, 1996, pp. 22ff). In particular, developing

---

[6] This happened for the first time in 1995 in the case of Russia (Victor, 1998, p. 155).

[7] There are several notions of credible sanctions of which the most convincing concept seems that of renegotiation-proof punishment. For a non-technical overview, see Finus (2003b) and for a technical exposition with references, see Finus (2001).

countries and Eastern European countries often submit incomplete monitoring reports. Obviously, there is a general incentive problem to provide an IEA secretariat with 'true' information. Moreover, it seems that governments are reluctant to accept an independent monitoring authority, fearing that external monitoring may interfere with their sovereignty. *Third*, even if almost complete and frequent monitoring were technically feasible, monitoring costs would probably exceed the gains from cooperation.

3. The Kyoto Protocol: A Review

In this section, we summarize the economic and environmental impacts that the Kyoto Protocol is likely to bring about, describe main institutional features of this treaty, and evaluate the Kyoto Protocol in the light of the fundamental incentive problems outlined in the previous section.

(a) *Preliminaries*

The UNFCCC was adopted during the Earth Summit in 1992 in Rio de Janeiro and provides the institutional framework for international climate policy. It has been ratified by the vast majority of states, though it has to be pointed out that this convention is only a declaration of intentions to deal with the climate-change problem in the future.[8] Periodic meetings of the parties to UNFCCC — the so-called Conferences of Parties (COP) — should promote and review efforts to combat global warming.

The Kyoto Protocol was negotiated in 1997 during the 'Third Conference of the Parties' (COP 3). It requires industrialized countries — as listed in Annex B of the Kyoto Protocol — to reduce their emissions of greenhouse gases, most notably CO_2 from fossil-fuel combustion. More specifically, Annex B countries committed themselves to reducing their greenhouse-gas emissions by 5.2 per cent on average below aggregate 1990 emission levels during the commitment period, 2008–12. The agreement can only enter into force when two conditions are fulfilled (the so-called double-trigger). First, at least 55 parties to the convention must ratify the treaty in their national parliaments. Second, among the ratifying parties, parties included in Annex I[9] of the Kyoto Protocol must account for at least 55 per cent of the total 1990 CO_2 emissions of all Annex I parties.

[8] As of mid-2003, the UNFCCC counted 187 parties, more than any other international environmental agreement (Barrett, 2003*a*).

[9] All parties included in Annex B of the Kyoto Protocol are also part of Annex I, except for Russia and Turkey.

COP 3 in 1997 left open several controversial details of the implementation of the Kyoto Protocol. Controversial issues include whether and by how much carbon sinks account for emission reduction. That is, land and forestry practices which remove carbon emissions through storage may be accounted for in a country's emission target. Moreover, the question whether and to what extent emission rights can be traded was not finally agreed upon between the European Union and the US government, with the former arguing for severe restrictions and the latter for unrestricted trade. In March 2001, the USA, under President Bush, announced that it would not ratify the Kyoto Protocol, reasoning that the costs for the US economy would be too high and arguing that the exemption of developing countries from binding emission targets would render this treaty ineffective.[10]

In the aftermath of the US withdrawal, the Conference of Parties met in Bonn in July 2001. Delegates from more than 180 countries came together, aiming to 'rescue' the Kyoto Protocol from collapse. However, the US withdrawal also supported some countries in their claim that previously negotiated abatement targets would be too tight. Finally, the negotiating parties achieved a compromise. Australia, Canada, New Zealand, Japan, and Russia were granted a substantial amount of credit for CO_2 sinks and some abatement targets were adjusted downwards. Moreover, the EU, which hitherto was strongly against 'paper trade' of hot air, gave up its restrictive position with respect to the permissible scope of emissions trading between industrialized countries. The latest version of the Kyoto Protocol does not include any restriction on the sale and purchase of permits. In practice, this means that Russia, the Ukraine, and Eastern Europe will be able to sell all their surplus emission permits (i.e. emission rights exceeding current emissions in these countries) — generally referred to as hot air — which may significantly increase the effective emissions under the Kyoto Protocol as compared to strictly domestic action.

COP 7 in Marrakesh (November 2001) confirmed the outcome of Bonn and clarified technical and legal details for the implementation and verification of emissions trading and the monitoring of emissions, as well as sanction mechanisms in the case of non-compliance. When Russia ratified the Kyoto Protocol at the end of 2004, the double-trigger

---

[10] In 1997, the US Senate unanimously passed the Byrd–Hagel resolution which makes 'meaningful' participation of developing countries a *conditio sine qua non* for ratification (The Byrd–Hagel Resolution, US Senate, 12 June 1997, 105th Congress, 1st Session, Senate Resolution 98). Given that US ratification requires a two-thirds majority in the Senate, the prospects for ratification have been rather small over the years, irrespective of the latest move under the Bush administration.

Table 1

Baseline Emissions and Emission Reduction Targets for Annex B Regions[a]

Region	Baseline emissions (MtC)[b]		Kyoto targets (% vis-à-vis 1990)[c]		Effective targets (% vis-à-vis 2010)		Effective targets (MtC)	
	1990	2010	Old	New	Old	New	Old	New
AUN	88	130	+6.8	+10.2	−27.7	−25.4	−36	−33
CAN	127	165	−6.0	+7.9	−27.7	−17.0	−46	−28
EUR	929	1,041	−7.8	−5.2	−17.7	−15.4	−184	−160
JPN	269	331	−6.0	−0.8	−23.6	−19.4	−78	−64
CEA	301	227	−7.1	−3.9	+23.2	+27.5	+53	+62
FSU	1,036	713	0.0	+6.4	+45.3	+54.6	+323	+389
Total US out[d]	2,750	2,607	−5.0	−0.5	+0.7	+3.8	+32	+166
USA	1,347	1,809	−7.0	−3.2	−30.8	−27.9	−556	−505
Total US in[e]	4,097	4,416	−5.0	−0.5	−11.9	−7.7	−525	−339

Notes: [a] For reasons of data availability, we apply the greenhouse-gas reduction targets only to CO_2, which is by far the most important greenhouse gas among industrialized countries. AUN − Australia and New Zealand; CAN − Canada; EUR − OECD Europe (incl. EFTA); JPN − Japan; CEA − Central and Eastern Europe; and FSU − Former Soviet Union (including Ukraine). [b] Based on IEO (2001): reference case. [c] Estimates by the European Commission (Nemry, 2001). [d] Annex B without US compliance (assuming full trade in 'hot air'). [e] Annex B with US compliance (assuming full trade in 'hot air').

criteria were met and thus the Kyoto Protocol will enter into force in 2005.

(b) Emission Targets and Timetables

Table 1 summarizes the potential environmental effectiveness of the Kyoto Protocol at different stages of the negotiation process for major Annex B countries. The reduction targets − as originally proposed − are reported in the column labelled 'Kyoto Targets − OLD'. The column 'Kyoto Targets − NEW' accounts for the 'softening' of targets through credits for CO_2 sinks and 'other adjustments' as agreed upon at the Sixth and Seventh Conferences of the Parties at Bonn and Marrakesh (see Nemry, 2001).[11] The reduction targets with respect to 1990 apply to historic emission levels. Since these targets will not become legally binding before the Kyoto commitment period, 2008–12, the appropriate reference for the *effective* cutback requirements are the business-as-

---

[11] Since credible data to measure effective sinks from forest management and agricultural activities *vis-à-vis* the business-as-usual emissions are missing, sink credits under the Kyoto Protocol largely come down to 'creative accounting'.

usual emissions during the commitment period. The column labelled 'Baseline Emissions — 2010' reports the projected business-as-usual emissions for the central year, 2010, of the commitment period based on the reference scenario of the most recent International Energy Outlook (IEO, 2001) by the US Department of Energy.

Except for the economies in transition, which include Central and Eastern Europe (CEA) as well as the Former Soviet Union (FSU), the Kyoto targets with respect to 1990 translate into much more stringent *effective* targets with respect to 2010, since industrialized countries are projected to have economic growth accompanied by a considerable increase in greenhouse-gas emissions from fossil-fuel combustion. Australia and New Zealand (AUN) receive emission rights that are 6.8 per cent higher than their 1990 reference emission levels. Nevertheless, they will face an effective cutback requirement of 27.7 per cent *vis-à-vis* their projected business-as-usual emissions in 2010. Apparently, the economies in transition have been endowed with emission entitlements under the Kyoto Protocol that are well in excess of their anticipated future business-as-usual emissions. The last column in Table 1 converts effective targets in percentages into absolute units.

Table 1 indicates that the Kyoto Protocol in its original form (i.e. US compliance and *OLD* targets) would have demanded a substantial cutback of business-as-usual emissions in industrialized countries. Even in the case of unrestricted Annex B trade in emission rights which would imply hot air in CEA and FSU, aggregate Annex B emissions were to fall by roughly 12 per cent compared to business-as-usual in 2010 (see the intersection of row 'Total US in' with column 'Effective Targets — *OLD*'). The row 'Total US out' illustrates the dramatic implications of US withdrawal and unrestricted permit trading. The total amount of hot air exceeds the cumulative cutback requirements across remaining Annex B countries. As a consequence, the Kyoto Protocol boils down to the business-as-usual scenario without compliance costs and emission reductions.

The story behind Table 1 supports the pessimistic predictions of standard economic theory about the prospects of effective and efficient international environmental cooperation. This would also be confirmed by much more sophisticated analyses that account, for instance, for the rationing of hot air within a multi-sector, multi-region computable general equilibrium model of global trade and energy use (Böhringer, 2002, Böhringer and Vogt, 2003) or a distorted permit market because of market power (Buchner *et al.*, 2002): compliance costs and environmental effects under the Kyoto Protocol are rather negligible.

Taken together, the result is in line with the literature measuring the effectiveness of other international environmental agreements, such as the Montreal, Helsinki, and Oslo Protocols (Murdoch and Sandler, 1997a,b; Finus and Tjøtta, 2002). Also the withdrawal of the US government does not really come as a surprise, taking public-choice aspects into consideration. For instance, Böhringer and Vogt (2004) argue that expected compliance costs exceed US voters' low willingness to pay substantially. Moreover, the US withdrawal provided the remaining non-EU Parties to the Kyoto Protocol (Canada, Australia, New Zealand, Japan, and Russia) with more veto bargaining power. Given the relatively small willingness to pay of voters in these countries, it was rational for these governments to negotiate far-reaching concessions from the EU for the account of carbon sinks and, in particular, for the tradability of hot air.

(c) Flexibility of Emission Targets

There are several instruments within the Kyoto Protocol that allow for some flexibility for the implementation of emission targets. First, under Joint Implementation (JI), Annex B countries can form a bubble in order to reach their targets. That is, individual countries do not necessarily have to meet their emission targets, but it is sufficient if a group of countries meets their aggregate target. Second, as pointed out above, the protocol allows for emission trading among Annex B countries without any restriction, including the trade of hot air. Moreover, a party may 'bank' its emissions rights if its emissions in some commitment periods are less than assigned under the Protocol. Third, the Clean Development Mechanism (CDM) allows Annex B countries to meet their emission targets by financing 'project activities resulting in certified emission reductions' in developing countries. The purchased reductions must be additional to 'any that would occur in the absence of the certified project activity'. Fourth, each country can figure out how it translates its target into domestic policy. That is, no article requires specific technological standards or harmonized measures.

Since many empirical studies (see, for example, Weyant (1999) for a review) confirm larger differences of marginal abatement costs across the participants of the Kyoto Protocol, global abatement costs can be reduced through JI and permit trading, considering effective emission targets, as shown in Table 1, and expecting further cut-backs in emissions in future commitment periods. Also banking of permits allows for some flexibility that is capable of reducing abatement costs. Since marginal abatement costs in developing countries are generally lower than in industrialized countries, the CDM will also contribute to reducing abatement costs. Moreover, it has to be judged positively that no uniform measures have been imposed by the treaty. However, the question arises as to what JI is good for if there is a functioning permit system. It has to be expected that the transparency and efficiency of emission trading may suffer from the coexistence of JI and the permit scheme. Obviously, the founders of JI did not believe in the permit system. Clearly, the problem of the CDM is how to measure 'additional measures'. Since they can only be determined via contra-factual reasoning, it may happen that measures are certified which would have been undertaken by developing countries anyway. This may cause a crowding out of domestic investment by foreign investment. Moreover, monitoring and verification of the CDM (as well as JI and permit trading) will probably prove very difficult. From an incentive point of view, however, the advantage of the CDM is that transfers will most likely take the form of in-kind transfers. Thus, transfers under the CDM may be less jeopardized by compliance problems. Moreover, the CDM reduces not only abatement cost of industrialized countries but also provides benefits to developing countries (see, for example, Böhringer et al., 2003, or Böhringer and Löschel, 2002).

(d) *Monitoring and Enforcement*

Originally, each party had to establish a national emission inventory system by 2004 (Articles 5, 7, and 8) though it looks currently as though most parties will not be able to meet this deadline. The methodologies to estimate emissions, as well as the conversion factor into global warming potentials, have been agreed upon in previous COP meetings. Once established, the emission report has to be submitted annually and will be reviewed by a panel for compliance. The panel experts will be nominated by the parties to the Protocol.

The clear and uniform guidelines on how to prepare inventories have to be judged positively. They should not leave much room for different interpretations and should make it easier to identify violations of the treaty. However, this statement has to be qualified, considering the composition of the expert panel that does not guarantee independent judgment. The frequency of the reports generally ensures that violations are swiftly detected. However, since the inventory is conducted by the parties themselves, reliable reports can hardly be expected. This is particularly true for countries which are undergoing a transition to a market economy. This problem may also be a major obstacle for establishing an efficient emission-trading scheme for which reliable certified emission reductions are a basic prerequisite. A similar problem faces the CDM. Taken together, monitoring is far from being perfect under the Kyoto Protocol. These deficiencies may be a potential source of instability of the treaty and will provide many loopholes for cheating.

In terms of sanctioning non-compliance, the parties to Kyoto Protocol agreed at their meeting in Marrakesh in 2001 on 'Consequences Applied by the Enforcement Branch'. Similar to the Montreal Protocol, most measures include assistance to meet the targets rather than tough sanctions, and complicated voting procedures precede any formal statement of non-compliance. Nevertheless, two punishment options have been decided that may have some effect on compliance: a party (a) may be excluded from the emission-trading system and (b) must reduce its assigned emissions by another 30 per cent in the second commitment period (2013–17).

Clearly, both sanctions are not convincing when viewed from the perspective of 'renegotiation-proof punishment'. The exclusion from the permit-trading system will not only harm the free-rider but also all other participants since trading takes place voluntarily and hence trading must imply a win–win situation. For instance, excluding a potential permit seller such as Russia will raise the permit price, which may be welcomed by other permit sellers, but not by permit purchasers. The additional abatement efforts by free-riders also have some shortcomings, though two positive aspects can be identified. First, additional abatement efforts by treaty violators compensate countries that comply with their treaty obligations. Thus, punishers suffer no disadvantage from sanctions. Second, punishment in the second and not in the first commitment period allows the treaty violator more flexibility to meet its obligations. This may provide some incentives for treaty violators to go along with the punishment. However, there are also three serious flaws. First, the time gap between treaty violation and sanctions reduces the threat potential of sanctions if governments discount time. In particular, the government responsible for treaty violation and the government which has to conduct additional abatement efforts may not be the same. Hence, it is easy for the successor government to claim that it is not responsible for the misconduct of previous governments. Second, the very fact that the Kyoto Protocol allows for parties to opt out after 3 years by giving notice to the secretariat, means that postponing punishment does not make much sense. Third, sanctions are too weak in case a country continuously violates a treaty and shows no repentance. Basically, no option has been set up that would enforce compliance if the free-rider does not accept the weak punishment option.

4. The Kyoto Protocol: Perspectives

Antagonists of the Kyoto Protocol see its failure in terms of environmental effectiveness as a natural consequence of a flawed architecture.[12] Overall, they conclude 'that the Kyoto Protocol is an impractical policy focused on achieving an unrealistic and inappropriate goal' (McKibbin and Wilcoxen, 2002, p. 127). An incomplete list of key arguments against the Kyoto structure includes the following.

(i) 'The Kyoto Protocol is defective on both efficiency criteria [spatial and temporal equalization of abatement costs] because it omits a substantial fraction of emissions (thus failing the spatial criterion) and has no plans beyond the first period (thus not attending to the temporal dimension)' (Nordhaus, 2001, p. 8);

(ii) 'The Kyoto Protocol has an arbitrary allocation of transfers. . . . Moreover, since developing countries are omitted, they are completely overlooked in the transfers' (Nordhaus, 2001, p. 9);

(iii) 'The most fundamental defect of the Kyoto Protocol is that the policy lacks any connection to ultimate economic or environmental policy objectives' (Nordhaus, 2001, p. 13);

(iv) 'International permit trading [as the principal policy instrument of the Kyoto Protocol] runs the risk of being highly inefficient, given uncertainties in the marginal cost of abating greenhouse gas emissions. . . . it would probably generate large transfers of wealth between countries' (McKibbin and Wilcoxen, 2002, p. 126); and

(v) 'no individual government has an incentive to police the agreement. . . . The Kyoto Protocol can only work if it includes an elaborate and expensive international mechanism for monitoring and enforcement' (McKibbin and Wilcoxen, 2002, pp. 126-7).

Against this criticism, two central questions arise with respect to forthcoming climate-policy negotiations. First, does the Kyoto Protocol really fall short of *any* basic economic principles? Second, are there *fundamentally* better approaches to climate policy and — if not — how could the Kyoto Protocol be amended into a more practical and efficient strategy?

(a) Is the Kyoto Protocol Totally Flawed?

Economists are generally uneasy if decision-making is not based on a comprehensive cost–benefit analysis. As pointed out in section 2,

---

[12] For example, Nordhaus and Boyer (1999*b*, p.125) find that the Protocol does not 'bear any relation to an economically oriented strategy that would balance the costs and benefits of GHG [greenhouse gas] reductions'.

because of the huge uncertainties in the science of climate change, the targets and timetables underlying the Kyoto Protocol were not derived from a cost–benefit analysis, but rather emerged from a (partially *ad hoc*) political process involving tough bargaining on the scope, timing, and distribution of emission reductions. Negotiating countries revealed different perceptions on the urgency and scale of abatement by putting different weights on the relative severity, irreversibility, and risks associated with action and a wait-and-see strategy. After all, the final version of the Kyoto Protocol implies only moderate emission reductions (even with inclusion of the USA) when considering hot air and the generous approval of carbon sinks. Thus, the agreement may be seen as roughly in line with recommendations based on tentative numerical cost–benefit analyses conducted by some opponents to the Kyoto Protocol (suggesting only moderate reductions from business-as-usual levels in the near future). Furthermore, it seems unfounded to accuse Kyoto of a total lack of economic and environmental policy objectives, pointing out that policy plans beyond the first commitment period are missing. In qualitative terms, the Kyoto Protocol reflects scientific evidence from the IPCC for the need of long-term emission reduction. Reconciling diverging views of the Parties in the short term seems a wise strategy to kick off a political process on climate change. Subsequent amendments may improve upon the current Kyoto Protocol.

Kyoto is certainly not perfect, either, in terms of cost-efficiency, which would require full 'where'- and 'when'-flexibility. However, the Kyoto Protocol is the *first* IEA which uses market-based instruments at all to achieve environmental targets. With respect to 'where'-flexibility, the JI, permit trading, and the CDM are a good start. As pointed out above, JI is redundant once a well-functioning permit-trading system has been established. Also the CDM improves upon 'where'-flexibility as long as developing countries have not accepted abatement targets.

In principle, the use of the CDM implies that developing countries become part of the abatement coalition. As noted before, the CDM may encounter severe problems of verification: not only do developing countries have incentives to offer projects that would have been undertaken anyway, but the Annex B countries also have incentives to select these projects if they can be acquired at lower cost (Barrett, 1998). Nevertheless, the CDM provides a good start to broaden the climate coalition and may be replaced by permit trading at a later stage.

Also some first steps have been taken to allow for 'when'-flexibility through the possibility of banking permits. While the exclusion of borrowing entails some potential efficiency losses in theory, it can be seen as a hedging strategy to prevent strategic incentives for 'postponing and doing nothing'.

Furthermore, the frequent accusation that the quantity-based approach in the Kyoto Protocol is rather inefficient and doomed to lead to excessive adjustment costs seems too strong. As has been pointed out before, the appropriate policy for limiting greenhouse-gas emissions — given the uncertainty on costs and benefits — would be a mixed system in which a 'finite penalty' provides an 'escape valve' under a quantity regime in case abatement costs turn out to be 'too' high. However, as observed above, the actual emission caps are not very restrictive. Thus, the risk of unacceptably high permit prices seems not very high. Larger price shocks and fluctuations could be dampened by permit banking which is available under the Kyoto Protocol. Moreover, the quantity element under the Kyoto architecture offers, from a practical policy perspective, the advantage of a transparent metric that allows for a direct control of the environmental outcome.

The issue of transfers, which is associated with the initial allocation of emission rights, may seem *ad hoc* and not well founded with respect to equity. However, there is no generally accepted definition of equity anyway. Equity principles refer to normative concepts of distributive justice or fairness that are perceived very differently.[13] The typical approach of economists is to separate efficiency from equity considerations and rely on (non-distortionary) lump-sum transfers in order to meet some exogenous equity criterion. However, in practice, efficiency and fairness are closely interwound, considering that equity issues are most likely related to the incentives of participation and compliance (Carraro, 2003). The outcome of the Kyoto conference in December 1997 supports this proposition, though concepts of equity have remained rather vague during the negotiation process. Industrialized countries have committed themselves to higher emission-reduction targets than economies in transition (both of them referred to as Annex B countries), whereas developing countries have not accepted any commitment. This allocation may be interpreted as if targets have been allocated according to the principle of different 'abilities to pay for emission reduction' and/or different 'responsibilities for the current stock of greenhouse gases'. Ultimately, the Kyoto Protocol targets can be traced back to the

---

[13] Ringius *et al.* (1998) distinguish five equity principles: *egalitarian*, i.e. people have equal rights to use the atmosphere; *horizontal*, i.e. actors under similar (economic) conditions have similar emission rights and burden sharing responsibilities; *vertical*, i.e. the greater the capacity to act or ability to pay is, the greater the (economic) burden should be; *polluter pays*, i.e. the greater the contribution to the problem is, the greater the burden should be; and *sovereignty*, i.e. current emissions constitute a status quo right now.

Berlin Mandate in 1995 that reflected a widespread consensus that countries 'graduate' into a set of obligations commensurate with their abilities to pay.

It is also certainly true that the effectiveness of the Kyoto Protocol is undermined by the fact that developing countries have not taken on any abatement responsibilities. This is particularly true when considering predictions of economic growth as well as fuel and energy consumption in countries such as India and China in the future. However, given the record of historical emissions, it seems sensible and probably the only political feasible strategy that industrialized countries which account for the bulk of past emissions start by setting a good example through a credible commitment to emission reduction. Only if industrialized countries prove that economic growth and greenhouse-gas abatement are not a contradiction, can it be expected that developing countries follow suit. Moreover, as pointed out above, the CDM may be a first start to expand the current climate coalition which may be fostered through transfers, technical assistance, and joint ventures in the development of abatement technology.

Finally, it is evident that the issue of enforcement has not been solved satisfactorily under the Kyoto Protocol. However, taking the record of past IEAs, as reported in section 2, into account, this criticism would be even more true for other IEAs. At least clear guidelines for monitoring have been established and the annual reports will provide at least some indication about the performance of individual parties. Moreover, apart from the Montreal Protocol, the Kyoto Protocol is the first treaty that goes beyond the simple establishment of a dispute-settlement regime and proposes at least two measures with which to punish violations of treaty obligations. Both measures provide at least a framework of a punishment architecture that may be developed further.

(b) *Giving Up or Amending Kyoto*

Since the beginning of the Kyoto process in 1997, numerous proposals on alternative architectures of global climate policy have been developed (see Aldy *et al.* (2003) for a recent cross-comparison of some proposals). They may be broadly divided in two categories. First, some proposals suggest adopting direct price and quantity instruments or a combination of both. Second, some proposals support common R&D efforts. Within the first category, proposals typically incorporate a price cap to limit the costs of greenhouse-gas mitigation policies. The price cap may form part of a hybrid policy mix, combining some cap-and-trade setting with a safety-valve (e.g. Aldy *et al.*, 2001, or Jacoby and Ellerman, 2002). Alternatively, the price cap may come as a harmonized carbon tax across regions forming part of the abatement regime (e.g. Cooper, 1998; Pizer, 1999*b*; and Victor, 2001). While the harmonized carbon tax approach bears some theoretical appeal, monitoring and enforcement will also be extremely difficult.[14] However, there are obviously strong incentives for countries to offset emission taxes with less visible compensatory policies, or to 'miscount' initial energy taxes and subsidies.[15] Another major problem of harmonized carbon taxes is that this will imply very asymmetric impacts across countries. Hence, compensation schemes with side payments would have to be negotiated which might be even more controversial than the international debate about alternative emission entitlement rules or abatement duties.[16] The second category of proposals (e.g. Barrett 2001, 2003*a*, and, partly, Benedick, 2001) puts emphasis on the inherent difficulties of enforcing participation and compliance to the provision of global public goods. These proposals depart from emission-reduction commitments as well as market-based instruments. Instead, these proposals suggest 'cooperative climate-friendly R&D agreements' and common technology standards that would make the enforcement of emission mitigation easier. However, such an approach reveals severe shortcomings. There are severe problems with windfall gains with respect to R&D subsidies, as well as with incentives to free-ride on R&D spillovers. Also environmental effectiveness may suffer without explicit targets and (dynamic and static) efficiency will definitely be lost through uniform technology standards.

Overall, it seems that alternative proposals to the current Kyoto architecture will not necessarily do better with respect to the key criteria — environmental effectiveness, efficiency, equity, and enforcement. Given that the current Kyoto Protocol provides substantial flexibility, it seems reasonable to think about ways to improve upon the current design of this treaty. After all, the Kyoto process has achieved — with considerable efforts — a relatively broad participation in international climate policy and introduced a market-based approach for the first time in an IEA. Thus, the key question that we would like to answer in the remainder of this section is: what could possible amendments look like?

[14] Nordhaus (2001) provides a list of additional, rather *ad hoc*, arguments for harmonized carbon taxes, such as higher transparency, less susceptibility to corruption, and preserved national sovereignty.

[15] In this context, Victor (2001, p. 86) warns of a 'goulash of prior distortions, new taxes, and political patches'.

[16] One proposal to avoid asymmetries is to implement an international tax with an international environmental agency that balances asymmetries via the reallocation of tax revenues (Bradford, 2002).

First, it is inevitable that the developing world is gradually becoming involved. The developing countries account for a large and growing share of emissions. Thus, in the mid term, climate protection cannot be successful without substantial participation by the developing countries. Assignment of emission entitlements to lock developing countries into the abatement coalition will inevitably involve controversial equity debates. To relax these debates, the short-term objective of broadening participation should not be so much to redistribute costs from the industrialized to the developing world as to lower the overall abatement bill. In this vein, an earlier draft of the Protocol allowed developing countries to choose, at any time and on a voluntary basis, a level of emission control that would be appropriate for their circumstances.[17]

Second, the current provisions for sanctioning violators can be improved (Finus, 2002, 2003a). For instance, the incentive problem associated with the current proposal to exclude violators from the permit-trading system could be mitigated through the following modification. Instead of excluding a seller of permits from trading, the seller's revenues could be transferred to an environmental fund for some time. Instead of excluding a buyer of permits from trading, this country should pay a mark-up on the current permit price. In both cases, the surplus can be used for compensation of other parties, leaving punishers not worse off than before the violation.

These measures also point to another role of transfers for sanctioning treaty violators in a renegotiation-proof manner. If each party were required to deposit some money with the secretariat of COP, then, in the same way that union funds are used to back up strikes by reducing the negative effect of strikes on their members (suspension of payment, lay-off of workers, and so forth), this money could be used to mitigate the negative effects of sanctions for punishers. Moreover, the deposit can function as a pledge. Parties that comply earn interest on their pledges and are rewarded; violators lose their pledges and interest rates and are punished. This would improve upon the credibility of sanctions, offers an option to punish violators that show 'no repentance', and puts up some hurdle against governments leaving the treaty after violation to get around punishment. A similar option to use transfers as an enforcement device could be inspired by the Montreal Protocol. Provided developing countries join the Kyoto Protocol at a later stage, a fund could be established to which industrialized countries contribute and from which developing countries receive assist-

---

[17] A more comprehensive emissions-trading system would also reduce concerns on counter-productive leakage through relocation of emissions from participating to non-participating countries.

ance. If developing countries do not comply with their abatement obligations, transfers could be suspended for some time and could only be taken up gradually again if violators show progress in meeting their targets. If transfers cover more than the incremental abatement costs of developing countries, suspension of transfers will harm these countries. Moreover, this type of sanction is credible because suspension of transfer provides a reduction of transfer obligations to industrialized countries.

Also the shortcomings of the second punishment option under the Kyoto Protocol of additional abatement duties in the future could be partly fixed. Instead of postponing punishment to the second commitment period, punishment could start immediately at low levels, with a gradual increase over time. In order to provide governments with an incentive to accept additional abatement duties as punishment, immediate action should be rewarded with generous reductions of future additional abatement obligations. Moreover, the Kyoto Protocol should include an option where parties reduce their abatement efforts as some form of reciprocal punishment (that is widely accepted in international law) if the treaty violator continuously ignores the rules of the protocol.

Third, during the initial commitment periods, Kyoto could be endowed with a safety valve (see Roberts and Spence, 1976; Kopp *et al.*, 1997; Victor, 2001; Jacoby and Ellerman, 2002; McKibbin and Wilcoxen, 2002) to hedge against uncertainty and volatility of permit prices. Under the safety valve, the national authorities can sell permits in unlimited amounts at a pre-set price. This would provide an upper limit on the marginal cost of the emission cap. If the penalty or, for that matter, the safety valve is set far below the expected marginal cost at the level of the cap, it would relax the target emissions reduction and effectively change the control instrument from quantity to price.[18]

However, as put forward by Jacoby and Ellerman (2002), the safety valve is not desirable as a long-term feature of the cap-and-trading system because it involves complex coordination of price and quantity instruments. Finally, assuming it will not prove easier to coordinate a global safety valve than it has been to decide on a global carbon tax, the phasing-out of any safety valves in national programmes will require the creation of a well-functioning emission-permit market. Once the cap-and-trade system is in place, similar results can be achieved by banking.

---

[18] In the extreme — if the price is low enough to be triggered frequently — this will lead to a globally harmonized carbon tax.

5. Final Remarks

More than 10 years of climate-policy negotiations have led to the Kyoto Protocol, the first international agreement on climate protection, coming into force in 2005. Given the large uncertainties of scientific evidence on climate change and the fundamental incentive problems associated with cooperation, it is clear that a first-best and even second-best climate policy cannot be achieved in practice. Thus, the Kyoto Protocol is certainly only one out of many possible imperfect architectures to address the risks posed by global climate change.

Opponents to the protocol have refused it as a 'deeply flawed agreement that manages to be both economically inefficient and politically impractical' (McKibbin and Wilcoxen, 2002, p. 107). This article views the Kyoto architecture more positively. Key elements of the protocol are in line with basic economic principles. The protocol is based on a mechanism that allows an iterative adjustment and movement towards new goals. A system of periodically negotiated 5-year compliance periods provides a flexible approach that allows policy-makers to adjust their decisions according to better information obtained in the future. The treaty constitutes the first international environmental agreement that builds upon market-based instruments and that allows for cost-efficient responses to the undisputed need for greenhouse-gas abatement. After tedious and controversial negotiations, the Conferences of the Parties came up with a burden-sharing scheme for the first commitment period that all major parties (with the exception of the USA) have accepted as a 'fair' compromise, reflecting historic responsibilities for the current stock of greenhouse gases as well as the ability to pay for emission reductions. Admittedly, it is also fair to say that the Kyoto Protocol — as it stands now — has not achieved a decisive breakthrough in international climate policy. Sink credits, hot air, and, in particular, the US repudiation will make Kyoto not very effective in environmental terms during the first commitment period. Moreover, it has not yet been negotiated which abatement targets will apply after the first commitment period, 2008–12.

The apparent 'failure' of the Kyoto Protocol with respect to environmental effectiveness does not come much as a surprise, given the huge incentive problems of providing a global public good. Ironically, and in retrospect, it may be more of an advantage than a disadvantage that Kyoto, which originally aimed at large early emission reductions (with potentially large costs for some nations), has been converted to a 'soft agreement' with very low compliance costs: (i) this lowers concerns on the disadvantages of a too rigid quantity-based approach, (ii) it appeases opponents who insist that Kyoto has been way too ambitious in short-term emission reductions, and (iii) it increases the chance that the USA as a key player might rejoin the protocol at a later stage. This conjecture may not be unwarranted, given that compliance costs to the US economy seem rather moderate, which could increase domestic pressure on the US government to contribute to an internationally coordinated abatement strategy.

Thus, even without effective emission reductions in the first commitment period, the ratification of Kyoto may be crucial for the further policy process of climate protection. It has established a broad-based international mechanism that provides a valuable starting point for efficient climate policies in the future. Given the shared belief that substantial global emission reduction will be required in the long run, the major challenge remains as to how more comprehensive and more ambitious international cooperation can be induced. Most importantly, this will require incentives for developing countries for participation. Ultimately, this comes down to how abatement duties — or emission entitlements — should be allocated across countries over a longer time horizon. This issue has already dominated previous climate negotiations and proved extremely difficult to solve, even though the overall abatement targets under discussion were very moderate in comparison with the long-term requirements suggested by the IPCC. Consequently, some pragmatic reconciliation of the equity and efficiency issues must be at the top of the research and policy agenda. Moreover, a credible system of direct or indirect sanctions, that is capable of deterring free-riding, must be developed. This requires the joint efforts of theoretical and applied research from economists, game theorists, and lawyers in order to develop sanction mechanisms that work not only in theory but also in practice.

13

Kyoto Plus

SCOTT BARRETT*

1. Introduction

The global climate regime today consists of the Framework Convention on Climate Change (FCCC) and its associated Kyoto Protocol. The Framework Convention establishes a general goal — preventing 'dangerous anthropogenic interference with the climate system'. The Kyoto Protocol is but the first of many protocols intended to achieve this ambition.

As I was finishing this paper, news broke that Russia had ratified the Kyoto Protocol. As a consequence, Kyoto will now enter into force and be binding upon all its parties. Romano Prodi, president of the European Commission, called this 'a huge success for the international fight against climate change'. However, history may judge the moment differently. Entry into force may only expose Kyoto's fundamental weaknesses.

One thing is clear: Kyoto will not stabilize concentrations at *any* level, let alone one that avoids 'dangerous interference' with the climate. Kyoto only constrains the emissions of some (not all) countries by a little bit for a very short period of time. Stabilization will require deeper cuts, by more countries; and these will need to be permanent. By design, Kyoto's importance lay in creating a foundation upon which *further* emission reductions could be achieved. Kyoto was intended to be a first step.

So, what really matters is whether Kyoto provides a solid foundation for a long-term programme for substantial emission cuts. In my view it does not. The intention was for Kyoto to be succeeded by another agreement much like it, for this agreement to be followed by another in turn, and so on in serial fashion. But if the basic architecture

* School of Advanced International Studies, Johns Hopkins University.
I am grateful to Dieter Helm and Lee Lane for commenting on an earlier draft.

remains faithful to this model of diplomacy, even a sequence of such agreements — what I call the 'Kyoto Only' approach — will fail to reduce emissions substantially. The reason is that the Kyoto model can only work with strong enforcement and Kyoto fails to provide the needed incentives for enforcement. Worse, it is hard to see how the agreement could be modified to create such incentives. The 'Kyoto Only' approach to climate mitigation is incapable of supporting substantial cuts in greenhouse-gas emissions. A different approach is needed.

This assessment is neither obvious nor universally shared. In a September 2004 speech, for example, the British Prime Minister, Tony Blair, confidently declared that Kyoto provided 'a solid foundation for the next stage of climate diplomacy'. However, in the same speech, the Prime Minister said that we need a 'new green industrial revolution that develops the new technologies that can confront and overcome the challenge of climate change'. I agree that a new technological revolution is needed. I simply disagree that Kyoto will be able to produce it.

My criticism about Kyoto is thus about means, not ends (though I shall have something to say about ends, too, in the next section). From this perspective, Kyoto is only to be opposed if it is perceived as having 'solved' the climate problem. A better approach would be to broaden climate diplomacy, to negotiate a wider set of mutually reinforcing protocols. These can encompass Kyoto, and so my proposal might be called the 'Kyoto Plus' alternative to the 'Kyoto Only' status quo. Broadening alone, however, is insufficient. The fundamental weakness in Kyoto must be overcome. Incentives must be created for countries to change their behaviour, and this requires a *strategic approach to treaty making* (Barrett, 2003a). It is not just broadening that matters. *How* we broaden is crucial. For this particular problem, strategy is needed in two dimensions, time and space.

Time. Climate change is a very, very long-term problem; behaviour must be influenced over decades and centuries, not months and years. Kyoto is a short-term agreement that creates no incentive for future emission reductions. Of course, focusing only on the long term will not suffice. States cannot make credible a promise today to do something in the future. What is needed, therefore, is a *strategic link between the short run and the long run* — one in which actions taken now make it more attractive to take additional actions in the future.

Space. Only global emissions count for the climate; the emissions of individual states are irrelevant. Kyoto requires that only a subset of countries reduce their emissions. But even if Kyoto worked as intended, this restraint shown by some countries would not cause others to reduce *their* emissions. It is often claimed that some countries must lead by example. But if the Kyoto parties were to reduce emissions substantially, the costs borne by their industries would rise, and the incentive for others to follow would be weak to say the least. Indeed, it seems more likely that other countries would *increase* their emissions in response. This would result not from a deliberate policy to increase emissions. It would result from market forces acting through a liberalized trade regime. Imposing costs on greenhouse-gas-intensive production in one set of countries simply shifts comparative advantage in emissions-intensive industry towards other countries, a phenomenon known as 'leakage'. What is needed is precisely the opposite effect. What is needed is a *strategic link among countries*: a mechanism whereby, as some countries reduce their emissions by more, incentives are created for others to reduce *their* emissions by more.

In short, the strategic approach creates incentives for positive feedbacks in emission reductions over both space and time.

As already noted, climate-change policy must reduce emissions substantially in the long run, and this will require a technological revolution. Kyoto tries to create incentives for innovation and diffusion indirectly, by raising the cost of emitting greenhouse gases. But because Kyoto cannot be enforced, these incentives will never materialize. A strategic approach, however, can create the needed incentives. Rather than leave it to the market only to choose future technologies, my proposal is for these decisions to be made by government–industry partnerships, cast in a multilateral framework. There can be advantages to standard setting by committees (Farrell and Saloner, 1988), but the motivation behind this proposal is strategic. There are two sides to the technology coin. Incentives are needed to spur innovation. But the availability and adoption of technology also changes behaviour. It is the latter effect that my proposal seeks to exploit.

One argument against my proposal (expressed most enthusiastically, I might add, by the architects of the Kyoto agreement) is that, flawed or not, so much has been invested in the Kyoto process that we cannot contemplate an alternative. This is illogical: past investments in this process are sunk. And these efforts will not have been wasted provided we learn from them. The climate problem is immensely complex. To expect that diplomacy would settle on the best approach from the start is to expect too much. Indeed, an effective climate regime must not only create incentives for change but also retain flexibility as regards both means and ends.

If my reasoning is correct, the failings of the Kyoto Only model will become more apparent even as the need for action becomes more manifest. Since there is no need to reject Kyoto (indeed, as I shall explain later, an element of my proposal can easily embrace Kyoto and any succeeding agreements), what should be emphasized is the need to construct mutually reinforcing pathways.

History, of course, often repeats itself; and it may do so here. This is not the first time that a treaty has been painstakingly negotiated only to stall at the starting gate, or to enter into force but not be implemented, or to enter into force and be implemented but fail to make a material difference. A striking example is the approach taken to limit the deliberate release of oil at sea by tankers. Negotiation of agreements to limit oil-tanker releases began in 1926. But the first attempts failed to enter into force, mainly because countries could see no way in which agreed obligations could be enforced. Eventually, an agreement to reduce deliberate oil releases (the International Convention for the Prevention of Pollution of the Sea by Oil or OILPOL, adopted in 1954) did enter into force, but this provided little more than a framework for further negotiations, as the quantitative limits set out in this agreement were not enforced. Later attempts to improve on this agreement encountered similar enforcement problems. The problem was with the approach to setting quantitative limits, not the aim.

Eventually, in 1978, a very different approach was tried: a new agreement establishing a technology standard to separate oil from ballast water. The new agreement, known as the International Convention for the Prevention of Pollution from Ships (MARPOL), entered into force 5 years after being adopted and has since been strengthened by a number of mutually supporting amendments (the most recent requires double hulls for new tankers). In contrast to the earlier agreements, MARPOL has been an enforcement success. Participation is nearly universal (today, it covers 97 per cent of global tonnage); compliance has been perfect (Mitchell, 1994).

MARPOL succeeded where earlier attempts failed by strategically manipulating incentives. First, in contrast to quantity releases at sea, compliance with the technology standard is easily verified. Second, coastal states had nationalistic incentives to enforce compliance, to protect their shorelines and near-shore ecosystems. Third, a positive feedback was created whereby, as more countries participated, the incentive for tanker owners to comply increased (the value of owning a tanker increases in the number of ports to which the tanker is permitted access). And as more tankers complied, the incentive for port states to participate and enforce compliance increased (the cost of excluding standard-violating tankers fell). Essentially, the agreement created a 'tipping' effect (Barrett, 2003a).

Of course, climate change is a much more challenging problem, and different problems require different remedies. But the lessons of this diplomatic history have much to teach climate negotiators. Unfortunately, most negotiators are unfamiliar with this story. The history of the Montreal Protocol negotiations is better known, but as I have explained elsewhere (Barrett, 2003a), the wrong lessons have been drawn from this experience.

As I was about to send this paper back to the editor for publication, another event forced me to make one last revision. President George W. Bush was re-elected for a second term, this time with a majority of the popular vote. This is a problem for the multilateral process. President Bush withdrew US support for Kyoto, and it is almost inconceivable that he would contemplate negotiation of a follow-on agreement styled after Kyoto. Shortly before the election, I asked a democratic senator what kind of treaty the US Senate would ratify. He thought the Senate would not approve a treaty that imposed quantitative limits on greenhouse-gas emissions, but that it might welcome a treaty approach of the kind I have recommended. This is important because a treaty requires a two-thirds majority of the Senate for ratification — and after the 2004 election, the Senate will be even less friendly to an emissions limitation agreement than before. It must also be remembered that President Clinton, who negotiated and signed the Kyoto Protocol, failed to send it to the Senate for ratification. This is because he knew the Senate would reject it. Finally, all of this is important because the United States is the world's largest emitter of greenhouse gases. Like it or not, an effective climate agreement must secure the participation of the USA.

This is where my proposal may have another advantage. President Bush has said that he supports 'approaches to reduce greenhouse-gas emissions, including those that tap the power of markets, help realize the promise of technology, and ensure the widest-possible global participation'.[1] An advantage of Kyoto Plus is that it allows the Kyoto parties to go ahead with this agreement while at the same time engaging with the United States and other countries in alternative approaches.

I am not trying to paint a pretty picture. My approach has flaws, too; it is a second-best treaty. And like all approaches, it only stands a chance of succeeding if the important players believe that climate mitigation is a goal worthy of sacrifice. If countries do not believe this — if the USA, especially, does not believe this — then it will not be possible to make much headway. There is no getting around this.

2. Framework Convention

Climate change represents a clash between two worlds, the earth's atmospheric system and its political system, a world of one atmosphere

[1] Speech by President George W. Bush, given on 11 June 2001; see http://www.whitehouse.gov/news/releases/2001/06/20010611-2.html

and a world of two hundred or so countries. The science of climate change draws our attention to the first world. Climate policy and negotiation require that we also look to the second. The international system created the climate-change problem; the international system will have to address it.

The first milestone in this effort — the FCCC — was adopted at the Rio Earth Summit in 1992. As of October 2004, 188 countries have ratified this agreement: a remarkable consensus. The achievement is perhaps best understood by listing the non-parties to this agreement: Andorra, Brunei, Holy See, Iraq, and Somalia. Quite plainly, this is not an agreement suffering from free riding.

To be sure, one reason for the nearly universal support is that the agreement does not require that parties reduce their emissions of greenhouse gases. And yet the consensus achieved by the agreement is impressive. It demonstrates broad support for the goal of stabilizing atmospheric concentrations of greenhouse gases. Indeed, the only environmental agreement with as wide a following is the Vienna Convention for the Protection of the Ozone Layer. And this is encouraging, since the Vienna Convention provided the framework for the very successful ozone regime — one of the greatest achievements of international cooperation ever. If there were a problem with the existing climate regime, it would seem not to be the Framework Convention.

The Convention's main contribution is to establish a goal: 'stabilization of greenhouse gas concentrations in the atmosphere at a level that would prevent dangerous anthropogenic interference with the climate system.' This would seem sensible enough. But stabilization will require a monumental effort, and identifying the concentration level that avoids 'dangerous interference' with the climate system is an impossible task.

Stabilization of atmospheric concentrations cannot be achieved merely by stabilizing emissions. Stabilizing concentrations implies an atmospheric balance, with the quantity of molecules being added to the atmosphere equalling the quantity being subtracted. Today, only a fraction of the gases added to the atmosphere are removed (by ocean absorption and biomass growth), with the result that concentrations (measured in parts per million, or ppm) have been rising. If emissions were stabilized at the current level, concentrations would continue to rise. Limiting concentrations to a level close to twice the pre-industrial level (about 280 ppm) would require '50 years of flat emissions, followed by a linear decline of about two-thirds in the following 50 years, and a very slow decline thereafter that matches the declining ocean sink' (Pacala and Socolow, 2004, p. 968). Current projections are that emissions will more than double over the next 50 years, in the absence of climate policy (Pacala and Socolow, 2004). So a goal of limiting concentrations to twice the pre-industrial level will require more than a 75 per cent cut in emissions from the business-as-usual trajectory.

To put this into perspective, the Kyoto Protocol would only limit the emissions of about 30 of the world's 200 or so countries by only about 5 per cent for a period of just 5 years. Even if Kyoto worked as intended, the emissions of the countries unconstrained by the agreement would rise, making it very unlikely that Kyoto would even stabilize global emissions, let alone reduce them, even over such a short period.

What level of concentrations is 'dangerous?' We do not know. Moreover, I do not think we will be able to know.

The basic physics of climate change are simple.[2] There naturally exist gases in the atmosphere—primarily carbon dioxide (CO_2) and water vapour—that trap the sun's heat, keeping the earth about 34°C warmer than it otherwise would be. It stands to reason that if more heat-trapping gases are concentrated in the atmosphere, more heat will be trapped. Since the industrial revolution, concentrations of greenhouse gases have increased by about 30 per cent (to about 365 ppm in 1998). Concentrations will increase even more in the future, though by how much depends on a number of things: emissions growth, which depends in turn on economic growth, technology, and policy; take up by the oceans and other carbon sinks; and the effect of CO_2 fertilization on terrestrial absorption. By 2100, concentrations are expected to be 90–350 per cent above the pre-industrial level. Beyond 2100, concentrations are expected to keep on rising. Already, concentrations are higher than they have been in the past 420,000 years—probably in the last 20m years.

Global mean temperature has already increased about 0.6°C. By 2100, it is expected to rise by 1.4–5.8°C. Sea level is expected to rise by 0.09–0.88 metres over this same period, as a result of thermal expansion and the melting of glaciers and ice caps. Of course, if concentrations are not stabilized, the climate will change still more beyond 2100. Even if concentrations were stabilized today, changes would continue for a very long time because of lags in the system. We are already committed to some amount of climate change.

The uncertainties in the science of climate change are substantial. Most importantly, the direct changes caused by climate change may trigger yet more changes, because of a number of feedbacks (positive

[2] My discussion here draws from Intergovernmental Panel on Climate Change (IPCC, 2001d).

and negative). One such change is a weakening or even collapse of the Gulf Stream (part of the global thermohaline circulation or THC). Abrupt climate change has occurred in the past, and could be triggered by human-induced climate change. As noted in a recent report by the National Academy of Sciences (Committee on Abrupt Climate Change, 2002, p. 1), 'future abrupt changes cannot be predicted with confidence, and climate surprises are to be expected'.

That predictions about the nature of climate change are uncertain should hardly come as a surprise. The climate system is complicated. And we are conducting a huge experiment with it. We will not know its full consequences for sure until they become manifest (even then, disentangling human-induced climate change from natural climate change will be difficult). It would be imprudent to wait for uncertainties to be resolved because not all uncertainties will be resolved, and because change, once it occurs, will take a very long time to reverse. Indeed, change may be irreversible.

Plainly, there is unanimous agreement that dangerous interference with the climate ought to be avoided. But do we know what level is dangerous? The expression itself implies a discontinuity, and O'Neill and Oppenheimer (2002) have identified three discontinuous changes that would be very serious indeed: the destruction of large-scale coral-reef ecosystems; the disintegration of the West Antarctic Ice Sheet (WAIS); and the collapse of the THC. They then suggest that these three changes can probably be avoided by limiting long-term warming to 1°C; that the last two can probably be avoided by limiting change to 2°C; and that the last can probably be avoided by limiting change to 3°C above 1990 global mean temperature. Noting that CO_2 stabilization at 450, 550, and 650 ppm would correspond roughly to a century's long warming of about 1.2–2.3°C, 1.5–2.9°C, and 1.7–3.2°C, respectively, O'Neill and Oppenheimer conclude:

> Full protection of coral reefs is probably not feasible for this concentration range. It is plausible that achieving stabilization at 450 ppm would forestall the disintegration of WAIS, but it is by no means certain, because additional warming would occur beyond 2100. Avoiding the shutdown of the THC is likely for 450 ppm.

Though O'Neill and Oppenheimer aim to show how we might identify the level of atmospheric concentrations that might trigger dangerous interference, their analysis really shows how difficult the task is. Why adopt 450 ppm if this will not protect coral reefs, if this will possibly forestall but not avoid disintegration of the WAIS, if this will likely, but not for certain, avoid a shutdown of the THC? Why not aim for 400 ppm? Or 500 ppm? Or some other level? The answers are not clear from their analysis.

Another problem with this approach is that it ignores the consequences of mitigation. Reducing greenhouse-gas emissions will be costly. Reducing emissions by enough to stabilize concentrations at 450 ppm will be very costly. It would require that emissions be cut by much more even than in the scenario examined by Pacala and Socolow. Looked at differently, mitigation introduces different risks. For example, and as Pacala and Socolow explain and Prime Minister Blair acknowledged in his 14 September 2004 speech, stabilization requires an expansion in nuclear power.

Ignoring the cost is a morally empty logic (Schelling, 2002). Should the rich countries reduce their emissions, even if only to help the poor countries, which will certainly be the most vulnerable to climate change? My answer would be 'Yes', not least because the rich countries are responsible for the historic build-up of atmospheric concentrations. But should the rich countries reduce their emissions by a huge amount, rather than by somewhat less, with the difference in costs being invested in alternative activities that could help poor countries increase life expectancy, improve the standard of living, and reduce their vulnerability to climate change? Ask poor people in poor countries, and they are likely to answer 'No'. Of course, the same people who would argue that we should stabilize at 450 ppm would likely reply by saying that they would also want more money to be spent improving life expectancy and the standard of living, and in reducing vulnerability to climate change. But the point is that it is not possible to do everything. Money spent doing one thing cannot be spent doing another. Choices have to be made. Any approach that ignores costs ignores this unavoidable reality.[3] Of course, it is precisely for this reason that other chapters in this volume — by Ingham and Ulph, Mendelsohn, Pearce, and Tol — devote so much attention to this issue.

Another problem is with who makes these choices. The refrain of this paper is that, while there is one atmosphere, decisions are made by 200 countries. A goal of capping global concentrations implies a global emissions path. So if some countries fail to participate in an agreement

[3] This same point is made in a letter to the editor of *Science*, in response to an article published in January 2004 by Sir David King, Prime Minister Blair's Chief Scientific Advisor. King's response, published in the same issue (1 October 2004), begins, 'There is no real choice between action on climate change and action on poverty, disease, hunger, and other millennium development goals. These are part of the same sustainable development agenda.' I agree that climate is best looked at as a sustainable development problem. After all, climate change will affect development, and development will shape the future climate. But there is no getting around the fact that choices must be made.

seeking to implement such a path, the others would need to pick up the slack; if they did not the goal would be missed. But this means that non-participants avoid the cost of mitigation without suffering any loss in benefit. It also means that the remaining participants incur yet higher costs without any increase in benefit. These incentives plainly reward non-participation, and so favour collapse of such an agreement. Of course, it might be argued that an agreement needs to be structured in such a way that this will not happen. But how can this be done? Indeed, can this be done? A theme of this paper is that, in moving forward, we need always to look over both shoulders. Over one, we need to look at the climate system. Over the other, we need to look at the international political system.

The stunningly successful ozone regime developed very differently. The Vienna Convention for the Protection of the Ozone Layer does not establish even a qualitative goal. Article 2 instead enjoins parties to 'take appropriate measures . . . to protect human health and the environment against adverse effects resulting or likely to result from human activities which modify or are likely to modify the ozone layer'. And take measures is exactly what the parties to this convention did, first under the Montreal Protocol and later under the adjustments and amendments to this agreement. The final result: virtually every country has done about as much as could be done to protect the ozone layer. Astonishingly, ozone levels are expected to return to their 'natural' (pre-1980) levels by around 2050.

The climate regime was strongly influenced by this earlier diplomacy, but drew the wrong lessons. The 'appropriate measures' taken under the Montreal Protocol were expressed as quantitative emission limits. But in Montreal these limits served as a means, not as an end. As Richard Benedick, the chief US negotiator of this agreement, explains in his insightful account of the negotiations (Benedick, 1998, p. 105),

> By cutting the market in half at a fixed date, the protocol was in fact tipping CFCs towards obsolescence. US negotiators had reasoned that, when substitutes were developed to such an extent, the remaining CFC market could probably not be sustained.

Kyoto established quantitative targets as an end. My view is that we need to turn our attention away from particular, arbitrary targets. We need to focus more on taking appropriate measures. The reason for this is not that the goal established by Kyoto is wrong. The reason is that Kyoto discourages the taking of appropriate measures. The main problem with Kyoto is that it will do nothing, or next to nothing, to mitigate climate change.

3. Kyoto Protocol

Why will Kyoto do nothing, or almost nothing, to mitigate climate change? The reason is not that Kyoto asks that only a small number of countries reduce their emissions by just a little for a short period of time. As noted in the introduction, Kyoto was only meant to be a first step. The reason is that Kyoto is unable to sustain even the little that it sets out to achieve. And if it cannot sustain this effort, it certainly cannot sustain a greater effort. The essential challenge for Kyoto is enforcement—in particular, the need to enforce both participation and compliance.[4]

Consider, first, the compliance problem: this is the problem of how to get parties to the agreement to comply. The agreement negotiated in Kyoto in 1997 did not incorporate a compliance mechanism, though it did require that parties approve 'appropriate and effective procedures and mechanisms' for compliance at the first meeting of the parties. However, according to Article 18 of the agreement, 'any procedures and mechanism . . . entailing binding consequences shall be adopted by means of an amendment to this Protocol'. Under the rules of international law, an amendment is binding only on the countries that ratify it (and on the countries that accede to the original agreement after the amendment enters into law). Since any party to Kyoto could decline to ratify a subsequent compliance amendment, each can avoid being punished for failing to comply. In other words, there is nothing in the agreement that actually makes countries do what they said they would do. As matters now stand, the Kyoto emission limits are more 'political' than 'legal'.

Does this matter? Chayes and Chayes (1995) argue that binding compliance mechanisms are not needed. Indeed, they argue that such mechanisms can be counterproductive. However, the evidence—even limiting our attention to the climate regime—fails to support this view. The industrialized parties to the FCCC pledged to stabilize their emissions at their 1990 levels, and yet very few did so. Moreover, those that did limit their emissions (primarily, Britain and Germany) did so for reasons having little to do with climate policy (Britain was helped by the 'dash for gas', Germany by industrial restructuring following reunification).

Plainly, many countries believed that compliance *would* be a problem. After all, they negotiated a compliance mechanism in subsequent meetings held in Bonn in 2001. Under this agreement, a party that failed

---

[4] See Barrett (1998, 2003a), Schelling (2002), and Victor (2001) for critical assessments of the Kyoto Protocol, including discussions of the enforcement challenge.

to meet its emission ceiling in the first control period (2008–12) would have to make up for the shortfall and reduce its emissions by an additional 30 per cent of this amount in the *next* control period (presumably, 2013–17). The 30 per cent value was meant to reflect 'interest' earned on the shortfall (removing the incentive for countries to 'borrow' emission reductions from the future) plus a penalty (for failing to comply).

Unfortunately, this is a defective mechanism, and not only because it cannot be binding (except by means of an amendment, as noted previously) for the first control period. First, the mechanism relies on self-punishment. That is, the mechanism is silent on the consequences for any country that fails to comply with the compliance procedure. Second, the emission limits for the second control period have yet to be negotiated. A country that worries that it may not be able to comply in the first control period may thus hold out for easy targets in the second control period—so that the punishment, if triggered, would not actually bite. Finally, and perhaps most importantly, a country can always avoid the punishment by not ratifying a follow-on protocol for 2013–17, or even by withdrawing from the Protocol at a later date. This is why participation is important.

Why do countries participate in a treaty? The answer is not obvious, given that an effective treaty must make countries do things that they would not otherwise do—reduce their greenhouse-gas emissions, for example. Countries may be willing to make such a sacrifice because others are making a similar sacrifice or because doing so is simply the right thing to do. They may also be willing to make such a sacrifice because, were they not to do so, others would not do so. It turns out that this last reason is especially important. It is the main reason treaties are necessary in the first place. Cooperation in a treaty is usually sustained by a strategy of reciprocity.

In a climate agreement, reciprocity would require that, were one country not to reduce its emissions, others would not reduce *their* emissions. In a bilateral setting, reciprocity is often very effective. Indeed, this is how the multilateral trading rules are enforced under the World Trade Organization (WTO). Climate-change mitigation, however, is a global public good, and when some countries punish another for failing to mitigate emissions, they harm themselves in the process. In other words, for global public goods, severe punishments are often not credible.

Intuitively, a punishment must 'fit the crime'. A small deviation can be deterred by means of a small punishment. A larger deviation can only be deterred by means of a larger punishment. The largest credible deviation from cooperation for any country would be for the country to emit as much as it would were it not to participate in an agreement. Hence, large punishments are needed to deter non-participation, whereas smaller punishments will normally suffice to deter non-compliance. Since small punishments are more credible, this means that if parties to a treaty can deter non-participation then they should also be able to deter non-compliance. In other words, participation should be the binding constraint on international cooperation, not compliance (Barrett, 2003a).

The Kyoto Protocol provides very weak incentives for participation. As of this writing (early November 2004), Kyoto has been ratified by 125 countries making up 44.2 per cent of the emissions of industrialized countries (Annex I emissions). Russia's ratification will increase both numbers and bring Kyoto into force in February 2005.

Kyoto's entry into force, however, has come at a price. In negotiations held in Bonn and Marrakesh, years after the emission limits were negotiated in Kyoto, country-specific concessions (more generous allowances for sinks) were given to Canada, Japan, and Russia, to facilitate their participation. Other modifications, such as the decision not to impose a quantitative limit on trading, also helped promote participation, by lowering the cost of compliance to countries facing net emission reduction obligations. At the same time, this relaxation in the trading rules will limit the environmental effectiveness of the treaty by releasing more 'hot air'.[5] In other words, Kyoto was renegotiated through the back door, as it were. If Kyoto enters into force, the reason will be that it requires that very little be done. This is not much of a victory for the environment.

Most importantly, Kyoto failed to secure participation by the United States—the world's largest emitter and only superpower. Now, to be sure, the manner in which President George W. Bush rejected Kyoto was grating. But, as mentioned before, it is almost certain that the United States Senate would have rejected Kyoto, had it ever been given the chance, even if a different president were in the White House. Why? One reason is that the emission-reduction obligations for United States are especially stringent. Most countries that have ratified Kyoto do not need to reduce their emissions at all under the agreement. Some must reduce their emissions by modest amounts. The United States was required to reduce its emissions 7 per cent below the 1990 level, and it

[5] 'Hot air' refers to the surplus of emission reductions for the former communist countries of Europe. Russia, for example is required to stabilize its emissions under the Kyoto agreement, and yet its actual emissions in 2000 were about 70 per cent of the 1990 level. Trading with Russia can thus allow countries to comply with the agreement, not by reducing emissions, but by paying Russia to transfer a portion of its surplus.

is widely believed that US emissions under a business-as-usual scenario will be at least 30 per cent higher in 2008–12 than in 1990 (in 2000, US emissions were already 17 per cent higher than in 1990). The USA would need to reduce its emissions very substantially to comply with the agreement, and this would be costly.

The failure by the USA to participate is striking but it is part of a general pattern. The USA failed to participate (at least in part) because the costs of participation were high. Other countries agreed to participate (at least in part) because the costs to them of participating were low (as is true for some EU states), zero (as is true of all non-Annex I states) or even negative (as is true for the states given 'hot air' allowances). The Annex I countries likely to have the hardest time complying (Canada and Japan) agreed to participate only on the condition that their initial reduction obligations be diluted. Russia's ratification will bring Kyoto into force, and yet, ironically, Russia's participation ensures that Kyoto will fail to reduce emissions by much. Indeed, it may not reduce global emissions at all (Buchner *et al.*, 2001).

And what are Russia's reasons for ratifying Kyoto? Russia has certainly dragged its heels. Partly, this was to gain concessions from Europe on other issues, including Russia's entry into the World Trade Organization (WTO). So, what would prevent Russia from threatening to withdraw later, to gain more concessions? And what incentive would Russia need to join any follow-on agreement? If Russia needs even more hot air or other concessions, this will only raise the cost to other countries of participating in the agreement — and so diminish *their* incentive to participate. Romano Prodi, President of the European Commission, said that, in approving Kyoto, President Vladimir Putin of Russia 'sent a strong signal of his commitment and sense of responsibility'. But is that really true?[6]

Even if Kyoto entered into force and succeeded in reducing the emissions of Annex I parties to this agreement, the total effect of the agreement would be diluted by trade leakage. As noted in the introduction, if the Annex I countries limit their emissions, comparative advantage in the emitting industries would shift towards other countries, causing emissions by these countries to rise.

To sum up, the Kyoto Protocol has two possible fates. It may enter into force but not be complied with; or it may enter into force and be complied with but only because it is so diluted that it fails to change

[6] Commenting on an earlier draft of this paper, Dieter Helm suggested to me that Russia's ratification is likely to weaken the climate regime. Russia, he argues, is likely to spend its revenues from permit sales on further oil and gas development, and use its position as a party to Kyoto to block more meaningful measures from being adopted in subsequent protocols.

behaviour substantially. The problem with Kyoto is not just that it will make little difference. To repeat one more time, by design this agreement only requires very modest emission reductions by very few countries over a very short period of time – not enough of a difference to change the course of climate change. The problem with Kyoto is that it does not provide a platform on which deeper and broader cuts in emissions can be sustained.

The only counter argument to this reasoning that I have heard is the rather hopeful assertion that, if some countries take the lead on this issue, others will follow. But why would they follow? Taking the lead does not by itself create incentives for change.

Could a redesign of the agreement do better at sustaining compliance and participation? The obvious suggestion is to use trade restrictions. After all, it was by this means that the Montreal Protocol was enforced. However, Montreal was enforced without the need to restrict trade based on how a product was made – an approach that is technically almost impossible and currently WTO-illegal, but that would be necessary in the case of climate change. As well, to be effective, trade restrictions must be both credible and severe. The history of environmental diplomacy shows how hard it is to meet both of these requirements (Barrett, 2003a). And in the case of a climate treaty, all trade would need to be affected – creating the risk that trade restrictions would strain the multilateral trading system to the breaking point. There are good reasons why trade restrictions were not a part of Kyoto from the beginning.

4. A New Treaty System

The Kyoto model is linear, with one agreement following the last in succession. A better approach, in my view, would be to adopt a number of different, mutually reinforcing protocols – agreements that would need to be adjusted and amended over time.

To make a difference to the climate, a treaty has to create incentives for long-term technical innovation. Kyoto tries to create a short-term 'pull' incentive. In limiting emissions, it seeks to raise the cost of emitting carbon dioxide, creating a market for carbon-saving technologies and thus an incentive for the invention and diffusion of such technologies. This is a good way to design a domestic environmental policy (an example being the acid-rain trading programme in the United States), but not an international agreement. A substantial pull incentive requires robust enforcement – and, as I have already explained, Kyoto fails to provide this. Indeed, since the Kyoto process began, most industrialized countries have actually scaled back their R&D funding, just the opposite of what is needed (Battelle, 2001).

As well, Kyoto provides no incentive for *long-term* technological innovation. Not only is Kyoto silent on post-2012 emission controls, it provides no incentive for investment that can lower the cost of reducing emissions in the future.

In any event, a 'push' programme for R&D is also needed, and yet Kyoto makes no provision for this. Basic research is, in part, a public good. For some problems, we can rely on individual countries to undertake the needed research unilaterally. For climate change, however, no country has a strong enough incentive to invest. Hence, a new R&D protocol is needed. Examples of 'big science' collaboration include nuclear fusion research (especially the International Thermonuclear Experimental Reactor, or ITER), the new Large Hadron Collider being built at CERN; the International Space Station; and the Consultative Group on International Agricultural Research (CGIAR). A climate R&D agreement, however, would have to be more ambitious than any of these.

How might such an agreement be structured? Each country's contribution to the collaborative effort should be contingent on the level of participation. That way, as more countries join, the contributions made by existing members would increase — creating an incentive for more countries to participate. Base-level contributions would need to be negotiated. They could be determined on the basis of ability and willingness to pay. Alternatively, they could be determined with reference to precedent-setting agreements (such as the United Nations scale of assessments). Either way, the agreement would fix the maximum total contribution for each country (this is in contrast to Kyoto, which fixes emission caps but not expenditures; and it differs from 'price caps' by fixing total costs and not marginal costs). The existing regime asks the question: By how much should concentrations be limited in the long term? This agreement asks a different question: How much are countries willing to invest in R&D so as to make it more attractive to reduce emissions in the long term? The R&D agreement thus focuses attention on the need to take appropriate measures.

Just as important as the size of the R&D budget and its financing is the way in which the money should be spent. R&D should be strategic. Technologies that capture and store CO_2, for example, may allow fossil fuels to be burned without adding to atmospheric concentrations. Such an innovation would reduce both leakage and domestic political opposition to emission reductions. It would also enhance the incentives for both participation and compliance in related agreements. However, there may also be limitations and problems with this technology, and that is why research is needed. The essential point is that the innovation undertaken under this protocol has to reinforce the efforts of related agreements.

These related agreements must create pull incentives for innovation and the diffusion of new technologies. Rather than prescribe emission limits that must be enforced, new protocols are needed that establish common standards for technologies that can be developed using the R&D (and so the R&D should also be strategic in focusing on technologies requiring standards). Economists normally reject the setting of technology standards by governments. However, market forces cannot be relied upon to be superior (Gandal, 2002). Markets may fail to set a standard when standardization is welfare improving. Markets can also select a welfare-inferior standard. Committees can help market processes work better in picking standards (Farrell and Saloner, 1988), and governments can also help (Funke and Methe, 2001). The main reason for advocating standards, however, is different. Standards can have a strategic advantage in a world of 200 sovereign countries. This was the lesson of the MARPOL agreement, discussed in the introduction.

There are a number of incentives that can be created to encourage the development and diffusion of new technologies:

(i) *R&D*. Current expenditure on R&D lowers the cost of developing new technologies in the future. Directed R&D would further steer development towards technologies requiring standards, technologies yielding domestic as well as global environmental benefits, and so on.

(ii) *Economies of scale*. With economies of scale in production, as more countries adopt a technology, the cost to others of adopting the same technology would fall. This would make it more attractive for others to adopt it.

(iii) *Economies of learning*. As experience in producing a technology increases, the average cost of production falls. Hence, as more countries adopt a technology, the incentive for others to adopt it in the future would increase.

(iv) *Network externalities*. When part of a network, the returns to every country of adopting a technology increase in the number of other countries that adopt the technology. So, as more countries adopt a network-based technology, the incentive for others to adopt it increase.

(v) *Non-climate-related benefits*. Technologies that reduce local air pollution, and not only greenhouse-gas emissions, increase the local benefit of adoption—and so make it more attractive for countries to adopt the technology.

(vi) *Trade restrictions*. Technology standards impose trade restrictions almost automatically, and these are both legal and easy to enforce.

Importantly, catalytic converters have become a global standard even though not required by any international treaty. The reason is that the adoption of this technology was influenced by all the factors listed above (Barrett, 2003a). But this means that a treaty that *did* require catalytic converters would not need to be enforced. In other words, the problems that plague Kyoto can potentially be avoided by a technology-centred approach.

There are, to be sure, problems with the standards approach. One problem is that standards will work better for some sectors than for others. For automobiles, network externalities are relatively important, leading to a positive feedback in the adoption of new technologies. For other sectors, such as electric power generation, network externalities will be less so. Another disadvantage is that standards are not always the most cost-effective way of reducing emissions. Certain parts of the economy will not be affected by the standards protocols. And standards may 'lock in' a technology, rather than promote continuous innovation and improvement. Of course, this problem can be reduced by the adjustment and amendment process. And even the Kyoto approach could create technologies subject to lock in. Nevertheless, it remains true that the standards approach is very much a second-best proposal. However, the nature of this problem means that first-best solutions cannot be implemented.

The standards protocols, like the cooperative R&D protocol, should be open to every country to sign. It is almost certain that the technologies needed to meet the standards will be more costly than those currently available, and this raises two problems. The first is why industrialized countries should participate in such an agreement. The second is why developing countries should participate.

For the industrialized countries, participation really needs to be based on the belief that something needs to be done to mitigate climate change. As noted in the introduction, there is no getting around this. The difference between this proposal and Kyoto Only is that the latter cannot be enforced while the former would be self-enforcing. Both approaches are alike, however, in that both entail costs. Success of the standards approach also depends on establishing a threshold effect, as the positive incentives outlined above would only materialize if a critical mass of participation were achieved. My guess is that, at a

minimum, the United States, Europe, and Japan would need to participate. Once the 'big' industrialized countries participate, however,
incentives should be created for others to participate. The minimum
participation level for this treaty must thus be chosen strategically; it
must ensure that participation exceeds the 'tipping point' before the
treaty enters into force (Barrett, 2003a).

Tipping would create an incentive even for developing countries to
participate, but these countries should be compensated for agreeing to
adopt the new technologies. A relevant model here is of the Montreal
Protocol Fund, which compensates developing countries for the 'agreed
incremental costs' of complying with the agreement to phase out ozone-
depleting substances. Note the difference between this approach and
the flexible mechanisms (the clean development mechanism, or CDM,
and trading among Annex I countries) under Kyoto. With the CDM,
industrialized countries must demonstrate the effect of CDM transactions on the emissions of developing countries. But the baseline level of
emissions is unknown, and estimating the baseline will make transactions costly. Trading in emission entitlements can lower transactions
costs, but would also result in the transfer of surpluses from one
country to another—possibly without emissions even being reduced.
Funding technology transfer is different. Baselines need not be calculated, and the number of transactions would be fewer. Also, as under
the Montreal Protocol Fund, developing countries would only be
compensated for reducing emissions. And their compensation need not
include surpluses. They could be compensated only for the 'incremental
cost' of adopting a new technology. Cutting out the transfer of
surpluses has an advantage in an international setting. In reducing
surpluses, the cost to the industrialized countries of financing emission
reductions in developing countries is lowered—and so the incentive to
offer the finance is increased. There are also political economy advantages in paying developing countries to adopt a technology likely to
have been developed and produced in the industrialized countries.[7]

The need to change the technology of economic development is
manifest. Poor countries such as China and India are growing very
rapidly, and it is important that the investment underlying this new
growth be climate-friendly. Capital invested now will have a long life.
In the rich countries, by contrast, growth will be more modest, and the
rate of capital turnover lower. Rather than have the poor countries
grow like the rich countries and then make a transition to a new

---

[7] This approach also avoids the political economy disadvantage of Kyoto. What
will be the reaction if European countries seek to comply with Kyoto by paying
Russia for its surplus permits? Money would be transferred without emissions being
cut—all for the purpose of meeting arbitrary allocations of emission entitlements.

technology base, as implied by the Kyoto model, it would be better for these countries to grow using new technologies.

The R&D and standards protocols address climate change in the longer run. But they can and should be complemented by a protocol that seeks to reduce emissions in the short run. Indeed, rather than be seen as an alternative to Kyoto, the R&D and standards protocols should be seen as complementary instruments. The difficulty with Kyoto, as mentioned before, is that its success depends entirely on effective enforcement. An agreement like Kyoto would be more helpful, I believe, if the pretence of international enforcement were dropped. The focus would then shift to the 'appropriate measures' that countries can and should undertake domestically and in the short run. Countries could, as in Kyoto, establish targets and timetables. They could also develop trading arrangements, as are now being developed in Europe. Alternatively, they could pledge to adopt policies and measures (ironically, an approach suggested much earlier in the negotiation process). In contrast to Kyoto, these pledges would be domestically enforced, though cast within a multilateral framework. The process of pledging might create a kind of 'tote board' for action, and so have some minimal effect over and above pure unilateralism (see Levy, 1993).

Finally, it must be acknowledged that climate change is almost sure to happen, no matter what we do now to try to mitigate it. Since the developing countries are relatively the most vulnerable, and since the industrialized countries are largely responsible for the cumulative build-up of atmospheric concentrations, these countries should help developing countries adapt. Adaptation assistance is a necessary ingredient for establishing fairness in the international response. Incorporating 'cooperative adaptation' also creates an incentive for parties to balance adaptation and global mitigation.

Though the approach proposed here is radically different from Kyoto, it would not in any way undermine Kyoto. Nor is it inconsistent with the current policy of the United States or any of the new policies being proposed for the United States. For both reasons, it is a politically feasible proposal—an arrangement towards which the international system can evolve. It is, I believe, our best chance for ensuring that collectively 'appropriate measures' are taken to address this extraordinary challenge.

5. Conclusions

The global climate regime consists of two agreements, the FCCC and the Kyoto Protocol. Participation in the Framework Convention is almost universal, but this agreement only establishes a collective goal for global action; it does not allocate responsibilities to individual countries for meeting the goal. This is the harder challenge—the task left to the Kyoto Protocol.

The goal of the Framework Convention—to stabilize 'greenhouse gas concentrations in the atmosphere at a level that would prevent dangerous anthropogenic interference with the climate system'—is reasonable enough. In practice, however, it will be impossible to identify the 'right' level of atmospheric concentrations with any precision. Rather than try to identify such a level, it would be better to focus attention on the 'appropriate measures' that can and should be adopted to reduce the damages and risks associated with climate change. This choice must also reflect concerns about the costs and risks associated with mitigation.

The Kyoto Protocol will not stabilize concentrations. To do that would require a much more ambitious agreement, one that constrains the emissions of all the major countries by a substantial amount indefinitely. Kyoto was meant to be a first step; its architects believed it could be broadened and deepened over time. But Kyoto will only work if it can be enforced, and it cannot be. It certainly cannot enforce very substantial cuts in emissions—the levels needed if concentrations are to be stabilized.

And yet Kyoto need not be rejected or abandoned. It is only essential that Kyoto not stand in the way of alternative approaches. It was a conceit to think that climate change could be addressed by the Kyoto Only model alone. This top-down approach will simply not work in a horizontal world of sovereign states. Serious mitigation will require a broader approach, one in which a number of mutually supporting protocols are adopted. These must include protocols that create a positive feedback between the short term and the long term (collective R&D into a new generation of energy technologies) and among countries (technology standards agreements, used to diffuse the new technologies).

Mitigation must be undertaken globally. Put a little crudely, any climate agreement that does not constrain the emissions of countries such as the United States and China (and this is precisely how Kyoto was designed) will simply not be effective. The USA is the world's largest emitter, and must be a party to any agreement aiming to reduce global emissions. China's participation is also important, for China is growing rapidly. China wants to develop and is entitled to develop. But concerns about climate change mean that the world as a whole can gain if China shifts to a different development path, using a different energy technology. The world thus needs to make it attractive for China to make such a shift.

Getting countries on a different development path will require new technologies, and this in turn will require investment in R&D. Kyoto provides virtually no incentive for R&D. It aims to reduce emissions by only a little for just 5 years. It is entirely silent on what comes after 2012. No wonder parties to this agreement have actually cut their energy R&D budgets. This situation needs to change.

Finally, the climate is likely to change no matter how successful we are at mitigation, and the greatest victims (in relative terms) are likely to be the developing countries. Provisions must therefore also be made to assist these countries to adapt to climate change. Climate change is not just an environmental challenge. It is a development challenge. It is a development challenge from the perspective of mitigation, which will require a technological revolution, diffused throughout the world. And it is a development challenge from the perspective of adaptation. Just as benefits and costs must be balanced in choosing 'appropriate measures,' so must climate-change mitigation and adaptation be balanced in future development policy.

Part Five: Institutional Design and Energy Policy

14

Credible Carbon Policy

DIETER HELM, CAMERON HEPBURN, AND RICHARD MASH*

1. Introduction

Most developed countries have adopted targets for the reduction of carbon-dioxide (CO_2) emissions. Some of these are aspirational, some are recorded in voluntary international agreements, others have the force of law and are enshrined in national legislation. That CO_2 emissions should be reduced is now largely accepted: how such reductions might be achieved is still a matter of controversy and debate.

The case for using market-based instruments is well known and increasingly accepted by government.[1] The instruments under active consideration are emissions-trading schemes and carbon taxes. The former focuses on quantities—which are the variables that lend themselves to international agreements;[2] the latter on price—lending themselves to revenue raising.[3]

Such instruments are typically effective in the medium to longer term. In the short run, demand for carbon-creating activities, such as electricity generation and transport, tends to be inelastic, and supply tends to be linked to fixed, sunk, and lumpy capital stocks. To reduce carbon emissions requires both adjustments on the demand side and in non-carbon supply technologies.

* New College, Oxford, St Hugh's College, Oxford, and New College, Oxford, respectively.
The authors are grateful for comments from Toke Aidt, Christopher Allsopp, Alan Budd, Edward Calthrop, David Pearce, and Kevin Roberts. Any errors, however, remain their own.

[1] Marshall Task Force (1998), HM Treasury (2002*a*, 2003*a*).
[2] The experience of OPEC, which switched from price to quantities at the end of the 1980s, provides evidence of this. Moreover, oligopoly theory shows that firms should collude on quantities when their goods are substitutes (see Singh and Vives, 1984).
[3] See, for example, Tietenberg (1990) and McKibbin and Wilcoxen (2002).

The credibility of emissions-trading schemes and carbon taxes is an important factor in their success or failure. Reducing emissions is likely to require significant irreversible investment from the private sector. The profitability of such carbon-reducing investments is highly sensitive to carbon policy. Whether firms invest will depend upon whether they believe the government can be taken at its word. Faced with the political demands of elections, will the government renege on promises to tax carbon in the future at pre-specified levels? Or, in the case of emissions trading, will governments and regulators rigorously enforce property rights and keep to promises about the number of permits available in the future?[4]

The private sector has good grounds for scepticism. Credibility from governments is a rare commodity for the very good reasons that politicians have multiple objectives and parties alternate in government. It is not surprising that there is a history of past default. Governments can (and do) 'change the rules' in a way that the private sector cannot.

A credible carbon policy must overcome two hurdles. First, clear rules must be defined for the resolution of trade-offs between conflicting objectives. Second, and more importantly, the government must convince firms that it will not renege on its promises once investment costs are sunk. Yet it is clear that there is an *ex-post* incentive to renege; the government faces a classic 'time-inconsistency' problem. A credible carbon policy is one which solves this time-inconsistency problem and provides firms with a degree of security that promises will be met.

Fortunately, the problems of credibility and uncertainty are generic, rather than specific to carbon policy, and have been particularly well researched in the area of monetary policy. The lessons that have been learned from the setting of monetary targets and interest rates are very helpful in thinking about carbon policy, and this paper carries these insights over into the carbon arena. We propose that the time-inconsistency problem in carbon policy can be solved through delegation to an independent agency. In addition to solving the time-inconsistency problem, delegation has two further benefits. First, it reduces uncertainty and political and regulatory risk, which is typically hard to diversify, thereby reducing the cost of capital. Second, it reduces the possibility that governments, which are driven by the next election and other short-term political economy considerations, will set carbon policy inappropriately.

The paper is structured as follows: the next section (section 2) sets out the credibility problem in carbon policy, the sources of non-

---

[4] Since the social cost of carbon is likely to rise over time, the policy will require appropriate adjustment over time (see Mendelsohn, 2003).

credibility, and the costs of failing to address it explicitly. There then follows a review of the time-inconsistency problem, and the outline of a conceptual framework (section 3). A plausible 'solution' requires an institutional context, and the design of an energy/carbon agency is sketched (section 4). A number of conclusions for the policy design are then drawn (section 5).

2. The Credibility Problem and the Low-carbon Strategy

(a) *Conflicting Objectives*

The British government set out its carbon policy in a White Paper, *Our Energy Future: Creating a Low Carbon Economy*, in February 2003 (DTI, 2003*a*). The central objective is a 60 per cent reduction in CO_2 emissions from the current level by 2050. This overarching target was recommended by the report of the Royal Commission on Environmental Pollution (RCEP, 2000) and augments two pre-existing carbon targets—the Kyoto objective of reducing a bundle of greenhouse gases by 12.5 per cent over the period 2008–12 and the 1997 Labour Manifesto target of a 20 per cent reduction in CO_2 by 2010 from the 1990 level (see UNFCCC, 1997; Labour Party, 1997).

To achieve the 2050 target, the White Paper has proposed three main policy initiatives—for renewables, energy efficiency, and emissions trading. These augment a host of other existing policies such as the Climate Change Levy and associated agreements.[5] Although there was intense lobbying in the build-up to the 2003 White Paper by the renewables and energy-efficiency interests, the government declined to set binding targets for 2020 for the contribution from each of these sources, leaving in place the existing target for renewables to contribute 10 per cent of electricity generation by 2010, and setting only aspirational 20 per cent targets for both renewables and energy efficiency for 2020. On emissions trading, the UK system has had, at best, limited success so far,[6] and future success depends upon the EU-wide scheme proposals, due to come into force in 2005 (see CEC, 2001, 2002).

This plethora of targets and policies presents the private sector with considerable difficulties in investment appraisal of carbon-free projects. It has to calculate the carbon-free benefits which may arise by weighing up its expectations on a host of targets and schemes, and try to predict

---

[5] Other policies include the Energy Efficiency Commitment and the Fuel Poverty Strategy (see Defra, 2001*b*; DTI, 2001).

[6] See, for example, ENDS (2002*a,b*, 2003).

how future governments will react to new information on actual emissions (the feedback rules), the evidence on the science of climate change, and, most importantly, how governments will react to perceived public opinion and voting behaviour.

This calculation is informed by the government's statements of objectives and the scope for *ex-post* revisions to policies. On the objectives, there have been a variety of relevant statements. The overarching objective is set as 'sustainable development', which is broken down into four components: social progress, environmental protection, prudent use of natural resources, and the maintenance of economic growth (DETR, 1999).

These components can obviously conflict, and it is apparent that specific carbon-reduction policies can conflict with social and economic growth objectives. No trade-off rules have been defined and, indeed, the plasticity of the definition of sustainable development is politically very attractive. A wide range of outcomes can be presented as 'successful'.

In the energy sector, the trade-off problems of objectives are explicit. In the PIU (2002) report, the Prime Minister's Foreword states that the objectives are, 'securing cheap, reliable and sustainable sources of energy supply'. This was further refined in the 2003 White Paper as: 'the four pillars of the environment, energy reliability, affordable energy for the poorest, and competitive markets for our businesses, industries and households'.

This ambiguity has been integrated directly into policy. The Renewables Obligation placed upon energy suppliers to purchase 10 per cent of their supplies from renewables by 2010 has a buy-out price, intended to put a cap on price effects.[7] The more general competition-policy priority focuses on the impact of energy policy on economic growth, with the DTI also having an explicit Public Service Agreement (PSA) with the Treasury. The DTI must:

> Ensure that UK ranks in the top three most competitive energy markets in the EU and G7 in each year, whilst on course to maintain energy security, to achieve fuel poverty objectives; and improve the environment and the sustainable use of natural resources. (HM Treasury, 2002*b*)

This replaces an earlier PSA target which explicitly focused on prices and international price comparisons. Finally, the DTI is only one of the departments involved in carbon policy: Defra has its own climate-

---

[7] See DTI (2002). Roberts and Spence (1976) set out the classic argument for hybrid quantity and price regulation.

change remit, especially in respect of energy efficiency (Defra, 2001*b*); and the Treasury sets tax policy.

The problem of conflicting objectives in the energy sector has been institutionalized in the relationship between the DTI and Ofgem, the energy regulatory body. Whereas the DTI set the objectives in the 2003 White Paper, much of the implementation is left to Ofgem, whose primary statutory duty following the 2000 Utilities Act is to protect the interests of customers (rather than achieve the CO_2 target). Ofgem has particular responsibility for setting prices for the monopoly networks, and in doing so must take a view about the required level of capital expenditure. The development of renewables is reliant on network investment to facilitate small-scale embedded generation and its cost allocation. Given that Ofgem does not have a primary duty to promote renewables (or energy efficiency), the government issued it with 'guidance', and this guidance includes having regard to renewables and energy-efficiency policies. Taking account of such guidance is, however, a *secondary* duty and hence does not necessarily result in implementation.[8]

Though the interfaces between the DTI, Defra, and Ofgem may seem a matter of detail, it turns out that such institutionalization of the conflict of objectives has considerable consequences, and we shall argue later that institutional reform is an integral part of addressing the credibility problem.

(b) *Non-credible Policies*

Investors in low-carbon technologies and energy efficiency have plenty of examples of non-credible behaviour by government to draw upon. Particular examples include the so-called *Climate Change Levy* (CCL), which came into force on 1 April 2001, as a result of the Marshall Report (November 1998); the *UK Emissions Trading Scheme* (UKETS), which commenced on 1 April 2002; and the *Guidance* issued to the energy regulatory body, Ofgem, discussed above.

The CCL was designed with an explicit intention to address the domestic and international CO_2 and greenhouse-gas targets. Lord Marshall was tasked by the incoming Labour government with comparing the relative merits of a tax or permits solution. The economic merits of each are well documented,[9] and if the policy was designed to achieve the targets at minimum cost, then *either* a carbon tax with *ex-post*

---

[8] Revised draft guidance (DTI, 2003*d*) was issued after the White Paper, incorporating the White Paper objectives (DTI, 2003*a*).

[9] See, for example, Kolstad (2000, chs 9 and 10) and papers cited therein.

adjustments to attain the target, *or* a carbon permits scheme would have been appropriate.[10]

The *political* merits of taxes and permits are less well documented, and the government decided in the light of the Marshall Report to implement an energy tax (the CCL) *and* to develop an emissions trading scheme. The energy tax was designed to avoid adverse effects on the coal industry (which was being supported in the 1998 White Paper, *Energy Sources*; see Helm, 2003a, pp. 302–3); and the UK emissions trading scheme excluded the electricity generators, again to protect coal. To further placate large industrial customers, exemptions of up to 80 per cent from the CCL were permitted under 'climate change agreements' (see Defra, 2001a). Finally, to avoid imposing an explicit burden on domestic customers, the CCL was, for political reasons, confined to the business sector. (The *economic* incidence of the tax did not, of course, avoid domestic customers, given the inelastic characteristics of short-run energy production.) Thus, the CCL and the UKETS were designed with an eye to the political interests of the coal and electricity industries, large-scale industry, and domestic customers.

To these specific examples, the 2003 White Paper adds a further dimension of non-credibility to investors in non-carbon activities. The White Paper had a political balancing act to achieve, in that it had to combine what seemed like a very demanding target for CO_2 reduction with more immediate-term aims of avoiding price or tax shocks to voters and limiting the public-expenditure implications.

This balancing act was recognized by many of the lobby groups involved in the White Paper's development. The renewables and energy-efficiency lobbies were keen to ensure that the White Paper contained binding targets for 2020, which electricity suppliers would be required to achieve (see EST, 2002; Solar Century, 2003). With legally binding targets imposed upon suppliers, investors in renewables and energy efficiency would be able to write long-term contracts with suppliers to enable the latter to fulfil their obligations. Such a scheme already existed for renewables up to 2010 (subject to a buy-out price — see Helm, 2002). The contracts would then reduce the cost of capital.

To achieve binding targets for 2020, the various lobby groups argued that the costs would not be great — hence assuaging the fears of politicians. The DTI persuaded itself of this convenient proposition, through a modelling exercise called MARKAL. MARKAL is a bottom-up approach to calculating least-cost solutions to meeting electricity

---

[10] Pizer (2002) suggests that, given uncertainty, a carbon tax is more efficient than carbon permits, although a hybrid policy is better still. His results, however, rest upon the assumption of a relatively flat marginal damage curve.

demand. The DTI's utilization of this model (DTI, 2003*b*) required certain assumptions about the costs of renewables and energy efficiency. It ignored the additional costs to the network and the back-up power supplies to wind generation (with a load factor of typically around 35 per cent) in the case of renewables, and also ignored the 'barriers' and transactions costs to energy-efficiency measures. It assumed that the costs of these technologies would be low, and falling over time. The model then integrated these assumptions to produce the prediction that the cost of achieving the 2050 target of 60 per cent reduction in CO_2 would be negligible – around 0.1 per cent of GDP per annum and between 0.5 and 2 per cent of GDP over the whole period (see DTI, 2003*a*, p. 9, para. 1.12).

The main implication was that since the costs of the new technologies were low, the level of support needed would also be low – and a very low priority in public-expenditure terms. If, however, as many private-sector investors might believe, the costs turned out to be high, investors might not be able to rely on future political commitment to support the overarching target, precisely because the government accepted the target on the condition that voters would not have much of a burden to bear.

There is, then, a substantial credibility problem in UK carbon policy. There are multiple objectives, and highly optimistic assumptions about costs. The unwillingness to face up to higher prices means that promises about future carbon policy are unlikely to be believed. Investors with sunk costs are aware that they risk *ex-post* opportunism by governments who lower future prices. This is likely to result in a failure to invest in low-carbon technologies and a higher cost of capital, raising the overall cost of achieving the CO_2 objectives. It is a problem which is unlikely to be confined to the UK.

3. Modelling the Credibility Problem

Credibility is a generic problem in many regulatory contexts. The area in the economics literature where it has probably been most extensively explored is monetary policy. Given a monetary or inflation target, how can policy-makers condition market expectations to believe that the monetary authority will not renege *ex post*, given that there may be short-term incentives to reduce interest rates? How do governments convince the public that there will be no U-turn? If market expectations are so conditioned, people will act as if wage- and price-setting targets are credible, thereby helping to fulfil the targets at lower interest rates.

If, however, the policies lack credibility, expectations built into wage- and price-setting processes may mean that the targets will be missed.[11]

This credibility problem is essentially a problem of 'time inconsistency'. Its key characteristic is a sequence of decision making whereby private-sector agents make an irreversible decision before the policy-maker acts. Private-sector agents look ahead to what the policy-maker will do, but their action is already fixed when the policy-maker makes the choice. Time inconsistency refers to the fact that the policy-maker with conflicting objectives has different incentives before and after the decision taken by private-sector agents. The result is that a policy-maker with 'discretion' will act differently to a policy-maker who can commit to the action in advance. Many situations where time inconsistency occurs are effectively repeated games involving uncertainty, but neither characteristic is essential.

Several 'solutions' to the time-inconsistency problem are found in different domains. Odysseus had himself bound to the mast *ex ante* to protect himself from the *ex-post* lure of the Sirens. In monetary policy, delegation to an independent central bank is the conventional solution. Patent law provides a further example. *Ex-post* prices might be lower, and welfare higher, if innovations could be copied and produced by competing firms. *Ex ante*, however, an incentive for innovation is needed, which is provided by the limited monopoly rights granted by patents.[12]

In Helm *et al.* (2003) we set out a formal model of time inconsistency in environmental policy. Time inconsistency arises from the sequencing of decisions. First, firms invest (irreversibly), having chosen from a spectrum of technologies with different emissions per unit of energy (such as coal-fired power stations or wind farms). Second, the policy-maker chooses the carbon tax that will apply during the productive life of that capacity.

The model is built with four main simplifying elements: (i) a constant elasticity demand curve for energy; (ii) a 'technology frontier', describing the trade-off between cleaner technology and lower production costs; (iii) constant emissions per unit of energy for a given technology; and (iv) Cournot competition with free entry, such that prices reflect average costs. The model also assumes that there is full information and, for the time being, the policy-maker acts on the correct preferences of society as a whole.

---

[11] The classic early references are Kydland and Prescott (1977) and Barro and Gordon (1983). For a survey see Blackburn and Christensen (1989). For textbook treatments see Walsh (2003) or Romer (1996).

[12] For a recent study on optimal patent life see, for example, Denicolò (1996).

The social welfare function has three components;[13] (i) consumer surplus from energy, which falls with the price-raising effects of carbon taxes; (ii) tax revenue received by government; and (iii) damage from emissions (E), represented by E^g with $g > 1$. The model generates three possible cases, depending upon different parameter values. In the first case, the tax rate under discretion is lower than under commitment; there is an *ex-post* incentive to reduce the tax once firms have sunk their investment costs. In the second, the *ex-post* incentive is to increase the tax rate. In the third, the tax rates before and after private-sector investment are the same.

There are at least three considerations that determine which case applies. The first concerns the elasticity of the tax base. Because taxation is distortionary in practice, the marginal cost of public funds is generally slightly above one.[14] One unit of revenue from an environmental tax is therefore valued at more than one unit of consumer surplus because it allows other distortionary taxes to be reduced.[15] If the elasticity of the environmental tax base is lower than other taxes, environmental taxation is an even more attractive source of revenue.[16] Marsiliani and Renström (2000) exploit this feature in their model of time-inconsistent taxation — there, the policy-maker has an incentive to *increase* the tax *ex post* relative to its optimal level because irreversible investment reduces the tax-base elasticity. Their model, then, is one in which carbon tax rates under discretion are higher than under commitment.

Second, if the environmental tax is regressive, as is typically assumed, and the government cares about distribution, then taxation entails additional welfare costs.[17] In this case, the tax rate under discretion will be lower than under commitment. Indeed, Abrego and Perroni (2002) propose a model of time-inconsistent taxation where distributional effects imply that the policy-maker has an *ex-post* incentive to *reduce* the tax.

[13] Profits are not included in the welfare function; they are zero in a model of Cournot competition with free entry.

[14] See Pigou (1947), Harberger (1964), and Browning (1976, 1987). For a review of the literature on the marginal cost of public funds, see Ballard and Fullerton (1992).

[15] This corresponds to the 'weak form' of the double-dividend hypothesis. For a definition of the 'weak' and 'strong' forms of the hypothesis, see Goulder (1995).

[16] This essentially amounts to the 'strong form' of the double-dividend hypothesis, in which it would make sense to replace other taxes with the environmental tax, even in the absence of environmental improvement. Many economists reject the strong form: see, for example, Bovenberg and Goulder (1996), Parry (1995), and Bovenberg and van der Ploeg (1994).

[17] Note, however, that work by Poterba (1989, 1991) and Metcalf (1999), among others, suggests that environmental taxes are not as regressive as typically thought.

Third, if the tax impairs the competitiveness of an export sector earning rents from imperfect competition, then there is an incentive to reduce the tax after investment has taken place, in order to support the competitiveness of the export sector. It is questionable, however, whether this effect would be of particular importance in the case of a British energy tax.

While the net effect of these three considerations is unclear, our model suggests that time inconsistency is likely to occur. Moreover, when distributional and competitiveness considerations outweigh the possible benefits of an *ex-post* reduction in tax-base elasticity, the government faces an *ex-post* incentive to reduce the tax rate. This generates the credibility problem for the British energy sector and the associated welfare costs.

A solution to the time-inconsistency problem is needed. There are four available options which could solve this problem in carbon policy, namely to:

- reduce the number of objectives;
- increase the number of instruments (including hypothecation);
- delegate to an international body within a contractual framework; or
- delegate to a national body within a contractual framework.

In an 'ideal' world, the solution would be some combination of the first two options. The government could focus on one core objective – CO_2 – and relinquish the other aspects of the sustainable-development objective and/or it could use other instruments to address the social and economic growth components. The former is, however, practically impossible: it is highly implausible to imagine that a government could be democratically elected with a welfare function excluding social and economic-performance objectives. The second is more plausible: other policy instruments, such as social security policies, competition policies, and infrastructure and other market-failure interventions can be and are utilized alongside environmental-policy instruments. But yet again, there is no evidence that governments would be prepared to make the necessary adjustments to the other instruments to accommodate policies such as the carbon tax or emissions trading. The reasons are complex, political, and organizational. Objectives and policy instruments are delegated to departments of government, and the determination of each is subject to the bureaucratic and political processes. Each department has its own interests and priorities and budget considerations, and the history of departmental conflicts (in particular in this context between the DTI, Defra, and the Treasury) is well documented. Given that these reasons rule out the ideal solution, delegation to another authority may be a better option for resolving the time-inconsistency problem.

The case for delegation is strengthened by the fact that, in addition to solving the time-inconsistency problem, it provides two further benefits. First, it provides transparency of policy actions and greater predictability, especially if it prevents government changing the objectives at will. Delegation would therefore reduce uncertainty and lower the political- and regulatory-risk components of the cost of capital. As this political risk is typically hard to diversify, reducing it would increase willingness to invest in low-carbon technologies. Second, delegation prevents governments, who are driven by the next election and other short-term political economy considerations, from setting carbon policy opportunistically.

These three arguments for delegation—the solution of the time-inconsistency problem, the reduction of uncertainty and political risk, and the avoidance of political bias—make a compelling case. Several general forms of delegation suggest themselves:

(i) The agency could be asked to maximize the social welfare function, provided that it is able to develop and retain a good reputation. Concern for its reputation would provide it with an incentive to implement the commitment outcome, despite short-term gains from reneging. The underlying argument is that because the agency is a long-lived institution not subject to short-term political pressures, it will be better able to develop and retain a reputation than governments.

(ii) If reputation alone will not ensure the optimal outcome, the agency could be given a single objective (the optimal level of emissions) to achieve, twinned with an appropriate policy instrument (the carbon tax rate, the number of emissions permits, or a hybrid instrument).

(iii) The agency could be constituted so that it maximizes a welfare function with a higher weight placed on emissions, such that its discretionary outcome corresponds to the social optimum.

Each of (i)–(iii) can achieve the social optimum. Each requires the agency to act with a high degree of transparency. Of the three, (ii) is the most readily monitored, but perhaps also the least flexible. Furthermore, we have experience of (ii) from the monetary policy example.

In the monetary policy case, the institutional response has been delegation to the Bank of England and its Monetary Policy Committee

(MPC). There are three potential reasons for delegation. First, as in (i) above, reputation may be stronger in a long-lived institution such as an independent central bank, rather than government. Second, as in (ii) above, an independent central bank may be given a single objective (inflation) as a sole or at least higher-priority target than other components of the social welfare function, such as output. This corresponds to inflation targeting, widely practised by many central banks including the Bank of England, where the inflation target is paramount though the regime can allow for some concern for output as long as there is no threat to the medium- to long-run inflation target.[18] Third, as in (iii) above, delegation to a central banker with a different welfare function, or different parameters within it, can solve the problem. The classic example is Rogoff's (1985) conservative central banker.

Even without time-inconsistency problems in monetary policy, there are still potential benefits from an independent central bank that have analogies in the carbon-policy context. First, there may be political bias in governmental discretion, either because governments target output above the natural rate for political reasons (see Bean, 1998) or through political business-cycle effects (see Drazen, 2000). In these cases an independent central bank may be beneficial simply because it can pursue social objectives largely free from political interference. Second, there are benefits from transparency of objectives and policy processes as a way of anchoring expectations.[19]

Hence monetary-policy delegation and carbon-policy delegation have a number of factors in common. In both cases there is a possible but not inevitable time-inconsistency problem. An independent agency may overcome the problem through enhanced reputation; a single objective that corresponds to the social outcome; or by maximizing a modified welfare function. With or without time-inconsistency problems, there may be large benefits from the avoidance of political bias and the increased transparency and stability of the regime through the anchoring of expectations.

For completeness, two differences should also be highlighted. First, most current monetary policy models have the property that there is no long-run trade-off between inflation and output or unemployment. The task of the central bank is to balance the short- to medium-run trade-off between these variables. In contrast, in environmental policy, the trade-off between energy prices and emissions is long term. Second, the expectations involved in price- or wage-setting generally have a time

[18] For more detail on the Bank of England's remit and practices, see Budd (1998) and Balls and O'Donnell (2002).

[19] Balls and O'Donnell (2002), Geraats (2002), and Goodfriend (2003).

horizon of perhaps 1–2 years, whereas expectations of carbon-tax levels influence investment in generating capacity that may last for several decades. A further caveat is that while Bank of England independence is widely seen as a success, some have argued that it has yet to be put fully to the test in very difficult economic or political circumstances. Nevertheless, the monetary policy analogy nicely highlights the options for enhancing carbon policy credibility.

4. An Energy Agency

How might such a combination of objectives, contracts, and delegation work in the carbon context? One proposal is to set up an energy agency analogous to the MPC of the Bank of England.[20] The government might commit to a CO_2 target—such as the 60 per cent target in the 2003 White Paper, discussed above. The energy agency could then be set a number of duties forming its 'contract' with government. The options are:

(i)   a duty to meet the target by *any* means it deems suitable;

(ii) a duty to meet the target by setting a carbon-tax or emissions-trading limit; or

(iii) a duty to monitor the performance of the government in meeting the target, with published reports to the relevant secretaries of state indicating whether it is on target and with recommendations for appropriate action.

Clearly, (i) would be hard for any democratic government to concede. The nearest to the MPC version is (ii), but, given the reluctance of the Treasury to concede tax-setting powers, the most likely version of (ii) is delegation to a European body responsible for setting quantities for emissions trading, such that the price of permits (the analogy to the tax) is set by the less politically exposed process of the permits market. In the British context, (iii) is most plausible. It would increase transparency and hence credibility, but not be wholly convincing.

The opposition to the delegation of powers to an agency has a variety of forms, largely related to the political process. The creation of a new agency means a reduction in employment within existing government departments—in this case at the DTI and, to a lesser extent,

[20] This was first proposed in Helm (1992) and more fully articulated in Helm (2003b).

Defra. This is further complicated where it might involve the closure or slimming down of existing agencies or government offices outside the department, in this case Ofgem, the Energy Saving Trust (EST), and the Carbon Trust. On the reasonable assumption that the objectives of bureaucracy are to increase size and budget, there is an obvious conflict.

These instrumental and bureaucratic objections are compounded by the loss of control that delegation may entail. The time-inconsistency problem arises in part because governments have conflicting objectives, and electoral success depends upon the creation of coalitions of interest. It is often not an optimal *political* strategy to sharpen the trade-off and to expose the losers to a policy. A 60 per cent CO_2 reduction target for carbon will raise prices and reduce the competitiveness of the coal and large energy-intensive industries. Politically, it may be better to avoid the explicit recognition of these costs, and in consequence to pay the price of the lack of credibility. Unsurprisingly, then, the 2003 White Paper (DTI, 2003a) concludes that there is no need to change the machinery of government and then proceeds to make a series of changes *within* government, using the guidance to Ofgem (discussed above) as the mechanism to try to resolve the conflicts of objectives.

The institutional solution is complicated by considerations other than price and emissions specific to the energy sector — notably security of supply. Security of supply arises as a special problem in energy markets for several reasons. Electricity cannot be stored (except in limited forms, such as pump storage). Hence, there needs to be an instantaneous matching of supply and demand and, since demand is uncertain, a capacity margin is needed by way of insurance. But energy is also a complementary good — failure of supply has large-scale effects on the economy as a whole — as recently demonstrated by interruptions in supply in London, California, Tokyo, Norway, and Italy — and hence there is an additional reason for carrying excess capacity on the electricity system. [21]

Although it might be thought that these two energy-related problems could be addressed within separate agencies, there are good economic reasons for combining them. Given that the monitoring of CO_2 target performance and the setting of appropriate levels of carbon taxes or permits requires specialist knowledge of the energy sector, there are obvious institutional economies of scale in combining in one agency both the CO_2 and security-of-supply objectives. The conventional economic logic that there should be as many instruments as targets (see Tinbergen, 1952) does not carry over to institutions.

---

[21] There are parallel reasons why the government is unlikely credibly to commit to pay for sufficient excess capacity, to induce investors to build marginal plant (see Helm, 2003b).

Indeed, if economies of scale in expertise are sufficiently great, there is a case for one agency for each *sector*, and, indeed, the tendency towards sectoral agencies has been marked since the 1997 election, with the creation of the Strategic Rail Authority for railways and Ofcom for telecommunications and broadcasting. In addition, non-fossil-fuel technologies raise their own security-of-supply issues — notably the intermittency of wind power and the consequences of decentralization of plant within electricity networks.

The combination of security-of-supply and CO_2 objectives in one agency could, however, reduce the credibility of the CO_2 target, if there is a trade-off between these two objectives. But, even if there is a trade-off, it is relatively easily avoidable by using two instruments. Indeed, some argue that there is no trade-off and that the two are compatible, because energy efficiency and renewables *add* to security of supply, by increasing diversity (see EST, 2002; Hain, 2002). In the British case, there are likely to be conflicts, too: base-load coal-fired generation capacity is, in the short term, critical to supply continuity, but it is also the dirtiest form of generation.

The solution to this problem — of combining CO_2 and security-of-supply objectives — for the design of an energy agency is to have more than one instrument to address the two objectives: a carbon tax or permits scheme to deal with CO_2, and a capacity payment or similar mechanism to induce sufficient marginal investment. Thus, the energy agency could be designed with both objectives in mind at one of the following levels:

(i) a duty to meet both CO_2 and security-of-supply targets by any means it deems suitable;

(ii) a duty to set a carbon tax (or emissions trading limit) and a capacity payment (or similar mechanism) consistent with meeting both targets;

(iii) a duty to monitor the performance of the government in meeting both targets, with published reports to the DTI on security of supply, and to Defra on the CO_2 targets, together with recommendations for appropriate action.

Even if the agency has two instruments (a carbon tax/permits scheme and a capacity payment) with which to achieve two objectives, it might be argued that the political constraints on the delegation of the powers under (ii) and (iii) will result in reduced credibility. However, the costs of slightly reduced credibility are likely to be more than offset by gains from the combined expertise, with the consequence that the two instruments are likely to be more accurately set.

5. Conclusion

Governments have been quick to sign up to targets for CO_2 reductions, especially where short-term costs are perceived to be small, and other changes in the economy — such as the contraction of the coal industry in Britain — mean that the targets will be met anyway. As the concern over climate change grows, and the easy early gains in emission reductions are exhausted, new tougher policies will be required. In Britain, the adoption of the 60 per cent target for 2050 provides a demanding policy objective. Its achievement depends upon the transition from a carbon-intensive to a low-carbon economy, with the associated consequences for investment in energy efficiency, renewables, and low-carbon technologies.

These investments are risky, not just in the normal commercial sense, but because their profitability at the margin is often largely or entirely dependent on government policy *over time*. The credibility of government CO_2 policy is therefore at a premium, and we have argued that there can be acute time-inconsistency problems in environmental policy. Governments have multiple objectives, limited instruments, and a history of non-credible policies. The 2003 White Paper provides several examples of non-credibility, notably the way in which the objective is supported by very weak empirical evidence and analysis, the aspirational nature of the 2020 targets for renewables and energy-efficiency measures, and the lack of coherence between the institutions responsible for delivering the policy objectives.

We have shown how the time-inconsistency problem arises formally, and set out a number of options to solve it. The most promising is the creation of an energy agency, and in practice it is likely that this will combine security-of-supply objectives with CO_2 ones. We have recognized the potential inconsistency faced by such an agency if it has both carbon and security-of-supply objectives, but fortunately there are two instruments available (a carbon tax/permits scheme and a capacity payment) and the gains from the combined expertise are likely to outweigh the weakening of credibility.

The idea that the solution to a credible carbon policy lies in institutional design is not one that appeals immediately to environmentalists, energy policy-makers, or, indeed, the DTI. We noted that, in the 2003 White Paper, institutional reform along the lines suggested here was explicitly rejected. However, that rejection comes at a price: the consequence of the loss of credibility is that investment in energy efficiency and renewables will be lower than it might otherwise have been. The conclusion that the private sector may draw is that the government is not serious about its CO_2 targets and that investment in low-carbon technology is unlikely to be profitable. Political and bureaucratic objections to the transfer of functions from government departments will probably only be overcome when the costs of failure in CO_2 policy become so great, and so explicit, that the case for institutional change is overwhelming.

15

Climate Change and Energy Policy

DIETER HELM*

1. Introduction

Given the link between climate change and greenhouse-gas emissions, and given that carbon emissions are associated with the burning of fossil fuels to produce electricity and for transport, it follows that reductions of emissions depend upon changes to the energy sector and to the energy policy which provides the framework for the sector's development. Addressing climate change is, then, to a considerable extent about redesigning energy policy.

Much of the debate about reducing carbon and other emissions focuses on specific technologies. It is argued by some that climate change can be addressed through a combination of energy efficiency and renewables. The policy problem is to set targets for the contributions of each, and then mandate their take-up. Thus, the European Commission has a target to increase renewables' share of the European Union (EU)'s total energy supply to 12 per cent by 2010 (CEC, 1997), and the UK has a target to supply 10 per cent of electricity in 2010 from renewable sources (DTI, 1999) and an 'aspirational' target of 20 per cent by 2020 (DTI, 2003a). This approach has merits, but it takes little account of the market contexts within which these measures are to be set, or of the other objectives of energy policy — notably security of supply, reduction of fuel poverty, and international competitiveness.

Energy markets display multiple market failures and a successful policy to reduce carbon emissions will have to take these other concerns into account. The challenge is not simply to reduce carbon emissions, but to do so in a way which does not prejudice the other objectives. An

* New College, Oxford.

This chapter draws upon the more detailed analysis of British energy policy in Helm (2004a), to which the reader is referred.

energy policy designed to meet multiple objectives is a much more complex problem, which is likely to require multiple instruments.

The relative importance of both the different objectives and the market failures varies over time. Because investments are typically long-lived, fixed, and sunk, the sector is very much a prisoner of the past. Most of the power stations in the developed countries were either planned in the 1970s or with the demand assumptions of the 1970s in mind. Now the excess-supply years of the 1980s and 1990s are formative in the shape of energy investment decisions. Policy responds to context, too: the liberalizations of the 1980s and 1990s were the product of a period of excess supply and low fossil-fuel prices.

To design an energy policy that reduces carbon-dioxide (CO_2) emissions, the first step is, therefore, to recognize the historical context and the implications of liberalization for energy markets in the 1990s. It is this context—largely independent of climate-change considerations—on to which the carbon constraints need to be grafted. This context is described in section 2.

The next step is to clarify the conditions upon which investment in low-carbon technologies depends, if it is to be successful. There are two elements: the price of carbon, and the risk. The price of carbon sets up the trade-offs and incentives; the risk turns on the ability to contract, and the credibility of government policy. This is the subject matter of section 3.

Section 4 turns to the consistency between the carbon and other objectives. Security-of-supply considerations need to be reflected in an additional 'price' for the relative contributions of different investments to system security, which may not be advantageous to some renewable technologies. This calculation is further complicated by the fact that the security-of-supply value of such investments depends in part on the design of the infrastructure transmission systems. With regard to fuel poverty, social security plays a role as a separate instrument, and competitiveness requires appropriate R&D and other policy instruments.

Section 5 turns to institutions and the evolution of energy policy over time. Climate change cannot be solved by simply redesigning energy policy and then leaving it to deliver the results. Energy policy is not a discrete activity—it is a continuous tuning of policy instruments to the shocks and surprises that crop up from time to time. If, for example, calm returned to the Middle East, and oil prices fell back to $10 a barrel, the fall in the implicit price of carbon would have serious consequences for carbon-emissions abatement policies. Conversely, if oil prices rise to $100 a barrel, rather different responses would be called for. Policy, too, needs to be credible over the lifetime of investments, and institutions are the mechanisms through which credibility is maintained. Section 6 concludes.

2. The Policy Context: Higher Prices, Aging Assets, and Liberalized Markets

For most of the twentieth century, the primary objective of energy policy was to create and sustain sufficient supply capacity to keep up with demand. The great industrial expansion was facilitated by the development of the coal, oil, and gas industries, and the generation of electricity from these sources. Only towards the end of the twentieth century did these priorities shift. The Organization of Petroleum Exporting Countries (OPEC) oil shocks of the 1970s marked a turning point: from the early 1980s until the turn of the century, demand and supply conditions eased, leading to a collapse in oil (and gas) prices, and excess capacity in electricity systems in most developed countries. In developed economies, too, the traditional link between economic growth and energy demand broke down, and the focus of energy policy shifted towards privatization, liberalization, and competition, as mechanisms to sweat the assets rather than support investment. With the exception of France, most countries also gave up on their nuclear power programmes.

This asset-sweating approach contained the seeds of its own destruction, as assets, from refineries to power stations, aged. By 1999, the oil infrastructure in much of the USA and Europe was in poor shape, and new exploration and production activities had been heavily curtailed. The asset-sweating, which boosted short-term profits by reducing both operating and capital costs, tightened the demand/supply balance. Furthermore, the breaking of the link between economic growth and energy demand encouraged policy-makers to think that energy no longer mattered as it had in the 1970s. Economic growth continued, spurred by the great stock-market speculative bubble of the 1990s, but its form was different: in the 1980s the shift from manufacturing to services in developed economies reduced the energy intensity in GDP. In some countries, the arrival of natural gas as a fuel for electricity generation and the contraction of the coal industries helped further. But the energy-intensive industries did not disappear in this process. They merely moved to developing countries, of which China is the most notable example. Global energy demand carried on upwards, and the combination of aging, sweated assets in the developed countries, and demand for energy in developing countries, produced an oil shock in 1999/2000 that has subsequently been exacerbated by the Iraq War and instability in the Middle East.

This is the context into which the climate-change constraints have to be injected. It is one in which security of supply is again a major issue. But it is also one in which the price of oil has increased significantly, and hence, in effect, a large carbon tax has been imposed. It is a context in which many of the assets — in electricity and oil — are due to be replaced. Thus, the task for policy-makers is to ensure that the existing assets are replaced primarily by low-carbon technologies, and to design policy instruments in the context of volatile fossil-fuel prices.

These parameters are further contextualized by the design of energy markets, itself a product of policy. In the 1980s and 1990s, energy markets were gradually liberalized. Liberalization broke the link between customers and investors. In the traditional energy markets — notably in electricity — investors recovered the sunk costs of new power stations from captured customers. In effect, cost pass-through in vertically integrated structures, sanctioned by regulators, created a safe investment environment, with the result that the cost of capital was kept low. Liberalization changed this radically: customers could now choose among suppliers, and hence when *ex ante* investments, which passed appropriate investment criteria at the time, turned out to be out-of-the-market as fundamentals changed, and customers no longer had to honour the sunk costs, they could simply switch.

This is, in fact, what happened on a large scale in the 1990s to the investments made in the 1970s: first, to governments, as owners through the write-offs of much of the coal and nuclear industries, and then to private companies, with the price collapses of gas and then wholesale electricity in the late 1990s, notably in Britain and Germany.

In theory, the sunk-cost issue should have been solved by financial markets. Instead of customers carrying the risks through cost pass-through and monopoly, spot and futures markets would develop that transferred risks to financial markets. A full set of futures markets would enable investors in new power stations to hedge the forward price risk, and hence, in effect, write long-term fixed-price contracts. In practice, however, it did not happen, because the conditions for the development of deep, liquid and transparent futures markets were not (and could not be) met. Indeed, they had not even developed in oil markets.

The result is a serious problem in investment incentives, which has only partially been solved by the agglomeration of market power. Energy markets have seen very significant merger and acquisitions activity, to the extent that not only have the oil companies witnessed larger-scale mergers, but Europe's electricity market has also come to be dominated by three companies: E.ON, RWE, and EDF. This concentration might address the sunk-cost investment-incentive problem in one of two ways: very large companies have portfolios of investments in different technologies and over different time periods, and can therefore benefit from portfolio effects to reduce project-specific risk; and companies with market power can impose investment costs on customers through vertically integrated structures.

The development of significant market power in vertically integrated structures has several implications for investment and climate-change policies. The recovery of such costs through *de facto* monopoly implies that the price of energy will be higher than under competitive conditions. It also implies that physical hedging will limit the development of financial trading and distort the incentives to entrants. Concentrated oligopolies tend to converge in technological choices, and, in an attempt to protect large-scale investment, the effect is to squeeze out innovative and smaller-scale technologies.

From a climate-change perspective, the current policy context is one in which the *general* incentives to invest have been undermined by the removal of monopoly franchises of customers, without an alternative being fully developed. Given the historical context of the need for a major asset-replacement programme (regardless of climate change), the scale and technology choice is now largely in the hands of a small number of very large European electricity and gas companies. Unlike in oil markets, electricity cannot easily be stored, and security of supply requires an element of policy intervention. Solving the CO_2 problem, therefore, requires the design of an energy policy in the context of significant market power, but without appropriate *general* investment incentives, at a point when assets in any event need replacing, and when security of supply is again a policy priority.

3. Investment in Low-carbon Technologies — Price and Risk

There are many technologies for producing electricity, including oil, gas, coal, nuclear, solar, and wind. For much of the post-Second-World-War period, the choice of technology was a matter of planning. Now it is left largely to private companies. Under planning, policy considerations were internalized and decisions were based on a variety of factors, including the project costs, balance-of-payments considerations, security of supply, and the political influence of the trade unions. The balance of these factors was rarely transparent. After privatization, only the project-specific costs and risks faced by companies and the expected prices mattered, some of which are affected by taxes, subsidies, and other external policy constraints. The fuel of choice for power generation, where it is readily available in the North Sea, has been gas.

Except in very special circumstances, renewable technologies, such as wind and tidal, and nuclear power, are unattractive to the private sector at current market prices. The costs are much greater than the gas (and even coal) alternatives. In the wind case, there are the added problems of remoteness from the core centres of demand and the intermittency of generation; in the case of nuclear, there are the issues of waste and liabilities, in addition to the costs of building new plant. On present trends, left to the markets with their current distortions, carbon technologies will replace the aging assets described in the previous section.

Adding in a price for carbon would change the relative economic attractiveness of renewables and nuclear technologies. It would not, in itself, guarantee that non-carbon sources would be the investment of choice. The question is whether the price of carbon is set high enough to offset the relative economic cost disadvantages.

There are two ways of arriving at this carbon price. The first is the conventional one: decide how much carbon can be 'safely' allowed in the atmosphere, set concentration targets, and then set the price of carbon so as to achieve that target. This is the basis of the Intergovernmental Panel on Climate Change (IPCC) work, and the Kyoto Protocol is designed as a first (very limited) step towards it. With the 'safe' quantity exogenously fixed, the price of carbon then goes to whatever level is necessary to ensure that there is a sufficient switch to non-carbon sources, net of the price effect on demand.

Note, however, that the price of carbon here is the final price, net of the economic rent in the oil price. If the marginal cost of producing oil is, say, $2–3 a barrel, to which the environmental cost is added, the economic rent extracted by OPEC already accommodates some of the social cost adjustment. OPEC already sets a carbon tax. So, prior to the 1999 oil shock, when the price of oil was $10 a barrel, the additional carbon price mark-up required would have been much higher than when the price reached $50 a barrel in 2004. The carbon price should, therefore, be set so as to accommodate and adjust to the OPEC monopoly rents.

The second approach is the economists' one: assess the costs and benefits of carbon emissions, and arrive at the marginal price of carbon—called the 'social cost of carbon'. The cost and benefits are assessed using consumer preferences, and the outcome should take account of the costs of abatement and adaptation. There have been numerous attempts to estimate the social cost of carbon, notably by

Pearce, Mendelsohn, and Tol (see other chapters in this volume). Almost all of these give lower values than would be yielded by the targets approach above—i.e. they do not justify the IPCC target. The reason is that the overall targets have not been subject to cost–benefit analysis—or, put another way, people do not appear to place as high a weight as the targets would suggest on the costs of climate change as opposed to the forgone current consumption.

Neither of these approaches is without its problems. The science is uncertain, not only in the nature of climate change, but also in arriving at specific target concentrations. The choice of around 500–50 parts per million (ppm) as the IPCC target (and that of the Royal Commission on Environmental Pollution report (RCEP, 2000)) is a pragmatic one—if only because there is no practical expectation that a limit of 400 ppm— or a return to the pre-industrial 250–70 ppm—could be achieved. The economics, too, is perhaps even more uncertain, and consumers' revealed preferences depend upon the current economic and social context, and their information and understanding of climate change and its consequences. Technological change is notoriously hard to factor into these sorts of assessments, and the social cost of carbon is a marginal concept, in a context that many environmentalists and scientists see as possibly non-marginal.

In principle, the price of carbon could be added to the costs of the various fossil fuels in proportion to their carbon intensities. The resulting full cost could then be reflected either in the market price paid by consumers, or in planning decisions by policy-makers, as, for example, in the decision to reserve a share of the market for wind, or to build a nuclear power station.

There are a number of good reasons for preferring the first approach; however, as we shall see, because of the contracting problem, a purely price-based approach could not provide a complete solution. Setting the 'correct' price of carbon would create a level playing field for carbon, but only if all the other factors were level, too.

Private investors in power stations are also concerned with risk— specifically, the sunk, fixed, and long-term nature of the capital costs referred to in the previous section. This risk has two dimensions: how quickly the project will yield positive revenues, then break even and recover the capital costs; and whether they can insure against future price fluctuations (whether caused by demand fluctuations, the level of other investors' activities, or new technologies). Consider, for example, a nuclear power station. The upfront costs in design, licensing, and planning are typically significant—and sunk. The construction may take 5 years.[1] By that time, others may have built new gas stations, even to

---

[1] In the case of Dungeness B, it took 22 years, see Helm (2004a, ch. 2).

the extent that supply exceeds demand and prices fall. Given that the station may operate for 30–40 years, by 2050, there may be all sorts of new technologies that are also non-carbon, cutting away at nuclear's carbon premium.

The consequence of these investment characteristics is that such technologies will typically require long-term contracts, which give some guarantee that the sunk costs are recovered. Traditionally, the solution to this problem in electricity has been vertical integration and monopoly. In Britain, the coal industry had contracts which passed the costs of the mines and mining infrastructure through to the electricity generators, which in turn passed the coal industry's and their own costs of generation through to regional electricity boards, which then passed all of these upstream costs, plus their own costs of distribution and supply, on to final captured customers. In gas, the North Sea natural gas reserves were developed by the oil companies that signed long-term contracts with British Gas, which, again, had a monopoly over final supplies. Residual risks were absorbed by the government, through public ownership.[2]

This arrangement worked well, in that the great post-Second-World-War boom was backed up with enough electricity capacity. The rule of thumb was that, as GDP grew at about 3 per cent p.a., electricity demand grew at 7 per cent p.a. However, the combination of privatization and eventual liberalization changed this. Initially, for the first 8 years after privatization (1990–8), the retail monopoly remained, and the newly privatized firms exploited the opportunity to pass through costs with a 'dash for gas'. New investment in combined-cycle gas turbines (CCGTs) added to excess supply such that, when full liberalization came in 1998, prices collapsed. The introduction of the new wholesale market system (called the new electricity trading arrangements, or NETA) made matters worse since the combination of customer switching and the price volatility under NETA meant that the risks to new power station investments were magnified. Wholesale prices fell by about 40 per cent in the years immediately after liberalization and the introduction of NETA, only to increase again sharply in 2003 and 2004. This sort of volatility was unprecedented.

In theory, in the new liberalized market system, buyers and sellers of electricity would try to smooth out fluctuations by signing longer-term, fixed-price contracts. As discussed in section 2, the theory was that, with the emergence of a spot price, a futures market would develop, and this would then enable future prices to be hedged, with the risk transferring from customers, under the old monopoly model,

---

[2] See, again, Helm (2004a, ch. 2).

to financial markets. The practice was rather different: the conditions required for futures markets (such as standardization of contract form, liquidity, and transparency) would only be met if the market was competitive, in the sense of many buyers and sellers all using the market. Under NETA, the compulsory element for using the market was replaced with a voluntary approach. Generators were allowed to consolidate, and to integrate vertically. The result was a small number of companies, dominating the sector, able to hedge physically, with balanced generation and supply businesses. The futures market was therefore stymied from the outset, and its primary role is now to help the generators balance their positions.

NETA has the further problem that it produces a single price—in the sense that it does not separate out the value of capacity available to the system from the cost of the energy supplied. When the system is in excess supply, this does not matter much. However, when the market tightens, as it has done since 2003, the return to peaking investment relies upon prices being allowed to go to whatever level is necessary to match supply and demand. In this market, investors are expected to build peaking plant 'on spec', assuming that from time to time they will be able to hit the jackpot. This could work, but only if it were reasonable to assume that prices would in fact be allowed to spike to the required level. Given the political significance of electricity prices, such an assumption would be rash.

These general problems with investment in privatized and liberalized markets have a particularly adverse impact on renewables and nuclear technologies, albeit in very different ways. Some forms of renewables, such as wind, have well-known and predictable project-risk characteristics. There is now considerable experience with wind farms. The cost of a turbine is predictable. It can be built and erected quickly, and hence it can begin to earn revenues to recoup capital costs to make it relatively insensitive to short-term changes in the cost of capital, and over a time horizon in which other types of investment will not be able greatly to upset the supply/demand balance. Hence, price is relatively easy to predict over the period of recouping of the capital costs—a characteristic which wind generation shares with a CCGT.

The difficulties that confront wind farms include the intermittency of its supply, the distribution networks to which it connects, planning and other environmental constraints, and, crucially, its full cost level. Intermittency is a cost to both customers and the electricity system as a whole. Wind requires back-up capacity (typically fossil-fuel based). Beyond a certain threshold of scale, it requires networks designed for distributive power rather than large-scale base-load power stations, and it requires that the (sunk) costs of the planning process are overcome. The intermittency reduces the value (and base price) of its output, network design raises entry costs, and planning processes entail sunk costs (analogous to bidding costs in conventional markets).

If, however, these were all the problems with wind power, minor adjustments to energy policy would probably suffice. But they are not: even correcting for the planning and distribution network issues, the core problem that remains is that the costs of wind-generated electricity do not match market prices for such intermittent supplies. The problems for wind are cost related.

These higher costs could be recovered by a price of carbon. However, it is far from clear that the carbon price necessary to induce non-carbon or reduced-carbon sources would favour wind: its cost premium may be in excess of the price of carbon necessary to meet the carbon target.

This economic uncompetitiveness has necessitated a compulsory contractual agreement, the Renewables Obligation, whereby suppliers are compelled to purchase a rising proportion of their electricity from non-carbon sources (renewables), largely, in practice, from wind. Investors then have the security of knowing that this obligation will ensure that the higher costs are rewarded. The mechanism is, however, hedged by three considerations: there is a buy-out price which enables suppliers to cap the total costs (although the revenues from the buy-out are then recycled to renewables); governments can change the definition of renewables over time; and the price of the Renewables Obligation Certificates (ROCs), which suppliers must buy to show that they have met their obligations, will be affected by the *total* supplied in the market, so that, as the share of renewables tends to the target, the price of the ROCs tends to zero.

Nuclear technology has very different economic characteristics to wind. Nuclear power stations not only require planning permission, but also licences for safety regulations. The latter can be very drawn-out and may require major country-specific modifications to generic reactor designs. The stations themselves take a considerable time to build, with high up-front capital costs. Their running costs, once built, tend to be low, and because of the costs of turning on and off, the marginal cost tends towards zero. Their revenue, therefore, depends on the price of electricity being set by other (higher marginal cost) generators, so that the gap between their own (zero) marginal costs and the system marginal cost (the marginal cost of the last station needed to balance supply and demand on the system) provides a contribution towards capital (sunk) costs. The economics of nuclear power, therefore, depends critically on everyone else on the system, and typically the marginal price-setting coal or gas stations.

Nuclear power stations create waste (as does coal), and nuclear power stations need to be decommissioned (as do coal mines, gas platforms, and depleted reservoirs). In the nuclear case, the spent fuel is either reprocessed or stored, and decommissioning can be 40 years or more into the future.

Finally, nuclear power stations carry very low probabilities of high-consequence accidents, of which Chernobyl is the most spectacular example. However, the coal industry kills people more regularly, and can lead to large-scale health problems, and offshore platforms can explode, too—as in the Piper Alpha disaster. The economic difference in the cases relates to the availability of insurance and its costs—although in all three cases, where limited liability companies fail, the state will—and often does—have to absorb the residual risk and associated costs.

The difference between the nuclear and wind cases is that, for nuclear, it is less a problem of price once a carbon cost has been factored in, and more one of the structure of the costs, their timing, and the treatment of longer-term waste and decommissioning costs. Nuclear power stations need long-term contracts to cover price risk, so that investors can have confidence that the sunk costs will be recovered. The licensing issue is a regulatory risk over which investors have little control, while the insurance risks are such that probably only the state can absorb them.

Under NETA, nuclear power has seen wide fluctuations in price without any ability to change its costs, with the result that British Energy has seen most of its equity risk transferred to government. New nuclear capacity is being built in Finland and in France. A form of long-term contract is a core feature of the energy policy framework in Finland, through contracts with large industrial users, and in France directly through policy, backed up by EDF's near monopoly.

While wind and nuclear are the two well-known non-carbon sources of supply, there is a host of other potential contributors. These range from technologies such as tidal and wave, which are largely in the development phases, to hydrogen, which is very much still in the research phase. And in R&D, there are well-known additional market failures. Fundamental *research* is a public good, and, for this reason, has typically been funded by government through universities and re-search institutions. *Development* typically involves the private sector, as does the further stage of demonstration plants. Privatization, liberali-zation, and competition have reduced the private sector's contribution at all three levels. Nationalized industries acted in part as research institutions, as well as developers and demonstrators. Privatization raised the cost of capital, while liberalization and competition increased the risks associated with such classic sunk-cost activities. None of these market failures has been adequately addressed in energy policy since these changes in ownership and markets were implemented, with the result that technologies further from deployment have made little headway in comparison to wind and nuclear.

Reducing carbon emissions does not, however, need to be limited to non-carbon sources. There are also major gains to be had from reducing the level of emissions from carbon technologies, notably by improving the performance and emissions of coal-fired plant, and through carbon sequestration. Almost all of these technologies offer a way of making significant practical inroads into overall emissions.

On the demand side, many environmentalists put considerable weight on energy efficiency and even the reduction in energy demand. These opportunities are largely dependent on associated investments — in insulation, more efficient boilers, and intelligent metering. As with the supply-side technologies, liberalization has undermined the contracting bases over which to recover the investment costs. On the demand side, this is complicated by the problems householders face in information about returns, access to capital markets to finance investments, and the landlord/tenant relationship. Some form of longer-term contract to overcome the switching problem is required here too, although, as with wind (but not nuclear or newer technologies), the time horizons are relatively short.

These considerations of the demand and supply sides suggest that there are two generic problems for an energy policy that takes account of climate change. These are the need to reflect the costs of carbon in the price of energy, and the need to reform the energy markets which has resulted from liberalization to facilitate longer-term contracts, and hence reduce risk.

By solving the generic problems, the market will then provide the context within which the new investments will take place. It will not, however, guarantee that wind or nuclear, or any other 'preferred' technology, is built. It will not be a planned outcome; rather, the market will have been harnessed to deliver a more benign outcome for the climate.

4. Multiple Objectives

Although governments will put greater emphasis on particular aspects of energy policy in different historical context, energy policy has multiple objectives to match the sector's multiple market failures. These are security of supply, reduction of fuel poverty, competitiveness, and the environment. In the 1980s and 1990s, the focus was largely on competitiveness, in the sense of driving down prices, and this objective coincided to a considerable degree with the desire to reduce fuel poverty. Excess supply meant that security of supply was not a problem, and the gradual closure of the coal industry and the associated dash-for-gas meant that environmental performance was generally improving—indeed, domestic CO_2 targets and the Kyoto greenhouse-gas targets could be adopted without the need for much proactive policy intervention.

As discussed in section 2, this happy coincidence of events gradually unwound in the late 1990s, and by this decade the plant margin fell at one point to 16 per cent in the winter of 2002/3, power cuts were experienced in London and Birmingham in 2003, while CO_2 emissions have not fallen significantly since 1997. The oil price shock in 1999/2000 coincided with the government's commitment to end fuel poverty, and subsequent price rises, combined with the decline of North Sea oil and gas, have added a price and balance-of-payments concern to the traditional physical concerns about security of supply. The happy coincidence has given way to a much less fortunate context.

Designing an energy policy to meet all these concerns *and* climate change is clearly much more difficult than the challenge facing government in the 1980s and 1990s. At least as many instruments are needed to meet the number of objectives, and it is immediately apparent that liberalization and competition policy are insufficient. Indeed, liberalization has exacerbated the investment problem in the context of NETA, and competition policy has singularly failed to prevent a substantial concentration of the sector. Neither, however, is likely to be reversed.

Security of supply arises as an objective in large measure because electricity cannot be stored. It is therefore necessary for supply to exceed mean expected demand by a margin sufficient to absorb 'reasonable' variances. Consumers not only buy energy when the switch is pushed, but also buy the 'insurance' that the energy will be available on demand, and that requires sufficient capacity (and networks). As a corollary, there are two components to price—the cost of the energy itself, and the cost of capacity: an energy and a capacity charge. As set out in section 3, the capacity will be invested in if the sunk-cost risks are contracted for, and hence a capacity payment is in effect a form of long-term contract that reflects these sunk costs (and only the sunk costs). These are fixed, whereas fuel costs are variable (and hence do not need this sort of contract protection).

Thus, we have the link between security of supply and climate change: climate change requires the existing carbon-based assets to be replaced by non-carbon capacity; such investment typically requires long-term contracts; and capacity payments provide a mechanism for assigning this risk to customers. But the link is, of course, not complete. Security of supply requires a capacity beyond the level that individual companies may want to supply — since it is a *system* property — and hence some sort of obligation on suppliers or on the system operator is required, with cost pass-through. Particular CO_2-benign technologies affect security of supply in different ways. Wind cannot be relied upon at peak demand points, and nuclear is base-load, not peak capacity. Both may be helped by a carbon price or a non-CO_2 obligation. But wind will carry a security-of-supply cost, as a penalty for variable availability and the consequent requirement for back-up capacity, whereas nuclear will not. Newer technologies will also carry the penalty that reliability may be lower for proto-types and initial designs.

A properly designed capacity payment system could 'solve' the investment aspects of security of supply. It would not, however, deal with physical supply interruption (for example to gas pipelines) or exposure to market price shocks. CO_2-benign technologies tend to be domestically based, and largely independent of fossil-fuel prices. Hence, renewables, nuclear power, and, indeed, energy efficiency all increase physical security of supply, and may dampen the impact of oil (and gas) price shocks.

Thus, attempting to design an energy policy to address climate change can be partly, but not completely, in sympathy with security of supply and the trade-offs can be partly internalized through the combined effects of a carbon price and capacity payments. The trade-off with fuel poverty is much harder: it is at the core of the climate-change problem that the price of carbon-based energy is too low, insofar as it does not incorporate the costs of climate change. Since energy is a merit good, raising energy prices disproportionately harms the poor.

The traditional economists' response is to separate out the two objectives by assigning different instruments: increase the price to meet the climate-change problem; and increase social security to address fuel poverty. In practice, policy is rarely that well calibrated, and second-best solutions need to be found. One possibility is income-related pricing, on the grounds that the elasticity is lowest for the poorest. But here the evidence is weak, and the policy in any event hard to implement. With full competition, such price discrimination is hard to achieve, since it implies that some customers will have to be charged more to compensate for the subsidies to the poor. Distribution network charges can achieve this objective (since distribution is a monopoly service), but supply charges cannot.

An alternative approach is to address the energy consumption of the poor directly, through energy-efficiency measures. Thus, grants for insulation, subsidized boiler replacement programmes, and incentives for landlords to make investments on behalf of tenants all have the merit of contributing to both the climate-change objectives and the targets to reduce fuel poverty. Indeed, much of energy-efficiency policy has been in large measure a dimension of social policy.

In political terms, perhaps the hardest trade-off is between competitiveness and climate-change objectives. Large energy-intensive industries tend to lobby hard against environmental measures which raise their costs, on the grounds that, in internationally traded markets, the result will be a competitive disadvantage relative to other countries without similar environmental costs. Thus, the chemical industry argued against the Climate Change Levy,[3] and electricity generators with significant coal plant argued against the UK's initial National Allocation Plan for the EU.

The counter-argument put forward by some environmentalists is that, by investing in new non-carbon technologies, a competitive advantage is gained over carbon-based rivals, and hence policies that bear down on CO_2 emissions contribute to economic growth, and these new industries will displace older carbon-intensive ones. There will, it is argued, be a substitution from one sector to another. Such arguments are encapsulated in economic models, such as MARKAL, on which the Department of Trade and Industry (DTI) relied in its Energy White Paper (DTI, 2003a). By *assuming* low and falling costs for non-carbon technologies, the effects on economic growth appear to be minimized, and hence the competitiveness argument is claimed to be neutralized.

These calculations are far from convincing. MARKAL-type models are only as good as their assumptions and there are clearly transitional costs. It is, in effect, a least-cost planning tool, and it is a partial, not general, equilibrium model. Unlike conventional macroeconomic models, it is ill suited to draw general conclusions about economy-wide costs.

Perhaps a better way to think about the problem of competitiveness and overall economic effects is to focus on what is — and what is not — measured by GDP. It neglects the depletion of natural resources (since it is all about *current* income, consumption, and investment), and it fails to account for the costs of environmental damage. A better measure is green net national product (NNP) — that is, environmentally adjusted and incorporating asset adjustments. The trade-off in objectives arises because competitiveness is measuring the relative position of resource-

[3] The Climate Change Levy was the outcome of a debate about the relative merits of taxes and tradable permits. The Marshall Report in 1998 was the focus of this lobbying (Marshall Task Force, 1998).

consuming, environmentally damaging practices. But these cannot be sustained, and hence, in effect, conventional competitiveness objectives are the rejection of climate-change objectives. Countries such as the USA gain a relative economic advantage by free-riding on others' CO_2-reducing policies, but only by refusing to take the climate-change objective seriously. Put another way, GDP overstates economic value by neglecting two core, fundamental sources of value: the environment and natural resources.

In summary, climate change can only be addressed by an energy policy that recognizes that there are other—multiple—objectives. The policy-design problem is to consider how policy interventions might address the trade-offs, and where there is a strong conflict (such as carbon pricing and fuel poverty) to consider remedial actions, using additional instruments. Fortunately, the problems of investment and investment incentives are common to both security-of-supply and climate-change policy, particularly at this historical point where assets are, in any event, largely old and in need of replacement. In the fuel poverty case, energy-efficiency measures can mitigate some of the price effects and at the same time contribute to the climate-change objectives. Even for competitiveness, there are *some* industry gains from investing in new non-carbon technologies, although, in the absence of global agreement, the free-rider problem will remain a serious obstacle.

5. Institutions

The discussion so far has suggested that energy policy is context-dependent and, with several objectives, likely to be complex. In the 1980s and 1990s, it was comparatively easy: privatization, competition, and liberalization turned out to reduce costs, improve the environment, and address fuel poverty without any need for additional intervention. Little or no investment was needed, and closing the coal industry helped on the environment front, too. With this limited agenda, the institutional structure was set up to deliver it. Independent regulators were established (and subsequently merged to form Ofgem, the Office of Gas and Electricity Markets), with general public-interest objectives. In practice, these focused heavily on promoting competition, and using RPI– X incentive regulation to force down costs and prices. The former helped to push wholesale prices down towards short-run marginal costs (which, in excess supply, were below average costs and the entry price); the latter sweated the network assets.[4]

[4] In due course, the incoming Labour government made the general duties even more general, to incorporate an overarching consumer objective. See Helm (2004b).

As the new policy agenda began to emerge—climate change, fuel poverty, and security of supply—government tried to graft these rather different objectives on to a framework designed for a very different context. 'Guidance' was given to regulators, but it was only a secondary duty to take this into account. A new committee (the Joint Energy Security of Supply Working Group) had to be created between the DTI and Ofgem to deal with security of supply. Network investment to support renewables (largely wind) lagged in the face of a less than enthusiastic response from the regulator. Reform of NETA, capacity payments and other reforms were strongly resisted. Ofgem behaved precisely as would be expected by institutional theory: it pursued its interests, honed by its (and its predecessors') history.

As climate change moves centre stage in energy policy, its rather semi-detached institutional setting in Defra (the Department for Environment Food and Rural Affairs) will continue to limit its influence, in comparison with Ofgem and its sponsoring ministry, the DTI. New bodies, such as the Energy Saving Trust and the Carbon Trust have been set up as satellites, outside the Ofgem context. Yet regulation is at the heart of energy policy, and climate change cannot be exogenous to it. Energy policy cannot be implemented effectively without an appropriate institutional context, and if the objectives change substantially, it will need a new institutional framework. The shift from the 1980s and 1990s agenda is, indeed, substantive, as described in section 2 above. It is implausible that an institution such as Ofgem can switch its priorities accordingly. Indeed, Ofgem's attempt to finesse the shift in objectives is only met by the implausible claims that security of supply can be left to the market, and that climate change will be met by economic instruments set outside the regulatory framework. The former is spurious, without a clear definition of the constraints within which the market operates (which is a policy and regulation question); the latter is clearly wrong, in that the setting of economic instruments is part and parcel of the regulatory context.

Thus, if climate change is to be addressed through energy policy, it will need significant institutional reform to deliver the desired results and to calibrate the trade-offs as the external energy markets change. Though it is beyond the scope of this paper to describe the detailed institutional changes required, a number of principles can be identified. First, there needs to be an alignment of objectives between policy and the institution charged with delivering that policy. In particular, the core energy institution will need to have primary climate-change and security-of-supply objectives. Second, the institutions need to have credibility so that firms and consumers can rely on the policy instruments. Investors in new technologies rely on the obligations, tradable permits, and tax regimes put in place.[5] Third, the time horizon of the institution needs to marry up with that of the problem. Thus, when investment was not a priority, it mattered little that regulatory bodies had 5-year time horizons for price caps, and even less for wholesale markets. In an investment-oriented world, time horizons are longer, and hence departmental institutions, tied to general elections, are likely to be less effective than arm's-length agencies.[6] Finally, institutions need expertise appropriate to their priorities. Climate change and security of supply require expertise on these problems and, with it, the ability to model rather different problems and scenarios to those focused on the competition and asset-sweating agenda of the 1990s.

6. An Energy Policy Driven by Climate Change

In retrospect, 2000 is likely to appear alongside 1979 as a turning point in the history of energy policy. The last oil shock of the 1970s gave way to a very different world of low fossil-fuel prices and excess supply: the oil shock which began in 2000 coincided with the depletion of the North Sea reserves, a much greater emphasis on climate change and security of supply, and the need to begin to replace old assets.

In the 'new' post-2000 world, energy policy is altogether more complex, with new priorities and more difficult trade-offs between multiple objectives. The priority of investment necessitates that long-term contracts and capacity payments underpin the lacunae left by liberalization, and the absence of a way of assigning the risk of the sunk costs of new investment. The price of energy needs to be adapted to incorporate carbon values. Networks need to be coordinated to support new technologies and to ensure greater supply security.

These policy instruments need to be set simultaneously, and this requires expertise and the flexibility to adjust instruments as circumstances change. None of the existing energy institutions is designed with these purposes in mind, and hence an energy policy designed to address climate change needs new institutions to deliver it.

---

[5] See Helm, Hepburn, and Mash in this volume.
[6] It is notable that since the election of a Labour government in 1997, there have been six energy ministers.

Bibliography

Abraham, S. (2004), 'The Bush Administration's Approach to Climate Change', *Science*, **205**, 616–17.

Abrego, L., and Perroni, C. (2002), 'Investment Subsidies and Time-consistent Environmental Policy', *Oxford Economic Papers*, **54**, 617–35.

Adelaja, A., Menzo, J., *et al.* (1998), 'Market Power, Industrial Organization and Tradeable Quotas', *Review of Industrial Organization*, **13**(5), 589–601.

Aldy, J. E., Orszag, P. R., and Stiglitz, J. E. (2001), 'Climate Change: An Agenda for Global Collective Action', paper prepared for the conference on The Timing of Climate Change Policies, Pew Center on Global Climate Change, Washington, DC, October.

— Barrett, S., and Stavins, R. N. (2003), 'ThirteenPlusOne: A Comparison of Global Climate Policy Architectures', Working Paper, John F. Kennedy School of Government (CBG), Harvard University.

Altamirano-Cabrera, J.-C., and Finus, M. (2004), 'Permit Trading and Stability of Climate Agreements', forthcoming as Working Paper No. 367, University of Hagen.

Anderson, L. G. (1991), 'A Note on Market Power in ITQ Fisheries', *Journal of Environmental Economics and Management*, **21**(2), 291–6.

— (1995), 'Privatizing Open Access Fisheries: Individual Transferable Quotas', in D. W. Bromley (ed.), *The Handbook of Environmental Economics*, Oxford, Blackwell, 453–74.

Annala, J. H. (1996), 'New Zealand's ITQ System: Have the First Eight Years Been a Success or a Failure?', *Reviews in Fish Biology and Fisheries*, **6**, 43–62.

Arnason, R. (2003), 'Minimum Information Management in Fisheries', *Canadian Journal of Economics*, **23**(3), 630–53.

Arrow, K. (1962), 'The Economic Implications of Learning by Doing', *Review of Economic Studies*, **99**, 155–73.

— (1969), 'The Organisation of Economic Activity: Issues Pertinent to the Choice of Market versus Non-market Allocation', *The Analysis and Evaluation of Public Expenditure: The PPB System: Vol. 1*, US Joint Economic Committee, 91st Congress, 1st Session, Washington, DC, US Government Printing Office, 59–73.

Arrow, K., and Fisher, A. (1974), 'Environmental Preservation, Uncertainty and Irreversibility', *Quarterly Journal of Economics*, **88**, 312–19.

— Cline, W., Maler, K., Munasinghe, M., Squittieri, R., and Stiglitz, J. (1996), 'Intertemporal Equity, Discounting and Economic Efficiency', in J. Bruce, H. Lee, and E. Haites (eds), *Climate Change 1995: Economic and Social Dimensions of Climate Change*, Cambridge, Cambridge University Press, 125–44.

Arthur, W. B. (1989), 'Competing Technologies, Increasing Returns and Lock-in by Historical Events', *The Economic Journal*, **99**, 116–31.

Atkinson, A. B., and Stiglitz, J. E. (1980), *Lectures on Public Economics*, New York, McGraw-Hill.

Atkinson, G. (2000), 'Measuring Corporate Sustainability', *Journal of Environmental Planning and Management*, **43**(2), 235–52.

— Dubourg, R., Hamilton, K., Munasinghe, M., Pearce, D. W., and Young, C. (1997), *Measuring Sustainable Development: Macroeconomics and the Environment*, Cheltenham, Edward Elgar.

Azar, C. (1999), 'Weight Factors in Cost–Benefit Analysis of Climate Change', *Environmental and Resource Economics*, **13**, 249–68.

— Lindgren, K. (2003), 'Catastrophic Events and Stochastic Cost–Benefit Analysis of Climate Change', *Climatic Change*, **56**, 245–55.

— Sterner, T. (1996), 'Discounting and Distributional Considerations in the Context of Global Warming', *Ecological Economics*, **19**, 169–84.

Ballard, C. L., and Fullerton, D. (1992), 'Distortionary Taxes and the Provision of Public Goods', *Journal of Economic Perspectives*, **6**(3), 117–31.

— Shoven, J. B., and Whalley, J. (1985), 'General Equilibrium Computations of the Marginal Welfare Costs of Taxes in the United States', *American Economic Review*, **75**, 128–38.

Balls, E., and O'Donnell, G. (eds) (2002), *Reforming Britain's Economic and Financial Policy: Towards Greater Economic Stability*, Basingstoke, Palgrave.

Barker, T. (1998), 'The Effects on Competitiveness of Coordinated versus Unilateral Fiscal Policies Reducing GHG Emissions in the EU: An Assessment of a 10% Reduction by 2010 Using the E3ME Model', *Energy Policy*, **26**(14), 1083–98.

Barrett, S. (1992*a*), 'Alternative Instruments for Negotiating a Global Warming Convention', in OECD (ed.), *Convention on Climate Change: Economic Aspects of Negotiations*, Paris, Organization for Economic Cooperation and Development, ch. 1, 11–48.

— (1992*b*), 'International Environmental Agreements as Games', in R. Pethig (ed.), *Conflicts and Cooperation in Managing Environmental Resources. Microeconomic Studies*, Berlin, Springer, ch. 1, 11–35.

Barrett, S. (1994a), 'Self-enforcing International Environmental Agreements', *Oxford Economic Papers*, **46**, 804–78.

— (1994b), 'The Biodiversity Supergame', *Environmental and Resource Economics*, **4**, 111–22.

— (1998), 'Political Economy of the Kyoto Protocol', *Oxford Review of Economic Policy*, **14**(4), 20–39.

— (2001), 'Towards a Better Climate Treaty', *World Economics*, **3**(2), 35–45.

— (2002), 'Consensus Treaties', *Journal of Institutional and Theoretical Economics*, **158**, 529–47.

— (2003a), *Environment and Statecraft: The Strategy of Environmental Treaty Making*, Oxford, Oxford University Press.

— (2003b), 'Towards a Better Climate Treaty', *World Economics*, **3**(2), 35–45.

Barro, R., and Gordon, D. (1983), 'A Positive Theory of Monetary Policy in a Natural-rate Model', *Journal of Political Economy*, **91**, 589–610.

Bateman, I. J., and Willis, K. G. (eds) (1999), *Valuing Environmental Preferences: Theory and Practice of the Contingent Valuation Method in the US, EU, and Developing Countries*, Oxford, Oxford University Press.

Bates, J. (1995), *Fuel Cycle Atmospheric Emissions and Global Warming Impacts from UK Electricity Generation*, Energy Technology Support Unit, Harwell, London, HMSO.

Battelle (2001), *Global Energy Technology Strategy: Addressing Climate Change*, Washington, DC, Batelle.

Baumol, W. J. and Oates, W. E. (1971), 'The Use of Standards and Prices for Protection of the Environment', *Swedish Journal of Economics*, **73**, 42–54.

Bean, C. (1998), 'The New UK Monetary Arrangement: A View From the Literature', *The Economic Journal*, **108**, 1795–809.

Becker, G. S. (1968), 'Crime and Punishment: An Economic Approach', *Journal of Political Economy*, **76**(2), 169–217.

Begg, K., Gaast, W. V. D., Host, D. V. D., Jackson, T., Jepma, C., Smith, A., and Sorrell, S. (2002), *Guidance for UK Emissions Trading Projects: Phase 1 Report – Advice to Policymakers*, a report to the Department Of Trade And Industry, Guildford, University of Surrey.

Benedick, R. E. (1998), *Ozone Diplomacy: New Directions in Safeguarding the Planet*, enlarged edn, Cambridge, MA, Harvard University Press.

— (2001), 'Striking a New Deal on Climate Change', *Issues in Science and Technology Online*, **Fall**, 71–6.

Bennett, L. L., Ragland, S. E., and Yolles, P. (1998), 'Facilitating International Agreements Through an Interconnected Game Approach: The Case of River Basins', in R. E. Just and S. Netanyahu (eds), *Conflict and Cooperation on Trans-Boundary Water Resources*, Boston, MA, Kluwer Academic Publishers, 61–85.

Berland, H., Clark, D. J., and Pederson, P. A. (2001), 'Rent Seeking and the Regulation of a Natural Resource', *Marine Resource Economics*, **16**, 219–33.

Berman, E., and Bui, L. T. M. (2001), 'Environmental Regulation and Labor Demand: Evidence from the South Coast Air Basin', *Journal of Public Economics*, **79**(2), 265–95.

Bernal, P., and Aliaga, B. (1999), 'ITQs in Chilean Fisheries', in A. Hatcher and K. Robinson (eds), *The Definition and Allocation of Use Rights in European Fisheries. Proceedings of the Second Concerted Action Workshop on Economics and the Common Fisheries Policy, Brest, France, 5–7 May*, Portsmouth, UK, Centre for the Economics and Management of Aquatic Resources.

Betz, R., Schleich, J., and Eichhammer, W. (2004), 'Designing National Allocation Plans for EU-Emissions Trading — A First Analysis of the Outcomes', *Energy and Environment*, **15**(3), 375–425.

Black, N. D. (1997), 'Balancing the Advantages of Individual Transferable Quotas Against Their Redistributive Effects: The Case of Alliance Against IFQs v. Brown', *Georgetown International Law Review*, **9**(3), 727–46.

Blackburn, K., and Christensen, M. (1989), 'Monetary Policy and Policy Credibility', *Journal of Economic Literature*, **27**, 1–45.

Blundell, R., and MaCurdy, T. (1991), 'Labor Supply: A Review of Alternative Approaches', in O. Ashenfelter and D. Card (eds), *Handbook of Labor Economics*, New York, Elsevier.

Boardman, B., Palmer, J., Arvidson, A., Buerger, V., Green, J., Lane, K., Lipp, J., Nordstrom, M., Ritter, H., Timpe, C., and Urge-Vorsatz, D. (2003), *Consumer Choice and Carbon Consciousness: Electricity Disclosure in Europe*, Oxford, Environmental Change Institute.

Boemare, C., and Quirion, P. (2002), 'Implementing Greenhouse Gas Trading in Europe: Lessons from Economic Theory and International Experiences', Fondazione Eni Enrico Mattei, Working Paper 35.2003.

Boer, G., Flato, G., and Ramsden, D. (2000), 'A Transient Climate Change Simulation with Greenhouse Gas and Aerosol Forcing: Projected Climate for the 21st Century', *Climate Dynamics*, **16**, 427–50.

Bohi, D. R., and Burtraw, D. (1992), 'Utility Investment Behavior and the Emission Trading Market', *Resources and Energy*, **14**, 129–53.

Bohm, P. (1993), 'Incomplete International Cooperation to Reduce CO_2 Emissions: Alternative Policies', *Journal of Environmental Economics and Management*, **24**, 258–71.

Böhringer, C. (2002), 'Climate Politics from Kyoto to Bonn: From Little to Nothing?', *The Energy Journal*, **23**(2), 51–71.

— Helm, C. (2001), 'On the Fair Division of Greenhouse Gas Abatement Cost', ZEW Discussion Paper No. 01-67, Mannheim.

— Löschel, A. (2002), 'Risk in Project-based Emission Trading', ZEW Discussion Paper No. 02-68, Mannheim.

— Vogt, C. (2003), 'Economic and Environmental Impacts of the Kyoto Protocol', *Canadian Journal of Economics*, **36**(2), 475–94.

— Vogt, C. (2004), 'The Dismantling of a Breakthrough: The Kyoto Protocol—Just Symbolic Policy', *European Journal of Political Economy*, **20**, 597–617.

— Conrad, K., and Löschel, A. (2003), 'Carbon Taxes and Joint Implementation: An Applied General Equilibrium Analysis for Germany and India', *Environmental and Resource Economics*, **24**(1), 49–76.

Bothe, M. (1996), 'The Evaluation of Enforcement Mechanisms in International Environmental Law', in R. Wolfrum (ed.), *Enforcing Environmental Standards: Economic Mechanisms as Viable Means?*, Berlin, Springer, 13–38.

Bovenberg, A. L. (1999), 'Green Tax Reforms and the Double Dividend: An Updated Reader's Guide', *International Tax and Public Finance*, **6**, 421–43.

— de Mooij, R. A. (1994), 'Environmental Levies and Distortionary Taxation', *American Economic Review*, **84**, 1085–9.

— Goulder, L. H., (1996), 'Optimal Environmental Taxation in the Presence of Other Taxes: General-equilibrium Analyses', *American Economic Review*, **86**(4), 985–1000.

— — (2001), 'Neutralizing Adverse Impacts of CO2 Abatement Policies. What Does it Cost?', in C. E. Carraro and G. E. Metcalf (eds), *Behavioral and Distributional Effects of Environmental Policy*, Chicago, IL, University of Chicago Press.

— — (2002), 'Environmental Taxation and Regulation', in A. Auerbach and M. Feldstein (eds), *Handbook of Public Economics*, New York, Elsevier.

— van der Ploeg, F. (1994*a*), 'Consequences of Environmental Tax Reform for Unemployment and Welfare', *Environmental and Resource Economics*, **12**, 137–50.

Bovenberg, A. L., and van der Ploeg, F. (1994*b*), 'Environmental Policy, Public Finance and the Labor Market in a Second Best World', *Journal of Public Economics*, **55**, 349–90.

— — (1997), 'Costs of Environmentally Motivated Taxes in the Presence of other Taxes: General Equilibrium Analyses', *National Tax Journal*, **50**, 59–88.

Bradford, D. F. (2002), 'Improving on Kyoto: Greenhouse Gas Control as the Purchase of a Global Public Good', Working Paper, Princeton University.

Brainard, J., Lovett, A., and Bateman, I. (2003), *Carbon Sequestration Benefits of Woodland: Social and Environmental Benefits of Forestry: Phase 2*, Report to the Forestry Commission, Edinburgh.

Broome, J. (1992), *Counting the Cost of Global Warming*, Cambridge, White Horse Press.

Browning, E. K. (1976), 'The Marginal Cost of Public Funds', *Journal of Political Economy*, **84**, 283–98.

— (1987), 'On the Marginal Welfare Cost of Taxation', *American Economic Review*, **77**, 11–23.

Buchanan, J. M., and Tullock, G. (1975), 'Polluters' Profits and Political Response: Direct Controls versus Taxes', *American Economic Review*, **65**, 139–47.

Buchner, B., Carraro, C., and Cersosimo, I. (2001), 'On the Consequences of the US Withdrawal from the Kyoto/Bonn Protocol', Venice, Fondazione Eni Enrico Mattei.

— — — (2002), 'Economic Consequences of the US Withdrawal from the Kyoto/Bonn Protocol', *Climate Policy*, **2**(4), 273–92.

Budd, A. (1998), 'The Role and Operations of the Bank of England Monetary Policy Committee', *The Economic Journal*, **108**, 1783–94.

Caldeira, K., Jain, A. K., Hoffert, M. L. (2003), 'Climate Sensitivity, Uncertainty and the Need for Energy Without CO_2 Emission', *Science*, **299**, 2052.

Carraro, C. (1997), 'The Structure of International Environmental Agreements', Working Paper, Fondazione Eni Enrico Mattei, Milan; revised version appeared as 'The Structure of International Agreements on Climate Change', in C. Carraro (ed.) (1999), *International Environmental Agreements on Climate Change*, Dordrecht, Kluwer Academic Publishers.

— (2003), 'International Regimes and Policy Strategies for Climate Change Control', in L. Marsiliani, M. Rauscher, and C. Withagen (eds), *Environmental Policy in an International Perspective*, Dordrecht, Kluwer Academic Publishers, 1–17.

— Siniscalco, D. (1993), 'Strategies for the International Protection of the Environment', *Journal of Public Economics*, **52**, 309–28.

Carraro, C., and Siniscalco, D. (1998), 'International Environmental Agreements: Incentives and Political Economy', *European Economic Review*, **42**, 561–72.

CEC (1997), 'Energy for the Future—Renewable Sources of Energy', White Paper, Commission of the European Communities, COM(1997) 599 final.

— (2001), *Proposal for a Directive of the European Parliament and of the Council Establishing a Scheme for Greenhouse Gas Emission Allowance Trading within the Community and Amending Council Directive 96/61/EC*, COM(2001) 581 final.

— (2002), *Amended Proposal for a Directive of the European Parliament and of the Council Establishing a Scheme for Greenhouse Gas Emission Allowance Trading within the Community and Amending Council Directive 96/61/EC*, COM(2002) 680 final.

— (2003a), 'Directive 2003/87/EC of the European Parliament and of the Council of 13 October 2003 Establishing a Scheme for Greenhouse Gas Emissions Allowance Trading within the Community and Amending Council Directive 96/61/EC', Commission of the European Communities, *Official Journal of the European Union*, L 275/32, 25 October.

— (2003b), 'Proposal for a Directive of the European Parliament and of the Council Amending the Directive Establishing a Scheme for Greenhouse Gas Emissions Allowance Trading within the Community, in Respect of the Kyoto Protocol's Project Mechanisms', Commission of the European Communities, Brussels, COM(2003) 403 final.

— (2004), 'Commission Decision of 29/01/2004 Establishing Guidelines for the Monitoring and Reporting of Greenhouse Gas Emissions Pursuant to Directive 2003/87/EC of the European Parliament and of the Council', Commission of the European Communities, Brussels, COM(2004) 130 final.

Cesar, H., and de Zeeuw, A. (1996), 'Issue Linkage in Global Environmental Problems', in A. Xepapadeas (ed.), *Economic Policy for the Environment and Natural Resources: Techniques for the Management and Control of Pollution*, Cheltenham and Brookfield, Edward Elgar, ch. 7, 158–73.

Chamley, C. P. (1981), 'The Welfare Cost of Capital Income Taxation in a Growing Economy', *Journal of Political Economy*, **89**, 468–96.

Chayes, A., and Chayes, A. H. (1995), *The New Sovereignty*, Cambridge, MA, Harvard University Press.

Chichilnisky, G. (2000), 'An Axiomatic Approach to Choice under Uncertainty with Catastrophic Risks', *Resource and Energy Economics*, **22**, 221–31.

CJC Consulting, Willis, K., and Pearce, D. W. (2003), *Economic Analysis of Forestry Policy in England*, Report to Department for the Environment, Food and Rural Affairs, and HM Treasury.

Clarke, H., and Reed, W. (1994), 'Consumption/Pollution Tradeoffs in an Environment Vulnerable to Pollution-related Catastrophic Collapse', *Journal of Economic Dynamics and Control*, **18**, 991–1010.

Clarkson, R., and Deyes, K. (2002), *Estimating the Social Cost of Carbon Emissions*, GES Working Paper 140, London, HM Treasury, available at http://www.hm-treasury.gov.uk/Documents/ Taxation_Work_and_Welfare/Taxation_and_the_Environment/ tax_env_GESWP140.cfm

Climate Action Network Europe (2003), *Letter from CAN Europe regarding CDM/JI and ET Draft Proposal*, Brussels, 28 February.

Cline, W. R. (1992), *The Economics of Global Warming*, Washington, DC, Institute for International Economics.

Cohen, J. E. (1995), *How Many People Can the Earth Support?*, New York, W. W. Norton.

Cohen, M. A. (1998), 'Monitoring and Enforcement of Environmental Policy', Vanderbilt University, Owen Graduate School of Management, Working Paper, August.

Committee on Abrupt Climate Change (2002), *Abrupt Climate Change: Inevitable Surprises*, Washington, DC, National Academy Press.

Congleton, R. D. (1992), 'Political Institutions and Pollution Control', *Review of Economics and Statistics*, **74**(3), 412–21.

— (2001), 'Governing the Global Environmental Commons: The Political Economy of International Environmental Treaties and Institutions', in G. G. Schulze and H. W. Ursprung (eds), *International Environmental Economics*, Oxford, Oxford University Press, 241–63.

Conrad, J. (1997), 'Global Warming: When to Bite the Bullet', *Land Economics*, **73**, 164–73.

Cooper, R. N. (1998), 'Towards a Real Treaty on Global Warming', *Foreign Affairs*, **77**(2), 66–79.

Council of Economic Advisors (1998), *The Kyoto Protocol and the President's Policies to Address Climate Change: Administration Economic Analysis*, Washington, DC.

Cowell, F., and Gardiner, K. (1999), *Welfare Weights*, Report to the UK Office of Fair Trading, available at www.oft.gov.uk/NR/ rdonlyres/

Cramton, P., and Kerr, S. (1998), *Tradable Carbon Permit Auctions: How and Why to Auction and Not to Grandfather*, Resources for the Future, Discussion Paper 98-34, Washington, DC.

Cropper, M. (1976), 'Regulating Activities with Catastrophic Environmental Effects', *Journal of Environmental Economics and Management*, **3**, 1–15.

Dahl, C., and Sterner, T. (1991), 'Analyzing Gasoline Demand Elasticities: A Survey', *Energy Economics*, **2**, 203–10.

Davidse, W. (1999), 'Lessons from Twenty Years of Experience with Property Rights in the Dutch Fishery', in A. Hatcher and K. Robinson (eds), *The Definition and Allocation of Use Rights in European Fisheries. Proceedings of the Second Concerted Action Workshop on Economics and the Common Fisheries Policy, Brest, France, 5–7 May*, Portsmouth, UK, Centre for the Economics and Management of Aquatic Resources, 153–63.

De Canio, S. J. (2003), *Economic Models of Climate Change: A Critique*, Palgrave.

Defra (2001*a*), 'Climate Change Levy — Background Information', Paper PP5, London, Department for Environment, Food and Rural Affairs, July.

— (2001*b*), *Energy Efficiency Commitment 2002–2005*, London, Department for Environment, Food and Rural Affairs, August.

— (2002*a*), *Valuing the Social Cost of Carbon Emissions: DEFRA Guidance*, London, Department for Environment, Food and Rural Affairs.

— (2002*b*), *Global Atmosphere Research Programme, Bi-annual Report 2000–2002: Summary of Research Programme*, London, Department of Environment Food and Rural Affairs.

De Mooij, R. A. (1999), 'The Double Dividend of Environmental Tax Reform', in J. C. J. M. Van Der Bergh (ed.), *Handbook of Environmental and Resource Economics*, Cheltenham, Edward Elgar.

Den Elzen, M. G. J., and De Moor, A. P. G. (2003), 'Analysing the Kyoto Protocol under the Marrakesh Accords: Economic Efficiency and Environmental Effectiveness', *Ecological Economics*, **43**, 141–58.

Denicolò, V. (1996), 'Patent Races and Optimal Patent Breadth and Length', *Journal of Industrial Economics*, **44**, 249–66.

DETR (1999), *A Better Quality of Life: A Strategy for Sustainable Development for the UK*, London, Department of the Environment, Transport and the Regions, May.

— (2000), *Climate Change: The UK Programme*, Department of the Environment Transport and the Regions, London, The Stationery Office.

Diamond, P. A., and Mirrlees, J. A. (1971), 'Optimal Taxation and Public Production I: Production Efficiency and II: Tax Rules', *American Economic Review*, **61**, 8–27 and 261–78.

Dinan, T. M., and Rogers, D. L. (2002), 'Distributional Effects of Carbon Allowance Trading: How Government Decisions Determine Winners and Losers', *National Tax Journal*, **55**, 199–222.

Dixit, A., and Pindyck, R. (1994), *Investment under Uncertainty*, Princeton, NJ, Princeton University Press.

Downing, P. B., and White, L. J. (1986), 'Innovation in Pollution Control', *Journal of Environmental Economics and Management*, **13**, 18–29.

Downing, T., Olstshoorn, A., and Tol, R. (1996), *Climate Change and Extreme Events: Altered Risk, Socio-economic Impacts and Policy Responses*, Amsterdam, Free University of Amsterdam.

Drayton, W. (1978), 'Comment on A. M. Spence and M. L. Weitzman "Regulatory Strategies for Controlling Pollution"' in A. F. Friedlander (ed.), *Approaches to Controlling Air Pollution*, Cambridge, MA, MIT Press.

Drazen, A. (2000), *Political Economy in Macroeconomics*, Princeton, NJ, Princeton University Press.

DTI (1999), 'New and Renewable Energy—Prospects for the 21st Century', consultation paper, March 30th, Department of Trade and Industry, London: SO.

— (2001), *The UK Fuel Poverty Strategy*, London, Department of Trade and Industry, November.

— (2002), *The Renewables Obligation Order 2002*, Statutory Instrument No. 914, London, Stationery Office.

— (2003a), *Our Energy Future – Creating a Low Carbon Economy*, White Paper, February, Cm 5761, The Stationery Office.

— (2003b), *Options for a Low Carbon Future*, Economics Paper No. 4, London, Department of Trade and Industry, June.

— (2003c), 'Consultation Paper on the Implementation of the EU Emissions Trading Scheme', London, Department of Trade and Industry, August.

— (2003d), Draft Social and Environmental Guidance to the Gas and Electricity Markets Authority, Consultation Document, London, Department of Trade and Industry, June.

Easter, K. W., Dinar, A., *et al.* (1998), 'Water Markets: Transactions Costs and Institutional Options', in K. W. Easter, A. Dinar, and M. W. Rosegrant (eds), *Markets for Water: Potential and Performance*, Boston, MA, Kluwer Academics, 1–18.

Edmonds, J. (1998), 'Comment on Kolstad, 1998', in W. D. Nordhaus (ed.), *Economics and Policy Issues in Climate Change*, Washington, DC, Resources for the Future.

Egenhofer, C. (2002), 'The Compatibility of the Kyoto Mechanisms with Traditional Environmental Instruments', in C. Carraro and C. Egenhofer (eds), *Firms, Governments and Climate Policy: Incentive Based Policies for Long-term Climate Change*, Cheltenham, Edward Elgar.

Ekins, P. (1996), 'The Secondary Benefits of CO2 Abatement: How Much Emission Reduction do they Justify?', *Ecological Economics*, **16**(1), 13–24.

— (2000), 'Costs, Benefits and Sustainability in Decision-making, with Special Reference to Global Warming', *International Journal of Sustainable Development*, **3**(4), 315–33.

Ellerman, A. D. (2003), 'The US SO2 Cap-and-Trade Program', *Proceedings of the OECD Workshop 'Ex Post Evaluation of Tradable Permits: Methodological and Policy Issues*, Paris, Organization for Economic Cooperation and Development, 21–22 January.

Endres, A. (1996), 'Designing a Greenhouse Treaty: Some Economic Problems', in E. Eide and R. van den Bergh (eds), *Law and Economics of the Environment*, Oslo, Juridisk Forlag, 201–24.

— (1997), 'Negotiating a Climate Convention – The Role of Prices and Quantities', *International Review of Law and Economics*, **17**, 147–56.

— Finus, M. (1998), 'Renegotiation-proof Equilibria in a Bargaining Game over Global Emission Reductions – Does the Instrumental Framework Matter?', in N. Hanley and H. Folmer (eds), *Game Theory and the Global Environment*, Cheltenham, Edward Elgar, ch. 7, 135–64.

— — (1999), 'International Environmental Agreements: How the Policy Instrument Affects Equilibrium Emissions and Welfare', *Journal of Institutional and Theoretical Economics*, **155**, 527–50.

— — (2002), 'Quotas May Beat Taxes in a Global Emission Game', *International Tax and Public Finance*, **9**, 687–707.

ENDS (2002a), '"Hot Air" Blows Gaping Hole in Emissions Trading Scheme', *The ENDS Report*, 326, Environmental Data Services, March.

— (2002b), 'Rise in Emissions Threatens CO_2 Target', *The ENDS Report*, 327, Environmental Data Services, April, 3.

— (2003), 'Oversupply Cripples UK Emissions Market', *The ENDS Report*, 340, Environmental Data Services, May, 4.

Epstein, L. (1980), 'Decision Making and the Temporal Resolution of Uncertainty', *International Economic Review*, **21**, 269–84.

EST (2001a), 'Towards an Energy Efficient Strategy for Households to 2020: Supplementary Submission to the PIU Energy Policy Review', Energy Saving Trust.

EST (2001b), *Energy Saving Trust's Response to DEFRA's Consultation on the Energy Efficiency Commitment 2002–2005*, London, Energy Savings Trust.

— (2002), *Putting Climate Change at the Heart of Energy Policy*, London, Energy Saving Trust, September.

Eto, J., Vine, E., Shown, L., Sonnenblick, R., and Payne, C. (1994), *The Cost and Performance of Utility Commercial Lighting Programmes*, Berkeley, CA, Lawrence Berkeley Laboratories.

Eyckmans, J. (1997), 'Nash Implementation of a Proportional Solution to International Pollution Control Problems', *Journal of Environmental Economics and Management*, **33**, 314–30.

Eyre, N., Downing, T., Hoekstra, R., Rennings, K., and Tol, R. (1997), *Global Warming Damages*, Final Report of the ExternE Global Warming Sub-Task, DGXII, Brussels, European Commission.

Falk, I., and Mendelsohn, R. (1993), 'The Economics of Controlling Stock Pollution: An Efficient Strategy for Greenhouse Gases', *Journal of Environmental Economics and Management*, **25**, 76–88.

Fankhauser, S. (1995), *Valuing Climate Change: the Economics of the Greenhouse*, London, Earthscan.

— Tol, R., and Pearce, D. W. (1997), 'The Aggregation of Climate Change Damages: A Welfare Theoretic Approach', *Environment and Resource Economics*, **10**(3), 249–66.

— — — (1998), 'Extensions and Alternatives to Climate Change Impact Valuation: On the Critique on IPCC WG3's Impact Estimates', *Environment and Development Economics*, **3**, 59–81.

Farrell, J., and Saloner, G. (1988), 'Coordination Through Committees and Markets', *Rand Journal of Economics*, **29**(2), 235–52.

Felder, S., and Rutherford, T. F. (1993), 'Unilateral CO_2 Reductions and Carbon Leakage: The Consequences of International Trade in Oil and Basic Materials', *Journal of Environmental Economics and Management*, **25**, 162–76.

Feldstein, M. (1999), 'Tax Avoidance and the Deadweight Loss of the Income Tax', *Review of Economics and Statistics*, **81**, 674–80.

Finus, M. (2001), *Game Theory and International Environmental Cooperation*, Cheltenham, Edward Elgar.

— (2002), 'Game Theory and International Environmental Cooperation: Any Practical Application?', in C. Böhringer, M. Finus, and C. Vogt (eds), *Controlling Global Warming: Perspectives from Economics, Game Theory and Public Choice*, Cheltenham, Edward Elgar, ch. 2, 9–104.

— (2003a), 'International Cooperation to Resolve International Pollution Problems', in M. Cogoy and K. Steininger (eds), *Economics of Sustainable Development: International Perspectives, EOLSS, The Encyclopedia of Life Support Systems*, ch. 1.21.4.3., forthcoming.

Finus, M. (2003*b*), 'Stability and Design of International Environmental Agreements: The Case of Transboundary Pollution', in H. Folmer and T. Tietenberg (eds), *International Yearbook of Environmental and Resource Economics, 2003/4*, Cheltenham, Edward Elgar, ch. 3, 82–158.

— (2004), 'Modesty Pays: Sometimes!', FEEM Working Paper No. 68.04, Milan, Fondazione Eni Enrico Mattei.

— Rundshagen, B. (1998*a*), 'Renegotiation-proof Equilibria in Global Emission Game When Players Are Impatient', *Journal of Environmental and Resource Economics*, **12**, 275–306.

— — (1998*b*), 'Toward a Positive Theory of Coalition Formation and Endogenous Instrumental Choice in Global Pollution Control', *Public Choice*, **96**, 145–86.

— Tjøtta, S. (2003), 'The Oslo Protocol on Sulfur Reduction: The Great Leap Forward?', *Journal of Public Economics*, **87**, 2031–48.

Fisher, A. (2000), 'Investment Under Uncertainty and Option Value in Environmental Economics', *Resource and Energy Economics*, **22**, 197–204.

— (2002), 'Irreversibilities and Catastrophic Risks in Climate Change', in E. van Ierland, H. Weikard, and J. Wesseler (eds), *Risk and Uncertainty in Environmental and Resource Economics*, Environmental Economics and Natural Resources Group, Wageningen University.

— Hanemann, M. (1986), 'Environmental Damages and Option Values', *Natural Resource Modelling*, **1**, 111–24.

— — Narain, U. (2002), 'The Irreversibility Effect: Necessary and Sufficient Conditions', in E. van Ierland, H. Weikard, and J. Wesseler (eds), *Risk and Uncertainty in Environmental and Resource Economics*, Environmental Economics and Natural Resources Group, Wageningen University.

Folmer, H., and de Zeeuw, A. (2000), 'International Environmental Problems and Policy', in H. Folmer and H. L. Gabel (eds), *Principles of Environmental and Resource Economics*, Cheltenham, Edward Elgar, ch. 16, 447–78.

— van Mouche, P. (2000), 'Transboundary Pollution and International Cooperation', in T. Tietenberg and H. Folmer (eds), *The International Yearbook of Environmental and Resource Economics*, Edward Elgar, Cheltenham and Brookfield, ch. 6, 231–67.

Folmer, H., van Mouche, P., and Ragland, S. (1993), 'Interconnected Games and International Environmental Problems', *Environmental and Resource Economics*, **3**, 313–35.

Foxon, T. (2004), *Inducing Innovation for a Low Carbon Future: Drivers, Barriers and Policies*, London, Carbon Trust.

Freeman, A. M., III, Haveman, H., and Kneese, A. V. (1973), *The Economics of Environmental Policy*, New York, John Wiley.

Freixas, X., and Laffont, J.-J. (1984), 'On the Irreversibility Effect', in M. Boyer and R. Kihlstrom (eds), *Bayesian Models in Economic Theory*, Elsevier, 105–13 .

Frijters, P., and van Praag, B. (2001), 'The Effects of Climate on Welfare and Well-being in Russia', in D. Maddison (ed.), *The Amenity Value of the Global Climate*, London, Earthscan, 77–92.

Fuchs, V. R., Krueger, A. B., and Poterba, J. M. (1998), 'Economists' Views about Parameters, Values and Policies: Survey Results in Labor and Public Economics', *Journal of Economic Literature*, **36**, 1387–425.

Fullerton, D., and Metcalf, G. (2001), 'Environmental Controls, Scarcity Rents, and Pre-existing Distortions', *Journal of Public Economics*, **80**, 249–68.

Funk, J. L., and Methe, D. T. (2001), 'Market- and Committee-based Mechanisms in the Creation and Diffusion of Global Industry Standards: The Case of Mobile Communication', *Research Policy*, **30**, 589–610.

Gandal, N. (2002), 'Compatibility, Standardization, and Network Effects: Some Policy Implications', *Oxford Review of Economic Policy*, **18**(1), 80–91.

GAO (1992), *International Environmental Agreements Are Not Well Monitored*, Washington, DC, United States General Accounting Office, RCED-92-43.

Geraats, P. (2002), 'Central Bank Transparency', *The Economic Journal*, **112**, F532–65.

Ginter, J. J. C. (1995), 'The Alaska Community Development Quota Fisheries Management Program', *Ocean and Coastal Management*, **28**(1–3), 147–63.

Gjerde, J., Gredderup, S., and Kverndokk, S. (1999), 'Optimal Climate Policy under the Possibility of a Catastrophe', *Resources Policy*, **21**, 289–317.

Glachant, M. (2000), *How Can the Implementation of EU Environmental Policy Be More Effective and Efficient: Lessons from Implementation Studies*, Synthesis Report of the Project IMPOL, funded by EU DGXII under the Climate and Environment Programme, Contract No. ENV4-CT97-0569.

Gollier, C. (2002), 'Time Horizon and the Discount Rate', IDEI, University of Toulouse, mimeo.

Gollier, C. (forthcoming), 'Discounting an Uncertain Future', *Journal of Public Economics*.

— Jullien, B., and Treich, N. (2000), 'Scientific Progress and Irreversibility: An Economic Interpretation of the "Precautionary Principle" ', *Journal of Public Economics*, **75**, 229–253.

Golombek, R., Hagem, C., and Hoel, M. (1995), 'Efficient Incomplete International Climate Agreements', *Resource and Energy Economics*, **17**, 25–46.

Golove, W. H., and Eto, J. H. (1996) *Market Barriers to Energy Efficiency: A Critical Reappraisal of the Rationale for Public Policies to Promote Energy Efficiency*, LBL-38059, Berkeley, CA, Lawrence Berkeley Laboratory, University of California.

Goodfriend, M. (2003), 'Inflation Targeting in the United States', NBER Working Paper No. 9981.

Goodstein, E. (1996), 'Jobs and the Environment—An Overview', *Environmental Management*, **20**(3), 313–21.

Gordon, H., and O'Farrell, S. (1997), 'Transient Climate Change in the CSIRO Coupled Model with Dynamic Sea Ice', *Mon. Weather Research*, **125**, 875–907.

Goulder, L. H. (1995), 'Environmental Taxation and the "Double Dividend": A Reader's Guide', *International Tax and Public Finance*, **2**, 157–83.

— (1998), 'Environmental Policy Making in a Second-best Setting', *Journal of Applied Economics*, **1**, 279–328.

— Parry, I. W. H., and Burtraw, D. (1997), 'Revenue-raising vs. Other Approaches to Environmental Protection: The Critical Significance of Pre-existing Tax Distortions', *RAND Journal of Economics*, **28**, 708–31.

— — Williams, R. C., III, and Burtraw, D. (1999), 'The Cost-effectiveness of Alternative Instruments for Environmental Protection in a Second-best Setting', *Journal of Public Economics*, **72**(3), 329–60.

Gregory, J. (2004), 'Climatology: Threatened Loss of the Greenland Ice-sheet', *Nature*, **428**, 616.

Gross, R., and Foxon, T. (2002), 'Policy Support for Innovation to Secure Improvements in Resource Productivity', EPMG Working Paper, Imperial College, London.

Grubb, M. (1997), 'Technologies, Energy Systems and the Timing of CO_2 Emissions Abatement: An Overview of Economic Issues', *Energy Policy*, **25**(2), 159–72.

— (2003), 'The Economics of the Kyoto Protocol', *World Economics*, **4**(3), 143–88.

Grubb, M., and Walker, J. (1992), *Emerging Energy Technologies: Impacts and Policy Implications*, Dartmouth, RIIA/Dartmouth.

Gunningham, N., and Gabrosky, P. (1998), *Smart Regulation: Designing Environmental Policy*, Oxford, Clarendon Press.

Haas, R. (2002), 'Survey on and Review of Promotion Strategies for RES in Europe', *ENER Bulletin*, **25**(2), 19–27.

Ha-Duong, M., and Treich, N. (2003), 'Risk Aversion, Intergenerational Equity and Climate Change', *Environmental and Resource Economics*, forthcoming.

— Grubb, M., and Hourcade, J.-C. (1997), 'Influence of Socio-economic Inertia and Uncertainty on Optimal CO_2-emission Abatement', *Nature*, **390**, 270–3.

Hahn, R. W. (1984), 'Market Power and Transferable Property Rights', *Quarterly Journal of Economics*, **99**(4), 753–65.

— Hester, G. L. (1989), 'Marketable Permits: Lessons from Theory and Practice', *Ecology Law Quarterly*, **16**, 361–406.

Hain, P. (2002), Speech on Energy Security to Royal United Services Institute, London, October.

Haites, E., and Mullins, F. (2001), *Linking Domestic and Industry Greenhouse Gas Emissions Trading Systems*, Toronto, International Emissions Trading Association.

Hall, B. H. (2002), 'The Assessment: Technology Policy', *Oxford Review of Economic Policy*, **18**(1), 1–9.

Hamermesh, D. S. (1986), 'The Demand for Labor in the Long Run', in O. Ashenfelter and R. Layard (eds), *Handbook of Labor Economics*, New York, Elsevier.

Hanemann, W. M. (1989), 'Information and the Concept of Option Value', *Journal of Environmental Economics and Management*, **16**(1), 23–37.

Harberger, A. C. (1964), 'The Measurement of Waste', *American Economic Review*, **54**, 58–76.

— (1974), *Taxation and Welfare*, Chicago, IL, University of Chicago Press.

Harrington, W. (1988), 'Enforcement Leverage when Penalities are Restricted', *Journal of Public Economics*, **37**, 29–53.

Harrison, D., Jr (2003), 'Ex Post Evaluation of the RECLAIM Emissions Trading Programme for the Los Angeles Air Basin', *Proceedings of the OECD Workshop 'Ex Post Evaluation of Tradable Permits: Methodological and Policy Issues'*, Paris, Organization for Economic Cooperation and Development, 21–22 January.

— Radov, D. B. (2002), *Evaluation of Alternative Initial Allocation Mechanisms in a European Union Greenhouse Gas Emissions Allowance*

Trading Scheme, National Economic Research Associates, prepared for the DG Environment, European Commission.

Hartridge, O. (2003), 'The UK Emissions Trading Scheme: a Progress Report', *Proceedings of the OECD Workshop 'Ex Post Evaluation of Tradable Permits: Methodological and Policy Issues'*, Paris, Organization for Economic Cooperation and Development, 21–22 January.

Heal, G. M. (1997), 'Discounting and Climate Change', *Climatic Change*, **37**, 335–43.

Helm, D. R. (1992), 'Submission to the House of Commons Select Committee on Trade and Industry Report on British Energy Policy and the Market for Coal: Minutes of Evidence'.

— (1998), 'Environmental Policy: Objectives, Instruments, and Institutions', *Oxford Review of Economic Policy*, **14**(4), 1–19.

— (ed.) (2000), *Environmental Policy*, Oxford, Oxford University Press.

— (2002), 'A Critique of Renewables Policy in the UK', *Energy Policy*, **30**(3), 185–8.

— (2003a), *Energy, The State, and The Market: British Energy Policy since 1979*, Oxford, Oxford University Press.

— (2003b), 'The Energy Policy Britain Needs', IEE Maxwell Lecture, April, Institution of Electrical Engineers.

— (2004a), *Energy, the State and the Market: British Energy Policy since 1979*, revised edn, Oxford, Oxford University Press.

— (2004b), *The New Regulatory Agenda*, Social Market Foundation.

— Hepburn, C., and Mash, R. (2003), 'Time-inconsistent Environmental Policy and Optimal Delegation', Oxford University Department of Economics Discussion Paper 175.

Henderson, N., and Bateman, I. J. (1995), 'Empirical and Public Choice Evidence for Hyperbolic Social Discount Rates and the Implications for Intergenerational Discounting', *Environmental and Resource Economics*, **5**, 413–23.

Henry, C. (1974a), 'Investment Decisions under Uncertainty: The Irreversibility Effect', *American Economic Review*, **64**, 1006–12.

— (1974b), 'Option Values in Economics of Irreplaceable Assets', *Review of Economic Studies*, **41**(S), 89–104.

Heyes, A. (1998), 'Making Things Stick: Enforcement and Compliance', *Oxford Review of Economic Policy*, **14**(4), 50–63.

Higgins, P. A. T., Mastrandrea, M. D., and Schneider, S. H. (2002), 'Dynamics of Climate and Ecosystem Coupling: Abrupt Changes and Multiple Equilibria', *Philosophical Transactions of the Royal Society of London Series B – Biological Sciences*, **357**(1421), 647–55.

HM Treasury (2002a), *Tax and the Environment: Using Economic Instruments*, London, HM Treasury, November.

— (2002b), *Opportunity and Security for All: Investing in an Enterprising, Fairer Britain. New Public Spending Plans 2003–2006*, Cm 5570, London, HM Treasury, July.

— (2003a), *The Green Book: Appraisal and Evaluation in Central Government, Treasury Guidance (Draft)*, London, HM Treasury, available at www.hm-treasury.gov.uk

— (2003b), *Economic Instruments to Improve Household Energy Efficiency: Consultation Document on Specific Measures*, London, HM Treasury, August.

— (2004), *Science & Innovation Investment Framework 2004–2014*, London, HM Treasury.

Hoel, M. (1992), 'International Environment Conventions: The Case of Uniform Reductions of Emissions', *Environmental and Resource Economics*, **2**, 141–59.

Hoerner, J. A., and Bosquest, B. (2001), *Environmental Tax Reform: The European Experience*, Washington, DC, Centre for a Sustainable Economy.

Hollings, C. S. (1978), *Adaptive Environmental Assessment and Management*, New York, John Wiley.

Houghton, J. (2004), *Global Warming: The Complete Briefing*, 3rd edn, Cambridge, Cambridge University Press.

— Ding, Y., Griggs, D., Noguer, M., van der Linden, P., Dai, X., Maskell, K., and Johnson, C. (eds) (2001), *Climate Change 2001: The Scientific Basis*, Third Assessment Report of the Intergovernmental Panel on Climate Change (IPCC), Cambridge, Cambridge University Press.

Hourcade, J.-C., and Shukla, P. (2001), 'Global, Regional, and National Costs and Ancillary Benefits of Mitigation', in B. Metz, O. Davidson, R. Swart, and J. Pan (eds), *Climate Change 2001: Mitigation: Contribution of Working Group III to the Third Assessment Report of the Intergovernmental Panel on Climate Change*, Cambridge, Cambridge University Press, 499–599.

Hope, C. W. (1999), *Incorporating Sulphates into the Calculation of Impacts of Two Almost Identical Climate Change Scenarios*, INASUD final report, CEC DG XII.

— (2003), *The Marginal Impacts of CO2, CH4 and SF6 Emissions*, Judge Institute of Management Working Papers, 2003/10, University of Cambridge.

— (2004), 'The Climate Change Benefits of Reducing Methane Emissions', *Climatic Change*, forthcoming.

Ibenholt, K. (2002), 'Explaining Learning Curves for Wind Power', *Energy Policy*, **30**(13), 1181–9.

IEA/OECD (2000), *China's Worldwide Quest for Energy Security*, International Energy Agency and Organization for Economic Cooperation and Development, Paris, International Energy Agency.

IEO (2001), 'International Energy Outlook 2001', US Department of Energy, Energy Information Administration, http://www.eia.doe.gov

ILEX (2003), *Implications of the EU ETS for the Power Sector*, Report to DTI, DEFRA & OFGEM, Oxford, ILEX Energy Consulting. ·

IPCC (1995), Working Group I report, *Climate Change 1995, The Science of Climate Change*, Cambridge, Cambridge University Press.

— (1996), Climate Change 1995: The Science of Climate Change. Summary for Policy-makers and Technical Summary of the Working Group I Report, p. 29.

— (2001*a*), Working Group I report, *Climate Change 2001, The Scientific Basis*, Cambridge, Cambridge University Press.

— (2001*b*), Working Group II report, *Climate Change 2001, Impacts, Adaptation and Vulnerability*, Cambridge, Cambridge University Press.

— (2001*c*), Working Group III report, *Climate Change 2001, Mitigation*, Cambridge, Cambridge University Press.

— (2001*d*), *Climate Change 2001: Synthesis Report*, Intergovernmental Panel on Climate Change, Available at http://www.ipcc.ch/pub/reports.htm

Jacoby, H. D., and Ellerman, A. D. (2002), 'The "Safety Valve" and Climate Policy', MIT Joint Program on the Science and Policy of Global Change, Report No. 83, Cambridge, MA.

Jaffe, A. B., and Stavins, R. N. (1994), 'The Energy-efficiency Gap: What Does It Mean', *Energy Policy*, **22**(10), 804–10.

Jepma, C. J. (2003), 'The EU Emissions Trading Scheme (ETS): How Linked to JI/CDM?', *Climate Policy*, **3**(1), 89–94.

Johnson, P., McKay, S., and Smith, S. (1990), *The Distributional Consequences of Environmental Taxes*, London, Institute for Fiscal Studies.

Johnstone, N. (2002), *The Use of Tradable Permits in Combination with Other Policy Instruments*, Working Party on National Environmental Policy, Document No. ENV/EPOC/WPNEP/(2002)28, Paris, Organization for Economic Cooperation and Development.

— (2003*a*), 'Killing One Bird with Two Stones: The Use of Policy Mixes in Environmental Policy', *CESIFO Forum*, Spring.

— (2003*b*), 'Environmental Policy Tools and Firm-Level Management: Descriptive Overview of the Data and Preliminary Empirical Results', OECD Monograph ENV/EPOC/WPNEP(2003)13.

Joos, F., Muller-Fustenberger, G., and Stephan, G. (1999), 'Correcting the Carbon Cycle Representation: How Important is it for the Economics of Climate Change?', *Environmental Modelling and Assessment*, **4**, 133–40.

Jorgenson, D. W., and Wilcoxen, P. J. (1996), 'Reducing US Carbon Emissions: An Econometric General Equilibrium Assessment', in D. Gaskins and J. Weyant (eds), *Reducing Global Carbon Dioxide Emissions: Costs and Policy Options*, Stanford, CA, Energy Modeling Forum, Stanford University.

— Goettle, R., Hurd, B., and Smith, J. (2004), *US Market Consequences of Global Climate Change*, Arlington, Pew Center on Global Climate Change, www.pewclimate.org

Joskow, P., and Marron, D. (1992), 'What Does a Megawatt Really Cost: Evidence from Utility Conservation Programmes', *The Energy Journal*, **13**(4).

Judd, K. L. (1987), 'The Welfare Cost of Factor Taxation in a Perfect-foresight Model', *Journal of Political Economy*, **95**, 675–709.

Jung, C. H., Krutilla, K., and Boyd, R. (1996), 'Incentives for Advanced Pollution Abatement Technology at the Industry Level: An Evaluation of Policy Alternatives', *Journal of Environmental Economics and Management*, **30**, 95–111.

Kann, A., and Weyant, J. (2000), 'Approaches for Performing Uncertainty Analysis in Large-scale Energy/Economic Policy Models', *Environmental Modelling and Assessment*, **5**, 29–46.

Karp, L., and Zhang, J. (2002), 'Regulation with Anticipated Learning about Environmental Damages', Giannini Foundation of Agricultural Economics, University of California, Berkeley, mimeo.

Keeler, A. G. (1991), 'Noncompliant Firms in Transferable Discharge Permits: Some Extensions', *Journal of Environmental Economics and Management*, **21**, 180–9.

Keller, K., Tan, K., Morel, F., and Bradford, D. (2000), 'Preserving the Ocean Circulation: Implications for Climate Policy', *Climatic Change*, **47**, 17–43.

Kelly, D., and Kolstad, C. (1999), 'Bayesian Learning, Growth and Pollution', *Journal of Economic Dynamics and Control*, **23**, 491–518.

Kelman, S. (1981), *What Price Incentives? Economists and the Environment*, Westport, CT, Greenwood.

Kerr, S. (2003), 'Evaluation of the Cost Effectiveness of the New Zealand Individual Transferable Quota Fisheries Market', *Proceedings of the OECD Workshop 'Ex Post Evaluation of Tradable Permits: Methodological and Policy Issues'*, Paris, Organization for Economic Cooperation and Development, 21–22 January.

King, D. A. (2002), 'The Science of Climate Change: Adapt, Mitigate or Ignore?', Ninth Zuckerman Lecture, London, available at www.ost.gov.uk

— (2004), 'Climate Change Science: Adapt, Mitigate, or Ignore?', *Science*, **303**, 176–7.

Kleven, H. J., and Kreiner, C. T. (2003), 'The Marginal Cost of Public Funds in OECD Countries: Hours of Work versus Labor Force Participation', CESifo Working Paper 935, Munich University, Germany.

Kolstad, C. (1993), 'Looking vs Leaping: The Timing of CO_2 Control in the Face of Uncertainty and Learning', in Y. Kaya, N. Nakicenovic, W. D. Norhaus, and F. L. Toth (eds), *Costs, Impacts and Benefits of CO2 Mitigation*, Laxenburg, Austria, IIASA.

— (1996a), 'Fundamental Irreversibilities in Stock Externalities', *Journal of Public Economics*, **60**, 221–33.

— (1996b), Learning and Stock Effects in Environmental Regulations: the Case of Greenhouse Gas Emissions *Journal of Environmental Economics and Management*, 31, 1–18.

— (1998), 'Integrated Assessment Modeling of Climate Change', ch. 9 of W. D. Nordhaus (ed.), *Economics and Policy Issues in Climate Change*, Washington, DC, Resources for the Future.

— (2000), *Environmental Economics*, Oxford, Oxford University Press.

Kopp, R., Morgenstern, R., and Pizer, W. (1997), 'Something for Everyone: A Climate Policy That Both Environmentalists and Industry Can Live With', Policy Brief, Washington, DC, Resources for the Future.

Krause, F. (1996), 'The Costs of Mitigating Carbon Emissions: A Review of Methods and Findings from European Studies', *Energy Policy*, **24**(10–11), 899–915.

Kroeze, C., Vlasblom, J., Gupta, J., Boudri, C., and Blok, K. (2004), 'The Power Sector in China and India: Greenhouse Gas Emission Reduction Potential and Scenarios for 1990–2020', *Energy Policy*, **32**(1), 55–76.

Kruger, J., and Pizer, W. A. (2004), 'The EU Emissions Trading Directive: Opportunities and Potential Pitfalls' Resources for the Future', Discussion Paper 04-24, April.

— McLean, B., *et al.* (1999), *A Tale of Two Revolutions: Administration of the SO2 Trading Program. Draft Report*, Washington, DC, US Environmental Protection Agency.

Krutilla, J. V. (1975), 'The International Columbia River Treaty: An Economic Evaluation', in A. V. Kneese and S. C. Smith (eds), *Water Research*, Baltimore, MD, John Hopkins University Press, 68–97.

Kula, E. (1987), 'Social Interest Rate for Public Sector Appraisal in the United Kingdom, the United States and Canada', *Project Appraisal*, **2**(3), 169–74.

Kydland, F., and Prescott, E. (1977), 'Rules rather than Discretion: The Inconsistency of Optimal Plans', *Journal of Political Economy*, **85**, 473–91.

Labour Party (1997), *New Labour: Because Britain Deserves Better*, London, The Labour Party.

Lee, D. R., and Misiolek, W. S. (1986), 'Substituting Pollution Taxation for General Taxation: Some Implications for Efficiency in Pollution Taxation', *Journal of Environmental Economics and Management*, **13**, 338–47.

Leiby, P. N., Jones, D. W., Curlee, T. R., and Lee, R. (1997), *Oil Imports: An Assessment of Benefits and Costs*, Oak Ridge, TN, Oak Ridge National Laboratory.

Levine, M. D., Hirst, E., Koomey, J., McMahon, J., and Sanstad, A. (1994), *Energy Efficiency, Market Failures and Government Policy*, Berkeley, CA, Lawrence Berkeley Laboratory and Oak Ridge Laboratory.

Levy, M. A. (1993), 'European Acid Rain: The Power of Tote-Board Diplomacy', in P. M. Haas, R. O. Keohane, and M. A. Levy (eds), *Institutions for the Earth: Sources of Effective International Environmental Protection*, Cambridge, MA, MIT Press.

Libecap, G. D. (1990), *Contracting for Property Rights*, Cambridge, Cambridge University Press.

Link, P. M., and Tol, R. S. J. (forthcoming), 'Possible Economic Impacts of a Shutdown of the Thermohaline Circulation: An Application of FUND', *Portuguese Economic Journal*.

Lipsey, R.G., and Lancaster, K. (1956), 'The General Theory of the Second Best', *Review of Economic Studies*, **24**, 11–32.

Loomis, J., and Crespi, J. (1999), 'Estimates Effects of Climate Change on Selected Outdoor Recreation Activities in the United States', in R. Mendelsohn and J. Neumann (eds), *The Impact of Climate Change on the US Economy*, Cambridge, Cambridge University Press, 289–314.

Lovins, A. B., and Lovins, H. L. (1997), *Climate: Making Sense and Making Money*, Old Snowmass, CO, Rocky Mountain Institute.

Lucas, R. E. (1990), 'Supply-side Economics: An Analytical Review', *Oxford Economic Papers*, **42**, 293–316.

Lyon, T. P. (2003), *Voluntary versus Mandatory Approaches to Climate Change Mitigation*, Issues Brief 03-01, Washington, DC, Resources for the Future.

McCarthy, J., Canziani, O., Leary, N., Dokken, D., and White, K. (eds) (2001), *Climate Change 2001: Impacts, Adaptation, and Vulnerability*, Third Assessment Report of the Intergovernmental Panel on Climate Change, Cambridge, Cambridge University Press.

McCay, B. J. (1998), *Oyster Wars and the Public Trust: Property, Law and Ecology in New Jersey History*, Tucson, AZ, University of Arizona Press.

— Creed, C. F. (1990), 'Social Structure and Debates on Fisheries Management in the Mid-Atlantic Surf Clam Fishery', *Ocean & Shoreline Management*, **13**, 199–229.

— Gatewood, J. B., *et al.* (1989), 'Labor and the Labor Process in a Limited Entry Fishery', *Marine Resource Economics*, **6**, 311–30.

McKibbin, W. J., and Wilcoxen, P. J. (2002), 'The Role of Economics in Climate Change Policy', *Journal of Economic Perspectives*, **16**(2), 107–29.

McLean, B. (2003), 'Ex Post Evaluation of the US Sulphur Allowance Programme', *Proceedings of the OECD Workshop 'Ex Post Evaluation of Tradable Permits: Methodological and Policy Issues*, Paris, Organization for Economic Cooperation and Development, 21–22 January.

McNeill, J. (2000), *Something New under the Sun: An Environmental History of the Twentieth Century*, London, Allen Lane, Penguin Press.

Maddison, D. (1994), 'Economics and the Environment: The Shadow Price of Greenhouse Gases and Aerosols', Surrey Energy Economics Discussion Papers, SEEDS 76, Guildford, University of Surrey.

— (1995), 'A Cost Benefit Analysis of Slowing Climate Change', *Energy Policy*, **23**, 337–46.

— (2001a), *The Amenity Value of the Global Climate*, London, Earthscan.

— (2001b), 'The Amenity Value of the Climate of Britain', in D. Maddison (ed.), *The Amenity Value of the Global Climate*, London, Earthscan, 1–24.

— (2001c), 'The Amenity Value of Climate in India: A Household Production Function Approach', in D. Maddison (ed.), *The Amenity Value of the Global Climate*, London, Earthscan, 106–17.

Majone, G. (1989), *Evidence, Argument, and Persuasion in the Policy Process*, New Haven, CT, and London, Yale University Press.

Mäler, K.-G. (1990), 'International Environmental Problems', *Oxford Review of Economic Policy*, **6**(1), 80–108.

Malik, A. S. (1992), 'Enforcement Costs and the Choice of Policy Instruments for Controlling Pollution', *Economic Inquiry*, **30**, 714–21.

Maloney, M., and Brady, G. L. (1988), 'Capital Turnover and Marketable Property Rights', *The Journal of Law and Economics*, **31**(1), 203–26.

Malueg, D. A., and Yates, A. (2004), 'Citizen Participation in Pollution Permit Markets', Tulane University, Department of Economics, Working Paper.

Mann, M. E., *et al.* (2004), 'Global-scale Temperature Patterns and Climate Forcing over the Past Six Centuries', *Nature*, **430**, 105

Manne, A., and Richels, R. (1992), *Buying Greenhouse Insurance : The Economic Cost of CO2 Emissions Limits*, Cambridge, MA, MIT Press.

— — (1995), *The Greenhouse Debate — Economic Efficiency, Burden Sharing and Hedging Strategies*, EPRI.

— — (1997), 'On Stabilizing CO2 Concentrations — Cost-effective Emission Reduction Strategies', in *Proceedings of the IPCC Asia-Pacific Workshop on Integrated Assessment Models*, March 1997, CGER.

— Mendelsohn, R., and Richels, R. (1995), 'MERGE: A Model for Evaluating Regional and Global Effects of GHG Reduction Policies', *Energy Policy*, **23**, 17–34.

Marauhn, T. (1996), 'Towards a Procedural Law of Compliance Control in International Environmental Relations', *Zeitschrift für ausländisches öffentliches Recht und Völkerrecht*, **56**, 696–731.

Marshall Task Force (1998), 'Economic Instruments and the Business Use of Energy: Conclusions', Marshall Task Force on the Industrial Use of Energy, HM Treasury, London, November.

Marsiliani, L., and Renström, T. I. (2000), 'Time Inconsistency in Environmental Policy: Tax Earmarking as a Commitment Solution', *The Economic Journal*, **110**, C123–38.

Mastrandrea, M., and Schneider, S. (2001), 'Integrated Assessment of Abrupt Climatic Changes', *Climate Policy*, **1**, 433–49.

Matulich, S. C., and Sever, M. (1999), 'Reconsidering the Initial Allocation of ITQs: The Search for a Pareto-safe Allocation Between Fishing and Processing Sectors', *Land Economics*, **75**(2), 203–19.

— Mittelhammer, R. C., *et al.* (1996), 'Toward a More Complete Model of Individual Transferable Fishing Quotas: Implications of Incorporating the Processing Sector', *Journal of Environmental Economics and Management*, **31**(1), 112–28.

Mayshar, J. (1991), 'On Measuring the Marginal Cost of Funds Analytically', *American Economic Review*, **81**, 1329–35.

Menantau, P., Finon, D., and Lamy, M. L. (2003), 'Feed-in Tariffs Versus Quotas: How to Promote Renewables and Stimulate Technical Progress for Cost Decrease', *ENER Bulletin*, **25**(2), 47–54.

Mendelsohn, R. (1999), *The Greening of Global Warming*, Washington, DC, American Enterprise Institute.

— (2000), 'Efficient Adaptation to Climate Change', *Climatic Change*, **45**, 583–600.

— (2001*a*), 'A Hedonic Study of the Non-market Impacts of Global Warming in the US', in D. Maddison (ed.), *The Amenity Value of the Global Climate*, London, Earthscan, 93–105.

— (ed.) (2001*b*), *Global Warming and the American Economy: A Regional Analysis*, Cheltenham, Edward Elgar.

— (2003), 'The Social Cost of Carbon: An Unfolding Value', paper presented to the DEFRA International Seminar on the Social Cost of Carbon, available at www.defra.gov.uk/environment/climatechange/carbonseminar/mendelsohn.pdf

— Markowski, M. (1999), 'The Impact of Climate Change on Outdoor Recreation', in R. Mendelsohn and J. Neumann (eds), *The Impact of Climate Change on the US Economy*, Cambridge, Cambridge University Press, 267–88.

— Neumann, J. (eds) (1999), *The Impact of Climate Change on the US Economy*, Cambridge, Cambridge University Press.

— Schlesinger, M. (1999), 'Climate Response Functions', *Ambio*, **28**, 362–6.

— Williams, L. (2004), 'Dynamic Forecasts of Market Impacts of Global Warming', *Integrated Assessment*, forthcoming.

— Dinar, A., and Sanghi, A. (2001), 'The Effect of Development on the Climate Sensitivity of Agriculture', *Environment and Development Economics*, **6**, 85–101.

— Morrison, W., Schlesinger, M., and Andronova, N. (1996), 'Global Impact Model for Climate Change', unpublished manuscript, Yale University, School of Forestry.

Mensink, P., and Requate, T. (2003), 'The Dixit–Pindyck and the Arrow–Fisher–Hanemann–Henry Option Values Are Not Equivalent', CAU Kiel Economics Working Paper 2003–09.

Metcalf, G. E. (1999), 'A Distributional Analysis of Green Tax Reforms', *National Tax Journal*, **52**, 655–81.

Metz, B., Davidson, O., Swart, R., and Pan, J. (eds) (2001), *Climate Change 2001: Mitigation*, Cambridge, Cambridge University Press.

Millman, S. R., and Prince, R. (1989), 'Firm Incentives to Promote Technological Change in Pollution Control', *Journal of Environmental Economics and Management*, **17**, 247–65.

Mishan, E. J. (1975), *Cost–Benefit Analysis*, London, Allen & Unwin.

Misiolek, W. S., and Elder, H. W. (1989), 'Exclusionary Manipulation of Markets for Pollution Rights', *Journal of Environmental Economics and Management*, **16**(2), 156–66.

Mitchell, R. (1994), *Intentional Oil Pollution at Sea: Environmental Policy and Treaty Compliance*, Cambridge, MA, MIT Press.

Montero, J. P. (1999), 'Voluntary Compliance with Market-based Environmental Policy: Evidence from the US Acid Rain Program', *Journal of Political Economy*, **107**(5), 998–1033.

— (2000), 'Optimal Design of a Phase-in Emissions Trading Program', *Journal of Public Economics*, **75**(2), 273–91.

— (2002a), 'Permits, Standards, and Technology Innovation', *Journal of Environmental Economics and Management*, **44**(1), 23–44.

— (2002b), 'Prices vs. Quantities with Incomplete Enforcement', *Journal of Public Economics*, **85**, 435–54.

— Sanchez, J. M., and Katz, R. (2002), 'A Market-based Environmental Policy Experiment in Chile', *Journal of Law and Economics*, **45**(1, Part 1), 267–87.

Montgomery, W. D. (1972), 'Markets in Licenses and Efficient Pollution Control Programs', *Journal of Economic Theory*, **5**(3), 395–418.

Morrisette, P., and Plantinga, A. (1991), 'The Global Warming Issue: Viewpoints of Different Countries', *Resources*, **103**, 2–6.

Morthorst, P. E. (2001), 'Interactions of a Tradable Green Certificate Market with a Tradable Permits Market', *Energy Policy*, **29**(5), 345–53.

Moulin, H. (1990), 'Fair Division under Joint Ownership', *Social Choice and Welfare*, **7**, 149–70.

— (1991), 'Welfare Bounds in the Fair Division Problem', *Journal of Economic Theory*, **54**(2), 321–37.

Muller, R. A. (1994), 'Emissions Trading with Shares and Coupons — A Laboratory Experiment', *Energy Journal*, **15**(2), 185–211.

Murdoch, J. C., and Sandler, T. (1997a), 'The Voluntary Provision of a Pure Public Good: The Case of Reduced CFCs Emissions and the Montreal Protocol', *Journal of Public Economics*, **63**, 331–49.

— — (1997b), 'Voluntary Cutbacks and Pretreaty Behavior: The Helsinki Protocol and Sulfur Emissions', *Public Finance Review*, **25**, 139–62.

Narain, U., and Fisher, A. (1998), 'Irreversibility, Uncertainty, and Catastrophic Global Warming', Working Paper 843, Dept of Agricultural and Resource Economics, University of California.

National Research Council (2002), *Effectiveness and Impact of Corporate Average Fuel Economy (CAFE) Standards*, Washington, DC, National Academy Press.

NERA (2003), *Security in Gas and Electricity Markets*, Final Report for the Department Of Trade And Industry, Reference 003/08 SGEM/DH, London, National Economic Research Associates.

Nelson, R., Tietenberg, T., and Donihue, M. R. (1993), 'Differential Environmental Regulation: Effects On Electric Utility Capital Turnover and Emissions', *Review of Economics and Statistics*, **75**(2), 368–73.

Nemry, F. (2001), 'LULUCF39 v4—Quantitative Implications of the Decision CP.7 on LULUCF', personal communication.

Newbery, D. (2001), 'Harmonising Energy Taxes in the EU', paper presented at the conference Tax Policy in the European Union, Erasmus University, Ministry of Finance, The Hague, 17–19 October.

Newell, R., and Pizer, W. (2000), *Discounting the Distant Future: How Much do Uncertain Rates Increase Valuations?* Discussion Paper 00-45, Washington, DC, Resources for the Future, available at www.rff.org

— — (2001), *Discounting the Benefits of Climate Change Mitigation: How Much do Uncertain Rates Increase Valuations?*, Arlington, VA, Pew Center on Global Climate Change, Economics—Technical Series, available at www.pewclimate.org

— — (2003), 'Regulating Stock Externalities Under Uncertainty', *Journal of Environmental Economics and Management*, **45**(2, Suppl. 1), 416–32.

Ng, Y. K. (1980), 'Optimal Corrective Taxes or Subsidies When Revenue-raising Imposes an Excess Burden', *American Economic Review*, **70**, 744–51.

Nordhaus, W. (1991), 'To Slow or Not to Slow: The Economics of the Greenhouse Effect', *The Economic Journal*, **101**(407), 920–37.

— (1993*a*), 'Rolling the DICE: An Optimal Transition Path for Controlling Greenhouse Gases', *Resource and Energy Economics*, **15**, 27–50.

— (1993*b*), 'Optimal Greenhouse Gas Reductions and Tax Policy in the 'DICE' Model', *American Economic Review*, **83**, 313–17.

— (1994*a*), *Managing the Global Commons: the Economics of Climate Change*, Cambridge, MA, MIT Press.

— (1994*b*), 'Expert Opinion on Climate Change', *American Scientist*, **82**, 45–51.

— (2001), 'After Kyoto: Alternative Mechanisms to Control Global Warming', presentation at the 20th Anniversary Meeting of the International Energy Workshop, IIASA, Laxenburg, Austria.

— (2003), 'After Kyoto: Alternative Mechanisms to Control Global Warming', Discussion Paper, New Haven, CT, Yale University.

— Boyer, J. G. (1999*a*), *Roll the DICE Again: Economic Models of Global Warming*, Cambridge, MA, MIT Press.

Nordhaus, W., and Boyer, J. G. (1999b), 'Requiem for Kyoto: An Economic Analysis', *Energy Journal*, Special Issue, 93–130.

— — (2000), *Warming the World: Economic Models of Global Warming*, Cambridge, MA, MIT Press.

— Popp, D. (1997), 'What is the Value of Scientific Knowledge? An Application to Global Warming Using the PRICE Model', *The Energy Journal*, **18**, 1–47.

NRCC (1999), *Sharing the Fish: Toward a National Policy on Fishing Quotas*, National Research Council Committee to Review Individual Fishing Quotas, Washington, DC, National Academy Press.

Oates, W. E. (1993), 'Pollution Charges as a Source of Public Revenues', in H. Giersch (ed.), *Economic Progress and Environmental Concerns*, Berlin, Springer.

— (1995), 'Green Taxes: Can We Protect the Environment and Improve the Tax System at the Same Time?', *Southern Economic Journal*, **61**, 915–22.

OECD (1991), *The State of the Environment*, Paris, Organization for Economic Cooperation and Development.

— (1996), *Implementation Strategies for Environmental Taxes*, Paris, Organization for Economic Cooperation and Development.

— (1997), *Towards Sustainable Fisheries: Economic Aspects of the Management of Living Marine Resources*. Paris, Organization for Economic Cooperation and Development.

— (1999), *Implementing Domestic Tradable Permits for Environmental Protection*. Paris, Organization for Economic Cooperation and Development.

— (2000), *Ancillary Benefits and Costs of Greenhouse Gas Mitigation*, Paris, Organization for Economic Cooperation and Development.

— (2004), *Tradeable Permits: Policy Evaluation, Design and Reform*, Paris, Organization for Economic Cooperation and Development.

Office of Science and Technology (2003), *Analysis of Future Risks of Flooding and Coastal Erosion for the UK between 2030 and 2100*, London, Office of Science and Technology.

Olson, M., and Bailey, M. (1981), 'Positive Time Preference', *Journal of Political Economy*, **89**(1), 1–25.

O'Neill, B. C., and Oppenheimer, M. (2002), 'Dangerous Climate Impacts and the Kyoto Protocol', *Science*, **296**, 1971–2.

OXERA (2002), *A Social Time Preference Rate for Use in Long-term Discounting*, Report to Office of the Deputy Prime Minister, Department for Transport, and Department for the Environment, Food and Rural Affairs.

Pacala, S., and Socolow, R. (2004), 'Stabilization Wedges: Solving the Climate Problem for the Next 50 Years with Current Technologies', *Science*, **305**, 968–72.

Palsson, G. (1998), 'The Virtual Aquarium: Commodity Fiction and Cod Fishing', *Ecological Economics*, **24**(2–3), 275–88.

Parson, E. A., and Fisher-Vanden, K. (1997), 'Integrated Assessment Models of Global Climate Change', *Annual Review of Energy and the Environment*, **22**, 589–628.

Parry, I. W. H. (1995), 'Pollution Taxes and Revenue Recycling', *Journal of Environmental Economics and Management*, **29**, S64–S77.

— (1997), 'Environmental Taxes and Quotas in the Presence of Distorting Taxes in Factor Markets', *Resource and Energy Economics*, **19**, 203–20.

— (1998), 'A Second Best Analysis of Environmental Subsidies', *International Tax and Public Finance*, **5**, 157–74.

— (2002), *Adjusting Carbon Cost Analyses to Account for Prior Tax Distortions*, report prepared for Environmental Protection Agency, available at: www.rff.org/disc_papers/PDF_files/0247.pdf

— Bento, A. M. (2000), 'Tax Deductions, Environmental Policy, and the "Double Dividend" Hypothesis', *Journal of Environmental Economics and Management*, **39**, 67–96.

— Small, K. A. (2004), 'Does Britain or The United States Have the Right Gasoline Tax?', *American Economic Review*, forthcoming.

— Williams, R. C., and Goulder, L. H. (1999), 'When Can Carbon Abatement Policies Increase Welfare? The Fundamental Role of Distorted Factor Markets', *Journal of Environmental Economics and Management*, **37**, 52–84.

Pasek, J., and Beckerman, W. (2001), *Justice, Posterity, and the Environment: Environmental Ethics for a New Millennium*, Oxford, Oxford University Press.

Pearce, D. W. (1991), 'The Role of Carbon Taxes in Adjusting to Global Warming', *The Economic Journal*, **101**, 938–48.

— (1998a), 'Cost–Benefit Analysis and Environmental Policy', *Oxford Review of Economic Policy*, **14**(4), 84–100.

— (1998b), 'Valuing Statistical Lives', *Planejamento e Politicas e Publicas*, **18**, 69–118.

— (2001), 'Trucks, Tractors, Trains and Trash: Problems and Progress with Britain's Economic Approach to Environmental Policy', University College London, Economics, mimeo.

— (2003a), 'Will Global Warming be Controlled? Reflections on the Irresolution of Humankind', in R. Pethig and M. Rauscher (eds), *Challenges to the World Economy: Festschrift for Horst Siebert*, Berlin, Springer, 367–82.

Pearce, D. W. (2003*b*), 'The Social Cost of Carbon and its Policy Implications', *Oxford Review of Economic Policy*, **16**(3), 362–84.

— (2005), 'Conceptual Framework for Analysing the Distributive Impacts of Environmental Policies', in Y. Serret and N. Johnstone (eds), *Environmental Poliy and Distributional Issues*, Cheltenham, Edward Elgar and OECD, forthcoming.

— Ulph, D. (1999), 'A Social Discount Rate for the United Kingdom', in D. W. Pearce (ed.), *Economics and the Environment: Essays in Ecological Economics and Sustainable Development*, Cheltenham, Edward Elgar, 268–85.

— Cline, W. R., Achanta, A., Fankhauser, S., Pachauri, R., Tol, R., and Vellinga, P. (1996), 'The Social Costs of Climate Change: Greenhouse Damage and the Benefits of Control', in Intergovernmental Panel on Climate Change, *Climate Change 1995: Economic and Social Dimensions of Climate Change*, Cambridge, Cambridge University Press, 183–224.

Pearson, M., and Smith, S. (1991), *The European Carbon Tax: An Assessment of the European Commission's Proposals*, London, Institute for Fiscal Studies.

Peck, S., and Teisberg, T. (1993), 'Global Warming Uncertainties and the Value of Information: An Analysis Using CETA', *Resource and Energy Economics*, **15**(1), 71–97.

Pedersen, S. L. (2003), 'Experience Gained with CO2 Cap and Trade in Denmark', *Proceedings of the OECD Workshop 'Ex Post Evaluation of Tradable Permits: Methodological and Policy Issues'*, Paris, Organization for Economic Cooperation and Development, 21–22 January.

Pendleton, L., and Mendelsohn, R. (1998), 'Estimating the Economic Impact of Climate Change on the Freshwater Sportfisheries of the Northeast United States', *Land Economics*, **74**, 483–96.

Perroni, C., and Whalley, J. (1998), 'Rents and the Cost and Optimal Design of Commodity Taxes', *Review of Economics and Statistics*, **80**, 357–64.

Pezzey, J. (2002), 'Distributing the Value of a Country's Tradable Carbon Permits', paper presented at the second CATEP Workshop on the Design and Integration of National Tradable Permit Schemes for Environmental Protection, University College London, 25–26 March.

Pierson, P. (2000), 'Path Dependence, Increasing Returns, and the Study of Politics', *American Political Science Review*, **94**(2), 251–67.

Pigou, A. C. (1947), *A Study in Public Finance*, 3rd edn, London, Macmillan.

Pindyck, R. (2000), 'Irreversibilities and the Timing of Environmental Policy', *Resource and Energy Economics*, **22**, 233–59.

PIU (2002), *The Energy Review*, Performance and Innovation Unit, Cabinet Office, London, February.

Pizer, W. A. (1999*a*), 'Choosing Price or Quantity Controls for Greenhouse Gases', Climate Issues Brief 17, Washington, DC, Resources for the Future.

— (1999*b*), 'The Optimal Choice of Climate Change Policy in the Presence of Uncertainty', *Resource and Energy Economics*, **21**, 255–87.

— (2002), 'Combining Price and Quantity Controls to Mitigate Global Climate Change', *Journal of Public Economics*, **85**, 409–34.

Plambeck, E. L., and Hope, C. (1996), 'PAGE95: An Updated Valuation of the Impacts of Global Warming', *Energy Policy*, **24**(9), 783–93.

— — Anderson, J., (1997), 'The PAGE95 Model: Integrating the Science and Economics of Global Warming', *Energy Economics*, **19**, 77–101.

Poterba, J. M. (1989), 'Lifetime Incidence and the Distributional Burden of Excise Taxes', *American Economic Review*, **79**, 325–30.

— (1991), 'Is the Gasoline Tax Regressive?', NBER Working Paper No. 3578, January.

Prentice, I. C., *et al.* (2001), 'The Carbon Cycle and Atmospheric Carbon Dioxide', in J. Houghton *et al.*, Intergovernmental Panel on Climate Change (IPCC), 2001a, *Climate Change 2001: The Scientific Basis*, Third Assessment Report (TAR), Cambridge, Cambridge University Press.

Rabl, A., Spadaro, J., and van der Zwaan, B. (2004), 'Uncertainty of Pollution Damage Cost Estimates: To What Extent Does It Matter?', *Environmental Science and Technology*, forthcoming.

Ragland, S. E. (1995), 'International Environmental Externalities and Interconnected Games', Ph.D. Dissertation, University of Colorado, Boulder.

RCEP (2000), 'Energy: The Changing Climate', 22nd report, Royal Commission on Environmental Pollution, Cm 4749, London, HMSO.

Reilly, J., *et al.* (1996), 'Agriculture in a Changing Climate: Impacts and Adaptations', in IPCC (Intergovernmental Panel on Climate Change), R. Watson, M. Zinyowera, R. Moss, and D. Dokken (eds), *Climate Change 1995: Impacts, Adaptations, and Mitigation of Climate Change: Scientific–Technical Analyses*, Cambridge, Cambridge University Press.

Rentz, H. (1996), 'From Joint Implementation to a System of Tradeable CO2 Emission Entitlements', *International Environmental Affairs*, **8**(3), 267–76.

Rentz, H. (1998), 'Joint Implementation and the Question Of "Additionality" — A Proposal for a Pragmatic Approach to Identify Possible Joint Implementation Projects', *Energy Policy* **26**(4), 275-9.

Repetto, R., Dower, R. C., Jenkins, R., and Geoghegan, J. (1992), *Green Fees: How a Tax Shift Can Work for the Environment and the Economy*, Washington, DC, World Resources Institute.

Ringius, L., Torvanger, A., and Holtsmark, B. (1998), 'Can Multicriteria Rules Fairly Distribute Climate Burdens? OECD Results from Three Burden Sharing Rules', *Energy Policy*, **26**(10), 777-93.

Roberts, M. J., and Spence, M. (1976), 'Effluent Charges and Licenses Under Uncertainty', *Journal of Public Economics*, **5**(3-4),193-208.

Rogoff, K. (1985), 'The Optimal Degree of Commitment to an Intermediate Monetary Target', *Quarterly Journal of Economics*, **100**, 1169-89.

Romer, D. (1996), *Advanced Macroeconomics*, McGraw–Hill.

Rose, A., Stevens, B., Edmonds, J., and Wise, M. (1998), 'International Equity and Differentiation in Global Warming Policy', *Environmental and Resource Economics*, **12**, 25-51.

Ross, M. (1986), 'The Capital Budgeting Practices of 12 Large Manufacturing Firms', *Financial Management*, **15**(4), 15-22.

Roughgarden, T. (1997), 'Quantifying the Damage of Climatic Change: Implications for the DICE Model', Undergraduate Honors Thesis, Stanford University.

— Schneider, S. (1999), 'Climate Change Policy: Quantifying Uncertainties for Damages and Optimal Carbon Taxes, *Energy Policy*, **27**, 415-29.

Rubin, J. D. (1996), 'A Model of Intertemporal Emission Trading, Banking and Borrowing', *Journal of Environmental Economics and Management*, **31**(3), 269-86.

Runolfsson, B. (1999), 'ITQs in Icelandic Fisheries: A Rights-based Approach to Fisheries Management', in A. Hatcher and K. Robinson (eds), *The Definition and Allocation of Use Rights in European Fisheries. Proceedings of the Second Concerted Action Workshop on Economics and the Common Fisheries Policy, Brest, France, 5–7 May*, Portsmouth, UK, Centre for the Economics and Management of Aquatic Resources, 164-93.

Sandmo, A. (1975), 'Optimal Taxation in the Presence of Externalities', *Swedish Journal of Economics*, **77**, 86-98.

Sands, P. (1996), 'Compliance with International Environmental Obligations: Existing International Legal Arrangements', in J. Cameron, J. Werksman, and P. Roderick (eds), *Improving Compliance with International Environmental Law*, London, Earthscan, 48-81.

Sartzetakis, E. S. (1997), 'Raising Rivals' Costs Strategies via Emission Permits Markets', *Review of Industrial Organization*, **12**(5-6), 751-65.

Scharer, B. (1999), 'Tradable Emission Permits in German Clean Air Policy: Considerations on the Efficiency of Environmental Policy Instruments', in S. Sorrell and J. Skea (eds), *Pollution for Sale: Emissions Trading and Joint Implementation*, Cheltenham, Edward Elgar, 141-53.

Schauer, M. J. (1995), 'Estimation of the Greenhouse Gas Externality with Uncertainty', *Environmental and Resource Economics*, **5**, 71-82.

Schelling, T. C. (1992), 'Some Economics of Global Warming', *American Economic Review*, **82**, 1-14.

– (1995), 'Intergenerational Discounting', *Energy Policy*, **23**(4/5), 395-401.

– (1998), *Costs and Benefits of Greenhouse Gas Reductions*, Washington, DC, American Enterprise Institute.

– (2002), 'What Makes Greenhouse Sense?', *Foreign Affairs*, **81**(3), 2-9.

Schneider, S. H. (1997*a*), 'Integrated Assessment Modelling of Global Climate Change: Transparent Rational Tool for Policy Making or Opaque Screen Hiding Value-laden Assumptions?', *Environmental Modelling and Assessment*, **2**, 229-48.

– (1997*b*), 'Overview of Climate Modeling Fundamentals and their Implications for Integrated Assessment Modelling', *Proceedings of the IPCC Asia-Pacific workshop on IAMs*, March, 39-51.

Schöb, R. (2003), 'The Double Dividend Hypothesis of Environmental Taxes: A Survey', CESifo Working Paper 946, Munich University, Germany.

Schulz, P., and Kasting, J. (1997), 'Optimal Reductions in CO_2 Emissions', *Energy Policy*, **25**, 491-500.

Shabman, L. (2003), 'Compensation for the Impacts of Wetland Fill: The US Experience with Credit Sales', *Proceedings of the OECD Workshop 'Ex Post Evaluation of Tradable Permits: Methodological and Policy Issues*, Paris, Organization for Economic Cooperation and Development, 21-22 January.

– (2004), 'Compensation for the Impacts of Wetland Fill: The US Experience with Credit Sales', in OECD, *Tradeable Permits: Policy Evaluation, Design and Reform*, Paris, Organization for Economic Cooperation and Development.

– Stephenson, K., and Shobe, W. (2002), 'Trading Programs for Environmental Management: Reflections on the Air and Water Experiences', *Environmental Practice*, **4**, 153-62.

Sijm, J. (2003), 'The Interaction between the EU Emissions Trading Scheme and National Energy Policies: A General Framework', *Climate Policy*, forthcoming.

Singh, N., and Vives, X. (1984), 'Price and Quantity Competition in a Differentiated Duopoly', *RAND Journal of Economics*, **15**, 546–54.

Smith, J. (2004), *A Synthesis of Potential Climate Change Impacts on the US*, Arlington, Pew Center on Global Climate Change, www.pewclimate.org

— Tirpak, D. (1990), 'The Potential Effects of Global Climate Change on the United States: Report to Congress', Washington, DC, US Environmental Protection Agency.

Smith, S. (1998), 'Environmental and Public Finance Aspects of the Taxation of Energy', *Oxford Review of Economic Policy*, **14**(4), 64–83.

— (1999), 'The Compatibility of Tradable Permits with Other Environmental Policy Instruments', in *Implementing Domestic Tradable Permits for Environmental Protection*, Paris, OECD.

Snow, A., and Warren, R. S. (1996), 'The Marginal Welfare Cost of Public Funds: Theory and Estimates', *Journal of Public Economics*, **61**, 289–305.

Solar Century (2003), 'Energy White Paper Long on Spin but Short on Substance', News Release, February.

Sorrell, S. (1999), 'Why Sulphur Trading Failed in the UK. Pollution for Sale: Emissions Trading and Joint Implementation', in S. Sorrell and J. Skea (eds), *Pollution for Sale: Emissions Trading and Joint Implementation*, Cheltenham, Edward Elgar, 170–210.

— (2002), *The Climate Confusion: Implications of the EU Emissions Trading Scheme for the UK Climate Change Levy and Climate Change Agreements*, SPRU (Science and Technology Policy Research), University of Sussex, Brighton, available at http://www.sussex.ac.uk/spru/environment/research/ccfr.pdf

— (2003*a*), 'Who Owns the Carbon? Implications of the EU Emissions Trading Scheme for the UK Renewable Obligations and Energy Efficiency Commitment', *Energy and Environment*, forthcoming.

— (2003*b*), 'Making The Link: Climate Policy and the Reform of the UK Construction Industry', *Energy Policy*, **31**(9), 865–78.

— (2003*c*), *Back to the Drawing Board: Implications of the EU Emissions Trading Scheme for UK Climate Policy*, SPRU (Science and Technology Policy Research), University of Sussex, Brighton, available at http://www.sussex.ac.uk/spru/environment/research/drawingreport.pdf

Sorrell, S., O'Malley, E., Schleich, J., and Scott, S. (2004), *The Economics of Energy Efficiency: Barriers to Cost Effective Investment*, Edward Elgar, Cheltenham.

— Boemare, C., Betz, R., Haralampopoulos, D., Konidari, P., Mavrakis, D., Pilinis, C., Quirion, P., Sijm, J., Smith, A., Vassos, S., and Walz, R. (2003), *Interaction in EU Climate Policy*, final report to DG Research under the Framework V project, 'Interaction in EU Climate Policy', SPRU (Science and Technology Policy Research), University of Sussex, Brighton, available at http://www.sussex.ac.uk/spru/environment/research/interact.html

Spash, C. (1994), 'Double CO_2 and Beyond: Benefits, Costs and Compensation', *Ecological Economics*, **10**, 27–36.

Springer, U. (2003), 'The Market for Tradeable GHG Permits under the Kyoto Protocol: A Survey of Model Studies', *Energy Economics*, **25**(5) , 527–51.

Spulber, N., and Sabbaghi, A. (1993), *Economics of Water Resources: From Regulation to Privatization*, Hingham, MA, Kluwer.

Stavins, R. N. (2003), 'Experience with Market-based Environmental Policy Instruments', in K.-G. Maler and J. Vincent (eds), *Handbook of Environmental Economics*, Amsterdam, Elsevier.

Stirling, A. (1994), 'Diversity and Ignorance in Electricity Supply Investment: Addressing the Solution Rather Than the Problem', *Energy Policy*, **22**(3), 195–216.

Stoneman, P., and Vickers, J. (1988), 'The Assessment: The Economics of Technology Policy', *Oxford Review of Economic Policy*, **4**(4), i–xvi.

Stott, P. A., Stone, D. A., Allen, M. R. (2004), 'Human Contribution to the European Heatwave of 2003', *Nature*, **432**, 610

Stranlund, J. K., and Chavez, C. A. (2000), 'Effective Enforcement of a Transferable Emissions Permit System with a Self-Reporting Requirement', *Journal of Regulatory Economics*, **18**(2), 113–31.

— — Field, B. C. (2002), 'Enforcing Emissions Trading Programs: Theory, Practice and Performance', *Policy Studies Journal*, **30**(3), 343–61.

Stuart, C. (1984), 'Welfare Costs per Dollar of Additional Tax Revenue in the US', *American Economic Review*, **74**, 352–62.

Sutherland, R. J. (2000), '"No-cost" Efforts to Reduce Carbon Emissions in the US: An Economic Perspective', *The Energy Journal*, **21**(3), 89–112.

Svendsen, G. T. (1999), 'Interest Groups Prefer Emission Trading: A New Perspective', *Public Choice*, **101**(1–2), 109–28.

— Christensen, J. L. (1999), 'The US SO2 Auction: Analysis and Generalization', *Energy Economics*, **21**(5), 403–16.

376

Swift, B. (2001), 'How Environmental Laws Work: An Analysis of the Utility Sector's Response to Regulation of NOx and SO2 under the Clean Air Act', *Tulane Environmental Law Journal*, **14**.

Széll, P. (1995), 'The Development of Multilateral Mechanisms of Monitoring Compliance', in W. Lang (ed.), *Sustainable Development and Internationaol Law*, London *et al.*, Graham and Tritman, 97–109.

Szokolay, S. V. (2004), *Introduction to Architectural Science*, London, Architectural Press.

Terkla, D. (1984), 'The Efficiency Value of Effluent Tax Revenues', *Journal of Environmental Economics and Management*, **11**, 107–23.

Thomas, H. A. (1963), 'Animal Farm: A Mathematical Model for the Discussion of Social Standards for Control of the Environment', *Quarterly Journal of Economics*, 143–8.

Tietenberg, T. H. (1985), *Emissions Trading: An Exercise in Reforming Pollution*, Washington, DC, Resources for the Future.

— (1990), 'Economic Instruments for Environmental Regulation', *Oxford Review of Economic Policy*, **6**(1), 17–33.

— (1995), 'Tradeable Permits for Pollution Control When Emission Location Matters: What Have We Learned?', *Environmental and Resource Economics*, **5**(2), 95–113.

— Johnstone, N. (2004), 'Ex Post Evaluation of Tradeable Permits: Methodological Issues and Literature Review', in OECD, *Tradeable Permits: Policy Evaluation, Design and Reform*, Paris, Organization for Economic Cooperation and Development.

Tinbergen, J. (1952), *On the Theory of Economic Policy*, Amsterdam, North Holland.

Tol, R. S. J. (1995), 'The Damage Costs of Climate Change: Towards More Comprehensive Estimates', *Environmental and Resource Economics*, **5**, 353–74.

— (1996), *A Decision-analytic Treatment of the Enhanced Greenhouse Effect*, Free University, Amsterdam.

— (1998), 'On the Difference in Impact of Two Almost Identical Climate Change Scenarios', *Energy Policy*, **26**(1), 13–20.

— (1999), 'The Marginal Costs of Greenhouse Gas Emissions', *The Energy Journal*, **20**(1), 61–81.

— (2001), 'Equitable Cost–Benefit Analysis of Climate Change Policies', *Ecological Economics*, **36**, 71–85.

— (2002a), 'Estimates of the Damage Costs of Climate Change. Part 1: Benchmark Estimates', *Environmental and Resource Economics*, **21**, 47–73.

Tol, R. S. J. (2002b), 'Estimates of the Damage Costs of Climate Change. Part 2: Dynamic Estimates', *Environmental and Resource Economics*, **21**, 135–60.

— (2002c), *Emission Abatement Versus Development As Strategies To Reduce Vulnerability To Climate Change: An Application Of* FUND, Research Unit Sustainability and Global Change **FNU-12**, Centre for Marine and Climate Research, Hamburg University, Hamburg, forthcoming in *Environmental and Development Economics*.

— (2003a), 'Is the Uncertainty about Climate Change Too Large for Expected Cost–Benefit Analysis?', *Climatic Change*, **56**(3), 265–89.

— (2003b), *The Marginal Costs of Carbon Dioxide Emissions: An Assessment of the Uncertainties*, Research Unit Sustainability and Global Change **FNU-19**, Centre for Marine and Climate Research, Hamburg University, Hamburg, forthcoming in *Energy Policy*.

— (2004), 'The Marginal Damage Costs of Carbon Dioxide Emissions: An Assessment of the Uncertainties', *Energy Policy*, forthcoming.

— Downing, T. (2000), *The Marginal Costs of Climate Changing Emissions*, Institute for Environmental Studies, Free University of Amsterdam.

— Fankhauser S. (1998), 'On the Representation of Impact in Integrated Assessment Models of Climate Change', *Environmental Modeling and Assessment*, **3**, 63–74.

— Heinzow, T. (2003), 'External and Sustainability Costs of Climate', in A. Markandya (ed.), *GreenSense Final Report*, University of Bath, Bath.

— Fankhauser, S., and Pearce, D. W. (1996), 'Equity and the Aggregation of the Damage Costs of Climate Change', in V. Nacicenovic, W. Nordhaus, R. Richels, and F. Toth (eds), *Climate Change: Integrating Science, Economics and Policy*, Laxenburg, Austria, International Institute for Applied Systems Analysis, 167–78.

— — — (1999), 'Empirical and Ethical Arguments in Climate Change Impact Valuation and Aggregation', in F. Toth (ed.), *Fair Weather? Equity Concerns in Climate Change*, London, Earthscan, 65–79.

— Downing, T., Kuik, O., and Smith, J. (2003), 'Distributional Aspects of Climate Change Impacts', *Global Environmental Change*, forthcoming.

— Fankhauser, S., Richels, R., and Smith, J. (2000), 'How much Damage will Climate Change Do?', *World Economics*, **1**(4), 179–206.

Tsur, Y., and Zemel, A. (1996), 'Accounting for Global Warming Risks: Resource Management under Event Uncertainty', *Journal of Economic Dynamics and Control*, **20**, 1289–305.

— — (1998), 'Pollution Control in an Uncertain Environment', *Journal of Economic Dynamics and Control*, **22**, 967–75.

UKACE (2000), *RS06: Employment Impacts of Energy Efficiency Investment Programmes*, London, UK Association for the Conservation of Energy.

Ulph, A. (2004), 'Stable International Environmental Agreements with a Stock Pollutant, Uncertainty and Learning', *Journal of Risk and Uncertainty*, **29**, 53–73.

— Ulph, D. (1997), 'Global Warming, Irreversibility and Learning', *The Economic Journal*, **107**, 636–50.

UNEP/DEWA~Europe (2004), 'Impacts of Summer 2003 Heat Wave in Europe', *Early Warning on Emerging Environmental Threats*, www.grid.unep.ch/product/publication/earlywarning/php.

UNFCCC (1992), 'United Nations Framework Convention on Climate Change', New York, 9 May 1992, in force 21 March 1994, 31 ILM 849.

— (1997), 'Kyoto Protocol to the United Nations Framework Convention on Climate Change', FCCC/CP/L.7/Add.1, Kyoto, available at http://unfccc.int/resource/docs/convkp/kpeng.pdf

Unruh, G. (2000), 'Understanding Carbon Lock-in', *Energy Policy*, **28**(12), 817–330.

Utilities Act (2000), *Utilities Act 2000*, London, Stationery Office, August.

Utilities Journal (2001), 'Renewables Obligation Consultation', *Utilities Journal*, September, 30–31.

Van Asselt, M., and Rotmans, J. (1999), 'Uncertainty in Integrated Assessment Modelling: a Bridge over Troubled Water', ICIS Maastricht University, mimeo.

Van den Bergh, J. C. J. M. (2004), 'Optimal Climate Policy is a Utopia: From Quantitative to Qualitative Cost–Benefit Analysis', *Ecological Economics*, **48**(4), 385–93.

Van Egteren, H., and Weber, M. (1996), 'Marketable Permits, Market Power and Cheating', *Journal of Environmental Economics and Management*, **30**(2), 161–73.

Victor, D. G. (1998), 'The Operation and Effectiveness of the Montreal Protocol's Non-Compliance Procedure', in D. G. Victor, K. Raustiala, and E. B. Skolnikoff (eds), *The Implementation and Effectiveness of International Environmental Commitments: Theory and Practice*, Laxenburg, IIASA and MIT Press, ch. 4, 137–76.

Victor, D. G. (2001), *The Collapse of the Kyoto Protocol and the Struggle to Slow Global Warming*, Princeton, NJ, Princeton University Press.

— (2004), *Climate Change: Debating America's Policy Options*, Council For Foreign Relations.

Walsh, C. E. (2003), *Monetary Theory and Policy*, 2nd edn, Cambridge, MA, MIT Press.

Washington, W., Weatherly, J., Meehl, G., Semtner, A., Bettge, T., Craig, A., Strand, W., Arblaster, J., Wayland, V., James, R., and Zhang, Y. (2000), 'Parallel Climate Model (PCM): Control and Transient Scenarios', *Climate Dynamics*, **16**, 755–74.

Watson, R., Zinyowera, M., Moss, R., and Dokken, D. (eds) (1996), Intergovernmental Panel on Climate Change (IPCC), *Climate Change 1995: Impacts, Adaptations, and Mitigation of Climate Change: Scientific-Technical Analyses*, Cambridge, Cambridge University Press.

Weart, S. R. (2003), *The Discovery of Global Warming*, Cambridge, MA, Harvard University Press.

Weitzman, M. L. (1974), 'Prices vs Quantities', *Review of Economic Studies*, **41**, 477–91.

— (1998), 'Why the Far Distant Future should be Discounted at its Lowest Possible Rate', *Journal of Environmental Economics and Management*, **36**, 201–8.

— (1999), 'Just Keep on Discounting, but . . .', in P. Portney and J. Weyant (eds), *Discounting and Intergenerational Equity*, Washington, DC, Resources for the Future.

— (2001), 'Gamma Discounting', *American Economic Review*, **91**(1), 260–71.

Werksman, J. (1997), *Five MEAs, Five Years Since Rio: Recent Lessons on the Effectiveness of Multi-lateral Environmental Agreements*, London, FIELD (Foundation for International Environmental Law and Development), Special Focus Report.

Weyant, J. P. (1998), 'Comment on Kolstad, 1998', in W. D. Nordhaus (ed.), *Economics and Policy Issues in Climate Change*, Washington, DC, Resources for the Future.

— (ed.) (1999), 'The Costs of the Kyoto Protocol: A Multi-Model Evaluation', *The Energy Journal*, Special Issue.

— Hill, J. (1999), 'Introduction and Overview', *The Energy Journal* (special issue), vii–xliv.

— *et al.* (1996), 'Integrated Assessment of Climate Change: An Overview and Comparison of Approaches and Results', ch. 10 of IPCC Working Group III report, *Climate Change 1995, Economic and Social Dimensions of Climate Change*, Cambridge, Cambridge University Press.

Wigley, T. M. L., Richels, R. G., and Edmonds, J. A. (1996), 'Economic and Environmental Choices in the Stabilization of Atmospheric CO_2 Concentrations', *Nature*, **379**, 240–3.

Wildavsky, A. (1979), *The Art and Craft of Policy Analysis*, London and Basingstoke, Macmillan.

Williamson, O. (1985), *The Economic Institutions of Capitalism*, New York, Free Press.

World Bank (2002), *Globalization, Growth and Poverty*, Oxford, Oxford University Press.

Wossink, A. (2003), 'The Dutch Nutrient Quota System: Past Experience and Lessons for the Future', *Proceedings of the OECD Workshop 'Ex Post Evaluation of Tradable Permits: Methodological and Policy Issues'*, Paris, Organization for Economic Cooperation and Development, 21–22 January.

Wright, E., and Erickson, D. (2003), 'Incorporating Catastrophes into Integrated Assessment Science, Impacts and Adaptation', *Climatic Change*, **57**, 265–86.

Yohe, G. (2003), 'More Trouble for Cost Benefit Analysis', *Climatic Change*, **56**, 235–44.

Young, M. D. (1999), 'The Design of Fishing-right Systems — The NSW Experience', *Ecological Economics*, **31**(2), 305–16.

— (2003), 'Learning from the Market: Ex Post Water Entitlement and Allocation Trading Assessment Experience in Australia', *Proceedings of the OECD Workshop 'Ex Post Evaluation of Tradable Permits: Methodological and Policy Issues'*, Organization for Economic Cooperation and Development, 21–22 January.

Zapfel, P., and Vainio, M. (2001), 'Pathways to European Greenhouse Gas Emissions Trading', paper presented at the International Workshop on 'Trading Scales: Linking Industry, Local/Regional, National and International Emissions Trading Schemes', Venice, 3–4 December.

Zylicz, T. (1999), 'Obstacles to Implementing Tradable Pollution Permits: the Case of Poland', in OECD (ed.), *Implementing Domestic Tradable Permits for Environmental Protection*, Paris, Organization for Economic Cooperation and Development, 147–65.

Index